THE ROLE OF UNIONS IN THE
TWENTY-FIRST CENTURY

The editors gratefully acknowledge the Banco di Napoli's financial
support of the conference on which this volume is based.

The Role of Unions
in the
Twenty-First Century

A Report for the
Fondazione Rodolfo Debenedetti

Edited by

TITO BOERI
AGAR BRUGIAVINI
LARS CALMFORS

with

Alison Booth, Michael Burda, Daniele Checchi,
Bernhard Ebbinghaus, Richard Freeman,
Pietro Garibaldi, Bertil Holmlund,
Robin Naylor, Martin Schludi, Thierry Verdier,
and Jelle Visser

OXFORD
UNIVERSITY PRESS

OXFORD
UNIVERSITY PRESS

Great Clarendon Street, Oxford OX2 6DP

Oxford University Press is a department of the University of Oxford.
It furthers the University's objective of excellence in research, scholarship,
and education by publishing worldwide in

Oxford New York

Athens Auckland Bangkok Bogotá Buenos Aires Cape Town
Chennai Dar es Salaam Delhi Florence Hong Kong Istanbul Karachi
Kolkata Kuala Lumpur Madrid Melbourne Mexico City Mumbai Nairobi
Paris São Paulo Shanghai Singapore Taipei Tokyo Toronto Warsaw

with associated companies in Berlin Ibadan

Oxford is a registered trade mark of Oxford University Press
in the UK and in certain other countries

Published in the United States
by Oxford University Press Inc., New York

© Fondazione Rodolfo Debenedetti 2001

British Library Cataloguing in Publication Data

Data available

Library of Congress Cataloging in Publication Data

The role of unions in the Twenty-first century : a report for the
Fondazione Rodolfo Debenedetti / edited by Tito Boeri, Agar Brugiavini,
Lars Calmfors, with Alison Booth... [et al.].
p. cm.
Includes bibliographical references.
1. Wages. 2. Collective bargaining. [1. Labor unions.] I. Boeri, Tito.
II. Brugiavini, Agar. III. Calmfors, Lars, 1948–
IV. Fondazione Rodolfo Debenedetti.
HD6483 .R634 2001 331.88–dc21 2001021539

ISBN 0-19-924657-2
ISBN 0-19-924658-0 (pbk.)

1 3 5 7 9 10 8 6 4 2

Typeset by Newgen Imaging Systems (P) Ltd., Chennai, India
Printed in Great Britain
on acid-free paper by
T.J. International Ltd., Padstow, Cornwall

Preface

Whenever structural reforms are mentioned, almost inevitably reference is made to the unions. For the good or for the bad, as an obstacle to reforms of product and labour markets or as a powerful ally of reforming governments, unions feature eminently in the debate on Social Europe(s) and on the European (un)employment problem. Yet, there is little strategic thinking, at least on a scientific basis, about the role of the unions. They are considered as a fixed, immanent, feature of the European institutional landscape, something like the Alps or the River Thames. However, it is arguable that unions will continue to be as powerful as they currently are and to play the same role in Europe as at present. It is even arguable that they will continue to exist. Overall, there is nothing inevitable about unions.

Current theories of unions are mainly theories of what unions *were* and *did* rather than theories of what unions *will be* and *will do*. In so far as much literature on unions takes membership as given and treats unions as monopolists, it cannot deal with either the decline in membership that occurred in most OECD countries or the ongoing processes of segmentation of the union movement in some European countries.

The purpose of this book is to help make economic thinking about unions more forward-looking. What will the unions look like in the years to come? What kind of interest groups will they represent? How important will be the broader political role of unions and their resistance to competitive pressures on the European welfare states? Which time horizons do union strategies have, and to what extent do they care about future generations? These are some of the issues that are addressed in this book.

The volume consists of two reports, each written by a group of economists, political scientists, and sociologists working in different countries. They are the result of coordinated efforts by some of the most authoritative scholars of the field to look ahead, develop scenarios for the future, and compare them.

The first study—by Alison Booth, Michael Burda, Lars Calmfors, Daniele Checchi, Robin Naylor, and Jelle Visser—addresses a number of issues related to the question of how the primary role of trade unions—their role in bargaining over wages and work conditions—is likely to evolve in the early decades of the new millennium. After charting the trends and patterns in trade union membership, it discusses the impact of unions on wages, income distribution, and economic efficiency and considers the extent to which the influence of unions depends on the nature of bargaining arrangements, the legal environment, and the extent of product market competition. The free-rider problems associated with the administrative extension of the coverage of collective bargaining are also discussed. Finally, the importance of the level of bargaining and the extent of centralization and coordination of bargaining across countries are characterized in an attempt to gain insights into how deeper economic and monetary integration affect union influence.

The second study—by Agar Brugiavini, Bernhard Ebbinghaus, Richard Freeman, Pietro Garibaldi, Bertil Holmlund, Martin Schludi, and Thierry Verdier—shifts the emphasis to an issue that has been so far overlooked, namely the relationship between union policies and the welfare state. After reviewing the position of unions on welfare policies, notably the design of public pension programmes and unemployment benefits, it examines the issue of how unions cope with the intergenerational tension in the workforce, related to the financing of pay-as-you-go pension systems and the moral hazard problems associated with the provision of unemployment insurance. Particular attention is devoted in this context to the legal framework that sets the scene for unions' actions. This enables the authors to assess how these norms constrain unions' actions or provide an incentive for unions to support specific transfer policies, and reduce their resistance to cuts to other social welfare programmes.

The approach of both studies is eminently positive, in that the preferred sequence of reasonings of the contributors to this volume was first to define likely scenarios for the future, and only at a second stage to attempt to be normative, by ranking scenarios on the basis of their desirability. This does not mean that the two studies do not provide policy-makers with food for thought. Rather, a careful reading of the two studies can give valuable suggestions to advisers and professional economists with a political agenda in mind concerning reforms of labour markets and social policies. It also provides union leaders with insights concerning those strategies that could help to reduce the decline in union membership experienced in many European countries and to manage the intergenerational and free-rider problems associated with the provision of social insurance.

The few normative statements made in the two studies are consistent with a twofold view of the role of unions, which is recurrent in economic theory at least since the seminal contributions by Freeman and Medoff (1984) and Calmfors and Driffill (1988). Unions are, on the one hand, rent-seeking bodies; but on the other hand they may also contribute to increasing aggregate welfare by remedying market failures. The studies point to measures and strategies enhancing this second efficient role of the unions, their 'good' face, which draws mainly on their capacity to internalize to the employer–employee relationships costs that would otherwise fall on society at large.

As is natural for reports written mainly by economists, the two contributions do not deal with the ideology of unions. Unions are treated as organizations representing the interests of their members, as collective expressions of atomistic decision-makers. Unions' ideologies are in this context, if relevant at all, only a device to improve the internal communication mechanism, a way to highlight the commonality of interests of the members and to increase their loyalty to the organization.

Does such a neglect of ideology as a driving force of unions' actions reduce the heuristic content of the two studies? Does it represent a major shortcoming of contributions looking well into the new Millennium?

Recent work done at the Fondazione Rodolfo Debenedetti (fRDB), which provided background material to the two studies, suggests that this is not the case. In particular, a representative survey designed at the Fondazione and carried out in four European countries (Bertola *et al.*, 2001)—France, Germany, Italy, and Spain—all with welfare systems heavily unbalanced in favour of the old generations and seriously challenged by the demographic transition, suggests that the political role of unions is associated mainly with the interests of the members of these organizations rather than with their own ideology.

It is usually deemed that unions have a strong bias towards preserving the status quo, at least as far as reforms of the welfare state are concerned. At first sight, the four-countries survey seemed to confirm this claim. Indeed, union members in all countries are more inclined to preserve the status quo—defined as neither reducing the size of the welfare state (keeping taxes and social security contributions unaltered) nor redistributing in favour of the younger generations and the unemployed—than individuals who do not belong to any union. The (absolute) majority of union members is, in all countries except Italy, in favour of the status quo, as defined above. More importantly, the differences in attitudes towards redistribution between union members and non-union members are marked: being a union member significantly increases opposition to a retrenchment of the welfare state.

However, if control is introduced for the personal characteristics of individuals, then it turns out that union membership is no longer statistically significant in affecting opinions *vis-à-vis* reforms of the welfare state. In particular, multivariate econometric analyses of the probability of being in favour of the proposed redistribution from the old to the young generation, rather than favouring the status quo or the alternative option of redistributing from the young to the old, suggest that factors like age, the position of the worker in the household, education attainments, and the labour market status of individuals (including whether the contract held by the worker is temporary or permanent) can explain differences in attitudes towards the proposed reforms, while union membership dummies are never statistically significant at conventional levels. Put another way, union membership *per se* does not seem to affect opinions concerning an intergenerational reallocation of welfare spending. If, on average, union members are in favour of the status quo, it is just because they are older, have a permanent contract protecting them from the risk of dismissal, and/or are the heads of the household. It is not a matter of ideology, of political views playing a role independently of personal characteristics of individuals.

Thus, the economic approach followed by the authors does not seem to leave aside important determinants of unions' behaviour. It is true that union leaders often have their own ideology or political agenda and that they sometimes make decisions that only partly reflect the opinions of the members. However, even when unions lack a transparent internal decision-making process—and such organizations are highly imperfect democracies—the preferences of the members are bound, sooner or later, to prevail. Put another way, in the medium to long run—the horizon considered by the two studies in this volume—_what_ unions do will depend mainly on _who_ union members will be.

For this reason, the two studies in this volume are complementary and should perhaps be read as in a loop. The study in Part I documents the areas in which unions find it more difficult to recruit their members. These cover individuals with a weak labour market attachment (either unemployed or working with a temporary contract), the young, the most educated, and those working in sectors highly exposed to product market competition. The economic rationale for these membership problems is that preferences of workers are becoming increasingly diversified, sometimes altogether antagonistic. Temporary workers wish to have a permanent contract, and often the only way to motivate employers to convert temporary into permanent contracts is to make the latter more flexible—that is, to reduce the costs employers have to face in case of dismissal, something that 'insiders', workers who already have a permanent contract, cannot like very much. Similarly, the generational divide—in the presence of overly generous public pension promises made in the past—is growing increasingly important in affecting attitudes towards alternative reforms of the welfare state, a fact documented by the survey discussed above. Skill-biased technological change may also have amplified asymmetries in preferences and goals of union members, making it more difficult for unions to pursue their egalitarian wage policies. Finally, increasing product market competition and price transparency in the EMU is likely to reduce the surplus to be shared between employers and workers, something that tends to reduce the appeal of union membership, as there is less that can be obtained by belonging to a union in this context. Union density rates are typically higher in sheltered sectors, such as public utilities, and union membership is often stronger among civil servants than in the private sector.

Overall, the study reported in Part I suggests that there are factors at work making membership more and more concentrated on specific categories of workers and generations. Furthermore, there is a tendency towards greater decentralization in collective bargaining, which could magnify the effects on union strategies of this increasing specificity of unions. This process of decentralization is, according to the authors of Part I, likely to continue in the future. Does this mean that we will no longer have unions operating on a national scale? The authors are rather cautious, in assessing alternative scenarios, as to the degree of coordination of unions. They claim that the tendency to decentralization may be only partly reversed by social pacts of the type that occurred in several EU countries in the runup to the EMU. However, this type of coordination is likely to be increasingly unstable in a context where membership is falling and hence, inevitably, it may require government intervention.

Not all governments may wish to intervene in wage-setting, as there are, after all, strong reasons to believe that such interventions could impose wage rigidities in some parts of the economy and would not be enforced in other parts. Moreover, under EMU what matters is ultimately the coordination of bargaining at the pan-European level rather than simply at the national level. Such a higher-level, transnational coordination is not likely to occur for a long time, because of the huge coordination costs it involves. Some transnational coordination may occur within multinational firms, as coordination costs are likely to be much lower at this level.

The report in Part II characterizes the intergenerational conflicts within unions, and indicates that there are ways in which unions can more efficiently deal with the redistributive problems between their younger and older members. It also indicates that unions may be able to respond better to the needs of the unemployed without losing the support of the current employees, those who ultimately pay the unemployment benefits. This is what happens when unions get involved in the running of unemployment benefit systems (as occurs in the countries applying the so-called Ghent system) and succeed in making the system more efficient, for example by helping to reduce the moral hazard problems associated with the provision of unemployment insurance. The authors of Part II argue however that, while unions may exhibit a 'static-efficiency' role in providing insurance, they are likely to feature a 'dynamic inefficiency' role, in the sense of treating different generations of workers asymmetrically. A typical example is the implementation of 'soft landing plans' in public pension systems widely observed in Europe, as well as the incentives to early retirement in occupational pension plans run with a strong involvement of the unions in several countries. More generally, unions tend to preserve the status quo when it comes to cutting pension benefits or reducing the generosity of pension provisions, or when a retrenchment process of welfare spending is to be implemented. The cost of these dynamic inefficiencies may be accepted by younger generations as long as an intergenerational contract can be enforced, whereby unions guarantee that the status quo will be preserved, and unions are credible in their commitment. In this intergenerational implicit pact, the unions could play a key role because they are long-lived agents, certainly lasting longer than many governments.

Even if the state can be ultimately more efficient than unions in providing unemployment insurance, an involvement of unions in this context may help to prevent these organizations from focusing too narrowly on the interest group they represent. The good face of unions can prevail only if unions succeed in encompassing a sufficiently broad range of interests—otherwise, only their bad, rent-seeking, face will be in evidence.

This is something to keep in mind also when defining regulations covering industrial relations. As discussed in both parts of this volume, the administrative extension of collective bargaining coverage and other norms, spreading the influence of unions to beyond that fraction of workers who are members of these organizations, tends to increase the free-rider problem for unions. In other words, workers have fewer incentives to pay union dues and take an active part in unions since, in any event, they will get the pay rises the unions are negotiating for, along with all the union members. In so far as shrinking membership makes unions less and less representative of different interests, hence less encompassing, there is a strong case also for reconsidering the regulations that extend the unions' influence much beyond their presence. Needless to say, there may be other reasons for reducing the so-called 'excess coverage' of unions, among these the need to tackle the marked regional dimension of unemployment in Europe. There is an increasing body of empirical work pointing to the persistence of large regional unemployment differentials in countries where regional wage adjustment is hampered by the artificial extension to high-unemployment areas of the coverage of wage agreements reached in the low-unemployment regions.

Tito Boeri,
Milan

Acknowledgements

Both studies were originally prepared for the second European conference of the Fondazione Rodolfo Debenedetti, which was held in Naples in June 2000. This book draws much on the discussion in Naples, which involved a qualified audience of academicians, professional economists, representatives of unions and employers' associations, industrialists, and policy-makers.

Needless to say, we are very much indebted to all those who attended that conference and contributed actively to the discussion. In particular, we wish to express our gratitude to Sergio Cofferati, leader of the largest Italian union, CGIL, who carefully followed the discussion and contributed to the final wrap-up session. We are most grateful to Carlo De Benedetti, who allowed this event to occur and opened the Conference.

Special thanks to Giacomo De Giorgi, Pietro Garibaldi, Mattia Makovec, and Roberta Marcaletti, who assisted us in the organization of the conference and worked hard and skilfully in preparing the background material for this volume. We are also grateful to Mario Macis, Francesca Mazzolari, and Giovanni Bono, who contributed to the final stages of preparation of the conference.

We are indebted to the European Trade Unions Institute, notably to its director Reiner Hoffmann, for organizing a one-day workshop in Brussels in January 2001 in which the two reports were discussed. On that occasion we benefited from comments from European trade union leaders, including Emilio Gabaglio, general secretary of the European Trade Union Confederations, which proved very valuable in the final preparation of this volume.

Financial support from Banco di Napoli is gratefully acknowledged.

Contents

List of Contributors   xvi

Part I. The Future of Collective Bargaining in Europe   1

Lars Calmfors, Alison Booth, Michael Burda, Daniele Checchi,
Robin Naylor, and Jelle Visser

1. Introduction   3

2. Union Membership   11
  2.1. *Membership trends in the twentieth century:*
        increased cross-national variation   12
  2.2. *Union membership decline*   14
  2.3. *Why join a trade union?*   17
  2.4. *Cyclical explanations of union membership*
        developments   19
  2.5. *Structural explanations*   24
  2.6. *Institutional explanations*   32
  2.7. *Centralization and unionization*   34
  2.8. *Some additional empirical evidence on union*
        membership   36
  2.9. *New organizing strategies*   42
  2.10. *Conclusions*   45

3. Wage Bargaining, Union Power, and Economic Integration   47
  3.1. *Review of literature on union wage effects:*
        theory and evidence   47
  3.2. *The impact of trade, integration, and FDI*
        in Europe on union bargaining power   56
  3.3. *Conclusions*   59

4. Wider Dimensions of Unions' Presence   61
  4.1. *What else do European unions do?*   61
  4.2. *How do they do it?*   70
  4.3. *The future of union presence*   83
  4.4. *Conclusions*   85

5. Bargaining Structure and Macroeconomic Performance   86
  5.1. *The conventional wisdom*   86
  5.2. *The interaction between bargaining structure*
        and economic policy   98
  5.3. *Bargaining structure and macroeconomic shocks*   104

5.4. *Bargaining structure and the EMU*   109
5.5. *Conclusions*   112

6. The Future Prospects for Trade Unions in Europe   115
    6.1. *Prospects for union membership*   115
    6.2. *Four scenarios for collective bargaining
          in the future*   118
    6.3. *Possible union strategies*   132

    Comments   135

    Villy Bergström   135
    Robert Flanagan   138

    References   143

Part II. What do Unions do to the Welfare States?   157
*Agar Brugiavini, Bernhard Ebbinghaus, Richard Freeman,
Pietro Garibaldi, Bertil Holmund, Martin Schludi,
and Thierry Verdier*

1. Introduction   159

2. Unions' Involvement in the Welfare State   163

    2.1. *Unions and the welfare state development*   164
    2.2. *Unions and membership structure*   172
    2.3. *Unions as a political movement*   175
    2.4. *Unions and social insurance administration*   177
    2.5. *Unions and occupational welfare*   181
    2.6. *Institutional and political veto points*   183

3. Unions and Pensions: Theory, Evidence, and Implications   187

    3.1. *What unions do to pensions: economic theory*   187
    3.2. *The importance of institutional setting*   195
    3.3. *What unions do in practice: empirical
          evidence on unions and pensions*   197

4. Learning from Welfare Reforms: The Case of Public Pensions 211

    4.1. *Long-term and short-term reform pressures on
          pay-as-you-go systems*   215
    4.2. *Tax financing or payroll contributions?*   217
    4.3. *Reversing early retirement*   220
    4.4. *How to calculate benefits fairly*   223
    4.5. *Privatization by mandated or voluntary
          occupational pensions?*   225

4.6. *Towards more funded private pension systems* 228
4.7. *Unilateral or negotiated reforms?* 230

5. Unions and Unemployment Insurance 234

    5.1. *Unemployment insurance and the demand
for union membership* 234
    5.2. *Unemployment insurance, wage bargaining,
and unemployment* 238
    5.3. *How do unions influence unemployment
insurance policies?* 241
    5.4. *Unemployment insurance reforms* 244
    5.5. *How could a Ghent system help other
European countries?* 247

6. Conclusions 248

    6.1. *Do unions interact with the welfare state?
How do they do it?* 248
    6.2. *What explains union policies towards
welfare outcomes?* 250
    6.3. *Which institutional structure best increases union
welfare-enhancing activities relative to
rent-seeking activities?* 251
    6.4. *Can unions contribute to a reform of welfare systems?* 252

Appendix. Unions and Benefits: A Simple Analytical Framework 254

    A1. *A model of trade unions and long-term benefits* 254
    A2. *Bargaining* 264
    A3. *Political economy considerations within the union* 265
    A4. *Endogenous membership* 273
    A5. *Proofs* 275

Comments 278

    Gilles Saint-Paul 278
    Michele Salvati 281

    References 286

Final Remarks 292

Olivier Blanchard 292

Stephen Nickell 296

Index 299

Contributors

Villy Bengström, Central Bank of Sweden

Olivier Blanchard, Massachusetts Institute of Technology, Cambridge, Massachusetts, USA

Tito Boeri, Bocconi University, Milan; IGIER, Milan, and Fondazione Rodolfo Debenedetti, Milan, Italy

Alison Booth, Essex University, Colchester, UK

Agar Brugiavini, University 'Ca' Foscari' of Venice, Italy

Michael Burda, Humboldt University of Berlin, Germany

Lars Calmfors, Stockholm University, Sweden

Daniele Checchi, University of Milan, Italy

Bernhard Ebbinghaus, Max Planck Institute, Cologne, Germany, and CES, Harvard University, Cambridge, Massachusetts, USA

Robert Flanagan, Stanford University, California, USA

Richard Freeman, National Bureau of Economic Research, New York, USA

Pietro Garibaldi, Bocconi University, Milan, and Fondazione Rodolfo Debenedetti, Italy

Bertil Holmlund, Uppsala University, Sweden

Robin Naylor, University of Warwick, Coventry, UK

Stephen Nickell, London School of Economics and Political Science, UK

Gilles Saint-Paul, University 'Pompeu Fabra', Barcelona, Spain

Michele Salvati, member of the Italian Parliament

Martin Schludi, Max Planck Institute, Cologne, Germany

Thierry Verdier, DELTA, Ecole Normale Supérieure, France

Jelle Visser, University of Amsterdam, the Netherlands

PART I

THE FUTURE OF COLLECTIVE BARGAINING IN EUROPE

Lars Calmfors, Alison Booth, Michael Burda,
Daniele Checchi, Robin Naylor, and Jelle Visser

We are grateful for the interaction with Tito Boeri at the Fondazione Rodolfo Debenedetti, and for helpful comments from the discussants Villy Bergström and Robert Flanagan. We are also grateful for the secretarial assistance provided by Roberta Marcaletti at the Fondazione and Astrid Wåke at the Institute for International Economic Studies at Stockholm University.

PART I

THE FUTURE OF COLLECTIVE BARGAINING IN EUROPE

1

Introduction

In the past century, and especially in the postwar period, European trade unions have been central actors in both the political and economic fields. Unions have been a major source of power through their affiliation with the political labour movement in most Western European countries and they have exerted an important influence on the design of many labour market regulations and social welfare systems. Through their impact on wage-setting, unions have also exerted a fundamental influence on broad macro-economic developments, sometimes making it very difficult for governments to achieve their policy objectives, but sometimes facilitating macroeconomic adjustments.

It is a widespread impression that there has been a trend towards weakening union power in the last two decades of the twentieth century. Against this background, our analysis has two main objectives: the first is to document and analyse the causes of the decline in union power that has occurred; the second is to analyse likely future developments and their economic implications. We shall first look at membership developments, as this is a basic factor for union strength. But we shall also look at wider aspects of *union presence*, such as the degree to which unions coordinate their wage bargaining, and the extent of coverage of collective bargaining. In many cases these aspects have a more profound effect on union wage gains and macro-economic performance than does the simple headline measure of union membership.

We aim to answer questions like the following ones:

- Is union membership decline in Europe inevitable?
- Can unions retain their influence in the years ahead despite declining membership?
- Will deepening European economic integration render unions more power-less *vis-à-vis* employers?
- Will past trends towards more decentralized bargaining continue?
- What are the prospects for coordination of wage bargaining at the national level?
- Is transnational coordination of wage bargaining at the European level likely to develop?
- How is wage bargaining likely to be affected by European monetary integration?

- How will future developments of union influence affect macroeconomic outcomes?
- How might unions respond to the new challenges—and the new opportunities—that confront them?

The basic structure of our discussion is as follows. Chapter 2 charts the decline in union density experienced by most European countries in the last two decades of the twentieth century, and posits a number of reasons for this decline. Chapter 3 examines the determinants of union power and assesses the impact of European integration on union prospects for influencing wage bargaining. Chapter 4 discusses what unions do in addition to pure wage bargaining, and how union presence and influence may extend beyond membership figures because of the possibilities to coordinate bargaining across wide parts of the economy and extend the coverage of collective agreements to non-union members and non-unionized firms. Chapter 5 surveys the literature on the macroeconomic effects of different degrees of centralization and coordination of wage bargaining and discusses how European monetary unification may affect wage outcomes. Chapter 6, finally, assesses how union membership and bargaining structure is likely to develop in the future and how unions are likely to respond to the new challenges they meet. The principal conclusions of the various chapters are described below.

To address the question of how unionization in Europe developed in the closing years of the twentieth century, *Chapter 2* makes use of new data on *net* union membership density rates, i.e. membership as a share of wage-earners and salaried employees in employment. We show that in the last two decades of the twentieth century unionization rates in Europe declined in all but a few countries. This development has parallels with union decline during the 1920s and 1930s. A comparison with US data shows that recent trends are similar, but the decline in Western Europe has begun much later and has not eroded the basis for trade unionism to the same extent.

The chapter discusses which factors determine union membership. A distinction is made between cyclical, structural (compositional), and institutional factors. We argue that the downward trend in unionization in the 1980s and the 1990s is related to the rise in unemployment during these years and to structural changes in labour market participation and employment, bringing in groups with a lower propensity to unionize (service workers, workers finding employment in small firms) and groups that go into non-standard employment, like part-timers and workers on temporary contracts. The principal cause of decline is related to this restructuring of employment. Typically, membership losses in the core sectors of unionization—manufacturing and the public sector—fail to be balanced by membership increases in the growing new, mostly tertiary, sectors: here density rates are low in nearly all countries, and employment growth is difficult to translate into union growth.

On a positive note for the unions, we observe that the characteristic weakness of unions among female employees is disappearing. While in many countries there is still a considerable gap between male and female unionization rates, differences are narrowing, partly on account of the rising propensity of women to join unions, especially when they work in the public or subsidized sector.

Our findings suggest that a return to lower unemployment in Europe over the coming years may eliminate one factor that has worked in the direction of lower unionization. However, structural changes associated with industrial and demographic change and rising labour force participation rates (in most countries from rather low levels, if compared with the USA or the Scandinavian countries) are likely to continue to exert downward pressure on rates of unionization.

Another main finding in Chapter 2 refers to the large cross-national differences in unionization levels. We can think of few other labour market variables with such a pronounced and persistent variation. These variations are the result of long-term developments, rooted in highly unique, national combinations of institutional and political conditions. Whether such national conditions will erode as a result of the internationalization of trade and European integration, and press towards greater convergence in union presence, is hard to tell. As yet, European integration seems to have brought little convergence, but since market integration and greater product market competition is far from completed, pressures towards convergence may still have to build up.

Chapter 2 highlights three major institutional conditions conducive to union organization: union access to the workplace, union involvement in the provision and administration of unemployment insurance, and the centralization of collective bargaining. Where all three of these institutions are (or were) present (as in the Nordic countries and, to a large degree, Belgium), unions appear to have been able to fight off the negative influence on membership growth caused by unemployment and structural change.

Chapter 2 also points to the important fact that the decline in unionization in recent decades means that a few countries now combine relatively high bargaining coordination and coverage of union contracts with relatively low unionization. Whether or not such a labour market regime is sustainable represents a key question, which is analysed in later chapters.

Chapter 3 examines the determinants of unions' influence over wages and focuses on the likely impact of trade and economic integration on the capacity of unions to exert an influence on pay and remuneration. We argue that two principal conditions must be met: (1) there must be some surplus to share; and (2) union bargaining power must be substantial. The existence of any surplus will depend primarily on the extent of product market competition. Much of the single market programme is aimed at generating intensified European competition. To the extent that this occurs, monopoly-like profits should fall, thereby squeezing the capacity of unions to raise wages above non-union levels.

Against this tendency, however, European integration also facilitates the strategies of transnational firms, and may enable them to establish product market domination across Europe. If this happens, it is more difficult to predict how wage bargaining will be affected. On the one hand, the development of pan-European monopoly raises the likelihood that big firms will enjoy large profits and hence generate potentially rich rewards to powerful unions. On the other hand, the international basis of these firms enables them to switch production and hence undermine the bargaining position of unions.

Chapter 3 also addresses the question of what other factors influence union bargaining power. We emphasize the importance of the capacity of the union to control labour supply. This will depend in part on the extent of coverage of collective agreements and in part on the level of union membership, at both plant and industry level. Membership is obviously crucial for unions' capacity to threaten credibly to damage the firm's profitability in the event of a conflict. This is also to a large degree influenced by the legal framework in which bargaining takes place, and by the state of competition in both the product and labour markets. Thus, economic integration, trade, and foreign direct investment behaviour, as well as labour law, all shape union influence in wage bargaining.

A key argument is that economic integration is associated with forces that will not necessarily increase product market competition. This challenges the assumption implicit in most discussions on European economic integration: that it must enhance competition. Thus, policy-makers should not be complacent about the implications of integration for competition—and the consequent impact on the labour market. Instead, industrial and competition policy at the European level will have to be pro-active. With appropriate policies, integration can be used as a tool to generate greater competition. Our general conclusions are premised on the assumption that such policies will be in place, so that European labour markets can be expected to face conditions that increasingly reflect greater product market competition.

Chapter 4 examines wider issues of union presence. We try to give a broad picture of the activities of trade unions. Unions in Europe provide a much richer answer to the question, 'What do unions do?' than their North American counterparts. Not only do they bargain over the distribution of the joint surplus with firms, they usually have also had far-reaching ambitions to even out the wage distribution. In addition, European unions influence efficiency in a number of (positive and negative) ways, and provide a number of services to their members. Indeed, unions play a central role in European economic life, and it is premature to write them off on the basis of the declining union density figures observed over the last two decades.

The chapter argues that one must look carefully at aspects other than union membership in order to assess union influence. One such aspect is the centralization and coordination of wage bargaining. We document a trend towards formal bargaining at more decentralized levels in most—but not all—Western European economies. But this trend has been counteracted in several countries by attempts at more informal coordination, through the development of consensual norms and guidelines. Especially in the countries that joined the EMU, these attempts have often taken the form of so-called *social pacts*, sometimes involving both governments and employers. We describe the various social pacts, tripartite structures, etc., operating across different European countries.

Another key issue concerns the coverage of collective agreements. It is noted that there is a large discrepancy between coverage and union membership in many European countries because of various extension mechanisms, which widen the coverage of union contracts to non-union members and non-union firms. This 'excess coverage' serves to uphold union influence despite falling membership rates, but it represents a serious long-term risk, as the legitimacy of unions and union contracts may increasingly come to be questioned.

Less problematic in this regard is the 'excess' representation of trade unions in works councils, where this is the result of elections in which non-union members also participate. Where we have data, the turnout in these elections is relatively high and unions gain a large share of the vote of both unionized and non-unionized workers. Under national and European legislation, or as the result of basic (nationwide) agreements with employers, works councils in Europe fulfil a role in providing information and consultation, and in rare cases also co-determination, of workers concerning business and personnel decisions in firms.

Chapter 5 analyses the macroeconomic effects of various degrees of coordination in wage bargaining. The focus is on the impact on aggregate wage and unemployment levels. The extent of bargaining coordination may affect wage-setting both directly and indirectly because it interacts with other factors, such as economic policy and macroeconomic shocks. There exist two main hypotheses. According to the first one, more bargaining coordination will always promote wage moderation (a monotonic relationship), because a number of negative externalities of wage increases in individual bargaining areas can be internalized. According to the second hypothesis, the relationship between bargaining cooperation and the aggregate real wage (unemployment) level is instead hump-shaped, with both high coordination and decentralized bargaining at the level of the firm resulting in lower real wages (unemployment) than intermediate coordination (industry-level bargaining). The explanation is that bargaining at the industry level gives unions a high degree of market power.

Empirical studies give about as much support to each hypothesis. But the studies seem to agree that highly coordinated bargaining is associated with substantially lower unemployment than very decentralized bargaining, when other factors are controlled for. Differences in the degree of bargaining coordination seem also to have larger unemployment effects than differences in union density and coverage. This suggests that a change from systems with both high coordination and unionization to systems with both decentralized bargaining and low unionization might lead to adverse unemployment consequences in the absence of other changes in labour market institutions. Theoretical reasoning also points to a risk that less coordinated bargaining could be associated with less nominal wage flexibility.

Moreover, Chapter 5 suggests that European monetary unification is likely to change the incentives for union wage-setting under present institutional conditions. The reason is that the earlier policy game between the Bundesbank and unions in Germany may have put a lid on European wage increases, because unions perceived a need to hold back wage increases in order not to provoke interest rate increases. This deterring effect is likely to disappear in the EMU, which means a *de facto* decentralization of wage bargaining, as all unions will become too small relative to the ECB to have to consider any policy responses to their own actions. As a consequence, the EMU may weaken the incentives for wage restraint.

The final chapter, *Chapter 6*, discusses the future prospects for union presence and influence in Europe, using the material from the other chapters as an input. The first issue concerns future membership developments.

On the basis of our analysis in Chapter 2, our prediction is that union membership will continue to fall. Union decline may slow down if unemployment levels fall, but the continuing restructuring of employment, and rising participation levels, will bring into the labour force people with a lower propensity to unionize. Here, factors such as the shift in employment from manufacturing and the public sector to private services, an increasing importance of small firms, and the growing importance of non-standard work (temporary and part-time employment) are important. The decline in unionization among young people and the ageing of trade union membership also forebodes a higher attrition rate in the near future. Current trends in decentralization and declining political influence of trade unions suggest, moreover, that the institutional complex that is connected with continuing high levels of unionization may be weakening.

A second issue concerns the future structure of wage bargaining. Here, we outline four different scenarios and advance arguments in favour of and against them: (1) continued decentralization, with a much larger role for uncoordinated bargaining at the level of the firm; (2) national bargaining coordination through social pacts; (3) transnational coordination at the European level; and (4) a combination of decentralization to the firm level and transnational bargaining coordination within multinational firms.

Our assessment is that the forces working in the direction of decentralized wage bargaining at the level of the firm or workplace are likely to dominate in a *long-run* perspective. A need for pay systems tailored to the situation of the individual firm, decentralization of decision-making in business operations in general, an increased importance of wage levels relative to foreign rather than domestic competitors, lower unionization rates, and possibly lower coverage of collective agreements all provide incentives for such a development. However, the development in the *medium term* is more difficult to judge. Monetary unification in Europe will create incentives for national coordination as a means of substituting nominal wage flexibility for monetary policy autonomy. Such coordination is likely to be based on the development of consensual norms and guidelines within the context of social pacts of the same type as during recent years in many counties.

The strength of the incentives for national coordination attempts will depend on how asymmetric macroeconomic developments will be inside the EMU. But if present trends towards deunionization and decentralization of formal bargaining levels continue, national coordination will become increasingly difficult to achieve: in the end, the union side will not be able to deliver coordinated wage restraint. One possibility is that the attempts to draw up social pacts will just 'fade away'. Another possibility is that governments will feel compelled to take more drastic coercive steps to enforce wage restraint, in which case the dismantling of national coordination attempts may lead to a very 'bumpy ride', entailing serious social and political conflicts.

We see very important obstacles for the transnational coordination of wage bargaining at the European level among union confederations or sectoral unions in different countries, because of the huge coordination costs involved. More likely is transnational coordination with respect to specific labour market issues where decision-making is taking place at the EU level. This may have important effects on overall wage costs and employment conditions, but it amounts to much less than the actual transnational coordination of wage bargaining. To the extent that some transnational coordination of wage bargaining might occur, it is likely to develop *within* large trans-European firms. Here, coordination costs are much lower because of the similarities between workplaces in different countries within the same firm, and because employees will anyway interact with each other in their normal work. In addition, the statutory European works councils may provide a basis for such bargaining coordination. Transnational bargaining coordination of this type would be consistent with a trend towards decentralization of wage bargaining to the individual firm.

A trend towards decentralized wage bargaining could have positive effects on productive efficiency and labour market flexibility. In countries where sectoral bargaining is replaced by bargaining at the firm level, there may also be positive employment effects. But empirical research seems also to suggest that there are macroeconomic risks for the countries that have had high coordination: simultaneous moves from high bargaining coordination and unionization to decentralization and lower unionization could, everything else equal, lead to higher wages and lower employment. The difficult thing is to judge to what extent such a development would go hand in hand with changes in other labour market institutions that could promote employment. It may be very important that such changes take place in the countries that have earlier had high degrees of bargaining coordination if high employment is to be achieved.

The diversity in trends of union presence in different countries suggests that the strategies chosen by unions to cope with the new challenges will be an important determinant of their future role. Unions are typically not passive agents: they are organizations that respond and adapt to change. Our assessment is that future union strategies will build on new roles for unions as service providers and bargaining agents in local contexts. An important task is to strike a reasonable balance between employer demands for productive efficiency and the legitimate desires of employees to cope with the stresses of modern working life associated with a two-gender workforce, increased complexity of jobs, a higher speed of adjustment to new demands, and more requirements concerning the upgrading of skills. In response to the decentralization of collective bargaining and greater involvement of local representatives and works councils in negotiating and implementing agreements, unions may also specialize in training and selecting local representatives. The development of European works councils may in the future become a new task for the unions and an opportunity to build and reinforce transnational union networks.

The future of unions as political organizations is uncertain. Like the central employers' federations, trade unions have traditionally been invited to serve as members of national joint councils and advisory committees. In the context of the EU decision-making on social and employment policy, the European federations of employers and unions have in recent years gained a role as co-legislators. It may be attractive for trade unions in a situation of declining membership to seek extra support and legitimacy from being a social partner that is consulted by governments and that can conclude agreements with them affecting the welfare of union members. But this entails a risk when lower unionization and decentralization of bargaining reduce the credibility of unions as an actor.

Many trade unions in Europe have in recent years restructured their activities through mergers and takeovers. This restructuring process is directly related to the cost pressures on unions, in which higher costs of members' service must be matched by falling or stagnating revenues from members' contributions. Such further restructuring is likely to produce 'conglomerate unions', which will face new demands with respect to the management of internal diversity. Union mergers may result in centralized service provision and decentralized representation and wage bargaining at the same time.

Finally, we stress the difficulties of predicting the future role of trade unions. The membership, presence, influence, and strategy of unions are shaped by a complex set of interrelated factors. At any one point in history, conditions may be more or less favourable to unions, and their fortunes have therefore varied over time. A corollary of this argument is that changing conditions might very well affect the trends that we have identified. We do, however, believe that continued membership decline and a continued trend towards the decentralization of wage bargaining are the most likely long-run outcomes.

2

Union Membership

Trade unions are membership organizations. In this sense they differ from firms, as do political parties, most churches, and voluntary community organizations. To know which workers join unions, and why, is therefore an important source of knowledge about trade unions. This is why the answer to the question, 'what do unions do?' must begin with the question, 'who are the union members?' Although there is much more to a trade union than its membership (wider aspects of 'union presence' will be discussed in later chapters), a study of trade union behaviour is best started with an examination of membership trends. From statistics concerning the level and distribution of its membership, we may derive a first impression of the position of a union in society (Bain and Price, 1980; Visser, 1992).

Membership is a source of power for the union. A high level of membership in a firm means that fewer workers are available to the firm during an industrial conflict. In the language of game theory, higher membership reduces the firm's 'inside option' or conflict (strike) payoff. If union membership is high throughout the industry or economy, the firm's 'outside option', its choice to sack all its workers and hire workers in the external labour market, is similarly reduced.

Comparing membership levels and trends across countries and over a long time span is fraught with problems (Visser, 1991). Some of these problems are statistical and relate to differences in measurement and reliability of the data. Other problems are conceptual and relate to differences in what it means to be a trade union member. Membership is not a fixed or constant concept. Over time and across countries, industries, and occupations, trade unions have held members to different obligations. Membership in a traditional craft union involved far greater submission to union authority, and more involvement of time and effort in the running of the union's internal affairs, than is required from the average member in a modern union (Webb and Webb, 1894; Lester, 1958). Membership 'in good standing' today may mean no more than paying one's dues, rather than going to meetings, voting in elections, or helping fellow workers. There is no automatic link to worker militancy; high rates of strike involvement, however measured, are found in countries with both high and low union membership (Korpi and Shalev, 1979).

In this chapter we will describe and discuss the trends in union membership in Europe. In Section 2.1 we present the long-term picture with data covering the entire twentieth century and ask ourselves whether the last decades of that century constituted a break with past trends. In Section 2.2 we ask the same question from a different perspective, by making a comparison with US data and examining other indicators. In Section 2.3 we discuss the reasons for becoming a union member. In Sections 2.4–2.6, we examine cyclical, structural or compositional, and institutional factors that may explain membership trends. Particular attention is given to the impact of (un)employment, the shift of employment from manufacturing to services, the growing importance of non-standard employment, and union involvement in providing unemployment insurance and in grievance handling in the workplace. Section 2.7 explores the connection between unionization and centralization, and Section 2.8 presents some new regression results on the determinants of unionization in Europe. Organizational restructuring among unions as a strategy to become more cost-effective and attractive for members is discussed in Section 2.9. In Section 2.10, finally, we draw the balance of forces that are likely to shape the future of trade union membership.

As a rule, we have used throughout this chapter data on 'net union density rates', that is, on union members as a fraction of all wage-earners and salaried employees in employment, net of retired, unemployed, or self-employed union members. The data are from the DUES (Development of Unions in European Societies) project and have been reported in Ebbinghaus and Visser (2000).

2.1. MEMBERSHIP TRENDS IN THE TWENTIETH CENTURY: INCREASED CROSS-NATIONAL VARIATION

The (West) European development in trade union organization during the past hundred years can be illustrated as a long, rising trend with significant interruptions in the 1930s and 1940s, growing divergence among countries, and a clear dip after 1980 in all but a few countries. A first peak in membership was reached around 1920, when, following the end of the First World War, workers joined unions in droves (Table 2.1). However, with only a minority of workers covered by collective bargaining agreements, unions were unable to maintain the high membership levels of 1920. A further dip in membership occurred in the early 1930s under circumstances of the international recession and rising unemployment, although it is noteworthy that trade unions in the three Scandinavian countries appeared to grow in this time of rising unemployment. In many countries—Italy (1926–44), Germany (1933–45), Greece (1936–49, 1967–74), Portugal (1926–1974), Spain (1939–75), and during wartime in Finland, Belgium, France, the Netherlands, and Norway—unions were politically repressed and trade union activities suspended.

Following the end of the Second World War and the restoration of democracy, union membership reached a second peak around 1950. The position of unions was now much more secure, as they were recognized nationwide by

Table 2.1. *Union density rates, 1950–1997*

	1900	1910	1920	1930	1940	1950	1960	1970	1975	1980	1985	1990	1995	1998
Sweden	5	8	28	36	54	67	71	67	73	78	82	82	88	88
Finland	—	5	14	8	13	30	32	51	65	69	69	73	80	79
Denmark	13	17	33	37	41	56	62	63	69	78	79	75	78	76
Norway[a]	4	8	20	19	43	45	52	50	52	55	56	56	55	55
Belgium	—	5	39	29	34	43	42	42	52	53	51	50	54	—
Ireland	—	—	33	28	21	37	45	53	56	57	56	53	47	42
Austria	—	6	51	38	—	62	60	57	53	52	52	47	41	39
Italy[b]	6	8	35	—	—	45	28	37	48	50	42	39	39	38
UK[c]	13	15	45	25	33	42	42	45	49	51	45	38	32	30
Germany	6	18	53	33	—	—	—	—	—	—	—	36	29	26
West	—	—	—	—	—	38	35	32	35	35	34	32	—	—
East	—	—	—	—	—	—	—	—	—	—	—	47	—	—
Portugal	—	—	—	—	—	—	—	—	—	52	—	40	30	—
Netherlands	3	11	31	28	30	43	42	37	38	35	28	24	24	23
Switzerland	—	7	26	24	26	40	39	30	32	31	28	27	24	22
Greece	—	—	—	—	—	—	—	—	—	36	37	34	24	—
Spain[d]	—	2	9	12	—	—	—	—	—	8	9	11	17	16
France	6	9	11	8	23	30	24	20	22	22	19	14	10	10

Notes: Maximum rates are italized. Prewar data may include unemployed and (small numbers of) retired members, and may therefore overstate the level of membership compared to postwar figures.
[a] 1997 instead of 1998.
[b] Density rates are underestimated (by 10%–20% in recent years) since they do not include members of independent or 'autonomous' unions.
[c] Density rates for the 1990s are based on Labour Force Survey data for the UK.
[d] 1981 instead of 1980; 1997 instead of 1998.

Sources: Bain and Price (1980), Visser (1989, 1994) for 1900–40; Ebbinghaus and Visser (2000) for 1950–97.

employers and governments and many more workers were now covered by collective agreements that applied to entire sectors of the economy. As an indicator of increased 'union security', we find that after 1945 the annual fluctuations in membership numbers dropped significantly (Visser, 1986). The two European exceptions were France and Italy where, following the tensions of the Cold War and the sharp ideological divisions, the unions lost almost half their members in only a decade. A third peak in union membership can be situated around 1980. We see that by that time Italian unions had fully recovered from their losses and that, with the lone exception of France, trade unions had more members than ever before.

In 1991 the OECD published a survey of trends in union membership and union density during the 1970s and 1980s (OECD, 1991). One of the main conclusions was that in all but a few countries the postwar expansion of trade union organization had halted in the 1980s, sharply contrasting with what had in Europe been the main trend in preceding decades. On the basis of newer data, covering also the 1990s, we are able to confirm this conclusion: 1980 was a reversal of (postwar) trends in nearly all OECD countries. The four Nordic countries (five if one includes Iceland, with a union density level approaching 100%) and Belgium, which are the countries with the highest density levels in Europe (and in the world),[1] are the only cases in which union density rates have not fallen (see Table 2.1).[2]

Considering the variation across countries, one can only be struck by the very large and persistent divergences. Even within the same geographical regions, and among countries that otherwise are quite similar—for example Norway and Sweden, the Netherlands and Belgium, Ireland and the UK, or Italy and France—union density rates vary a great deal. There is no evidence of convergence. Overall, the divergence in union density in Western Europe and in the OECD area—as measured by the coefficient of variation—has increased since 1950 and accelerated since the late 1970s (Blaschke, 2000; Visser, 1993; Western, 1997). Persistent and increasing cross-national differences in unionization levels and trends are prima facie evidence that union membership decisions must be seen in the context of institutions specific to national labour markets.[3]

2.2. UNION MEMBERSHIP DECLINE

The last decades of the twentieth century were unhappy ones for the trade unions. In France and the UK, the desyndicalization trend has continued for two decades.[4] The French union density rate was halved, whereas British unions lost 40% of their strength. Italian unions faired better: in absolute numbers, the three main federations gained almost two million members since 1979 (Ebbinghaus and Visser, 2000), but more than half of current members are pensioners and retired. The union density rate (net of these groups, as shown in the table) dropped to 37, a loss of more than 25%. A part of this loss was probably compensated by the increased membership of independent unions with a strong presence in the public and subsidized sectors, and in banking. However, the precise membership of these unions, and its variation over time, is very hard to ascertain. The 1998 union density rate may lie between 10% and 20% above the rate shown in Table 2.1.

Unions in Germany, by far largest of the European economies, initially did better, but in the years following unification in 1989 they lost more than three million members, and the current density rate of 26% of the dependent

---

[1] See ILO (1997). We disregard countries such as China or some former communist states, with compulsory membership or data that cannot be verified.

[2] Note, however, that in Belgium and Sweden there were fewer employed union members in 1998 than in 1980.

[3] Further evidence is that splitting the membership figures by industry, occupation, or gender gives the same rank-order differences across countries. Variation across countries dominated within-country variation (Visser, 1993).

[4] In the UK, the 1999 Labour Force Survey reported a small rise in aggregate union membership, the first rise in twenty years! In France the decline began in 1976 and was largely determined by, though not restricted to, the communist trade unions. In the 1990s the CFDT, a reform-oriented union confederation, appears to have gained members and has moved into the first place among French unions.

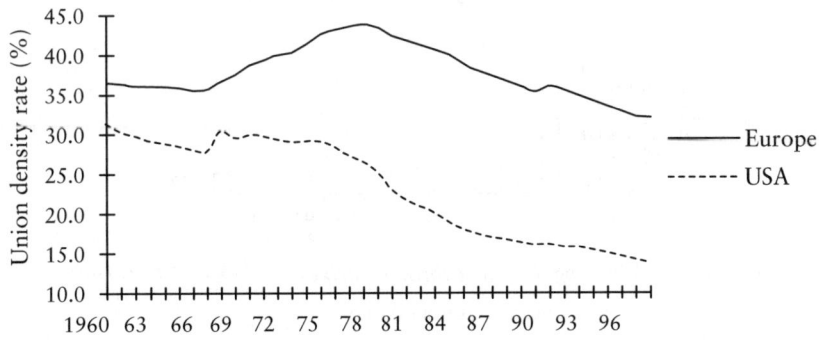

Figure 2.1. *Unionization trends in Europe and the United States, 1960–1996*

The rate for Europe is a weighted average of all countries listed in Table 2.1, except for Greece, Portugal, and Spain, for which no continuous data were available.

workforce is a quarter below the previous level in West Germany. In the smaller economies, also—with the exception of the four Nordic countries and Belgium—unions have witnessed a decline in their overall position. We note that in many countries the current period of union decline is now longer than at any time before. Current union membership in Austria, France, Germany, the Netherlands, Switzerland, and the UK is lower than at any time since the end of the Second World War.

Figure 2.1 summarizes the trend reversal in union fortunes, comparing the average union rate in Western Europe with the average rate in the United States.[5] In the USA the decline began two decades earlier, in the 1950s (interrupted by the surge in public-sector unionism during the Kennedy–Johnson administration in the 1960s) and has continued since. Currently, US labour unions organize 16.5 million out of a total of 119 million workers, which gives a union density rate of 13.9%.[6] In Europe, 41.5 million workers (in employment), out of a labour force of 130 million, joined unions in 1998, giving a union density rate of 32%. This is 12 points (or more than a quarter) below the postwar peak of 44% in 1979, lower also than the level in 1960.[7]

The reversal in unionization trends in Europe is paralleled by the development of three other possible indicators of union power: the decline in militancy, decreasing wage shares, and the rise in unemployment. In the EU, the number of working days lost as a result of labour conflicts has dropped from 85 million in

---

[5] Given the large cross-national variation, it may seem unnatural to take a European average, but interstate variation in union density in the USA vary from 33.9% in Michigan to 3.8% in Alaska (figures for 1995).

[6] Figure for 1999 provided by the US Bureau of Labor Statistics, Washington, DC.

[7] Note that the aggregate for Western Europe (based on the countries listed in Table 2.1) does not overlap with the EU, as it includes non-EU members Norway and Switzerland but excludes EU members Greece and Luxembourg.

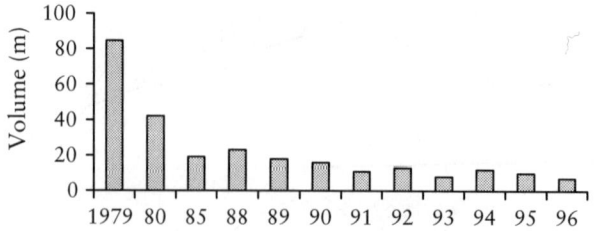

Figure 2.2. *Working days lost through strikes in the EU, 1979–1996*
Sources: CEC (2000); calculations from ILO data.

1979 to less than 7 million in 1996, which is less than half an hour per year per worker (Figure 2.2). Shalev (1992) underscores the connection with the rise in unemployment and observes that 'in nearly all countries where data on the number of strikes are available and there are enough data to justify the analysis we find an evident fit between general trends in strikes and the rate of unemployment. Once unemployment began its steady rise above the customary levels of the "Golden Age", an equally steady decline in strike frequency was not far behind' (Shalev, 1992: 115). The easing of the trend towards higher unemployment in the later 1980s did not lead to a reversal of the trend in declining militancy. On this basis, Shalev conjectures that the new labour quiescence, at least in the market sector, is 'more than a simple conjectural response'.

The most significant policy shift in the 1980s was probably the change in macroeconomic policy, when governments and central banks, with few exceptions (Sweden, for instance), adopted a non-accommodating stance. This came after the failure of most incomes policies and the inability of most trade union movements to deliver wage restraint (Flanagan *et al.*, 1983; Scharpf, 1991). In Western Europe, the reduction in inflation rates in the 1980s was based on policies that allowed unemployment to rise.

The steep rise in real compensation (corrected for inflation) from the mid-1960s to the late 1970s came to a halt in the 1980s. As in the case of the convergence to low inflation rates, the cross-national convergence to moderation is much stronger than is apparent in the data on union density (EIRO, 2000). A possible indicator of this development is the fall in the wage share, which again shows a sharp reversal of trend around 1980 (Figure 2.3).[8]

The crucial question is whether the decline of recent times forebodes continued 'lean times' for the unions, or whether the unions will eventually find a way to bounce back, as they did in or after the 1930s and 1940s. Can we arrive

---

[8] This interpretation presupposes that the elasticity of substitution between capital and labour is smaller than unity. An alternative interpretation is that the fall in the wage share is purely a result of a shift in technology (Blanchard, 1998; Blanchard and Wolfers, 2000). The latter interpretation presupposes a Cobb–Douglas production function, which has an elasticity of substitution equal to unity.

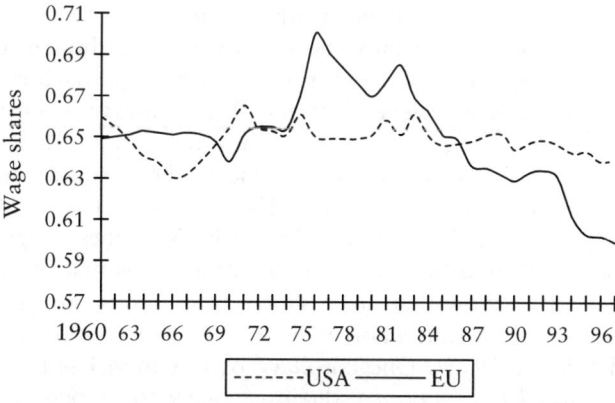

Figure 2.3. *Wage shares, USA–EU, 1960–1996*
Sources: CEC (2000), calculations from national account statistics.

at a reliable prediction of future membership trends? While this will be the main topic in Sections 2.4–2.7, we will lay the theoretical groundwork in the next section.

2.3. WHY JOIN A TRADE UNION?

The most obvious answer to this question is that unions have something to offer: better wages, employment terms and working conditions, job security, protection, a feeling of self-respect. The problem with this answer is that one actually does not have to be a union member to get many of these things: it is enough that other people have joined, as most of the 'goods' of the union are 'collective' in the sense that they cannot be withheld from non-union members. This situation gives rise to the so called *free-rider* paradox. According to the theory of public goods (Olson, 1965), no individual will rationally join in the cost of production, because they can enjoy the goods for free. The key problem is to explain why any worker would join a trade union when dues are costly and when the benefits are not immediately available or apply to all workers regardless of their union status (Crouch, 1982; Booth, 1985; Naylor, 1989).

In order to escape the free-rider paradox, Olson argued that collective action would occur only if there is either compulsion (analogous to the 'closed shop', in which union membership is a condition of employment) or if the union offers *selective incentives*, i.e. private goods to members only. In addition to material incentives, Booth (1985) interprets the selective incentives as being the 'reputation' utility that derives from complying with a social custom of membership. This idea stems from Akerlof (1980), who defines a social custom as 'an act whose utility to the agent performing it in some ways depends on the beliefs or actions of other members of the community'. In the context of union membership, the social custom is thought of as urging workers not to take a free ride. This social customs approach considers that the joining decision is interdependent and that, contrary to Olson's theory, workers may be more prepared to join if (they know that) others are joining. A similar result on collective action is found in the 'resource mobilization', 'critical mass', and 'tipping' models of Klandermans (1984), Marwell and Oliver (1993), and Schelling (1978). On the basis of these approaches, and assuming that workers differ with respect to their sensitivity to solidarity, it has been possible to show that 'open-shop' trade unions can exist at various levels of union density despite a potential free-rider threat (Naylor, 1989, 1990; Naylor and Cripps, 1993). One corollary of this model is that any fall in membership caused by *temporary* shocks is likely to be persistent. If membership is reduced, the process of rebuilding can be lengthy and, perhaps, unsustainable. Thus, in the Netherlands recent surveys have shown that the proportion of workers in establishments with a (perceived) high level of membership (of 40% and more) has decreased. Further analysis has shown that workers in establishments with low (perceived) density rates left the union in significantly higher proportions than workers in establishments with high density rates, and talked much less frequently with colleagues about 'union business' (Klandermans and Visser, 1995).

Beyond some minimum critical level of density, whether or not there are losses in having some free-riders will depend on the cost structure in the provision of union benefits and services, and on the relationship between union density and bargaining power. The union's provision of benefits and services may be crucial in obtaining its critical level of membership density in the absence of coercion. In the presence of uncertainty and high individual transaction costs, the union can act as an agent providing for its membership a variety of services (collection of information, contract services, evaluation of wage and fringe benefits, monitoring of firms' performance, aggregation of worker preferences, communication of these to the firm, improving the quality of works councils, offering favourable terms with insurance companies, etc.). Since the cost of provision of these services is subject to 'economies of scale and jointness' characteristics (Faith and Reid, 1987), workers gain from sharing an agent rather than individually arranging for provision of them.

Whenever unions offer exclusive services to their members, for example in the form of advice on retirement plans, job training, and legal support in disputes with employers, union density is obviously increasing with the quality of the services provided (Booth and Chatterji, 1995). Union size is also relevant, as larger unions can benefit from economies of scale. We may expect that pro-union legislation (lowering the cost of union activity, or allowing unions to monopolize certain services) and lower membership dues (direct monetary costs) increase equilibrium union density (Naylor and Cripps, 1993). Of course, the demand by workers for the services of an 'agent–union' depends on what services are available elsewhere; for instance, firms or the state may provide some of the services listed above. Workers' demand for union services cannot be considered in isolation, since it is likely to be interdependent with employers' personnel policies, the state's welfare policies, and any union involvement in these. The relationship between union and state welfare policies is the subject of Part II of this book; however, in the next section, where we deal with cyclical factors such as unemployment, we will discuss one particular aspect: whether unemployment insurance is administered by the union or by the state.

2.4. CYCLICAL EXPLANATIONS OF UNION MEMBERSHIP DEVELOPMENTS

Explanations of union growth and decline fall, by and large, within one of three approaches: cyclical, structural, or institutional (Ebbinghaus and Visser, 1999). Historians and economists have advocated the *cyclical* approach. In his history of the US labour movement in the nineteenth century, John Commons and his team discovered that in years of prosperity, when prices, sales, and profits rise and labour demand increases, workers 'grow dissatisfied' and 'are impelled, first as individuals, then as organisations, to demand higher wages and reduced hours' (Commons *et al.*, 1918). Under these circumstances, if they get established, unions gain concessions and attract members, but when the tide turns 'unions are sooner or later defeated, and when the period of depression ensues, with its widespread unemployment, the labour movement either subsidises or changes its form to political or socialist agitation, to ventures in cooperation of communism, or to other panaceas' (Commons *et al.*, 1918). This cycle has been 'so often repeated', that it was concluded that the history of trade unions is divided into separate phases of prosperity and crisis measured by the index of commodity prices (Commons *et al.*, 1918).

Later work has greatly improved the theoretical foundations and methodology of empirical studies (Ashenfelter and Pencavel, 1969; Bain and Elsheikh, 1976; Booth, 1983; Carruth and Disney, 1988; Carruth and Schnabel, 1990; Roche and Larragy, 1990; Van den Berg, 1996; van Ours, 1991; Western, 1997). Operationally, these business cycle studies have taken different forms, but the impact of two variables stands out. Sometimes *inflation* seems to increase membership, whereas *unemployment* usually halts membership growth.

2.4.1. *Inflation*

The usual explanation for a positive relation between inflation and union membership is based on an 'insurance motive': 'in as much as workers perceive an increase in the rate of change of retail prices as a threat to their standard of living... they are more likely to become and remain union members in an attempt to maintain this standard' (Bain and Elsheik, 1976). In addition to this 'insurance motive', Bain and Elsheik mention a 'reward motive', according to which workers join the union as a sort of 'reward' for its success in obtaining a wage rise (see also Checchi and Corneo, 1996). It is unclear, however, how these incentives can be strong in the face of the fact that wage rises are applied to members and non-members alike. In most European countries, bargaining coverage extends far beyond union membership, and within the same bargaining domains union members receive the same wages as non-members (see Chapter 4). In the econometric studies cited before, inflation proved an unstable predictor, and in many countries no effect was found.

2.4.2. Unemployment

With regard to unemployment, the literature is even more uncertain. Ashenfelter and Pencavel (1969) use unemployment in the previous trough of the business cycle as an explanatory variable for union membership, believing the effect to be positive since unemployment is supposed to have contributed to the workers' stock of grievances. However, most authors have followed Bain and Elsheik (1976) in their argument that unemployment strengthens the bargaining position of management: 'When unemployment is high or increasing, employers may be better able and more willing to oppose unionism. For in as far as unemployment reduces the level of aggregate demand, production lost as a result of strikes and other forms of industrial action will be less costly to employers' (Bain and Elsheikh, 1976).[9] The principal argument as to why unemployment would halt union membership growth, then, is quite similar to Commons's business cycle hypothesis: in times of high and rising unemployment, unions are less able to press demands and obtain advantages for members. Another reason may be that under conditions of slack the (perceived) cost of union membership may rise. Employees may to a larger extent be prone to 'appease' employers by staying out of unions. This may especially be the case when new entrants are employed on temporary contracts. However, these conjectures are highly contingent on legal conditions, such as union recognition rights and practices, employment protection, etc. It has been noted in the literature, for instance, that in the 1970s, when unemployment was rising in the OECD area, density levels continued their upward trend in Europe (Visser, 1991). During the 1970s, often as a *quid pro quo* to incomes policies and social

[9] They add that the relationship between unemployment and union membership depends on whether members continue or discontinue their membership upon becoming unemployed. However, this does not affect the net union density rate, defined as *employed* union members taken as a proportion of wage and salary-earners in employment. For models using (the rate of growth of) absolute membership rather than union density as the dependent variable, the behaviour of unemployed workers is of course relevant.

contracts, unions tended to gain more employment protection and recognition rights, especially among white-collar employees and in the public sector.

The ability of unions to influence layoff decisions is an important intervening variable, as this presents a private incentive good. When unions are able to bargain over layoff procedures and obtain preferential treatment for their members (in that non-union members are the first to be laid off), workers are likely to join the union in order to obtain (partial) insurance against the unemployment risk. If workers are heterogeneous in terms of risk aversion, more risk-averse workers will join the union and, other things being constant, an increase in aggregate unemployment risk raises union density (Booth, 1984). In this context we must consider two important conditions related to the union's ability to influence layoff and rehiring decisions: (1) the presence of unions in the enterprise or workplace (Hancké, 1993); and (2) the organization of unemployment insurance and how it affects wage-setting and the demand for union services (Holmlund and Lundborg, 1999).

2.4.3. *Workplace presence*

With the disappearance of working-class neighbourhoods and the replacement of local dues collection by centralized administrative procedures, union representation at the workplace has become the only direct means of contact between members and their union (except where unions administer social security programmes—see Section 2.4.4). The workplace appears to be the main locus to recruit new members ('members recruit members'), uphold the 'social custom' of membership, and offer services (e.g. grievance handling). Protection and support in case of conflict with management is often cited as the main reason why workers would join the union (see Section 2.5.4).

To understand the role of local unions or works councils in recessions, we must bear in mind that, under legislation or central agreements in many European countries, local management is under obligation to negotiate or consult with local union representatives or works councils over restructuring plans and layoff schemes (Rogers and Streeck, 1995). Formally or informally, local union and works council representatives favour policies that benefit their re-election chances, selecting 'qualities of the workers, which have trad-itionally been conducive to union membership and enhance job security at the same time: e.g., skill, tenure, male, married, indigenous, etc.' (Streeck, 1981). The fact that in Austria, Belgium, Denmark, Germany, and Italy the decline in manufacturing employment (and rise in unemployment of manual workers) during the 1970s and 1980s was accompanied by a rise in union-ization must mean that the share of those who lost their jobs was less among union members than among non-union members (Visser, 1990). Where entire 'high density' plants, for instance mining pits or shipyards, are closed, as was the case in France, the Netherlands, Spain, and the UK, local union influence may be irrelevant.

2.4.4. *Unemployment insurance: Ghent and non-Ghent*

Most countries introduced some form of public or publicly supported unemployment insurance system before the Second World War (ILO, 1955). These schemes took two forms (Rothstein, 1992): a compulsory system administered by government agencies, and a voluntary but publicly supported scheme administered by unions or union-dominated funds. The latter system is also called the *Ghent system*, after the Belgian town where it was first introduced, in 1901. State unemployment schemes became mandatory for workers at a relatively early stage in the UK (1911), Austria (1920), and Germany (1927). Norway (1938) and the Netherlands (1952) abandoned the Ghent system for statutory regulation. The mutual insurance schemes in France and Switzerland never grew to such importance for trade unions (Flora, 1986). Italy, Spain, Portugal, and Greece failed to achieve a comprehensive safety net for the unemployed (Ferrera, 1996). The Ghent system is still operating in Sweden, Denmark, Finland, and Iceland. In Denmark, the unemployment funds also administer the early retirement funds that were introduced in the late 1970s (Scheuer, 1992). In Belgium unemployment insurance was brought under the control of the state after 1945, but, following the Social Pact of 1944, the unions retained a role in the administration of the insurance and received a state subsidy for these services (Martens, 1985).[10]

In any unemployment insurance scheme, the paramount question is: who decides what kind of job the unemployed worker can refuse without losing the unemployment benefit? (Rothstein, 1992). It is here, in influencing these decisions for its members, that we discover the importance of the Ghent system as a 'selective benefit'. Thus, membership is likely to be higher under a 'Ghent system' in so far as (1) unions can make it difficult for non-members to obtain the insurance; (2) unions control, or greatly influence, what is considered a 'suitable job'; and (3) unions can, through the scheme, increase their control over the supply of labour. Although membership of the unemployment fund is formally disconnected from union membership, and the latter is not a qualifying condition for the former, employees are likely to perceive a close connection, as is shown in surveys among employees in Denmark (Scheuer, 1984).

In Ghent countries unemployed members, like workers who anticipate unemployment, tend to join the union. Hence, unionization levels tend to be higher for any given level of unemployment in these countries than in non-Ghent countries. In the Ghent countries union membership is also likely to increase in times of rising unemployment, whereas in non-Ghent countries the opposite effect is more likely. A study of Danish membership trends before 1940 (Pedersen, 1982) and one of Dutch trade union growth before and after 1945 (Van den Berg, 1996) found exactly these effects. The difference between

---

[10] Similar arrangements exist or have existed in non-Ghent countries in some industries, e.g. in Italian agriculture and in the Dutch construction industry (until 1997).

Ghent and non-Ghent systems helps explain the difference in unionization between Norway and its Scandinavian neighbours (Holmlund and Lundborg, 1999), between the Netherlands and Belgium (Visser, 1992), and the exceptionally high rates of unionization in Italian agriculture and the Dutch building industry (Ebbinghaus and Visser, 2000).

2.4.5. *Union organizing and labour force growth*

Most business cycle theories may be criticized for taking a 'thin' view on the union as an organizing agent. The key agents are workers, perhaps employers, rarely union organizers (Visser, 1994; Western, 1997). But it may also be fruitful to see the development of union membership from the perspective of existing unions: as the costs of union organizing activities fall on current members, union leaders, who feel that they have penetrated their primary jurisdiction deeply enough to be an effective bargaining agent for their members, may not want to 'waste' scarce resources on organizing activities (Shister, 1967). The assumption that union leaders are interested primarily in organizing the entire working class assumes a high degree of political motivation in these leaders.

Wallerstein (1989, 1991) has attempted to tackle the organizing problem of the union. He argues that unionization is inversely related to the size of the labour force. He treats union organizing drives as an investment. The benefit of higher union density is that the union's bargaining power is increased. This is to be set against the cost of organizing new members. The marginal cost of recruiting new members will be increasing if the least easy-to-organize workers—those working in small firms, or in unstable employment relations, or with religious and political views against unionism—are recruited last. Three main propositions follow from Wallerstein's analysis: (1) since organizing costs are borne in the present while benefits come in future bargaining rounds, unions will allocate less resources to organizing the less members care about the future (for instance, a union with only older members, or workers in temporary jobs); (2) since the costs of organizing new members (eventually) rise with an increased number of potential members, unions in large (and expanding) labour markets settle for a lower 'target unionization rate' than unions in small (and stagnant) labour markets; (3) anything that lowers the costs of recruiting new members (e.g. legal protection for union organizers, or a law that makes strikes less expensive for the union) increases the 'target unionization rate'. In conformity with his theoretical analysis, Wallerstein was able to explain a large share of the cross-national variation of the unionization rate (in 1989) with two variables: the size of the labour force, and the cumulative impact of social democratic or left-wing governments (measured as the number of years they were in power since the 1930s, weighted by their share in coalition governments). We will present some additional evidence in favour of a negative relationship between unionization and the size of the labour force in Section 2.8.

2.5. STRUCTURAL EXPLANATIONS

Sociologists have favoured the structural approach to union decline. In this view, decline results from changing class structures, new modes of production, flexible labour markets, and a spread of individualist values undermining the social custom of union membership. Union growth trajectories are expected to resemble a long-term 'parabola' rather than short-term 'cycles'. Union movements grew in the ascending phase of industrial capitalism with the rise of large industrial conglomerates, the institutionalization of collective employment relations, and the expansion of social and industrial citizenship. In the descending phase, with the coming of 'post-industrial' society, the trend is reversed. The key observation for structural explanations is that the distribution of union membership across sectors, occupations, and firms is highly unequal.

The composition of European labour markets has changed dramatically in past decades. Nearly the entire employment growth was due to increased female participation; women's share among European wage earners rose to 44.2% in 1997. Decline has hit mining and manufacturing and led to a sharp fall in employment of manual workers, who are now a minority in Europe's labour force. In 1970, half of all wage-earners found work in industry (ISIC II–V); in 1995 they represented one-third or less, equal to the employment share of social and personal services (ISIC IX). If the strong growth of the past twenty-five years continues, commercial and financial services (ISIC VI + VIII) will soon make up the other third. We observe, finally, that the share of public or collective (i.e. subsidized) employment, mostly in social and personal services (ISIC IX), has risen over the entire period from less than a quarter to one-third. However, most of this growth occurred in the 1960s and 1970s; in recent years the expansion of public sector employment has stopped or been reversed.

Judging by the union density rates in Table 2.2, it appears that most of these composition shifts must have had a negative effect on aggregate union growth. The shift of employment from industry and transport to sectors where unions were not well established reduced the highly organized population. The expansion of the public sector may have worked in the opposite direction until the recent halt in welfare state growth. Table 2.3 shows that unionization rates in the public sector are always much higher than in the private sector. The gap between union density in the private and public sectors is particularly large in the German-speaking countries, the UK, Norway, the Netherlands, France, and Spain. We also note that, where we have time-series data (not available for some of the high-density countries, and only since 1991 for Spain), unionization rates in the private sector have fallen since the early 1980s, whereas unionization levels in the public sector have been relatively stable. On average, current union density in Europe's public (and subsidized) sector is twice as high as in the private sector—an estimated 50% against 25% in the private sector. The public–private gap in union organization suggests that stability of

Table 2.2. *Union density by sector and gender* (%)

	Year	Male	Female	I Agriculture	II–IV Manufacturing	V Construction	VI Commerce	VII Transport	VIII Finance	IX Services
Sweden	1980	79	77	53	89	95	45	79	83	84
	1997	83	90	69	100	100	61	83	58	100
Denmark	1981	83	73	—	98	89	53	60	50	73
	1997	73	78	—	94	—	—	—	53	—
Finland	1989	69	75	83	80	—	—	—	—	—
Norway	1980	69	44	31	78	44	17	68	45	60
	1995	60	51	27	79	47	13	61	33	66
Belgium	1980	—	—	74	80	47	32	63	26	27
	1995	—	—	82	100	65	39	77	23	27
Ireland	1980	54	51	—	55	49	—	71	—	—
	1994	42	39	—	68	64	26	82	36	55
Austria	1980	58	39	54	57	48	15	60	15	41
	1997	44	27	40	56	36	22	77	33	38
Italy	1980	—	—	100	39	42	23	57	17	29
	1997	—	—	100	—	38	10	80	22	59
UK	1979	64	38	23	64	30	14	62	26	52
	1989	44	33	13	44	22	7	45	18	46
	1997	32	28	8	31	19	12	73	19	26
Germany—West	1980	44	18	20	50	19	12	71	7	24
	1990	38	19	22	48	25	16	76	8	27
Germany—all	1991	40	26	29	53	13	10	61	5	24
	1997	30	17	21	45	44	10	49	8	44
Netherlands	1980	44	18	17	43	41	14	39	16	28
	1997	33	20	20	33	—	11	—	19	28
Switzerland	1980	41	14	—	34	65	9	62	14	24
	1987	32	11	—	34	52	6	56	20	—
Spain	1991	—	—	9	22	10	6	32	20	10
	1997	—	—	11	24	11	4	32	27	14
France	1981	29	15	16	21	8	3	25	20	28
	1993	13	7	7	9	3	—	19	—	21

Notes: Entries in italic are based on labour force sample surveys; the other entries are based on administrative data of unions.

Sources: Calculations from Visser (1991), Ebbinghaus and Visser (2000), and OECD Labour Force Statistics (various years).

Table 2.3. *Union density, private and public sectors (%)*

	Year	Private	Public	Year	Private	Public
Sweden	1980	—	—	1995	77	93
Finland	1980	—	—	1989	65	86
Norway	1980	47	74	1994	44	79
Ireland	1980	—	—	1994	43	68
Italy[a]	1980	48	60	1997	36	43
Austria	1980	40	68	1998	30	69
Germany[b]	1980	29	67	1997	22	56
Switzerland	1980	24	71	1987	22	71
UK[c]	1980	45	69	1999	19	60
Netherlands	1980	26	60	1997	19	45
Spain	1991	14	26	1997	15	32
France	1981	18	44	1993	4	25

Notes: Public sector includes public administration, education, public health, railways, and PTT (before privatization).

[a]Public-sector density in Italy in 1997 was probably much higher, by 10–15 percentage points, if the membership of independent unions, which are especially active in the public sector, is added. However, given the poor and scanty nature of the membership statistics of these unions, the figures in this and other tables in this chapter are based on the membership in unions belonging to the three main confederations.

[b]1980 refers to West Germany.

[c]1999 refers to Great Britain.

Sources: Calculations from Ebbinghaus and Visser (2000).

employment and the absence of employer opposition are important elements in union organizing.

Structural explanations based on compositional shifts in employment explain only part of current union decline. A shift–share analysis over the period 1980–97, using the division in seven sectors based on ISIC coding (aggregating mining and utilities with manufacturing, as in Table 2.2), shows that at most one-third of the decline in unionization in any of these countries is explained by sectoral employment shifts. Of course, an analysis based on cross-industry shifts in employment does not take account of changes within industries, for instance from manual to non-manual work, from full-time to part-time work, and from large firms to small firms. Hence it tends to under-estimate the actual structural challenge to trade union organization (see also Green, 1992). In the following sections we discuss compositional effects related to gender, working time, and age.

2.5.1. *Male and female union density*

Surveys in Denmark, Sweden, the Netherlands, and the UK show no significant differences between men and women (if controlled for part-time or full-time employment status) in their attitudes with regard to the union (Bild *et al.*, 1998; Gallie, 1996; Kjellberg, 1997; Klandermans and Visser, 1995). In fact, the Danish survey showed that the strongest support for the unions came not from the 3M (male, manual, and manufacturing) workers, but from women in the public sector. Thanks to the strong presence of female workers in the public sector and in professions like teaching and nursing, the gender gap in union-ization has narrowed, and indeed, has disappeared in the Nordic countries (as is shown in Table 2.2). A particularly large gender gap with respect to union membership is, however, still found in the German-speaking countries and in the Netherlands.

It is worth noting that since the early 1980s all of the trade union mem-bership growth has come from women. Never before have so many women in Europe joined the trade union movement. Figure 2.4 gives further evidence on the convergence in male and female unionization rates for a selection of European countries. We observe that, outside Scandinavia, it is the fall in the male density rate, rather than the rise in the female density, that accounts for the narrowing of the gender gap in unionization.

2.5.2. *Part-time and full-time workers*

The difference in unionization between men and women is largely a com-positional effect: women work in sectors and jobs where unionization is lower (Spilsbury *et al.*, 1987). In Europe, part-time employment has increased to around 15 percent of total employment, though with pronounced varia-tions across countries—with the highest rates in the Netherlands, the UK and the Scandinavian countries. Part-time jobs are still mostly female jobs and have traditionally been considered by trade unions as sub-standard jobs. Union concern for part-time workers 'is at best marginal and spotty' (Cook *et al.*, 1983). Delsen (1995) reports data for the US, Australia, Canada and the UK, showing a large difference in unionisation rates for part-timers and full-timers. Unfortunately, we have only scattered recent data for European countries (Table 2.4). We observe that in Sweden there is hardly a difference in the union density rate of full-time and part-time workers. The fact that most part-time jobs in Sweden are standard jobs in the public sector matters greatly. The data for Norway and the Netherlands confirm that there are significant differences between 'long' and 'short' part-time jobs. An analysis of the Dutch labour force sample survey data of 1997 showed that it was the flexibility of the job, interpreted as absence of job protection and low tenure, that mattered as it decreased the likelihood of union membership in a large measure (Visser and Van Rij, 1999). In the Netherlands, as in the UK, there is a large overlap between 'small' part-time jobs, of less than a half-time week, and flexible employment conditions (Gallie *et al.*, 1998; Hakim, 1996).

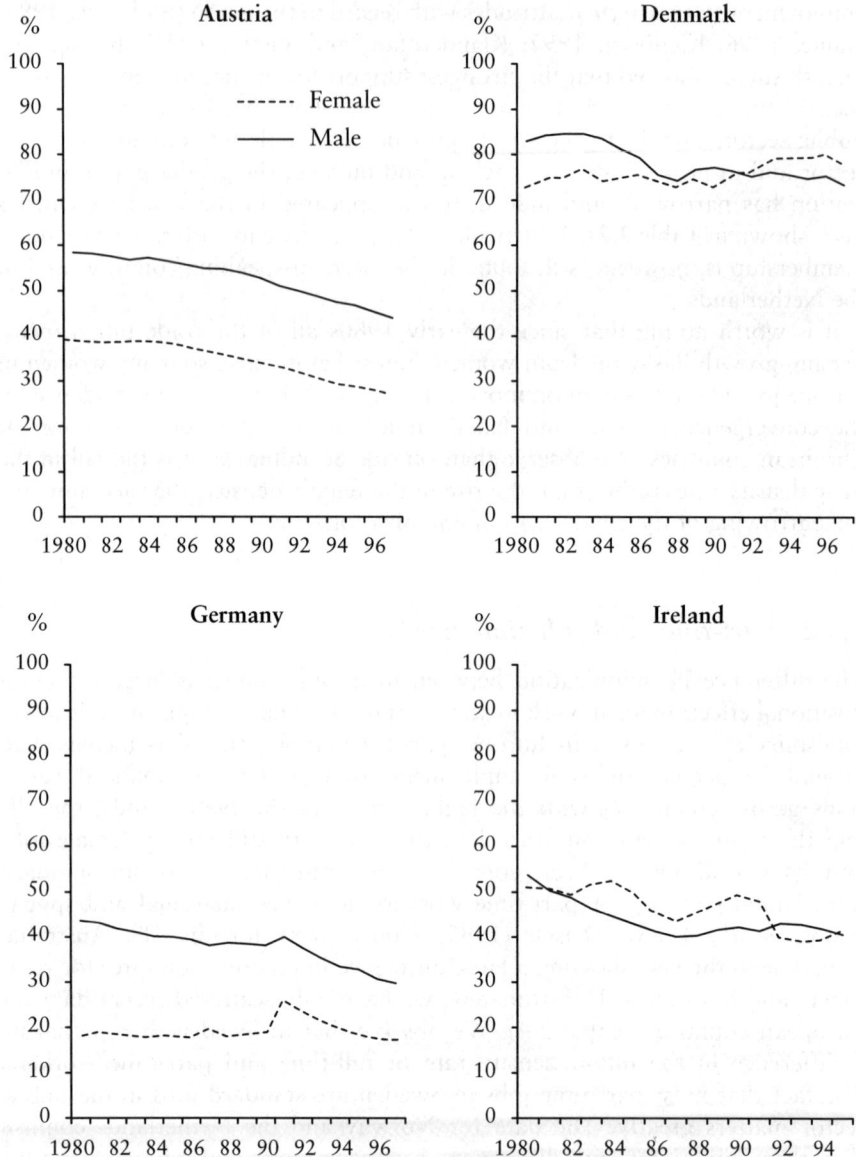

Figure 2.4. *Male and female density rates in some EU countries, 1980–1996/1998*

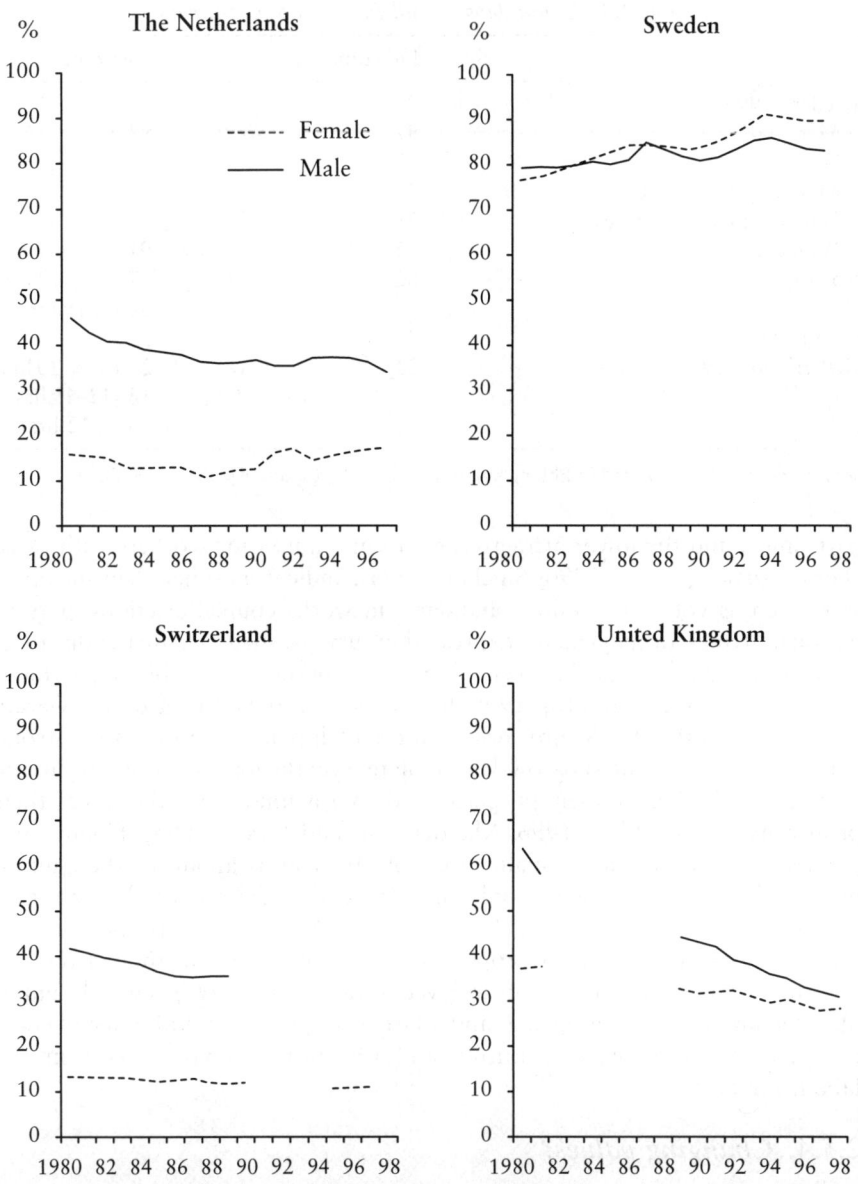

Figure 2.4. *(Continued)*

2.5.3. *Ageing of union membership*

The low unionization rate of part-time workers in Britain has been attributed to the lower availability of an organizing union in workplaces with many

Table 2.4. *Union density, full-timers and part-timers*

	Full-time	Part-time
Sweden, 1995		
Men	87	83
Women	90	83
Men, private services	75	70
Women, private services	78	68
Women, public services	95	91
Norway, 1994	62	57 (> = 19 hrs)
		36 (< 19 hrs)
Britain, 1997	34	20
Netherlands, 1997	31	25 (> = 20 hrs)
		13 (12–19 hrs)
		3 (< 12 hrs)

Source: Survey data reported in Ebbinghaus and Visser (2000), and Kjellberg (1997).

part-timers and the lower attractiveness of any union for workers with these characteristics (Green, 1990; Sinclair, 1995). Indicators other than membership, such as voting for union candidates in works council elections, participation in strikes, or judgements expressed in surveys, suggest a greater distance, emotional and otherwise, between unions and workers in unstable employment relations (Visser and Van Rij, 1999, for the Netherlands; Richards and Garcia de Polavieja, 1997, for Spain). British and Dutch panel data indicate a strong correlation between union growth and job tenure; the longer people stay in the same firm, the higher their propensity to join a union and the lower their propensity to quit (Elias, 1996; Klandermans and Visser, 1995). Finally, and possibly related to the 'casualization' of the youth labour market, union membership among young people has dropped sharply over the past two decades in all countries for which we have data (both as a proportion of total union membership and as a proportion of young workers), though the fall appears to have been only small in Sweden (Kjellberg, 1997). Overall, union membership in Europe is ageing, and a larger proportion of union members— between 10% in North-West Europe and 50% in Italy—has retired from the labour force.

2.5.4. *Changing values?*

It would be useful to consider changes in social values and expectations of workers towards unions. Such changes, in conjunction with the aforementioned compositional shifts in the labour market and the possible diffusion of 'post-materialist' values and 'individualist' life styles (Inglehart, 1977), are obvious candidates in an explanation of the decline of (the social custom of) union membership. Historically, the core of the trade union movement was the manual working class in industry and transport. Its strength derived from a number of distinctive conditions of traditional working life: concentration of employment in large factories, a sharp distinction in status and authority between (manual) workers and (non-manual) staff, the insecurity of jobs and income, and in some cases the strength of working-class communities. All these conditions generated a sense of collective identity and awareness that improvement was more likely through collective action than through individual effort. With the decline in manufacturing and the rise of small firms, fewer workers find themselves in structural conditions conducive to collective organization. We need not assume a decline in collectivist sentiments among workers in smaller firms or in post-industrial conditions in order to reach the conclusion that union organizing has become a more arduous task. Irrespective of collectivist values, it is easier for union organizers to recruit members, provide services, and retain effective organization in environments where large concentrations of workers congregate. Union density rates correlate strongly with firm size.

It must remain a matter of speculation whether employees are less motivated by collective values than, say, one or two generations ago. Van de Vall (1970) showed that Dutch union members in the late 1950s were overwhelmingly motivated by 'egocentric' motives, believing that they themselves would be better off with union membership. Sociocentric or other directed motives and social control motives, based on the perceived pressure from parents, friends, and colleagues, came second and third. In a replication of this study thirty years later, we found no large changes, except that social control related motives had almost disappeared (Klandermans and Visser, 1995). The British Social Attitude studies show a similar picture: union members overwhelmingly report as a motive for joining: 'to protect me if problems come up' (reported by over 90% as important) and 'to get higher pay and working conditions' (80%) (data for 1990 reported by Jowell *et al.*, 1990). Less self-regarding motives were 'to help other people I work with' (76%), 'I believe in them in principle' (67%), and 'most of my colleagues are members' (55%).

2.5.5. *Unavailable unions?*

In econometric and cross-sectional studies of union membership, the observed personal characteristics of individuals are usually found to be insignificant co-determinants of union membership (Bain and Elias, 1985; Booth, 1986; Guest and Dewe, 1988; Schippers, 1986). The characteristics of jobs and workplaces rather than personal attitudes seem to determine whether or not someone will join the union. Newer survey research in Britain and the Netherlands suggests that no large attitudinal differences exist between members and non-members (Gallie, 1996; Klandermans and Visser, 1995). What has changed in both countries is the labour market, especially for newcomers and young people (Gallie *et al.*, 1998; Visser and Van Rij, 1999). In the British case the 'key explanation of non-membership appears to be the inability of unions to make contact with, or provide sufficient support to, potential members' (Waddington and Whitston, 1997). This may also apply elsewhere, notably in France or the Netherlands, where surveys show that two out of three workers find themselves in a workplace where fewer than one in ten workers is known to be member of a union (Dufour and Nunes, 1998; Klandermans and Visser, 1995).

Based on the British Workplace Industrial Relations Survey, Millward recorded in 1990 that 10% of non-unionized workers declared that 'no-one ever asked me to join' as their reason for non-membership, while a full quarter of non-unionized workers cited the lack of a union as an 'important reason' for non-membership. From these findings he concluded that 'further potential for union recruitment may thus come as much from penetrating a wider range of workplaces as from signing up free-riders in those that are already unionised' (Millward, 1990). Union recruitment is notoriously inefficient. In the Netherlands, for instance, two out of three new recruits leave the union within five years. Separations are most frequent among young people (Klandermans and Visser, 1995). Gallie (1996) argues that joining a union does not require a strong collectivist value; often people join for instrumental reasons or are made to join by their colleagues or friends; with the passing of time, they may develop a commitment to membership. Given the lack of union organization in unstable work environments, it is unlikely that 'insiders' will remind newcomers of their 'duty' to organize. Workers in unstable labour and young people may simply not have time enough to develop any strong commitment to membership.

Even if compositional changes seem to be an important factor behind the fall in union membership, they cannot give the full explanation. The decline of industrial employment, in absolute and relative terms, began in many countries before the drop in membership. Moreover, unionization trends have differed across countries despite the fact that these compositional changes are quite similar. This, evidently, points to the role for union strategy, a role that is obscured in structuralist (and business cycle) explanations. To sum up, compositional change is a likely suspect in any judgement on union decline, but it is best conceptualized as a background presence, the true impact of which can be established only in multivariate analysis. We will return to this issue in Section 2.8.

2.6. INSTITUTIONAL EXPLANATIONS

Cyclical and structural approaches cannot explain cross-national diversity—trends and cycles are too similar between countries. Institutional approaches, in contrast, emphasize cross-national variation and historical contingency, and have been favoured by political scientists (Golden *et al.*, 1997; Griffin *et al.*, 1991; Western, 1997).

Examples of institutional variables with an impact on the costs and benefits of union membership are: tax deduction of union membership dues, acceptance and protection of the check-off system (in which dues are deducted from

Table 2.5. *Regression analysis of union density in 1995 and membership growth,*
1975–1995

	Union density 1995		Membership growth 1975–95	
	Model 1	Model 2	Model 3	Model 4
Constant	26.9***	− 9.1	− 41.3***	− 63.3***
Ghent system	28.7***	12.7**	14.8	
Workplace access (strong version)	27.9***	16.0***	29.2***	27.4***
Workplace access (weak version)			16.9**	13.7**
Closed shop	22.0**			
Density, 1975	—	0.9***	—	0.6
R^2	0.8936***	0.9623***	0.8620***	0.8864***

Notes: Number of observations = 15; level of significance: ** < 0.05; *** < 0.01. In models 1 and 2 the dependent variable is measured in percentage points. The institutional variables (Ghent system, workplace access, and closed shop) are dummy variables. Thus, according to model 1, everything else equal, union density in 1995 was 28.7 percentage points higher in countries with the Ghent system relative to other countries. In models 3 and 4 the dependent variable is measured as the percentage change in union density levels between 1975 and 1995.

Source: Ebbinghaus and Visser (1999).

salaries and transferred to the union by employers), works councils and union access to the workplace (see Section 2.4.3), unemployment insurance (see Section 2.4.4), legal basis for closed shop and secondary pickets, and legal protection for union organizers and union members. There is considerable variation across countries in such institutions.[11]

In a comparative analysis of union decline since 1975, Ebbinghaus and Visser (1999) found that the cross-national variation in union density in 1995 could be explained by just three institutional variables: union-affiliated unemployment insurance, a closed shop, and union access to the workplace (Table 2.5, model 1). However, the correlation between union density at the beginning (1975) and the end (1995) of the period under analysis is so strong that all three institutional factors are no longer significant within the same model when initial (1975) union density is added as an explanatory variable. In such an 'inertia model' (model 2 in the table), only 'Ghent' and 'workplace access' (strong variant, excluding statutory representation through works councils) remain. By far the most important factor explaining the variation in union growth or decline since 1975 appears to be whether or not, and to what degree, unions were present and recognized in the workplace. This is the only

[11] One example relates to secondary pickets. The legality of such boycotts and other forms of economic pressure may explain why workers at McDonald are unionized in Denmark, Finland, Italy, Mexico, and Australia, but not in the UK or the USA (Cobble, 1994).

institutional variable that remains significant, in both its strong and weak (including mandatory representation) variant, in models 3 and 4. This is in line with the findings of Hancké (1993) for a smaller group of seven countries and our argument in Section 2.4.3, and is unsurprising, given the general trend towards company restructuring and decentralization of industrial relations in these years. Note that 'business cycle' and 'compositional' variables did not add to the explanation—none of these variables proved significant when they were included in the regressions.

2.7. CENTRALIZATION AND UNIONIZATION

One of the main hypotheses in the institutional literature on union membership (Visser, 1991; Traxler, 1994; Golden *et al.*, 1997; Western, 1997) concerns the relationship between unionization and the level of collective bargaining. In countries where unions participate in higher-level or multi-employer systems of collective bargaining, unionization rates tend to be less prone to decline than in countries where bargaining is conducted at the company level. Blanchflower and Freeman (1990) argue that higher-level bargaining is likely to weaken employer resistance to union organizing, partly because the union premium or mark-up on wages will be lower than under single-employer bargaining. Another reason, mentioned by Sisson (1987), is that under multi-employer bargaining arrangements union interference in workplace management tends to be less intense. Moreover, under centralized and multi-employer bargaining arrangements unions have usually an easier task to establish themselves and gain recognition as the representative of workers in new sites and businesses, at least if newcomers sign up as members of employers' federations. On the other hand, workplace distance or lack of local representation, in combination with inclusive collective bargaining at higher levels (with non-members sharing in the results), is likely to make the unions more vulnerable to the free-rider problem. Cross-nationally, there appears to be a positive relationship between membership mobilization and central bargaining if bargaining is articulated in a strong tradition of local unionism (Hancké, 1993).

We discuss the structure of collective bargaining at greater length in Chapters 4 and 5, and present a combined index of union centralization and coordination in Section 4.2.1. Here, we have drawn two pictures of the relationship between this centralization/coordination measure and unionization (Figures 2.5 and 2.6). From the first picture, referring to the mid-1970s, we observe that there was an almost perfect fit between both indicators ($r = 0.835$): countries with a high level of centralization/coordination are those with a high level of unionization, and countries with low centralization/coordination are those with low unionization rates. If we now move on twenty years, to the mid-1990s, we observe that the fit between the two indicators has become much poorer ($r = 0.379$). There are now three countries (Sweden, Denmark and Finland) where, owing to the recent trend towards decentralization,

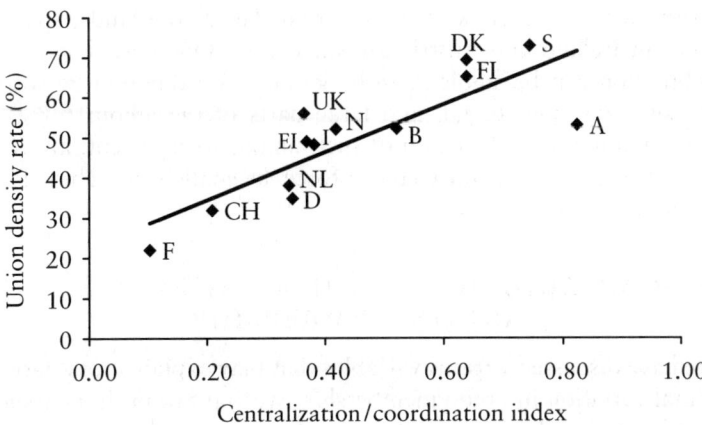

Figure 2.5. *Centralization/coordination and unionization in European countries, 1975*

Note: The density figures are those used in this chapter. The centralization index is explained in Section 4.2.1.

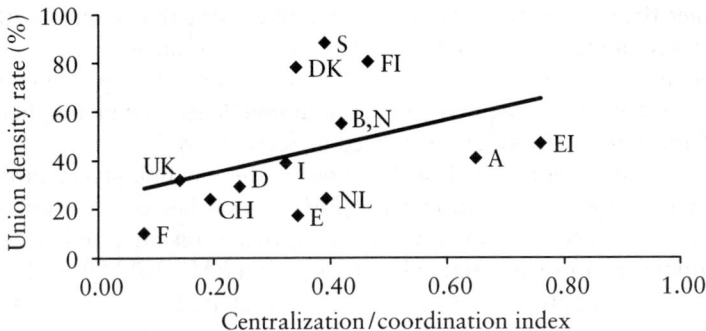

Figure 2.6. *Centralization/coordination and unionization in European countries, 1995*

Note: The density figures are those used in this chapter. The centralization/coordination index is explained in Section 4.2.1.

unionization levels are far 'in excess' of the current level of centralization/coordination. The current high level of unionization may be seen as the result of a combination of high centralization/coordination in the recent past (which gave these unions a high level of recognition), extensive workplace access, and the Ghent system (three conditions also reflecting the strong (party-)political position of the unions in these countries).

Following the decline in unionization in recent decades, together with a more moderate decline, and in some cases an increase, in centralization/coordination (see Section 4.2.1), a few countries now combine relatively high bargaining coordination with relatively low unionization. The Netherlands, Spain, and to a lesser extent Ireland and Austria are such cases. One may wonder whether this combination can be stable. Can bargaining coordination be sustained if union density continues to fall and large parts of the labour forces remain outside the unions? Will the claim of such unions to represent, and negotiate agreements that cover, the entire labour force, be challenged? These issues will be taken up in Chapters 4–6.

2.8. SOME ADDITIONAL EMPIRICAL EVIDENCE ON UNION MEMBERSHIP

While we have discussed various variables that may explain cross-national and longitudinal variation in union membership, we want to push the issue a little further and examine the impact of various factors in multivariate regressions. The main purpose of the analysis is to establish the influence of cyclical and structural changes in the labour market on union membership. Using a gross simplification, one can relate the cyclical influence to the unemployment rate (unemployment relative to the labour force). The structural influence can be related to the participation rate (the labour force relative to the population). The higher the participation rate, the more likely it is that groups with a low propensity to unionize have entered the labour force (young people; workers—mostly women—working part-time or with temporary employment contracts). So one should expect a negative impact on union density from a higher rate of labour force participation, as we argued in Section 2.4.5.

Formally, we make the analysis by entering the unemployment rate (UNE) and the employment–population ratio (EMP) as explanatory variables in our regressions. The unemployment rate, the participation rate, and the employment–population ratio are related by the equation $EMP = PART \times (1 - UNE)$, where $PART$ is the participation rate. It follows that, if a higher participation rate has a negative impact on union density, then one should also expect a negative coefficient for the employment–population ratio in the estimations.

In our regressions, we have also entered a number of other variables mentioned in the literature. Among these are the inflation rate (the change in the consumer price index), the strike participation rate, various indicators measuring structural (compositional) factors—such as the shares of women, young people, temporary workers, self-employed, and workers with higher education as well as the employment shares of industry, services, and government employment—and two political indicators aiming to capture the attitude of governments towards labour, one measuring the composition of the government and the other the unemployment benefit replacement rate.

In search of a common unionization pattern, we have pooled the data for fourteen countries (all countries in Table 2.1 except Portugal, for which we have no time-series data) and treated the data set as an unbalanced (time-series–cross-section) panel. The time period stretches from the early

1960s to 1997 or 1998. A fixed-effects model estimated over the available time span (the period 1961–95) is reported in Table 2.6. A fixed-effects estimation has been preferred to a random-effects alternative (where the model assumes the existence of a common data-generating process across countries), because several institutional features (e.g. the role and relative importance of firm-level union organization, the Ghent system, and bargaining centralization) are not controlled for. Using the fixed-effects model, we do not explain persistent differences in density levels among countries, but concentrate instead on the dynamics around these different levels. We have made the regressions in error-correction form: the change in union density is the dependent variable, and the lagged level of union density is included among the explanatory variables. The other explanatory variables are entered both in difference form (as changes), to capture short-run effects, and in level form, to capture long-run effects.

In Table 2.6 potentially endogenous variables, such as changes in unemployment and employment, or the change in the strike participation rate, have been lagged by one year. It turned out that imposing the same dynamics for all countries is effectively rejected by the data. For this reason we have interacted the lagged variables with country dummies, and have retained the statistically significant ones. The results in the table are encouraging but not overwhelming. The most striking result perhaps is that the labour market variables usually are significant and come out with the expected signs. A higher unemployment rate and a higher employment–population ratio seem to reduce union density in both the short run and the long run. The long-run effects are given at the bottom of the table. These effects may be interpreted as a partial corroboration of our hypotheses that cyclical factors matter and that the entry of new groups into new forms of employment tend to reduce union density.[12] The interaction terms between country dummies and lagged level variables are significant for three countries: Denmark, the Netherlands, and the UK. Taking the coefficients for the interaction terms into account in the calculation of long-term relationships, it comes out that Denmark and the UK exhibit positive relationships between union density and unemployment, whereas the negative effect is attenuated for the Netherlands. In the case of Denmark, this might be related to the Ghent system. The exceptional position of the UK and—to a lesser degree— the Netherlands is harder to explain.

As to the other variables, they are all insignificant in level form. The change in the inflation rate (variable *INFL* in the second column) also comes out insignificant. The change in educational attainment (variable *FHC* in the third column) obtains a positive sign. Other structural variables (gender composition, industrial composition, etc.) proved to be insignificant in both level and difference forms (and are not shown in Table 2.6). As in nearly all econometric

---

[12] Note that the effect on union density of a 1 percentage point increase in the participation rate is given by the coefficient for *EMP* divided by $(1 - UNE)$. The impact of a 1 percentage point increase in the unemployment rate at a given participation rate is given by the coefficient for *UNE* minus the coefficient for *EMP* multiplied by the participation rate.

Table 2.6. Determinants of union density (fixed effects)

No. obs: Dep. var.:	432 ΔDEN (1)	426 ΔDEN (2)	419 ΔDEN (3)	394 ΔDEN (4)	283 ΔDEN (5)	406 ΔDEN (6)
INTCPT	0.046*** (3.55)	0.045*** (3.38)	0.043*** (3.25)	0.051*** (3.65)	0.083*** (3.67)	0.042*** (3.15)
$\Delta UNEL1$	−0.100 (−1.29)	−0.102 (−1.27)	−0.114 (−1.44)	−0.118 (−1.46)	−0.173** (−2.26)	−0.124 (−1.54)
$\Delta EMPLL1$	−0.209** (−2.12)	−0.216** (−2.12)	−0.217** (−2.19)	−0.225** (−2.22)	−0.309*** (−2.97)	−0.220** (−2.18)
$\Delta INFL$		0.018 (0.76)				
ΔFHC			0.112* (1.65)			0.104 1.49
$\Delta SPART$				0.005 (0.96)		
GOVN					0.000 (0.32)	
$\Delta BENEFIT$						0.042 (1.47)
DENL1	−0.027*** (−3.12)	−0.027*** (−3.11)	−0.025*** (−2.80)	−0.030*** (−3.21)	−0.062*** (−3.01)	−0.026*** (−2.85)
DENL1 × DK	−0.231*** (−4.60)	−0.209*** (−3.58)	−0.244*** (−4.35)	−0.232*** (−4.10)	−0.269*** (−4.32)	−0.238*** (−4.22)
DENL1 × NL	−0.096* (−1.83)	−0.097* (−1.83)	−0.110** (−2.03)	−0.099* (−1.82)	−0.087* (−1.72)	−0.113** (−2.06)
DENL1 × UK	0.065* (1.80)	0.066* (1.81)	0.065* (1.79)	0.069* (1.87)	0.095** (2.53)	0.068* (1.85)
UNEL1	−0.128*** (−6.34)	−0.126*** (−6.13)	−0.132*** (−6.17)	−0.129*** (−5.79)	−0.143*** (−4.68)	−0.125*** (−5.65)
UNEL1 × DK	0.681*** (5.23)	0.60*** (4.11)	0.704*** (5.05)	0.692*** (4.90)	0.547*** (4.19)	0.696*** (4.96)
EMPLL1	−0.041 (−1.45)	−0.043 (−1.51)	−0.038 (−1.30)	−0.047 (−1.56)	−0.075* (−1.83)	−0.035 (−1.20)
R^2 (within)	0.212	0.199	0.202	0.211	0.253	0.204
Hausman	75.02	507.1	62.99	63.78	168.5	52.08
Long-term relationship of DEN (all countries) with						
UNE	−4.79	−4.71	−5.29	−4.25	−2.30	−4.85
EMPL	−1.51	−1.60	−1.51	−1.55	−1.20	−1.36

Notes:

t-statistics in parentheses.

DEN = union net density (active dependent members, excluding unemployed or retired).

UNE = unemployment rate (unemployed/labour force).

INFL = inflation rate of consumer price index.

EMPL = employment rate (employed/population).

FHC = population share with secondary or college degree (interpolation on quinquennial observations).

GOVN = government political orientation (pro-labour +1; conservative −1).

BENEFIT = replacement rate.

SPART = strike participation (strikers/employees).

L1 = variable is lagged by one year.

Δ = rate of change.

Levels of significance: * < 0.10; ** < 0.05; *** < 0.01.

studies of union growth, the political orientation of the government and the strike participation rate are insignificant, whereas we find some indication of a positive effect of the (change in the) replacement rate (variable *BENEFIT*) in the sixth column).

The dynamic relationship is stable. (The coefficients on the lagged union density rate, *DENL*1, are negative, thus implying convergence to a long-run relationship.) But it should be noted that the speed of adjustment is very low. Only between 2% and 3% of a deviation from the long-run relationship is eliminated per year. This has important implications for the interpretation of the results. On the one hand, the long-run effects of changes in the unemployment rate and the employment–population ratio appear very large. On the other hand, the low adjustment speed would seem to imply that, for example, the rise in European unemployment from the mid-1970s to the mid-1980s have not had their full impact on unionization. Therefore, it also follows that a return to somewhat lower unemployment (but not as low as in the early 1970s) over the coming years does not have to imply a reversal of unionization trends.

We have checked the robustness of our results by using instrumental variable estimation (Table 2.7). Starting from the last column of Table 2.6 as a reference model, we replicate it using current (first column) and lagged values (second column) for changes in the unemployment rate and the employment–population ratio. The third and fourth columns use as instruments the changes of total population and of government consumption at constant prices. The fifth and sixth columns replace these instruments with the (current and lagged) participation rate in the labour force. The results here suggest that the unemployment rate and the employment–population ratio exhibit a contemporaneous negative impact on density rates, whereas the effect disappears when we consider lagged variations. Among the other regressors, the change in the educational composition of the population is now insignificant. As far as the long-run relationship is concerned, the unemployment rate and the employment–population ratio remain negatively related to union growth, though the long-run impact of unemployment is now much smaller.

In a further attempt to establish the impact of structural changes in employment, we have used information on the age and gender composition of the labour force, and the precariousness of the employment conditions. The main problem with this part of the analysis is that it is restricted to a subset of countries and covers only recent years. Since the intersection of non-missing observations on all variables is rather limited (256 observations from six countries), we consider two alternative sub-samples. In the first one (reported in Table 2.8) we include the variables that performed the best in the earlier regressions (lagged unemployment and employment rates, educational attainments, and unemployment benefits) together with gender composition (columns (2)–(6)) and sectoral variables (industry share in column (2), private services share in column (3), public employment share in column (4), natural monopoly share in column (5), and self-employment share in column (6)). The

Table 2.7. Determinants of union density (instrumental variables fixed effects—robust estimates)

No. obs.:	395	395	395	395	395	395
Dep. var.:	ΔDEN	ΔDEN	ΔDEN	ΔDEN	ΔDEN	ΔDEN
	(1)	(2)	(3)	(4)	(5)	(6)
INTCPT	0.057***	0.046***	0.115	0.135*	0.051***	0.045***
	(5.43)	(4.46)	(1.59)	(1.81)	(4.75)	(3.94)
ΔUNE	−0.381***		−0.386		−0.60**	
	(−4.58)		(−0.75)		(−2.11)	
$\Delta EMPL$	−0.540***		−0.507		−0.602***	
	(−4.68)		(−1.20)		(−4.63)	
$\Delta UNEL1$		−0.130*		0.204		0.334
		(−1.63)		(0.52)		(1.11)
$\Delta EMPLL1$		−0.227**		−0.017		−0.106
		(−2.17)		(−0.03)		(−0.96)
ΔFHC	0.113	0.101	0.044	0.021	0.077	0.073
	(1.45)	(1.34)	(0.45)	(0.23)	(0.95)	(0.91)
$\Delta BENEFIT$	0.034	0.038	0.038	0.035	0.040*	0.034
	(1.42)	(1.47)	(1.43)	(1.15)	(1.61)	(1.26)
DENL1	−0.024	−0.029*	−0.031	−0.040**	−0.025	−0.040***
	(−1.50)	(−1.76)	(−1.55)	(−2.27)	(−1.47)	(−2.33)
DENL1 × DK	−0.213***	−0.234***	−0.126	−0.063	−0.199***	−0.131
	(−3.65)	(−3.90)	(−1.27)	(−0.49)	(−3.17)	(−1.52)
DENL1 × NL	−0.121***	−0.113***	−0.223	−0.279*	−0.10***	−0.133***
	(−3.50)	(−2.50)	(−1.59)	(−1.90)	(−2.59)	(−2.37)
DENL1 × UK	0.076**	0.070*	0.080**	0.054	0.102***	0.066
	(2.09)	(1.79)	(1.73)	(1.18)	(2.83)	(1.45)
UNEL1	−0.140***	−0.128***	−0.083**	−0.105**	−0.074***	−0.119***
	(−7.26)	(−6.45)	(−2.14)	(−2.20)	(−2.55)	(−2.76)
UNEL1 × DK	0.616***	0.696***	0.406**	0.348	0.488***	0.463***
	(4.73)	(4.86)	(2.19)	(1.30)	(3.31)	(2.34)
EMPLL1	−0.069***	−0.042*	−0.294	−0.352	−0.090***	−0.049*
	(−2.72)	(−1.69)	(−1.33)	(−1.58)	(−3.14)	(−1.76)
R^2	0.421	0.379	0.262	0.101	0.375	0.295
Sargan (pval)	—	—	0.25	0.29	0.89	0.00

Long-term relationship of DEN (all countries) with

UNE	−5.85	−4.46	−2.66	−2.61	−2.93	−2.96
EMPL	−2.88	−1.45	−9.46	−8.73	−3.55	−1.22

Notes: see Table 2.6.

Table 2.8. *Compositional effects on union density (fixed effects)*

No. obs.:	256	256	256	256	256	256
Dep. var.:	ΔDEN (1)	ΔDEN (2)	ΔDEN (3)	ΔDEN (4)	ΔDEN (5)	ΔDEN (6)
INTCPT	0.055*** (3.20)	0.043*** (2.50)	0.049*** (2.87)	0.046*** (2.68)	0.057*** (3.31)	0.049*** (2.78)
ΔUNEL1	−0.218* (−1.73)	−0.138 (−1.03)	−0.256** (−2.02)	−0.218* (−1.66)	−0.308*** (−2.44)	−0.270*** (−2.12)
ΔEMPLL1	−0.466*** (−2.74)	−0.475*** (−2.69)	−0.529*** (−2.97)	−0.571*** (−3.25)	−0.605*** (−3.47)	−0.569*** (−3.21)
ΔFHC	0.180** (2.01)	0.151* (1.72)	0.151* (1.68)	0.169* (1.89)	0.152* (1.72)	0.161* (1.80)
ΔIND		0.392*** (2.79)				
ΔGENDER		0.638*** (3.08)	0.371* (1.89)	0.544*** (2.58)	0.532*** (2.70)	0.417** (2.13)
ΔSE			−0.238 (−1.43)			
ΔPA				−0.246 (−1.55)		
ΔMON					0.717*** (2.63)	
ΔINTO						0.012 (0.10)
ΔBENEFIT	0.065* (1.65)	0.062 (1.61)	0.063 (1.61)	0.063 (1.60)	0.046 (1.17)	0.063 (1.60)
DENL1	−0.013 (−1.24)	−0.011 (−1.05)	−0.014 (−1.35)	−0.012 (−1.09)	−0.016 (−1.54)	−0.015 (−1.34)
UNEL1	−0.166*** (−5.69)	−0.165*** (−5.67)	−0.152*** (−5.17)	−0.168*** (−5.53)	−0.157*** (−5.41)	−0.156*** (−5.22)
EMPLL1	−0.085** (−2.20)	−0.059 (−1.54)	−0.075** (−1.93)	−0.068* (−1.75)	−0.092*** (−2.38)	−0.075* (−1.92)
R^2	0.194	0.234	0.216	0.217	0.232	0.209

Notes:
t-statistics in parentheses.
GENDER = female share of dependent employment.
IND = industry share in dependent employment.
PA = public employment share in dependent employment.
MON = employment share of 'natural monopolies' (energy-gas-water-transport-telecommunications) in dependent employment.
INTO = self-employment share in total employment.
Levels of significance: * < 0.10; ** < 0.05; *** < 0.01.
Other variables are the same as in Table 2.6. Data refer to the following country/year: Finland (1962–95); Belgium (1962–92); Sweden (1960–95); Norway (1962–95); Italy (1962–94); Great Britain (1962–95); West Germany (1962–95); France (1975–89); Switzerland (1971), Spain (1982–95). See also Table 2.6.

general model retains its validity, but there is additional variation that can be explained by these compositional variables. The female component in the dependent employment shows a positive sign, thus suggesting that women have higher rather than lower propensities to unionize. As expected, industrial employment is positively related, and, private services employment is negatively related (but only weakly significant), with union density. The negative sign for the public employment variable is difficult to explain, as we know that unionization rates are particularly high there, as previously discussed. However, employment in 'natural monopoly' sectors (energy–gas–water–transport–telecommunications) shows, as expected, a strong and positive effect on density. Finally, the share of self-employment (which in some countries—like Italy or Spain—proxies the extent of the informal sector of the economy) does not seem to affect union density.

In Table 2.9 we consider a different sub-sample of countries and years, drop previous compositional variables, and introduce age composition and temporary employment. In general, the regression models here do not work well. The unemployment rate and the employment–population ratio usually turn out insignificant, and educational attainment obtains an opposite sign to what we had before. With these caveats in mind, we observe that both the youth component in the employment (workers aged less than 35) and the temporary component of dependent employment (both entered in difference form) have a negative impact on union density. However, when both variables are jointly considered, they lose significance, which suggests that they are capturing the same effect.

2.9. NEW ORGANIZING STRATEGIES

In response to membership decline, structural shifts in employment, decentralization, and a more intense demand for adequate services, unions have searched for methods to increase efficiency through scale economies. In recent years, many unions—especially in Belgium, Denmark, Germany, the Netherlands, Norway, and the UK—have amalgamated their activities. This process of restructuring is directly related to the cost pressures on unions as service providers (Streeck and Visser, 1998). As unions are labour-intensive service organizations, their capacity to increase productivity through technological innovation is limited. At the same time, their labour costs tend to rise with the general wage level, determined, by and large, by the productivity increase in manufacturing. Where there are data, we know that subscription rates have fallen relative to wages in the past thirty years (Visser, 1990). These financial problems are especially serious when membership stagnates or decreases.

Whether or not unions may avail themselves of economies of scale depends also on the distribution of their membership by firms. If members are employed by a small number of large firms, with many union members in each, servicing

Table 2.9. *Further compositional effects on union density (fixed effects)*

No. obs.:	95	95	95	95
Dep. var.:	ΔDEN	ΔDEN	ΔDEN	ΔDEN
INTCPT	0.045	0.076	0.037	0.066
	(0.56)	(0.96)	(0.47)	(0.83)
ΔUNEL1	−0.116	−0.101	−0.120	−0.106
	(−0.82)	(−0.73)	(−0.86)	(−0.76)
ΔINFL	0.233***	0.202***	0.232***	0.206***
	(3.02)	(2.61)	(3.02)	(2.65)
ΔEMPLL1	−0.192	−0.189	−0.160	−0.171
	(−0.94)	(−0.94)	(−0.79)	(−0.84)
ΔFHC	−0.183	−0.271**	−0.265**	−0.305***
	(−1.46)	(−2.08)	(−1.96)	(−2.24)
ΔTEMPOR		−0.108**		−0.091*
		(−2.01)		(−1.57)
ΔYOUNG			−0.263	−0.156
			(−1.50)	(−0.84)
DENL1	−0.083*	−0.108***	−0.085**	−0.105**
	(−1.93)	(−2.45)	(−1.99)	(−2.37)
UNEL1	−0.10	−0.105	−0.046	−0.073
	(−0.84)	(−0.91)	(−0.38)	(−0.59)
UNEL1 × DK	0.659***	0.812***	0.686***	0.803***
	(3.49)	(4.05)	(3.64)	(3.64)
EMPLL1	−0.018	−0.072	−0.013	−0.060
	(−0.11)	(−0.45)	(−0.08)	(−0.38)
R^2	0.308	0.343	0.328	0.349

Notes:
YOUNG = share of dependent employment below the age of 35.
TEMPOR = share of temporary workers in dependent employment.
Levels of significance: * < 0.10; ** < 0.05; *** < 0.01.
Other variables are the same as in Table 2.6. Data refer to the following country/year: Belgium (1984–93); Denmark (1984–91); Italy (1984–95); Great Britain (1984–95); Ireland (1984–95); West Germany (1984–95); Netherlands (1988–95); France (1984–95); Spain (1987–97). See also Table 2.6.

them is less costly for the external union than if members are dispersed over a large number of small firms, each of which has only few members. Current trends in outsourcing and decentralization of production, as well as the shift from industry to services, where the average size of establishments is smaller, thus diminish the scale economies that unions may make use of. In addition, unions are confronted with rising claims on the part of their members arising from changes in employment conditions, which increase insecurity and require more frequent and more costly assistance. Cutting costs in response to declining membership or revenue is extremely difficult for unions. A union can hardly refuse solidarity to workers on the grounds that their area has been particularly hard hit by industrial decline.

Merging unions can eliminate inefficient local offices without increasing the spatial distance between office and membership by realizing economies of scale between different unions within the same territory rather than within the same union between adjacent territories. Early retirement of national and local officials who are no longer needed can be funded by selling off local and central office buildings that the combined organization no longer needs.

In recent mergers between British unions, it was found that an important motive for an acquiring union was to move its centre of gravity out of declining and into expanding areas (Willman *et al.*, 1993). In the British context, this meant a cross-over from declining and unprofitable manual into expanding and high-income non-manual employment. In Dutch unions a similar logic can be detected, where the cross-over is from industrial into service sectors, combining a rich and large manufacturing sector union with a declining membership base, with a poorly endowed service-sector union with a growing membership base that it has difficulties in organizing. A merger of this kind immediately puts the well-developed organizational capacities of the larger and older union to the purpose of organizing workers in the expanding service sector.

The 'conglomerate unions' that result from such mergers are internally highly heterogeneous (Streeck and Visser, 1997). Like conglomerate firms, they straddle sectoral as well as occupational boundaries. These unions face new demands with respect to the management of internal diversity, especially under conditions of decentralized bargaining. Sacrificing industrial homogeneity for economic efficiency, conglomerate unions have only a limited capacity to speak with one voice for all their members. While member demands for generic services force unions to build large-scale organizations that extend beyond sectoral and occupational boundaries, differences in member interest and identity require diversified policies, especially in collective bargaining. Union mergers thus tend to result in centralized service provision and decentralized representation and participation at the same time.

Conglomerate unions, after the model of the British 'general unions', have typically adopted a decentralized, non-unitary approach to collective bargaining, negotiating separately for different membership sections with different (groups of) employers. Whether this will result in larger wage differentials is an open question. As long as conglomerate unions operate a combined strike fund—as industry unions in most European countries do—some element of coordination of their local bargaining strategies must be retained. Small groups of members cannot be allowed to strike at the expense of the common strike fund for wage demands far in excess of what the same union can get for other members. To protect organizational cohesion, negotiations are therefore typically handled by appointed full-time officials controlled by headquarters and not attached to specific subsections of the membership, and the procedures for the ratification of claims and settlements become a critical constitutional issue. To realize its potential for growth and optimally exploit the match between old assets and new membership markets, a conglomerate union must be capable of a 'corporate policy' of cross-subsidization, in which resources are mobilized for and shifted to markets where the union has a potential for growth.

2.10. CONCLUSIONS

In this chapter we have shown that in the last two decades of the twentieth century unionization rates in Europe have declined in all but a few countries. We have argued that this downward trend in unionization is related to the rise in unemployment during these years and to structural changes in labour market participation and employment, bringing in groups with a lower propensity to unionize (service workers, workers finding employment in small firms) and groups that go into non-standard employment (e.g. part-timers and workers on temporary contracts). The fact that fewer young workers have joined the unions in recent years implies that the average age of union members has increased. As a result of the decline in retirement age, the average duration of union membership careers tends to become shorter. This in itself means that the recruitment task of unions has become more difficult. As a significant proportion of members will leave the unions in coming years, unions face a formidable challenge to make up their numbers with more and younger recruits.

On a positive note for the unions, we observe that the characteristic weakness of unions among female employees is disappearing. While in many countries there is still a considerable gap between male and female unionization rates, differences are narrowing partly on account of the rising propensity of women to join unions, especially when they work in the public or subsidized sectors. How this change in the composition of union membership translates into new issues on the agenda of negotiators and into collective bargaining would be a highly interesting subject for further research.

Our findings suggest that a return to lower unemployment in Europe over the coming years may eliminate one factor that has worked in the direction of lower unionization. However, structural changes associated with industrial and demographic change and rising labour force participation rates (in most countries from rather low levels, if compared with the US or the Scandinavian countries) will probably continue to exert downward pressure on rates of unionization.

Another main finding in this chapter refers to the large cross-national differences in unionization levels. We can think of few other labour market variables with such a pronounced and persistent variation. These variations are the result of long-term developments, rooted in highly unique, national combinations of institutional and political conditions. In the present chapter we have highlighted three major institutional conditions conducive to union organization: union access to the workplace, union involvement in the provision and administration of unemployment insurance, and centralization of collective bargaining. Where all three of these institutions are (or were) present (as in the Nordic countries and, to a large degree, Belgium), unions appear able to fight off the negative influence on membership growth caused by unemployment and structural change. Centralization alone, or workplace access by itself, is hardly enough, as can be demonstrated by the large decline in unionization in, for instance, Austria and the UK. Even if, in the latter case, political and legal interventions after 1979 seem to have played a large role in the downfall of the unions (Freeman and Pelletier, 1990; Brown *et al.*, 1997), the question to be asked is how unions can conduct policies that avoid such negative interventions.

While we may think of centralization and workplace representation as independent variables that help explain variation in union growth patterns, causation may also flow in the opposite direction. Thus, a high level of unionization may have helped unions to be effectively present in most work-places, to gain or uphold a right of recognition in macroeconomic and social policy-making, to prevent unfriendly legislation, and to gain widespread recognition rights. Employers and public authorities may have contributed to such outcomes and to centralization, mainly in response to union strength. Current trends towards decentralization suggest that union strength is now countered by other, more market-related factors, as we shall be discussing in the following chapters.

3

Wage Bargaining, Union Power, and Economic Integration

This chapter examines the determinants of union influence over wages. We briefly review the existing literature on this issue, before examining specific issues in more detail. In particular, we focus on the impact of trade and economic integration on union wage influence. In our discussion on the effects of trade, our main theme is that if changing patterns of trade do not enhance product market competition—and there should be no presumption that they must—then there is little reason to suppose that the conditions for unions to influence wage outcomes will necessarily deteriorate as a consequence of product market integration. We explore the theory and evidence relevant to this issue. Our discussion connects with the analysis presented in Nicoletti *et al.* (2001).

3.1. REVIEW OF THE LITERATURE ON UNION WAGE EFFECTS: THEORY AND EVIDENCE

For a trade union to be able to increase wage rates above the competitive level, two conditions must be satisfied. First, there must be some surplus that can be shared between the firm and the union, and second, the union must have sufficient bargaining power to induce the firm to share any such surplus. In the following sections, we consider the product market conditions in which a surplus arises that may be shared with unions. We then consider briefly the conditions necessary for a union to achieve sufficient power to induce firms to share any such rents. Both of these issues are crucial in assessing the likely future influence of unions.

3.1.1. *What determines the size of the available surplus?*

Even if a union controls labour supply, it will not necessarily be able to negotiate a large wage increase relative to the competitive wage level. The magnitude of the union wage effect depends crucially on the elasticity of labour demand in that sector, which is a derived demand, and which depends on product market factors, among other things. Product market power generates monopoly (or, in the case of market dominance by a small number of firms, oligopoly) rents, which may be captured by employees in the form of higher wages or better working conditions. In perfectly competitive labour markets, in which firms pay market-determined wage rates, there is no rent-sharing with (or 'rent capture' by) employees. The firm will typically share its monopoly (oligopoly) rents only if the workers have sufficient bargaining power to induce it to do so, or if sharing increases the size of the surplus. Finally, we note that under certain labour market conditions—those associated with 'monopsony'—firms may have sufficient power in their labour market to be able to push wages below competitive wage levels. In such cases, union bargaining power can be thought of as a countervailing power, offering resistance to employers' attempts to force on workers conditions inferior to those that would obtain under competitive conditions.

The size of any available surplus is thus related to the nature of competition in the product market. If the firm is the sole supplier of a good—a true monopolist—then the surplus depends on the elasticity of product market demand. If the product market is perfectly competitive, at the other extreme, there will be a surplus only where the competitive firm's production function is characterized by decreasing returns in the neighbourhood of the equilibrium (see Booth, 1995). Between the extremes of pure monopoly and perfect competition lie the cases of oligopoly, where a small number of firms dominate the product market for a homogeneous good, and of monopolistic competition, where competing firms produce differentiated products. In the oligopoly case, the surplus depends not only on the industry elasticity of demand, but also on the nature of strategic interactions between firms: for example, whether they choose to collude in the manner of a cartel, or instead choose to adopt aggressively competitive strategies against one another. In the monopolistic competition case, the surplus depends on the product demand elasticity faced by each producer, which in its turn is determined by how close substitutes the products of different producers are. In general, the less competitive are the firms, the greater will be the capturable profits for unions. Importantly, the surplus available will also depend on the extent of barriers preventing new firms entering the market, on product market regulations, and on the threat of foreign trade where markets are international or global (Stewart, 1990; Nickell, 1999).

An interesting question, then, concerns what might happen to the extent of monopoly power as the Single Market Programme in Europe deepens. Jacobson and Andreosso-O'Callaghan (1996) found that there was diversity of movement in four-firm EU concentration ratios in different industries. They found that through the 1980s the concentration ratios rose in industries such as food, drink and tobacco, engineering, and metals (production and processing). Interestingly, comparison of forty-firm concentration ratios for the manufacturing industry shows that there is more market domination in the United States than in Europe (Jacquemin *et al.*, 1989): this may indicate that over time, with market integration, concentration ratios in Europe may grow.

The necessary conditions for a union to be able to appropriate any surplus in a competitive product market, without driving the firm out of existence, are: high levels of unionization, no non-union foreign competition, entry barriers, and inelastic product demand. Without the first three conditions, domestic firms—or foreign firms, or new firms entering the industry—could simply hire non-union labour and produce at a lower cost than unionized competitors, thereby driving them out of business (Booth, 1995).

In the European context, it is natural to focus on the extent of foreign competition to unionized firms as a crucial determinant of the capacity of unions to raise wages. Even if a unionized firm has a domestic monopoly, the existence—or merely the threat—of foreign competition is likely to restrict the ability of the firm to charge prices high enough to generate super-normal profits, or *surplus*. Hence, one might surmise that European integration will tend to erode the capacity of unions to establish wage premia: so long as integration generates a greater degree of product market competition. It is possible, however, that the predominant economic forces associated with the changing patterns of trade—and foreign direct investment (FDI)—in Europe are not competitive, but oligopolistic. If this is the case, European integration might not weaken union bargaining power to the same extent. We explore these issues further in the next section.

3.1.2. *Unions, surplus, and efficiency*

Economic theory states that, if unions emerge in competitive and efficient markets, high union wages will introduce allocative inefficiencies into the economy through the distortion of factor prices. With higher wages in the union sector, union firms employ fewer workers. Displaced union workers crowd into the non-union sector, lowering wages there. As a result, too few workers are employed in the union sector, where output falls, while too many workers are employed, and too many goods produced, in the non-union sector. There is a deadweight efficiency loss, because the values of marginal products in the two sectors are not identical. In addition, there are distributional issues to consider, and longer-run effects arising from the substitution of capital for labour. Furthermore, in unionized sectors there may be under investment in capital (Grout, 1984).

However, this analysis of allocative inefficiency assumes that unions emerge in an economy characterized by competitive product and labour markets. But in modern industrialized countries many product markets are characterized by imperfect competition. In addition, it is a well established empirical regularity that imperfections in product and labour markets are correlated (Stewart, 1990; Peoples, 1998; Neven *et al.*, 1998; Duca, 1998; Nicoletti *et al.*, 2001). Thus, it is far from clear that the competitive product market paradigm is the appropriate benchmark from which to examine the impact of trade unions. And when we consider unions in an imperfectly competitive setting, our view of their impact is very different from that associated with the competitive model.

In addition, labour markets themselves may not be perfectly competitive even in the absence of trade unions. For example, non-union firms may also face an incumbent workforce with a degree of bargaining power, perhaps because of transactions and worker turnover costs (Lindbeck and Snower, 1988). Thus, even in the absence of unionization, management and workers may be in a situation of bilateral monopoly. An important and little addressed question arises as to whether or not the replacement of individual bargaining by collective bargaining generates additional inefficiencies and misallocation of resources in situations where markets were previously not functioning in accordance with the textbook model of perfect competition.

Even within the competitive model, there are arguments suggesting that, in the presence of imperfect information and uncertainty, unions may enhance efficiency. To the extent that unions reduce labour turnover and negotiating costs, and act as the agent of workers, they may increase the available surplus to be shared between parties (Freeman and Medoff, 1984; Faith and Reid, 1987). Of course, there may be an interdependence between the monopoly and efficiency roles of trade unions: unless the union has some bargaining power, it may be unable to increase efficiency. (Chapter 4 provides a further discussion of some of these issues.)

3.1.3. *What determines union bargaining power?*

Union leaders are well aware of the fact that a major source of union power is the capacity to organize all workers in an industry, thereby acting as a monopolist over the supply of labour. Union bargaining power derives from the ability of the union to inflict damage (or to *credibly threaten* to inflict damage) on the firm or employer by withdrawing labour. This is most effective when there is no substitute pool of non-union workers—for instance, if there are high labour turnover costs, or if the union controls labour supply through entry restrictions, or through having high levels of membership relative to the size of the sector. But in an increasingly integrated global economy, union control of labour supply in an industry becomes ever less likely. The more footloose is industry through increased mobility of physical capital—for example through foreign direct investment and transnational enterprise—the less able are unions to control the supply of labour within an industry.

In recent years, however, many commentators have reported a trend towards a decentralization of bargaining in a number of countries, with an increasing incidence of firm or plant-level bargaining. This places more importance on the local bargaining power of the union. Chapters 4 and 5 examine in some detail both the causes and consequences of changing levels of centralization and the coordination of bargaining. In the rest of this section we outline the factors that will influence union bargaining power when bargaining is decentralized and takes place at the local workplace level. Because local bargaining has an established tradition in the UK, and because of the extensive empirical analysis based on British workplace industrial relations surveys, our discussion is illustrated predominantly by examples and results from the UK. However, we argue that the analysis has more general application to countries experiencing a decentralization of bargaining.

It has been commonly argued that forces related to globalization have been rendering unions powerless to achieve their traditional objectives. It is perhaps too easy to exaggerate this position and neglect other influences on union bargaining power. In this context, it is important to identify the conditions affecting the capacity of unions to influence pay and other working conditions. For example, understanding these various aspects is vital for union organizers if they wish to maintain/increase membership at a time of 'deunionization' and thereby retain a significant degree of influence in the workplace. It is also important for policy-makers to understand how unions affect pay and working conditions, and how union–firm interactions vary with factors such as product market conditions.

What determines the degree to which a *local* union can bargain for wages and/or working conditions superior to non-union levels? Important influences include local membership density, the nature of bargaining arrangements, the legislative environment, management attitudes, and union structure and modes of governance. We now discuss each of these in turn.

Local union membership density

Union membership density within the workplace may play a part in determining the bargaining power of the local union. As membership density increases, there is a shrinking pool of workers available to the firm should it choose not to employ union labour. Local membership density is thus a key determinant of the credibility of the strike threat (e.g. Booth and Chatterji, 1995; Barth *et al.*, 2000). It does not follow, however, that the relationship between density and influence is simple. For example, it may well not be a linear mapping between density and wage influence. There is likely to be a minimum critical level of membership below which firms will refuse to recognize and bargain with the union (Osborne, 1984). Interestingly, in their analysis of UK establishment-level data, Metcalf and Stewart (1992) found that, in the absence of closed-shop bargaining arrangements, unions are unable to raise wages above non-union levels unless membership density in the establishment is as high as 95%. It is likely that the critical or threshold level varies across establishments according to legal rights, technology, and labour market conditions. In the language of game theory, higher local membership reduces the firm's 'inside option' or conflict (e.g. strike) payoff.[1]

---

[1] The 'outside option' is also important: in theory, the firm can sack all its employees and go to the outside labour market to hire, so the available pool of workers in the industry—and hence industry union coverage—is also a relevant factor. In practice, employment protection legislation will define both the inside and the outside option. In the UK, as in the USA, legislation gives firms some latitude to replace striking workers both temporarily and permanently: this is not possible in most European countries.

The nature of bargaining arrangements

Even if bargaining occurs at the local level within the firm or workplace, there is great variation in the form that the bargaining might take. One way in which local bargaining structures can diverge arises from union organization, which may be based on industrial lines or be craft or occupationally based. The evolution of craft unions in the UK provides a partial explanation of the widespread—though diminishing—incidence of multi-unionism, which occurs when a heterogeneous workforce at a single workplace is represented by more than one union. In such a situation various forms of bargaining might arise. Most obviously, bargaining might be either 'separate'—with the employer bargaining separately with each union—or 'joint'—with the employer and representatives of all the local unions bargaining together. Machin *et al.* (1993) have examined the impact of these different bargaining arrangements on various outcomes. They find that multi-unionism itself has no significant effect on bargained outcomes: there is no difference in outcome according to whether there is a single union in the establishment or a joint bargain involving a number of unions. Instead, there is a significant difference between separate bargaining by multiple unions (which is associated with higher wage levels and has a deleterious effect on financial performance), and single or joint bargaining (which have less significant effects).

Horn and Wolinsky (1988) have presented a theoretical analysis of the factors influencing the choice between joint and separate bargaining. They show how the degree of substitutability between different types of labour input affects the incentives for unions to bargain separately or jointly. The intuition behind the result is as follows. Suppose that a firm employs workers to carry out two different kinds of task, and that if one of these work-groups is on strike, then the other work-group is unable to carry out its own tasks effectively. (This would happen, for example, if the first group produced an intermediate output which was an input for the activities of the second group, and if the firm did not hold inventory stocks.) In the language of economists, the two work-groups are said to be 'complementary'—rather than 'substitutable'—factors of production. In such a situation, Horn and Wolinsky show that the workers will be able to bargain higher wages if they bargain separately with the firm in two distinct unions than if they bargain jointly: effectively, by dividing they rule the firm! This is because each union by itself is in a strong position in the event of a conflict: each knows that the firm's production will be severely constrained by a strike by either work-group. Conversely, if the two groups of workers are substitutes for one another—i.e. if, in the event of a strike by one group, the firm can continue to produce by using the other group (perhaps more intensively)—they are best off forming a single union (or, at least, bargaining jointly), as this will prevent the firm from dividing and ruling *them*. The Horn–Wolinsky model provides an example of how the production technology may influence the nature of bargaining and, by implication, the bargained outcome itself (see also Naylor, 1995).

In some countries, such as the UK, there has been a shift away from union contracts and towards individual contracts. This shift is associated with diminishing union power, and may further exacerbate problems of declining union power. However, the new UK recognition machinery, introduced by the Labour government in its 1999 Employment Relations Bill, may reverse this trend. The machinery is intended in part to give recognition rights to workers in establishments in which a majority of workers demand union recognition. Prior to this legislation, employers have traditionally controlled the recognition decision in the UK. The new recognition machinery (loosely based on US representation elections in order to formalize and legitimize union recognition) may also lead to even more decentralization, in the US style, with its emphasis on establishment-level worker organization.

Finally, bargaining arrangements also diverge with respect to the extent of union control over labour supply. For example, pre-entry union closed shops in the UK were widely held to be an extreme—and rather rare—example of unions exercising significant control over labour supply. To a large degree, the extent of union control over labour supply will depend on the legal framework and legislative environment in which bargaining takes place. This is discussed below.

The legislative environment
Bargaining theory predicts that the bargained outcome is likely to be sensitive to the conflict payoffs available to the two sides in the event of a strike by workers (or a lockout by employers). Conflict payoffs can be thought of as the income that firms and workers can continue to command in the event of a dispute. Moene (1988), for example, has shown how the nature of the conflict threat available to workers will influence the bargained wage. Union wage influence will vary according to whether workers can credibly threaten strike action or a go-slow or work-to-rule, for example. Clearly, the legislative environment is an important factor in determining which of these options will be used by unions. Of great importance are the legal possibilities for unions to let only small key groups of employees, who are vital for production, go on strike and stop production. In some countries, for example Denmark, Germany, Italy, and the Netherlands, so-called *proportionality rules*, requiring a balance between the extent of strike action and the consequences for the employer, or between the extent of strike action and the bargaining goal of the union, limit these possibilities (SOU 1998: 141). Legal provisions regarding the right to sympathetic, solidaristic, and secondary supporting action of other unions are also very important.

The conflict payoff of the union itself will be another important determinant of the credibility of the union to threaten industrial action. The eligibility of striking workers to state welfare payments will be one influence on this; another will be the extent of union funds available to award strike pay to striking workers.

The extent to which unions can control the available supply of labour to a firm depends in part upon the legal status of the individual worker's right to remain outside a union, as opposed to the right of the union to require all workers to be union members. In the UK there were until the mid-1980s two forms of closed-shop arrangements under which unions could require workers to be union members. The pre-entry closed shop gave the union more power over labour supply, as it enabled the union to dictate to firms the pool of workers (i.e. the set of registered union members) from which the firm could recruit. The post-entry closed shop, in contrast, merely enabled the union to require that all employed workers (not the entire pool of all possible workers) become union members *ex post*, i.e. after they had been employed by an (unconstrained) employer decision on recruitment. Stewart (1987) showed that the pre-entry closed shop gave a big boost to the capacity of the union to raise wages above non-competitive levels, the post-entry closed shop much less so. Metcalf and Stewart (1992) further showed that the abolition of the closed shop under the Thatcher administration accounted for much of the reduction in the capacity of British unions to influence wages over that period.

Indeed, the Thatcher governments in the UK instituted a number of legislative changes that had the intention of reducing trade union bargaining power. As well as legislation to abolish the closed shop, policies were targeted at making strikes more costly to organize and less damaging to firms. Thus, strict conditions regarding strike ballots were introduced, as were fines and the legal sequestration of union funds in the case of illegal strike actions. The legal status of secondary and sympathetic actions was gradually undermined and in the end such actions were outlawed. Furthermore, striking workers and their families were disqualified from claiming supplementary social welfare payments.

Additionally, the legislative environment is likely to be an important influence on the extent of union membership itself. This issue has been examined in some detail in Chapter 2 above. Here, we note simply that Freeman and Pelletier (1990) have argued that much of the decline in union membership in the UK can be attributed to an increasingly hostile legislative environment facing unions after 1979. We note also that this view is not without its critics (see e.g. Disney, 1990), and that other explanations have been put forward, namely compositional effects, changing attitudes towards neo-conservatism, and the business cycle. (See also Booth, 1995, and references therein.)

The role of management attitudes to unions

Historically, many UK firms have been favourable to union organization.[2] This is less well appreciated among economists and in much public discourse. There

---

[2] Brown (1981) found, from survey evidence, that management at that time strongly supported the closed shop. The UK experience in this regard contrasts with that of the USA. This may be due in part to the fact that British employers in much of the nineteenth century were sheltered from international competition through their technical lead from the Industrial Revolution (Phelps Brown, 1986).

are, however, many reasons why firms might actually wish to encourage some form of union organization in the workplace, and some of these reasons are discussed in Chapter 4. An interesting research project would involve examining how firms' attitudes to unions vary across Europe and why. Not all firms, of course, are favourable to union organization, and some are particularly hostile. Management opposition to unions in a more anti-union legislative environment has been put forward as an explanation of union decline both in the USA and in the UK. Building on the work of Freeman and Medoff (1984), Dickens and Leonard (1985), and Freeman (1986), Freeman and Kleiner (1988) argued that the growth of management opposition to unions in the USA was a major cause of the decline in private-sector unionism. For the later decline of union membership in the UK, Freeman and Pelletier (1990) concluded that a major factor was the change in the legislative environment, which 'strengthened management's hand in opposing unions'. As previously discussed, legislation in the UK is introducing US-style union representation elections. If US experience is relevant to the UK, however, it is possible that this step will foreshadow more explicit hostilities between organized labour and anti-union employers.

Union governance and union preferences

Chapter 2 documented the extent and causes of the decline of union membership in a number of European countries in the last two decades of the twentieth century—in what has sometimes been referred to as a period of 'deunionization' (see e.g. Acemoglu *et al.*, 2000). But can trade unions recover in the early decades of the twenty-first century? We shall be addressing this question in Chapter 6. But it is worth noting here that the answer to this question depends on whether or not trade unions can still play a role in representing their workers' interests better than workers can do themselves.[3] Bargaining coverage and workplace representation—which is discussed in Chapter 4—are important here. Equally important are the governance of trade unions and the extent to which they are democratic.

Unions are typically large organizations with a complex hierarchical structure comprising an executive, a shop-steward system, and a body of rank-and-file union members. Clegg's (1979) taxonomy of unions is still relevant today. At one extreme, unions can be viewed as oligarchic, unresponsive to members' wishes, and with an executive securing a monopoly of power to stay in office with low membership participation and apathy. Alternatively, unions may be quasi-democratic, owing to the presence of informal parties or factions, the growth of workplace organization, and the existence of workplace or postal balloting.

---

[3] In the UK, for example, unions have traditionally represented the interests of men, leaving the welfare of youth and working women to be determined by legislation. Such considerations are of obvious importance with the increasing feminization of the workforce.

Because of these complexities in union internal structure, there are likely to be considerable time lags in the transmission of preferences from membership to executive. Moreover, the executive may have aims that conflict with the desires of the membership. There is no guarantee that the union will be the perfect agent of workers, although fluctuations in membership levels affect the union's power base as well as its finances, so this may moderate leaders' behaviour. Union organizers might find it useful to consider these factors when assessing their relevance in the twenty-first century.

3.2. THE IMPACT OF TRADE, INTEGRATION, AND FDI IN EUROPE ON UNION BARGAINING POWER

Bertola *et al.* (2001) have argued that, even with increasing cross-border competition, persistent cross-country price disparities demonstrate relatively weak competitive pressures in EU product markets. They suggest that this results from the continuing presence of significant market power even in apparently competitive industries such as manufacturing. They observe that it is of particular concern that price convergence in the EU seems to have slowed down after the establishment in 1992 of the Single Market. Nicoletti *et al.* (2001) have presented a discussion of the economic theory relating product market competition to labour market performance. The analysis shows that an increase in product market competition would be expected to lead to an increase in employment. One channel is the output effect on labour demand stemming from a reduction in price–wage margins when product demand elasticities increase. Another channel is the reduction of wage pressure that will follow from the increases in labour demand elasticities associated with higher product demand elasticities. The effects on wages, however, are theoretically ambiguous: on the one hand, a greater labour demand elasticity will tend to lower any union-bargained wage level; but, on the other hand, the outward shift in labour demand (stemming from the output effect of greater competition) will lead unions to demand higher wages (see also Naylor, 1998; 1999).

3.2.1. *Trade and product market competition*

Here there are two essential points to note. The first is that opening up domestic markets to international trade may favour large-scale transnational firms, which might actually undermine the extent of competition in national product markets. Economic integration does not necessarily imply greater product market competition. The second point is that intra-industry trade can have 'reciprocal dumping' characteristics, meaning that more trade can actually be welfare-damaging, even while having small positive effects on the extent of competition. Dumping is said to occur when a firm sells into a foreign market in which the price is set at a high level by a resident foreign monopolist. When two markets are dominated by resident monopolists, then each monopolist has an incentive to sell into the potential rival's market: this is described as reciprocal dumping. Although reciprocal dumping might be profit-enhancing, the duplicated transport costs can render such forms of intra-industry trade welfare-damaging. Reduced trade costs will serve in part to increase the incentives to carry out reciprocal dumping. Thus, it is possible that economic integration might simply enable large European firms to penetrate rivals' markets more deeply. This may increase the extent of competition between them, depending on the conduct of the firms. Yet there remains a fundamental lack of competition in a market dominated by a small number of dominant firms. This underlines the importance of direct policy measures aimed at enhancing the competitive functioning of product markets: public policies may be a necessary element in a package of measures to ensure that increased product market integration in Europe also enhances product market competition. If one is interested in predicting the effects of integration on the prospects of unions to bargain for high remuneration, this understanding of the importance of the distinction between integration and competition is fundamental.

It is informative to consider the patterns of trade within Europe over the 1980s and 1990s, a period in which the volume of intra-EU trade grew substantially. Typically, a distinction is drawn between two types of trade: inter-industry and intra-industry. Inter-industry—or one-way—trade can be thought of as resulting from the traditional international trade argument concerning comparative advantage. It is consistent with the existence of highly competitive (international) markets. Intra-industry—or two-way—trade in similar products could reflect more competition, but it is also often modelled as arising out of the profit-motivated behaviour of dominant firms in imperfectly competitive markets.

In recent years there has been a clear tendency for intra-EU trade to shift in the direction of two-way rather than one-way trade. It has been estimated that in the early 1980s approximately 45% of all intra-EU trade took the form of inter-industry trade (see, e.g. CEPII, 1996; or Fontagné and Freudenberg, 1999); by 1996, however, this proportion had fallen to about 38%, with intra-industry trade coming to dominate intra-EU trade. The implications for competition of such a shift are not obvious: more trade in similar products could enhance competition, but it could also be associated with non-competitive markets and reciprocal dumping. We also observe that there is some tendency for those industries in which trade is predominantly inter-industry to be characterized by typically low levels of trade union density, for example agriculture, food and beverages, and textiles. Conversely, unionization rates tend to be relatively high in industries associated with two-way or intra-industry trade, such as the machinery, chemicals, and motor industries. We conclude that the predominant trend in trade in the key period of the Single Market Programme has been away from one-way trade and towards intra-industry trade, and that this is consistent with our argument that economic integration in Europe has not so far been necessarily damaging to the prospects for unions' capturing a share of rents generated in (persistently) imperfectly competitive product markets.

3.2.2. *Foreign direct investment and union bargaining power*

Of course, trade is not the only way in which enterprises may seek to supply foreign product markets. An alternative route—which may actually be either a substitute or a complement for trade—is through foreign direct investment (FDI). FDI takes different forms: it might, for example, be 'greenfield' investment in new establishments, or it might be a merger or acquisition of existing firms. The fact that multinational enterprises are the main source of most FDI flows implies that the impact of FDI on the extent of product market competition is ambiguous. While an influx of FDI in an economy may be welfare-improving in the short run if relatively fewer competitive domestic firms are forced to raise efficiency or to fail, it may have a less beneficial long-run effect if it results in market domination by a small number of multinational firms.

Furthermore, it is worth underlining that there are several different possible motives for FDI. First, there is the incentive to move into a country in order to capture a share of product market rents. Second, there is the incentive to expand market coverage in order to exploit increasing returns to scale. Third, FDI may be motivated by strategic labour market objectives: having production units in different countries can increase the bargaining power of firms, which, during an industrial dispute, can credibly claim to be able to shift production. The different motivations towards FDI may have differing and complex implications for the capacity of unions to bargain for higher wages. If FDI enables large-scale transnational or pan-European enterprises to dominate EU product markets, then this will be anti-competitive, and will lead to welfare reduction and profit enhancement. There may be more surplus generated for workers to capture, and this may drive unions to a stronger position than if product markets were competitive. Against this, however, transnational firms may, through a divide-and-rule strategy, strengthen their bargaining hand and diminish union bargaining influence. In part, then, the impact of FDI on the bargaining position of unions in Europe will depend upon whether FDI is motivated by product or by labour market considerations.

That the issue is an important one is clear from the sheer magnitude of FDI in Europe. It has been estimated that, while worldwide FDI flows grew about five-fold between 1984 and 1990 (CEPS, 1996), the rate of growth within Europe was even greater. By 1993, two-thirds of FDI flows to developed countries were to the EU.

It is likely that FDI represents a potential challenge to union bargaining power. However, we note that there is some evidence that FDI has product market motivations—not just labour divide-and-rule objectives. Inward FDI flows have tended to concentrate on European countries with large domestic product markets (like the UK and France) rather than on those with relatively low-wage economies (like Greece and Portugal). Another indication is that the overwhelming majority of FDI in the EU is concentrated in the services sector. Because the alternative to FDI—i.e. trade—is not an option in the case of services, the motivation must be product market capture. All this suggests that product market motivations for FDI may be stronger than is sometimes reflected in political discussions.

Furthermore, the divide-and-rule argument concerning FDI and multi-national enterprises requires that, within the enterprise, plants in different countries are performing the same tasks. This is necessary to render credible the threat to supply from abroad in the event of an industrial dispute. Simple observation shows, however, that this need not be the case: in the car industry, for example, there is sometimes the possibility that a certain car could be produced at alternative sites, but in many cases a company's plants in different countries perform different tasks—production is organized vertically rather than horizontally across countries. Potentially, far from weakening the bargaining power of trade unions, the latter mode of production could actually enhance union power. Indeed, in this case unions may even do better by bargaining independently of fellow company unions in foreign plants. The logic is the same as in our earlier discussion of separate and joint bargaining by unions within a workplace: when employees who are complements bargain separately, they can 'share the surplus' twice with the employer because of their strong bargaining position when they can individually affect output very much (see Section 3.1.3). Where production is organized horizontally, however, coordination across unions within multinational enterprises is likely to affect the degree to which unions can capture rents, as the employer bargaining position is otherwise strengthened by the possibility to shift around production.

The difficulties of obtaining reliable data on FDI, however, have so far prevented any clear conclusions emerging over the effects of FDI on the overall bargaining position of European trade unions. However, to some extent the question of how union bargaining power will be affected depends on the time perspective of the analysis. Even in multinational firms with vertical integration of production between units in different countries, there remains the possibility of relocating production (for example when a new car model is introduced) in a long-time perspective. This is likely to have a restraining effects on union wage claims.

3.3. CONCLUSIONS

In this chapter we have reviewed the major factors conditioning the extent to which unions will be able to exert an influence on bargained wage outcomes. We have argued that a precondition is that there must be rents available for unions to attempt to capture: and the most likely source of such rents lies in profits generated in imperfectly competitive product markets. We then addressed the issue of what factors shape the capacity of unions to succeed in capturing a share of any available rents. We argued that the main factors include the level of union membership density and coverage, the level of coordination across bargaining groups, the legislative environment conditioning the rights of trade unions, and the attitudes of employers.

We then focused on the question of how the bargaining position of unions might be affected by the increasing integration of European economies. We have argued that many of the economic forces associated with economic integration and with the developing patterns of trade and foreign direct investment are unlikely of themselves to produce anything resembling perfect competition in Europe's product markets. *More* trade should not be confused with *more competitive* trade: freedom to trade—when it is dominated by large multinational corporations—does not engender free or 'perfect' competition. Instead, we have suggested that there is evidence consistent with the view that European product markets are failing to converge towards an acceptable competitive position. We have argued that this is likely to have major consequences for the behaviour of agents—firms, workers, unions—in European labour markets. We have reviewed the evidence on union wage effects and, among other important findings, we have argued that the capacity for unions to raise wages and generally improve working conditions depends critically on the extent of product market competition: the less competitive are product markets, the better the prospects for unions to raise wages. Thus, a key determinant of the evolution of union influence will be the extent to which economic integration and European public policy succeeds in enhancing product market competition.

The impact of the possibility of multinationals to have production units in several countries on union bargaining strength depends on whether production is horizontally or vertically integrated. In the former case, union bargaining strength will be reduced by the awareness that production can be relocated among countries. In the case of vertical integration, union bargaining power in an individual plant is increased because of the potential to disrupt the whole production chain. But this may apply only in a rather short-term perspective. Unions taking a longer-term perspective are likely to realize that the mere existence of production units in different countries (even under vertical integration) gives multinational firms the possibility of moving production once they have had the time necessary for adjustment. So we would conjecture that, overall, union bargaining power is reduced by the growing importance of multinational corporations.

4

Wider Dimensions of
Unions' Presence

Up to now, the presence of unions has been discussed primarily by way of reference to union membership as a fraction of employment, i.e. union density. Yet focusing only on this aspect can be misleading, particularly in European countries. In this chapter we examine wider aspects of union presence, including forms of bargaining and issues of union coverage. In particular, two questions arise. First, what do unions do besides bargain over wages? Second, and just as important for policy-makers, how do unions make their presence felt beyond mere density statistics? To answer these questions in a European context, one needs to think harder about how unions influence the economic environment of their members and, in particular, that of non-members. Section 4.1 asks what unions do in the broadest sense. Section 4.2 focuses on the harder question about available means: what mechanisms enable trade unions to perform these functions? Finally, Section 4.3 concludes with some commentary on the deviation between union membership and presence over the past decades, and what one might expect from the future.

4.1. WHAT *ELSE* DO EUROPEAN UNIONS DO?

There is a long-standing debate over what unions do. In one view, associated primarily with the Anglo-American economists Marshall, Hicks, Dunlop, Leontief, Slichter, and Lewis, unions seek primarily to improve the pay of their members. An alternative, broader, sociological view of unions more frequently encountered on the European continent stresses general political advocacy of issues related to the labour movement. In an acclaimed book, Freeman and Medoff (1984) bridged this gap by expanding the economic purview of organized labour to include what Mancur Olson (1965) called 'the logic of collective action'. Invoking Hirschmann's (1970) famous distinction of *exit versus voice*, Freeman and Medoff argued persuasively that unions are not only monopolists, but also vehicles for the collective expression of concerns and desires in the workforce. Given limited individual bargaining power and high costs of renegotiation and mobility, unions may be an effective communication mechanism which would be difficult to replicate in a theoretical market setting of atomistic workers and firms.

For most European economies, the message of Freeman and Medoff might have been seen as obvious. While the decline of unionism in the USA continued into and through the 1990s, the same cannot be said of all Western European countries, as has been documented in Chapter 2. Moreover, despite falling membership in most of Europe, unions have been able to defend or even maintain their role in economic relations beyond mere membership numbers. In other words, union presence is manifested in ways other than that measured simply by membership. And, through different facets of presence, unions have been able to maintain sometimes surprisingly high levels of influence over different aspects of economic and political life.

4.1.1. *Non-wage compensation and working conditions*

It is clear that improving—and maintaining—income levels of working members is a primary objective of the trade unions. Success in this area will depend on the ability of unions to exert control over aggregate labour supply at the level of the workplace or local labour market—or, more precisely, to prevent outsiders from underbidding wages determined in collective bargaining. Many theorists have used the monopoly model as a metaphor for the trade union, arguing that simple tools such as the Marshall–Hicks rule and Nash bargaining rules go a long way in predicting outcomes.[1] This has already been examined in detail in Chapter 3.

Yet negotiating base pay is only one dimension of union activity. More general forms of pecuniary compensation are also subject to union influence: overtime and weekend pay rates, holiday bonuses, and other fringe benefits. The fact that unions also bargain over these items, instead of their equivalent in pay, is a signal that unions' interactions with their members and with management may be considerably more complex.

Similarly, unions strive to influence average working conditions of their members, which include standard working hours (the work week), work schedules, workplace safety and environmental quality, promotion systems and bonuses, and leave policy. Perhaps most important, unions have traditionally tried to exert control over conditions of termination of employment, one of the thorniest issues in labour relations. Conditions for severance are often—especially in Europe—designed to protect the weaker and more

---

[1] The Marshall–Hicks rule (see e.g. Hamermesh, 1993; Booth, 1995) states that the elasticity of labour demand is positively related to (1) the elasticity of demand for the product that uses labour in production; (2) the ease of substitution of other factors for labour in production; (3) the elasticity of supply of these factors; and (4) the share represented by labour in total costs. Nash bargaining theory can be seen as either a normative theory of bargaining which relates outcomes to the (relative) fall-back positions of bargaining parties, or a positive theory predicting the outcome of bargaining rounds among agents with different rates of time preference or other attributes (see Binmore *et al.*, 1986; or Booth, 1995).

vulnerable members of the workforce, and the rhetoric of unions is normally directed at stirring emotions for these groups, which include women, older unskilled workers, workers with high levels of firm-specific human capital and high seniority, and minorities. Raising these aspects of the employment relationship above some 'market level' presumes the availability of surplus, as stressed in Chapter 3. As with fringe benefits, these aspects are amenable in principle to the same analysis applicable to compensation; in a world with imperfect markets and indivisibilities, however, the union may represent an economically superior vehicle for bringing about better employment conditions.

4.1.2. *Distribution: equity and fairness*

An important sphere of influence concerns the overall *distribution* of wages, working conditions, and severance rules across individuals, plants, and industries. The distributional element of union activity is ubiquitous. The slogan 'equal pay for equal work' seems to have an equivalent in almost every major language of the world and seems to accord with notions, however vague, of fairness and equity. Perhaps because of informational asymmetries, perhaps because of idiosyncratic characteristics of the employment relationship, it is known that variation of pay in local labour markets can be significant.[2] It is also well established that a large share of the wage variation that cannot be explained by worker attributes (education, experience, ability) occurs between and not within establishments, and that this variation is highly correlated with the ability to pay (i.e. profits).

From the perspective of an individual worker, it may seem a matter of luck (and unfair) whether or not one is employed by a firm that can afford to pay good wages. For this reason, unions tend to favour standardized single-rate remuneration over individual pay, pay attached to jobs rather than persons (Machin, 2000), and industry or even nationwide bargaining to plant-level negotiations.[3] This also explains the application of egalitarian principles to pay structures across sectors and the blue–white-collar distinction, as well as across enterprises. 'Taking wages out of competition' may thus be seen as an attempt to fill in where insurance markets have failed (Agell and Lommerud, 1992; Burda, 1995). It should be noted that a critical dissenting interpretation sees the levelling of wages as a restraint on competition; it is true that incumbent firms welcome measures that prevent competitors from cost-cutting and thus maintain available surplus for capital and labour.

---

[2] Slichter (1950) and Slichter *et al.* (1960), among others, have noted the large variation of earnings in local labour markets for workers of similar skill grade and experience, which union influence could in principle mitigate.

[3] Another justification has been adduced by Freeman and Medoff (1984) and Metcalf *et al.* (2000): if the union implements the preferences of the median voter, and if relative wages matter, the equilibrium wage distribution is likely to be compressed and skewed relative to the distribution of productivities.

More generally, unions strive to impose uniform workplace conditions. This is often articulated as the protection of workers from arbitrary job quality shifts for which they are not responsible. This type of insurance can also be directed towards reducing or eliminating pay decisions arising solely from managerial discretion, and replacing them with automatic progression schemes. Unions have been known to influence training and so-called 'active labour market policy' in a number of OECD countries; one way of interpreting this is as an attempt to eliminate productivity differences that might lead to wage differentiation.

Evidence that unions compress pay is common.[4] Some additional suggestive evidence from Germany's Socioeconomic Panel is provided in Table 4.1. The regressions in the table are extensions of a traditional Mincer model for explaining log earnings. In the regressions, the explanatory variables, i.e. education, experience (and the constant), are all interacted with a dummy variable for union membership. The coefficients on these interaction terms should be thought of as a descriptive characterization of the earnings of German trade union members relative to non-union members. Not only was the joint hypothesis rejected that all interactions with the union dummy were zero, but the signs of the coefficients uniformly point to a *reduction* in the wage-differentiating effect of potential experience and education.

An important and related issue concerns the impact of unions on gender pay differences. Unions have been important in the fight against sex discrimination, and the gender gap seems to be lower in countries in which union presence is strong (Blau and Kahn, 1996). At the same time, it is not clear whether the gender gap is affected primarily by unionization (1) directly (because of explicit pro-women, anti-discrimination policy; (2) indirectly via implementation of pay scales and job ladders; or (3) indirectly via an overall reduction of inequality.

One should expect the scope for pay compression to be larger when bargaining is more centralized and coordinated, as this gives unions greater possibilities to even out pay also between enterprises and sectors. For example, national agreements that cap overall wage increases or provide for a fixed base increase are more likely to accomplish this end than firm-based agreements influenced by individual enterprise profits. It is a robust empirical finding in studies trying to explain cross-country variations in pay distribution that centralization of wage bargaining is conducive to pay compression (see e.g. OECD, 1997a; or Wallerstein, 1999). Evidence from Sweden also indicates that pay differentiation started to increase after the move from nationwide centralized bargaining to industry bargaining in 1983 (Hibbs and Locking, 1996; Iversen, 1999; Davis and Henrekson, 2000).

---

[4] See e.g. Metcalf *et al.* (2000), who examine union effects in the UK, or Freeman and Medoff (1984) and sources cited therein for the USA.

Table 4.1. *Returns to human capital and work experience: West Germany, 1985–1998 (selected years)*

Characteristics	1985 Unrestricted	1985 Fully interacted	1989 Unrestricted	1989 Fully interacted	1993 Unrestricted	1993 Fully interacted	1998 Unrestricted	1998 Fully interacted
EDUC	0.0670 (24.2)	0.0776 (24.3)	0.0645 (23.3)	0.0759 (23.7)	0.0687 (26.6)	0.0760 (26.2)	0.0627 (22.1)	0.0698 (22.1)
EXP	0.0318 (15.0)	0.0347 (13.2)	0.0306 (14.5)	0.0340 (13.3)	0.0333 (14.6)	0.0373 (13.9)	0.0335 (12.1)	0.0337 (10.5)
EXP2	−0.000493 (−11.1)	−0.000524 (−9.3)	−0.000479 (−10.8)	−0.000520 (−9.5)	−0.000545 (−11.6)	−0.00610 (−10.9)	−0.000495 (−8.9)	−0.000495 (−7.5)
CONST	1.647 (42.3)	1.469 (31.9)	1.858 (49.0)	1.668 (37.4)	1.982 (52.3)	1.831 (42.2)	2.095 (44.8)	1.986 (37.4)
EDUC × D		−0.0360 (−5.7)		−0.0378 (−6.0)		−0.0256 (−4.1)		−0.0279 (−3.8)
EXP × D		−0.0105 (−2.4)		−0.0134 (−3.0)		−0.0175 (−3.5)		−0.00249 (−0.4)
EXP2 × D		0.000122 (1.3)		0.000170 (1.8)		0.000283 (2.785)		0.00000712 (0.1)
CONST × D		0.591 (6.9)		0.644 (7.8)		0.554 (6.4)		0.437 (3.9)
R^2	0.27	0.29	0.26	0.29	0.31	0.33	0.25	0.26
s.e.e	0.284	0.281	0.279	0.275	0.273	0.270	0.301	0.298
F-test of all interactions		$F_{(4,2360)}$ = 14.92 (0.0000)		$F_{(4,2344)}$ = 18.20 (0.0000)		$F_{(4,2151)}$ = 14.63 (0.0000)		$F_{(4,2004)}$ = 9.80 (0.0000)

Notes: *t*-values in parentheses.
Sample: male, fully employed (> 25 hrs a week), excluding the self-employed and those currently in VET. Moreover, those working in fishing, agriculture, non-profit organizations, or in a family business have been excluded from the sample. The sample is restricted to those living in former West Germany.
Dependent variable: the log of the gross hourly wage.
Regressors: EDUC = yrs of education; EXP = yrs of work experience; EXP2 = yrs of work experience squared; CONST = constant; D = dummy variable for union membership.
s.e.e.: Standard error of the estimated regression errors.

Source: Own calculations using GSOEP data.

4.1.3. *Increasing efficiency*

It is a commonly held (but not universal) view among labour economists that labour unions represent a source of allocative *inefficiency*, just like those caused by taxes or monopolist pricing. While unions are certainly responsible for some resource misallocation, this reflects only one relevant aspect of their overall activity. Even abstracting from equity and fairness considerations, which on their own can represent welfare improvements, it is imaginable that under certain conditions unions could *increase* efficiency.[5] In history, unions often emerged in response to perceived abuses of monopsony power, which is another source of inefficiency. Standardization of pay may help to lift the effort and productivity of workers if they feel secure and unexploited. Standardization of labour contract terms in a particular industry could also help to prevent 'ruinous competition' for workers by firms and avoid the unnecessary mobility that may arise when different firms chase after the same workers.

A common theme in the discussion of how unions improve efficiency is that collective action entails considerable transaction costs, as well as sizeable public goods aspects. For example, one-off communication and coordination costs can easily inhibit individual workers from lobbying for higher pay or spontaneously organizing enterprise- or firm-level restructuring efforts. Unions offer a practical way of reaching workers efficiently and of communicating proposals for change directly.

An instructive (but not necessarily representative) example taken from the recent press is the case of Chantiers de l'Atlantique, the tradition-bound French shipyard in St-Nazaire that in the late 1920s built *Le Normandie*, the world's fastest passenger ship at the time.[6] The recent introduction of part-time and *temps souple* was hardly met with enthusiasm, but, faced with the prospect of closure with the EU ban on shipbuilding subsidies in 2001, the unions persuaded workers to accept a massive restructuring which abolished old-fashioned job assignment procedures and implemented 'modern' shift and flexible work time schedules. Such radical regime changes may require a centralized intervention; if none is forthcoming, management will generally close such enterprises. While France is certainly not known for the cooperation of its trade unions, it is interesting to note that the *Loi-Aubry*—which reduces the French work week from 39 to 35 hours—involves a large number of union concessions which were extracted in return for the work-week reduction. Most of these concessions involve workplace flexibility and organizational issues (Askenazy, 2000).

To be sure, it is difficult for an outside observer to know when efficiency is helped and when it is hindered by collective action. Unions can employ

---

[5] This view has been put forward by Freeman and Medoff (1984). Metcalf (1993) has shown that the inefficiency relationship is theoretically ambiguous. Recently, Agell (1999) has made this point in a more general context.

[6] 'France Reforms on the Sly', *International Herald Tribune*, 29–30 April 2000.

dilatory tactics to prevent restructuring solely in the interest of its members, and often appear to do so; they can feign ignorance of the market situation or even deny it, attempting to shift restructuring costs to the owners of capital. Although there are examples of union-assisted restructuring—witness the heroic concessions of the German construction union IG Bau to save the construction company Holzmann AG from bankruptcy, including five hours per month of unpaid overtime[7]—there are also many examples of unions blocking reform, such as in the case of liberalization of the shop-closing laws in Germany and Austria.

Exit versus voice and transaction costs

At a deeper level, it is useful to return to the notion of 'exit versus voice'. While the economic theory behind these ideas was not formally elucidated either by Hirschman or by Freeman and Medoff, the notion lends itself readily to at least two modern interpretations. The first is the existence of transaction costs at the level of the individual employment relationship, including renegotiation costs and fixed costs of starting a new employment relationship in general. But according to a second interpretation, this argument can be extended to the theory of real options and quitting as well.

Suppose workers observe or merely perceive that their productivity has risen, and suppose further that this would justify a pay rise under competitive conditions. To obtain a pay increase, each worker must first approach his superior and make a convincing case. This step alone may involve important psychic and possibly, pecuniary costs. Now suppose the manager refuses to recognize the higher productivity as a rationale for a pay increase, even though objectifiable data supported the workers' case. The workers could in principle (1) all quit and search for a better job with a higher wage elsewhere; or (2) stay (albeit with a considerable loss of face) and continue to agitate for better pay, either alone or, more likely, as part of a larger group. The first option corresponds to 'exit', while the second corresponds to 'voice'. If the costs involved with renegotiation are significant, or if the creation of new employment matches always contain a fixed cost component, then there can be a rational incentive for staying on board rather than quitting. Quitting will help contribute to higher wages in the end, but the quitter is unable to internalize the economic effect for himself. Collective action can bring about the same pay rise without the resource costs of mobility. This incentive is greater the higher the fixed costs are, but also the higher the probability that collective action will yield results.

An argument based on real option value theory is also applicable here. Quitting extinguishes an option of being employed by the current firm in the future, leaving a familiar if imperfect job situation for uncertain benefits; the new job may be more susceptible to the business cycle than the current one, and

---

[7] Interestingly, this effort was resisted not by the construction union, whose *erga omnes* wage deal would have been undermined by Holzmann's workers' pay concessions, but by the employers' association, which saw Holzmann gaining a competitive advantage as a result of wage cuts.

may require extensive investment before an acceptable level of productivity has been attained. Staying on implies being given a chance to improve working conditions from within, while retaining the option of quitting should the situation not improve.

The reduction of turnover has additional benefits, one of which is an increase in on-the-job training. As long as unions reduce labour turnover, long-lasting work relationships favour investment in firm-specific human capital (Lynch, 1994; Esping Andersen and Regini, 2000). In Britain panel data, Booth et al. (1999) find that union-covered workers receive significantly more training and are less likely to quit than their non-union counterparts. They also find that union-covered workers who receive work-related training earn lower wages before training and higher wages after training than do otherwise comparable non-union-covered workers. While these findings may be peculiar to the UK, they provide support for the hypothesis that unions create more incentives for human capital investments.

Efficiency and the 'Produktivitätspeitsche' or Rehn-Meidner (Swedish) model

Another potential channel for efficiency is the relationship between wages and structural change. To the extent that new investment is associated with positive productivity spillover effects, unions may be internalizing them when they adjust wage structures to favour the formation of new vintages of capital and a shortening of the expected operating lives of older ones (Agell, 1999). Implicitly, this is done via a 'single-wage-fits-all' policy when capital and firms are heterogeneous. More generally, a common wage policy across firms tends to punish inefficient companies and accelerate their demise while encouraging the expansion of more efficient firms.[8] In German trade union circles this effect is known as the Produktivitätspeitsche ('productivity whip'), which allegedly spurs firms to adopt state-of-the-art methods to reduce labour costs. The obvious limitation of this policy, however, is the alternative use of labour set free when the whip is cracked; if this labour goes into long-term unemployment, it is not clear that the economy as a whole is better off.

Efficiency and the indemnification for inflation/elimination of nominal rigidity

Over the last half of the twentieth century, the inflation rate fluctuated widely. Workers presumably care about the real value of their compensation, and want to be compensated for losses of purchasing power resulting from inflation. Yet, wages are set in nominal terms for some discrete period; if renegotiation has costs, it may be difficult to maintain real wage levels in the face of high and

[8] This argument has been made by Moene and Wallerstein (1992) and by Flassbeck and Scheremet (1995). It is only valid as long as the least profitable companies really do go bankrupt, i.e. if they do not become the recipients of government subsidies to stave off their demise!

variable inflation. It is likely to be efficient for unions to act on behalf of the membership, especially as regards a common factor such as inflation over which there is little disagreement. Defending real pay against fluctuations of inflation has frequently been seen as a central task of unions, and unions tend to set terms for 'compensation' for losses arising from unanticipated increases in the price level.

In economies where unions are weak, it may take labour markets some time to transmit a nominal price shock to nominal wages. This is because, as argued above, managers may exploit local monopsony power by refusing at first to acquiesce to demands of higher nominal wages, even if these are justified. Sufficient workers would need to quit the plant or firm in question before nominal wages would begin to rise to compensate for inflation. With frequent union bargaining, nominal wages are more likely to reflect inflationary tendencies more rapidly.[9] The way unions do this varies widely. They may set national terms for a backward-looking inflation 'compensation' based on the past, or formulate a forward-looking national inflation expectation (often employing resources at the central organization). In any case, the traditional formula of 'inflation plus average expected productivity growth' continues to guide union policy-making.

4.1.4. *Unions as a provider of services*

As their ideological appeal wanes, unions have become increasingly intent on attracting and retaining members by offering a range of tangible benefits of membership. The range of services offered is considerable: from retirement counselling and tax advising (outsourcing of government functions, or *patronato* in Belgium and Italy), training and retraining policies (in Germany unions are actively involved in annual negotiations concerning the number of training positions industry will offer, and the Danish unions, Catholic CISL in Italy, and the CFDT in France have also dabbled in this), to worker education and the training of works council representatives. In the USA, the UK, and the Netherlands some unions have offered financial services, issuing credit cards. In Sweden it has been common for unions to negotiate favourable terms for private insurance with insurance companies for their members.

The most promising area for union services appears to be the provision of legal advice to members, since this is directly related to the needs of union members, as expressed in surveys. Three out of four new members mention 'support should I have a problem at work' as the primary motive for joining

---

[9] Support for this hypothesis can be found in Bruno and Sachs's (1985) estimates of the responsiveness of nominal wages to consumer prices for a number of OECD countries, among which the lowest were in the USA and Canada and the highest in Germany and the UK; this is consistent with the fact that union contract periods are longer in the former two countries than in the latter two. Similar evidence can be found in Alogoskoufis and Manning (1988) and Layard *et al.* (1991).

(Klandermans and Visser, 1995; Waddington and Whitston, 1997). The requirement of greater professionalism, and the increased complexity and flexibility of employment rights and conditions, has made it ever more expensive for unions to provide these services. The burgeoning costs of legal advice were a major factor in the current wave of union mergers in Germany and the Netherlands, as unions tried to achieve greater economies of scale in servicing their members (see Section 2.9, and Streeck and Visser, 1997). Under pressure of low-cost competition from insurance companies, unions have also attempted to draw narrower boundaries, rather than expand servicing into new areas, and they have begun thinking about charging members on the basis of their use of services (Visser, 1998a).

Unions frequently also provide another important service, namely that of political advocacy. Historically, unions have championed the causes of the political left, and are actively engaged in the political lobbying of legislatures and decision-makers. In continental European countries an important strand of unionism has been, and in some countries still is, associated with Christian Democracy and Catholicism. In recent decades, however, the organizational and political ties between unions and political parties have been de-emphasized and have become more contentious in nearly all countries (Ebbinghaus and Visser, 2000; Taylor, 1989). Informal ties may still count, however, and European trade union leaders usually present themselves, and are more often than not seen, as champions of 'social principles' and 'solidarity', standing vigilant to guard social *acquis* against incursions.[10]

4.2. HOW DO THEY DO IT?

It is one thing to describe what one wants, another to be able to achieve those goals. In Europe, the institutional constraints that determine what can be achieved vary widely across countries. In this section we study mechanisms that increase union influence beyond membership. We focus on (1) the extent of bargaining coordination; (2) social pacts with or without governments; (3) the coverage of union contracts; and (4) alternative institutions for employee influence.

4.2.1. *The structure of collective bargaining*

The locus of influence is central to understanding the presence of unions, and can be thought of as the level(s) at which unions can credibly press their

---

[10] The English language does not capture the ideological flavour encountered in continental languages: the French *acquis sociales* and the German *soziale Errungenschaften* transmit much more directly the notion that these benefits represent fruits of a political or social struggle between workers and capital. Not surprisingly, this ideological aspect often serves as a rallying point for opponents to reform.

demands. The Marshall–Hicks rule predicts that the elasticity of labour demand will be lower at the industry than at the firm level, so it is easy to understand why unions are generally interested in coordinating wage negotiations at the industry or even the national level. The most far-reaching form of bargaining coordination is *formal centralization*, i.e. delegation of the conclusion of wage agreements to industry or national (regional)-level unions. This approach has been observed in many European countries at different points in time. If formal centralization is difficult to achieve, independent unions may strive instead to coordinate their efforts, either implicitly or explicitly, as a substitute. Both centralization and coordination between different unions and employers will be of crucial importance for wage outcomes, as Chapter 5 will make clear.

Since the authority within unions or employers' associations is closely tied to the level at which collective agreements are negotiated (Clegg, 1976; Sisson, 1987), the formal level at which bargaining actually takes place represents a first crucial aspect of the wage determination process. Under single-employer bargaining, each employer (firm) negotiates independently; under multi-employer bargaining, employers combine in employers' associations with a mandate to conduct negotiations and reach binding decisions for an entire industry, region, or country. Since the 1930s, multi-employer bargaining has become the dominant type of wage-setting in Western Europe—unlike in Japan and the United States. Sectoral bargaining is still the dominant pattern today, though it is rare that all bargaining occurs at one level. Instead, most bargaining systems are characterized by multi-level negotiations. Two major exceptions are the UK, where multi-employer bargaining has disappeared in nearly all sectors, and France, where company or enterprise bargaining over wages and working hours is of greater importance than sectoral or national bargaining. In Austria, Denmark, Germany, Italy (since 1993), the Netherlands, Sweden, and Switzerland sectoral bargaining is dominant; in Portugal and Spain more intermittently so. Sectoral agreements can be concluded at the national level or on a regional basis (Germany). In Finland, Ireland, Norway, and Portugal central agreements incorporate wage guidelines; in Austria peak associations influence the timing of negotiations; in the Netherlands targets are set through coordination within and among peak associations. In Belgium weak coordination at the national level by peak associations is often compensated—or frustrated—by state intervention.

In recent years centralized bargaining has been subjected to considerable stress: diverse factors such as technological innovation, globalization of the world economy, and the decline of national support for unions have increased pressure on workers to conclude wage agreements that are consistent with local labour market conditions. Decentralization of wage-setting practices, leading to increasing within-sector wage variation, can be observed in many European countries and appears driven primarily by sectors of the economy exposed to international competition and technical change. But a generalized collapse of industry bargaining, and its replacement by company or individual bargaining, has yet to be observed. More usual is the introduction of an additional level of bargaining, usually in the firm, articulated within national or—more commonly—industry-level bargaining.

When trying to measure the extent of centralization/coordination, it must be acknowledged that there is both a vertical and a horizontal dimension. The vertical dimension captures how bargaining authority is divided between different levels (firm, industry, and national) within a union confederation. A high degree of bargaining authority for the national or industry level is usually related to control over strike funds, which makes it possible to enforce contracts concluded at these levels, even when there is subsequent bargaining at lower levels. Weaker authority for the national and industry levels obtains when they have only partial control over strike funds, and have to rely instead on measures such as appointments of union officials and moral persuasion to make lower bargaining levels follow more general guidelines. The horizontal dimension of coordination has to do with the number of actors: with a given distribution of bargaining authority between levels within each union confederation (industry union), the degree of centralization/coordination is obviously lower the more union confederations (industry unions) there are.

Table 4.2 presents a measure of centralization/coordination of the bargaining systems in the European economies, which is based on work by Visser (1990, 2000) and Iversen (1999).[11] Our index is defined as

$$C = \sum_{ij} (w_j \cdot p_{ij}^2),$$

where w_j is the weight accorded to each bargaining level (the sum of all $w_j = 1$), and p_{ij} is the share of union members organized by the union (or confederation) i at level j. w_j measures the distribution of bargaining authority within each union. The fact that p_{ij} is squared means that bargaining is regarded as more coordinated if unions are of uneven size. This is reasonable, as coordination should then be facilitated, for example because the possibility of pattern bargaining (wage leadership) is opened up. The index captures both the horizontal

---

[11] The existence of regional bargaining complicates the picture, though it is often the case that these variants can be subsumed under one of the three principal levels. Thus, although branch-level agreements in Germany are concluded at the level of *Länder* (states), negotiations are tightly coordinated by the national union leadership, and the first regional agreement usually sets the pattern for the entire industry. Similarly, we have treated the provincial, regional, and cantonal agreements in Spain, Portugal, and Switzerland as industry or branch agreements. The recent area agreements in Italy, however, are treated as local agreements, since they involve nationally supervised local bargaining over wages that may be up to 30% lower than the national (industry) minimum. Local bargaining of this kind also exists in Belgium, but is fully prescribed by national (statutory) norms.

Table 4.2. *Bargaining authority and coordination*

	Distribution of bargaining authority			C-index
	w_1	w_2	w_3	
Austria				
1973–77	0.8	0.2	0	0.823
1983–87	0.6	0.2	0	0.624
1993–97	0.6	0.4	0	0.648
Belgium				
1973–77	0.52	0.48	0	0.521
1983–87	0.36	0.04	0	0.311
1993–97	0.4	0.56	0.04	0.422
Denmark				
1973–77	0.8	0.2	0	0.639
1983–87	0.56	0.44	0	0.470
1993–97	0.4	0.4	0.2	0.341
Finland				
1973–77	0.72	0.28	0	0.642
1983–87	0.72	0.28	0	0.577
1993–97	0.64	0.28	0.08	0.465
France				
1973–77	0.4	0.2	0.4	0.104
1983–87	0.4	0.04	0.56	0.065
1993–97	0.4	0.2	0.4	0.079
Germany				
1973–77	0.36	0.64	0	0.346
1983–87	0.2	0.8	0	0.257
1993–97	0.2	0.72	0.08	0.243
Ireland				
1973–77	0.44	0	0.56	0.365
1983–87	0.32	0	0.68	0.267
1993–97	0.8	0	0.2	0.759
Italy				
1973–77	0.4	0.28	0.32	0.382
1983–87	0.28	0.32	0.4	0.110
1993–97	0.4	0.4	0.2	0.324
Netherlands				
1973–77	0.48	0.52	0	0.340
1983–87	0.6	0.4	0	0.449
1993–97	0.48	0.4	0.12	0.393
Norway				
1973–77	0.76	0.24	0	0.419
1983–87	0.72	0.28	0	0.427
1993–97	0.72	0.28	0	0.419
Portugal				
1973–77	0.4	0.2	0.4	0.223
1983–87	0.48	0.2	0.32	0.229
1993–97	0.6	0.2	0.1	0.284

Table 4.2. *(Continued)*

	Distribution of bargaining authority			C-index
	w_1	w_2	w_3	
Spain				
1975–77	0.6	0.2	0.2	0.395
1983–87	0.44	0.28	0.28	0.223
1993–97	0.36	0.24	0.4	0.343
Sweden				
1973–77	0.8	0.2	0	0.745
1983–87	0.48	0.52	0	0.490
1993–97	0.4	0.4	0.2	0.389
Switzerland				
1973–77	0.2	0.8	0	0.209
1983–87	0.2	0.8	0	0.204
1993–97	0.2	0.72	0.08	0.194
UK				
1973–77	0.44	0.28	0.28	0.370
1983–87	0.2	0.4	0.4	0.181
1993–97	0.2	0	0.8	0.141

Source: Visser (2000).

and vertical dimensions in bargaining coordination and varies between 0 and 1. Let 1 denote the national (confederation) level, 2 the industry level, and 3 the local (firm) level. If all bargaining is concentrated at the national level and conducted by one central organization, then both $w_1 = 1$ and $p_{i3} = 1$, and thus $C = 1$. If all bargaining is at the industry level, then $w_2 = 1$, whereas all p_{i2} are numbers between 0 and 1. It follows that C will then also be a number between 0 and 1. When bargaining is occurring only at the local level, $w_3 = 1$ but all p_{i3} will approximate 0, and C thus will approach 0. Table 4.2 presents the C-values and weights for three periods (1973–7, 1983–7, and 1993–7) for fifteen European countries. The index not only captures formal centralization, but also aims to capture more informal coordination, as the membership rates of independent but cooperating unions have been added together before squaring. (See Visser, 2000, for further details on the index.)

Table 4.2 reveals considerable variation across countries. In the 1970s, unions in the four Nordic countries, Austria and Belgium achieved high levels of coordination (as well as high levels of union density, as we saw in Chapter 2); medium levels of coordination at that time characterized wage bargaining in Germany, the Netherlands, Spain, Italy, Ireland, and the UK, while very low levels of coordination were found in France, Portugal, and Switzerland, countries with weak and divided union federations. Two decades later, however, the picture is quite different. In almost all countries there has been a trend towards decentralization. The largest changes according to this measure have taken place in Denmark and Sweden, where earlier nationwide bargaining has strongly lost importance. The picture is not uniform, however, as there are a few exceptions to this picture. In Ireland there has been a strong move towards more centralization and coordination; movements in this direction have also occurred in the Netherlands and Portugal (and in Belgium, Italy, and Spain, if one compares the 1980s with the 1990s). In Norway, France, and Switzerland there has not been much change in either direction.

4.2.2. *Social pacts and the role of unions in macroeconomic policy-making*

One form of coordination of wage-setting and other working conditions that has become increasingly important in recent years is represented by so-called *social pacts*. These are broad agreements between peak-level unions and employers' associations, which try to set guidelines for nominal wage growth. Sometimes such agreements have involved the government as a third party; sometimes they have been bipartite but concluded under pressure from governments. One can view these types of agreement as a way of substituting consensual norms and moral suasion for formal centralization of wage bargaining in a situation when the general development towards lower-level bargaining has made such centralization impossible (Visser, 1998c; Hassel, 1999; Fajertag and Pochet, 2000; Crouch, 2000a,b). Such social pacts were observed in the 1980s and 1990s in several of the EU countries that opted for a non-accommodating monetary regime within the European Exchange Rate Mechanism (ERM) and later for membership of EMU. Strong incentives for such coordination were created when it became increasingly clear that the high unemployment necessitated downward real wage adjustments, which could be accomplished only through money wage restraint.[12]

There is a long tradition in many European countries of unions disclosing their wage and other demands for public discussion, either with or without the presence of the government at the negotiating table. In doing so, they have recognized the macroeconomic effects their nominal wage demands can have on the overall conditions of aggregate supply and demand. Sometimes social pacts have been negotiated by labour and management under the watchful influence of the state, which may at times involve cajoling or even thinly veiled threats. These highly public events can help focus public

---

[12] According to Streeck (1998), the convergence criteria of Maastricht and the subsequent decisions on implementation of the monetary union have inspired 'more or less explicit alliances' between the government, business, and labour aimed at 'making the country fit for Monetary Union'. National pride, or 'the almost irresistible economic and political imperative for countries not to be excluded', proved a strong incentive for such action.

attention on the necessity of macroeconomic adjustment, and can also help to coordinate expectations.

Perhaps the most outstanding example of a national macroeconomic consensus between unions and employers was the Wassenaar Consensus in the Netherlands, forged in 1982.[13] This agreement has received a great deal of attention for achieving real wage moderation, although the exact mechanism remains the subject of some dispute.[14] In any case, the Wassenaar deal resulted in nominal wage moderation on the part of private-sector unions and was followed by government-initiated labour tax cuts (mostly social security contributions) and spending reductions. Indeed, since the mid-1980s real wage growth in the Netherlands has been the most moderate in Europe, even matching the US experience, while a number of tax reforms have mitigated the effect on net family income and enhanced the attractiveness of part-time work.

Social pacts, sometimes of a bipartite character, sometimes of a tripartite character involving also the government directly, have in recent years also been concluded in many other countries (see Table 4.3). One outstanding example is Ireland, where the government has been a direct party, exchanging tax concessions for wage moderation. Other clear examples are Finland, Norway, Italy, Portugal, and Spain. In Belgium several attempts have failed, but have then been superseded by direct government intervention in wage-setting through legislation. Less clear-cut cases are Denmark, where elements of coordination are retained through the system of conflict settlement (where the government can resort to compulsory arbitration), and Sweden, where an agreement between a number of industry unions and employers' associations in 1997 (the Industrial Agreement) aimed at creating a bargaining framework conducive both to industrial peace and wage moderation (Elvander, 1999). Another example for which the jury is still out is Germany's 'Bündnis für Arbeit' (Alliance for Jobs) which was initiated by Chancellor Schröder's SPD government but has been less than tripartite, since the government's role was limited. Yet it has been credited with the pay moderation shown in the 2000 wage round, despite high initial pay demands. As can be seen in Table 4.3, failures are frequent. However, the fact that there continue to be attempts to reach these national pacts or agreements may in itself still have an effect on bargaining behaviour.

---

[13] The Wassenaar agreement of 1982 has since been followed by successor agreements: 'New Course' in 1993 and 'Flexibility and Security' in 1996. Noteworthy is the fact that one key Dutch union leader at the time, Kok, later became prime minister, and thus bore responsibility for staying the tough course of the accord.

[14] See Visser (1998b) and Nickell and van Ours (2000). The Wassenaar agreement involved the peak organizations of employers and unions, and was reached in the Foundation of Labour (a private union–employer organization, recognized by the government). In these agreements (especially in 1982 and 1993), the government ostensibly was present behind the scenes, threatening intervention with wage controls or other norms.

Table 4.3. *Social pacts and national agreements in Europe*

Country	Social pact/agreement	Remarks
Austria	Institutional Social Dialogue (*Paritätische Kommission*)	
Belgium	(Global Pact 1993)	Law
	(Future Pact 1996)	Law
	Central agreement 1998–9	Within narrow legal limits
Denmark	Informal wage moderation norm (D-mark zone) 1987	
Finland	(Stability Pact 1991)	
	Social Pacts I 1996–7 and II 1998–9	
	(Social Contract 2000)	
France	(Attempt to establish national social dialogue in 1997)	Law
Germany	(Alliance for Jobs 1995–6)	
	Alliance for Jobs, Training and Competitiveness 1999	
Greece	Pact of Confidence 1997	'Stop-go social dialogue'
Ireland	PNR, National Recovery 1987–91	
	PESP, Economic and Social Progress 1991–4	
	PCW, Competitiveness and Work 1994–7	
	Partnership 2000 1997–2000	
Italy	National agreement to end *scala mobile* 1992	
	Ciampi Protocol 1993 (reform wage setting)	
	Pension reform 1995	Govt with unions
	Employment Pact 1996 (labour market reform)	
	Social Pact for Growth and Employment 1998 (Christmas Pact)	
Netherlands	Wassenaar (wage moderation) 1982	Bipartite
	Convergence and Concertation (institutions) 1992	
	A New Course (decentralization) 1993	Bipartite
	Flexibility and Security ('flexicurity') 1996	Bipartite
Norway	Incomes policy agreement 1987–8	Bipartite
	Solidarity Alternative 1992–7	
	(Basic Agreement 1998–9)	

Table 4.3. *(Continued)*

Country	Social pact/agreement	Remarks
Portugal	Economic and Social Agreement 1990	Without largest union
	Short Term Social Concertation Agreement 1996	Without largest union
	Strategic Concertation Agreement 1997–9 (Europact 2000)	Without largest union
Spain	Toledo Pact on Future of Social Security 1996	Govt with unions
	Stability of Employment and Bargaining Pact (reforms) 1997	Bipartite
Sweden	(Attempts at establishing 'Euro' wage norm 1995)	
	Industrial Agreement 1997	Bipartite
	(Pact for Growth 1998)	Bipartite

Note: The agreements are tripartite (i.e. involving unions, employers, and government) unless indicated otherwise. Failed attempts are shown within parentheses.

Sources: CEC (2000); Fajertag and Pochet (1997, 2000).

The social pacts of the 1990s differed fundamentally from the social contracts and incomes policies of the 1970s (Regini, 1997; Pochet, 1999*a*; Hassel, 1999; and Crouch 2000*a*,*b*). Those policies were attempts to buy union support for anti-inflationary wage-setting so as to allow governments and central banks to pursue the expansionary fiscal and monetary policies needed to defend high employment levels. With the political commitment to full employment, trade unions held an important power resource in this process of political exchange in so far as they could defeat the government's inflation goal or create political and social unrest (Goldthorpe and Hirsch, 1976; Pizzorno, 1978). As a result, they could then often obtain concessions from the government on taxes and welfare state provisions favouring their members (a 'social wage') in exchange for wage moderation.

Unions had a much weaker bargaining position in the 1990s owing to high unemployment and product market deregulations. Their bargaining aims in many countries seem to have been the defensive ones of limiting labour market and welfare state reforms designed to increase the flexibility of the economy, instead of obtaining new concessions (Crouch, 2000*a*,*b*). It is a typical feature of the social pacts in many countries that wage restraint has often been part of a package that has also included elements of welfare state reforms: the reduction of ancillary wage costs through a change in the financing of social security; pension reforms; the adjustment of social security on new patterns of working-life; and working-time arrangements. The inclusion of these aspects in social pacts has been natural in view of the participation of unions in the administration of welfare state systems in many European countries: unions help determine the minimum wage in France, and they administer the unemployment benefit system in Belgium, Denmark, Finland, and Sweden, and the health and pension systems in France and Germany (see also Part II of this volume).

4.2.3. *The coverage of union contracts*

In the first instance, the influence of unions is determined by the willingness of management or employers' associations to negotiate with them. This is by no means a given in the USA, Canada, or the UK, but is considerably more likely in continental Europe. The ability of unions to conclude agreements with employers depends to a large extent on the legal framework for labour relations. While the right of unions to speak collectively for workers, including non-members, represents an incursion into the freedom to contract, most OECD countries have been willing to permit considerable limitations of this right. Enabling legislation has a significant effect on the ability of unions to perform their functions.

A crucially important means of extending union presence comes under the heading of extension or *erga omnes* mechanisms. These ensure that collectively bargained wages act as binding minima for all contracts in the relevant sector. *Erga omnes* can be achieved in a number of ways; legal extension of national or regional agreements by act of the labour minister, parliament, decree, or court ruling are mechanisms that are in use. In Germany the *Allgemeinverbindlichkeitserklärung*, a ruling in which the federal or *Land* labour minister extends provisions of a labour contract to employees in the sector, is more rarely used than is often thought, allegedly out of respect for the right of management and labour representatives to bargain over pay without state interference (*Tarifautonomie*). However, the threat serves as an important deterrent to bad faith practices. Legal mandatory extension also exists in Austria, Belgium, Finland, France, Greece, Ireland, the Netherlands, Portugal, Spain, and Switzerland; it is regularly used in Austria, Belgium, France, and Portugal. In Ireland the parties signing a collective agreement may apply to the Labour Court (an arbitration board, really) to have the agreement registered, whereupon it becomes legally binding upon the signatory parties and on other employers and employees. Interestingly, in Sweden, Denmark, and Norway organizations of employers and unions do not benefit from this form of legal extension.

Extensions of collective agreements may also frequently emerge as an implied response to the threat of collective action. The most important and pervasive means of increasing presence beyond membership levels, especially in Germany, Austria, and the Scandinavian economies—but remarkably absent from the Anglo-Saxon countries—is simply the extension provided by the contracting mechanism itself: employers extend union contracts to

Table 4.4. *Unionization, employer organization, and bargaining coverage in the market sector, mid-1990s*

Countries	% workers joining trade unions (1)	% workers in firms joining employers associations (2)	% workers covered by collective agreements (3)	'Excess coverage' (3) − (1) (4)	Extension of agreements through public law (5)
Sweden	77	56	72	−5	Absent
Finland	65	58	67	2	Limited
Norway	44	54	62	18	Negligible
Denmark	68[a]	48	52	−14	Absent
Austria	34	96	97	63	Significant
Germany	25	72	80	55	Limited
Belgium	44[a]	72	82	38	Significant
Netherlands	19	79	79	60	Limited
France	< 4	74	75	> 70	Significant
Spain	< 15	72	67	> 52	Limited
Portugal	< 20	34	80	> 60	Limited
Switzerland	22	37	50	28	Limited
Italy	36	40		?	Absent
Ireland	43	39	—	?	Negligible
UK[b]	19	54	35	16	Absent
Japan	24	—	21	−3	Absent
USA	10		13	3	Absent

[a]Estimate. [b]Figures do not include Northern Ireland.

Source: Visser (1999).

non-unionized employees, and employers outside employers' associations adjust voluntarily to the contracts concluded by the latter. To a large extent, unions derive their influence from the existence, as a bargaining counterpart, of a powerful employers' association which negotiates on behalf of its due-paying member firms. The framework agreement serves as a benchmark, and the agreement is self-enforcing, since a firm paying below contract wages would be vulnerable to action by both workers and competitor firms in the industry.[15]

As Table 4.4 shows, the result of various extension provisions is that the coverage of collective agreements (defined as the fraction of contracts in which wages are determined in collective bargaining) can easily exceed

[15] This may explain why this system is most successful in countries in which collective bargaining takes place along industrial lines, and explains why in recent years collective bargaining in Italy has been conducted along industrial lines by three unions (all with different religious and political affiliation) that act jointly as a single union. In a few cases, national contracts have been signed by only two of the three sectoral unions (typically, the Christian democratic CISL and the socialist UIL).

membership as measured by union density. At the same time, it is important to note a number of regularities in these data. First, the countries can be divided into three well defined groups: those with low membership and low coverage (USA, Japan, the UK), those with relatively high membership and high coverage rates (Denmark, Sweden, Finland, Norway), and those countries with 'excess coverage' of 38 percentage points or more (Austria, Belgium, France, Germany, the Netherlands, Portugal, Spain).

Table 4.4 shows that in all but a few European countries—the UK, Denmark, and Switzerland—at least two out of three workers in the market sector are covered by a collective agreement. Comparison with earlier data (Traxler, 1994) indicates that until the early 1990s collective bargaining held its place in Sweden, Finland, Norway, the Netherlands, Belgium, France, Spain, and Portugal. (Unfortunately, we have no data for Italy and Ireland.) There are signs that employers' associations are losing members in Germany and that bargaining coverage is decreasing, especially in the eastern states and among smaller manufacturing firms and in services (see Section 4.3 below). Denmark and Switzerland are two more cases where employers' organizations seem to be in decline, in the Danish case through deliberate reform. In Britain bargaining coverage has continued to contract: the current rate (35%) is only half that of the late 1970s. This is the largest drop in a century (Milner, 1995) and is directly related to the collapse of multi-employer bargaining and the disorganization of employers' associations (Brown, 1993).

4.2.4. *Works councils and alternative channels of institutional influence*

The institution of works councils (*comité d'entreprise, Betriebsrat*, etc.) represents an innovative means of solving the exit–voice problem without explicitly endorsing union organizations or aiding organization efforts. Mandatory works councils exist in Austria, Belgium, France, Germany, the Netherlands, and Spain. In the Nordic countries and in Italy, similar structures of representation are guaranteed by collective agreements. In general, works councils in large enterprises act as conduits of information and are used by management as well, as a source of consultative feedback on such issues as workplace organization, environmental quality, and general workplace morale. In some instances works councils have usurped functions more traditionally performed by unions. In Spain they have a legally recognized role in wage bargaining, and under Dutch law collective agreements may create openings for additional bargaining by the council.

In many countries—but especially in the 'low membership' contexts of France and Spain—works councils serve as one of the most important mechanisms by which poor union membership rates can be transformed up into presence and influence. The reason is that union members tend to attract the votes of non-union workers in the election of council representatives.

Table 4.5. *Union representation and voter turnout in works council elections*

Country	Year	Unionization of council representatives (%)	Voter turnout (%)
Austria	1995	100	—
Germany	1994	74	78
Netherlands	1992–3	67	65
Belgium	1995	97	81
France	1995	71	66
Spain	1994	92	74
Italy	1994–5	80–90	70–80

Sources: Ebbinghaus and Visser (2000); Klandermans and Visser (1995); Rogers and Streeck (1995).

Where councils are mandated by public law (and in Italy), non-union members do participate in works council elections.[16] As a rule, turnout is high and unions attract a much wider support than is evident from their membership. Comparing the data on union membership among works councillors (in Table 4.5) with the data on union density in the market sector (shown in Table 4.4), we find again, as in the case of collective bargaining, a union presence far 'in excess' of plain membership. Works councils are usually mandated in medium-sized and larger firms only (above the threshold of 50 or 100 employees), covering about 40%–50% of the entire private-sector workforce, where union membership tends to be higher. Representation in 'excess' of membership through coverage of collective bargaining can be thought to have resulted from administrative practices. The wider presence of unions on works councils is, however, the outcome of elections in which non-union members participate. It therefore has a greater potential to add legitimacy, and constitutes an additional resource to European unions in spite of declining membership (see Table 4.5).

Most recently, works councils have moved into the policy discussion as European works councils (EWCs) have been established in the European Union. The relevant regulation of *European Works Councils* was adopted in 1994 (Directive (94/45/EC), applying to some 1,200 multinational firms, located in one of the eighteen member states of the European Economic Area (EU + Norway, Malta, and Liechtenstein) with at least 1,000 employees in total and a minimum of 150 employees in at least two countries. Although the UK was not included at the outset, since the Treaty of Amsterdam in 1997 it has been. In 1998 some 600 EWCs appeared to be operating.

At first glance, the EU Directive governing EWCs appears to contain little in the way of substance. Voluntary management–worker agreements on

---

[16] To make the system more accountable, the union workplace representation system in Italy was reformed (on the basis of elections, with some extra seats assuring a majority to those unions who signed the contract). This system appears to have worked well and was, after lengthy negotiations, reaffirmed in 1998.

labour–management consultation procedures concluded before the September 1996 deadline could replace legislative requirements, and the modest information and consultation rights provided for do not include co-determination rights as in German or Dutch works councils. Nevertheless, this institution is of particular interest since, as noted in Chapter 6, pan-European cooperation among unions is likely to be difficult. In view of the fact that they are standardized and institutionalized networks of employees across borders, the EWCs represent a new potential coordination mechanism and could operate in transnational firms as a Trojan horse for pan-European collective bargaining.[17]

4.3. THE FUTURE OF UNION PRESENCE

Secular declines in membership pose risks for the influence of the European labour movement. As membership of trade unions decreases, so in the long run does their influence on governments and social policy, as the relevant voting block becomes less important for politicians and the administrative extension of wage agreements loses public support. This effect is likely to be even more important if bargaining is already decentralized. The rise of the service sector, a growing number of smaller firms, and less standardized workplaces make unionization more difficult, as was discussed in Chapter 2, and decentralization is one reaction that allows flexible adaptation to the new environment. Active management of the process seems inevitable, as German 'opening clauses' have sought to achieve. A growing gap between membership and coverage may cause the legitimacy of collective agreements to become increasingly vulnerable in the policy debate. There is also some evidence to suggest that 'excess coverage' may tend to cause further membership decline, because the free-rider problem discussed in Section 2.3 is accentuated (Boeri and Burda, 2000).

The empirical evidence is rather clear that the decline in union membership observed in Europe is the product of slow erosion, rather than frontal assaults on unions by capital and management. Machin (2000) has shown that the massive deunionization observed in the UK is due primarily to new, non-union establishments rather than to derecognition in existing plants. He further shows that this trend is no different in services than in manufacturing. The failure of unions to gain legitimacy in new establishments has no doubt promoted outsourcing and greenfield investments. Kohaut and Schnabel (1999) have reached similar conclusions based on the new German firm panel. They find not only that coverage rates have declined by several percentage points since 1995, but that new firms are more likely to pay wages determined in establishment (rather than industry)-level wage agreements.

---

[17] A first contract-like agreement has been struck between the unions and the French food giant Danone. Negotiating the EWCs, moreover, had the effect that it gave a boost to the 14 or so sectoral European (cross-border) trade unions (affiliates of the European Trade Union Confederation) in giving them a new role in assisting and advising these councils. This effort received financial support from the European Commission and Parliament (Schulten, 1996).

The recent case of eastern Germany bears witness to the vulnerability of *erga omnes* collective bargaining arrangements in times of economic stress. As a result of the severe structural change and unemployment that followed unification, eastern Germany saw its unions lose more than half their members in the span of a few years, in itself strong evidence that employment is a primary determinant of membership. During this period a uniform wage policy, chosen by western German unionists and employers, was imposed on the eastern regions; ostensibly, the motives of those decision-makers did not include maintaining high employment in the capital-poor eastern states. Not only were unions weakened by employment losses following unification (Table 4.6), but employers increasingly resigned from employers' associations or even explicitly disregarded wage agreements (Table 4.7) and attempted to extract concessions

Table 4.6. *East German membership in DGB (Deutscher Gewerkschaftsbund),*
1991–1998

	Year end union membership ('000)			As % of total employment[a]		
	1991	*1995*	*1998*	*1991*	*1995*	*1997*
Berlin-Brandenburg	1085	755	608	38.0	36.6	32.3
Sachsen	1342	677	510	59.0	42.0	34.6
Sachsen-Anhalt	727	377	306	52.8	41.4	37.0
Thüringen	613	327	244	50.2	38.5	32.1
Mecklenburg-Vorpommern	439	225	227	48.3	36.7	31.1
All new states	4158	2360	1841	50.6[a]	39.0	33.4
Western Germany	7643	6994	6470	32.3	31.4	31.8

[a]Dependent-status employment.

Source: DGB, *Statistisches Bundesamt*.

Table 4.7. *The evolution of membership in employers' associations and non-union*
wages in Eastern Germany, 1993–1998 (%)

	1993	1995	1998
Share of all firms that are members of an employers' association	36	27	21
Share of all employees employed by members of employers' associations	76	64	45
Share of firms which generally pay below the union wage in their sector and region	35	33	41
Share of employees who are paid below the union wage	12	16	28

Source: DIW (1999).

from workers, sometimes through the conduct of the works councils.[18] Some would even argue that unification has accelerated a trend towards decentralized plant-level agreements in Germany; calls in both East and West for more deviations from blanket, industry-wide wage agreements have been followed by increasing use of exit clauses by firms in distress (Schnabel, 1999; Kohaut and Schnabel, 1999).[19] Nevertheless, Kohaut and Bellman (1997) showed that 72% of all employees in 1995 were still covered by industry-wide, collective agreements.

4.4. CONCLUSIONS

Unions in Europe provide a much richer answer to the question 'What do unions do?' than do their North American counterparts. Besides negotiating pay and fringe benefits, European unions have an unmistakable effect on the wage distribution, can influence efficiency in a number of positive (as well as negative) ways, and provide a number of services to their members, including political advocacy. As will be clear in the next chapter, they can have significant influence on macroeconomic outcomes, and often claim for themselves a role in macro policy-making. In this respect, unions play a central part in European economic life, and it seems premature to write them off on the basis of the recent trend towards lower membership.

We have chosen to stress the notion of union *presence*. Union presence may diverge from union membership. It is a striking finding that, despite falling membership, there is little by way of a clearly identifiable trend over the past two decades in qualitative indicators of union presence and influence. It is true that there appears to be a tendency towards decentralization of formal bargaining levels. But this seems, at least to some extent, to have been counteracted by attempts at more informal development of consensual norms and guidelines, sometimes with the help of social pacts with governments and employers. An intriguing question, to which we shall return in Chapter 6, is to what extent such attempts, as well as high coverage of union contracts, are compatible with lower membership rates than in the past.

[18] It is technically illegal under German law for works councils to engage in negotiations over wages or other issues that are normally the domain of the social partners.
[19] According to Schnabel (1999), the number of companies with company-level agreements has risen in Western Germany from 2,100 in 1990 to 3,300 in 1997; in Eastern Germany the rise over the same period was from 600 to 1,700.

5

Bargaining Structure and Macroeconomic Performance

One of the most important aspects of union presence is the extent of coordination of wage bargaining, as was discussed in Chapter 4. Bargaining coordination can occur in several ways: via formal delegation of bargaining to more centralized union levels, formal coordination between different bargaining units, pattern bargaining where aggregate wage developments are determined by a key sector, informal norms for wage-setting, social pacts between labour market organizations and governments, mediation procedures, or other government interventions. This chapter looks more closely at how the extent of wage-setting coordination affects the aggregate wage level and unemployment. As emphasized in the earlier chapters, this is only one of many channels through which bargaining structure can influence macroeconomic performance. The main motivation for the focus here is the importance attached to the unemployment problem in the European policy debate and the fact that the issue of centralized versus decentralized bargaining has been much discussed in this context. This makes it natural to survey existing knowledge. The survey is used as a basis for discussing how the EMU is likely to affect wage bargaining.

Bargaining structure may influence macroeconomic outcomes either directly, or because it interacts with other factors. We emphasize both these aspects. Section 5.1 surveys the 'conventional wisdom' on how bargaining structure may directly influence wages and employment. Section 5.2 discusses the interaction between bargaining structure and economic policy, while Section 5.3 focuses on the interaction with macroeconomic shocks. Section 5.4 analyses how wages in collective agreements are likely to respond to European monetary unification. Section 5.5 summarizes.

5.1. THE CONVENTIONAL WISDOM

The existing literature has emphasized two main mechanisms through which bargaining structure may affect real wage levels and macroeconomic performance: (1) internalization of externalities, and (2) market power.

5.1.1. Internalization of external effects

Higher wages for one group may have negative effects for other groups. Wage decisions under uncoordinated bargaining will not take these negative externalities into account, but under coordination they can be internalized. This works in the direction of stronger incentives for real wage restraint, and thus higher employment, under coordinated than under uncoordinated bargaining.

A number of such negative externalities have been discussed in the literature (see e.g. Calmfors, 1993*a*; Flanagan, 1999). The most obvious one is a *consumer price level externality*. A wage rise in part of the economy tends to raise the price of the consumption basket and thus to reduce the purchasing power of wages in the rest of the economy. Related to this is an *aggregate-demand* externality: to the extent that money wage increases in part of the economy raise the aggregate price level, real aggregate demand falls, which in turn reduces employment and profits elsewhere (Alesina and Perotti, 1997; Soskice and Iversen, 2000). A third example is an *input price externality*: because various sectors are interlinked through the input–output system, a wage rise in a sector that produces inputs for other sectors affects them adversely.

There is also a *fiscal externality*. Wage increases in one part of the economy, which raise unemployment and reduce output there, mean higher costs for unemployment benefits and a smaller tax base. As a consequence, tax rates have to increase. This reduces real disposable incomes throughout the economy. Yet another example is a direct *unemployment externality*: there are fewer alternative employment opportunities for everyone if wage rises in one part of the economy causes unemployment there. Finally, wage increases in one firm may in themselves have direct negative effects on the rest of the economy. There may be *envy* or *jealousy effects*, because employees value a given wage less when the wages of others go up. In addition, if relative wages are important for the productive efficiency of employees, wage increases in one part of the economy harm productivity and profits elsewhere.

5.1.2. *Market power*

If internalization of negative externalities were all that there was to it, more coordination would always lead to lower wages and higher employment. This possibility is illustrated by line I in Figure 5.1. But there is also another important aspect: the degree of market power. The argument then is that various categories of employees are substitutes. This will be the case, for example, for employees in different firms that produce goods that are substitutes in product markets. If wages are raised in one firm, its demand for labour will fall by more if wages are raised only there than if at the same time they are raised in competing firms as well. Coordinated wage bargaining will in this way give wage-setters more market power and will increase wage pressure.[1]

---

[1] An alternative way of regarding this market power effect of coordinated bargaining is as an internalization of a *positive* employment externality, which arises because wage rises in one part of the economy increase labour demand elsewhere.

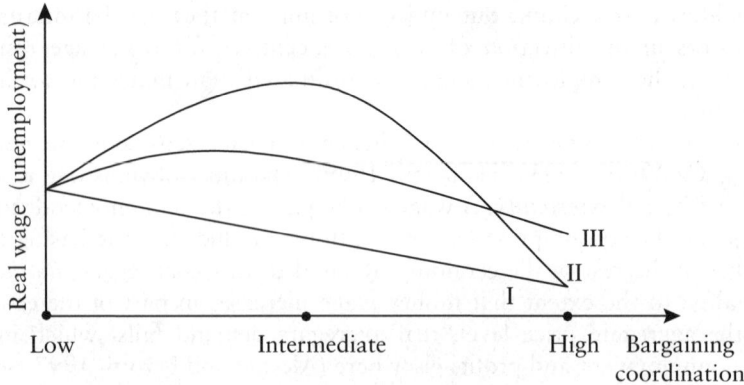

Figure 5.1. *The relationship between bargaining coordination and real wages (unemployment)*

I: The effect of internalization of negative externalities
II: Hump-shaped relationship with small foreign trade
III: Hump-shaped relationship with large foreign trade

The net effect of greater coordination is thus the outcome of two conflicting forces: more internalization of negative externalities, which tends to reduce wage pressure, and more market power, which tends to increase wage pressure. This could lead to a hump-shaped relationship between the degree of coordination and the real wage, with intermediate bargaining at the industry level producing higher real wages than either decentralized bargaining at the firm level or centralized multi-sector bargaining (Calmfors and Driffill, 1988). This possibility is illustrated by curve II in Figure 5.1.

To understand the result, the distinction between the *real product wage* (the money wage deflated by the product price) and the *real consumption wage* (the money wage deflated by the consumer price index) is crucial. When contemplating a wage rise, a union will trade off the welfare gain of a higher real consumption wage against the welfare loss of lower employment that follows when the real product wage increases. Different bargaining structures imply different terms of trade between rises in real consumption and real product wages (Moene *et al.*, 1993). A simultaneous wage rise in all firms in an industry will result in a substantial rise of the output price. The consumer price index will also increase, but by much less than the output price of the sector. So with industry-level bargaining, a given nominal wage increase will be seen to result in a much larger increase in the real consumption wage than in the real product wage. The consequence is a weak incentive for real wage moderation, as a large gain in the purchasing power of the wage can be obtained at a low cost in terms of reduction of employment.

Both highly decentralized and highly centralized wage bargaining will present wage-setters with less favourable terms of trade between increases in the purchasing power of the wage and employment losses. When bargaining occurs at the firm level, wage-setters will realize that there are few possibilities of raising output prices: wage rises will be perceived to give increases of real product and real consumption wages of a similar magnitude. When bargaining is highly centralized, so that wages increase across most of the economy, it will be realized that the resulting increases in product prices must lead to similar increases in consumer prices. So, again, wage-setters will see few possibilities of raising the real consumption wage without generating a similar increase in the real product wage.

A crucial determinant of the market power of unions is, as discussed in Chapter 3, the extent of product market competition. *Foreign competition* tends in general to flatten the relationship between domestic bargaining coordination and the real wage. This is illustrated by curve III in Figure 5.1. There are two reasons for this. On the one hand, competition from abroad restricts the possibilities to raise output prices in response to domestic wage increases. This will be particularly important for wage bargaining at the industry level. If an industry is exposed to a high degree of foreign competition, product prices cannot be raised by much even if the wages of all domestic competitors rise uniformly. So the wedge between increases in real consumption and real product wages is reduced. This promotes wage moderation and tends to flatten (or eliminate) the Calmfors–Driffill hump at an intermediate level of coordination (Danthine and Hunt, 1994). On the other hand, foreign trade weakens the incentive for wage restraint under high coordination relative to low coordination. Because the consumption basket is also made up of imported goods, the consumer price index will increase by less than domestic output prices when all wages in the domestic economy rise uniformly. Therefore, nationwide wage increases raise real consumption wages more than real product wages (Layard *et al.*, 1991; Calmfors, 1993*b*).

The existence of a *non-union sector* may have similar effects to those of foreign trade (Flanagan, 1999). With bargaining at the industry level, competition from non-union firms could exercise downward pressure on wages just like competition from foreign firms. And even with complete coordination within the union sector, there remains a wedge between increases in real consumption and product wages, because the non-union sector is not encompassed.

5.1.3. *Multi-level bargaining*

A feature of bargaining at sectoral (or national) level that is often neglected is that such bargaining systems in reality mean multi-level bargaining. In the Scandinavian countries, higher-level bargaining is typically followed by local bargaining about the implementation of the wage agreement at the level of the firm. Such second-tier bargaining occurs also in, for example, Austria, Germany, and Italy. Especially in the Scandinavian countries, local bargaining

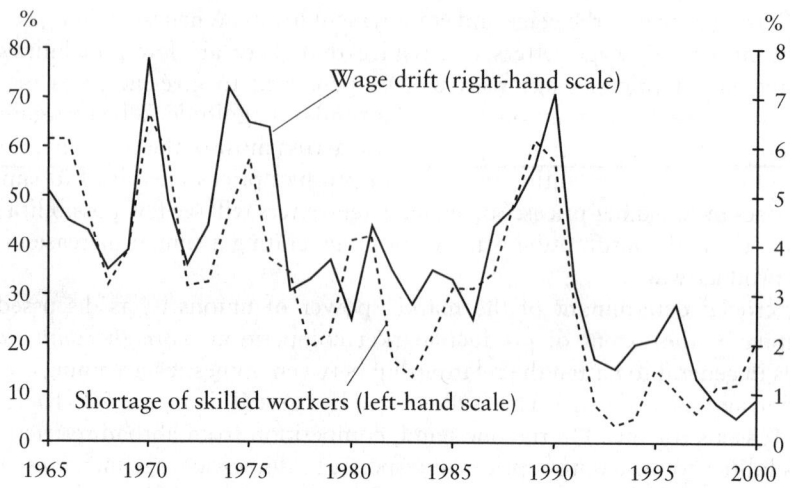

Figure 5.2. *Wage drift and shortage of skilled workers in Swedish manufacturing, 1965–2000*

Source: National Institute of Economic Research (KI) and Swedish Employer's Federation (SAF).

has regularly given rise to wage increases in excess of the increases negotiated at the higher level, so-called *wage drift*.

There exist several explanations of this phenomenon. According to one view, wage drift is a response to demand pressures in the labour market. If there are labour shortages, employers try to attract and keep labour by raising the relative wage they offer. This interpretation receives support from empirical studies that have found a strong correlation between the labour market situation and wage drift (e.g. Holden, 1990*a*; Holmlund and Skedinger, 1990; Hibbs and Locking, 1996). Figure 5.2 illustrates the relationship for Sweden.

Another explanation of wage drift focuses on the fact that local bargaining about the implementation of a higher-level contract is usually conducted under a peace clause, which in practice gives employees a stronger bargaining position than the firm (Holden, 1988; 1990*a,b*). The reason is that the peace clause effectively prevents the employer from taking industrial action, whereas employees can resort to informal conflict measures, such as go-slow actions, working-to-rule, sick leaves etc., which cannot in practice be regulated. Because employees are guaranteed to obtain at least the wage bargained at the higher level, they can always obtain an additional wage increase in local bargaining.

Finally, a third explanation emphasizes conflicts about wage dispersion. To the extent that higher-level unions seek to compress the pay structure, wage drift may be a market response to this 'distortion'. Hibbs and Locking (1996) find some support for this view.

It has been widely discussed whether or not wage drift affects the final wage outcomes. If higher-level negotiators can anticipate subsequent wage drift, they should be able to offset its influence on final outcomes through variations in the wages they negotiate. Both Rödseth and Holden (1990), and Hibbs and Locking (1996) find support for this hypothesis. However, in situations with low inflation and low demand, such offsetting variations could necessitate reductions in the money wages that are negotiated at industry level. As this is not likely to occur, it is possible that the wage drift implied by two-tier bargaining could in such situations lead to higher real wages, and thus lower employment, than would otherwise be the case (Calmfors, 1993b).[2]

5.1.4. Empirical studies

Considering all aspects, the question of how the bargaining structure affects real wages and unemployment is clearly an empirical one. A number of regression studies have been made of the determinants of unemployment in the OECD countries, in which measures of bargaining structure have been entered alongside measures of other labour market institutions and sometimes also controls for business cycle conditions. A few studies have tried to explain cross-country differences in unemployment only over longer time periods, but many of the studies have used panel data and thus seek to explain variations both across countries and over time.

Chapter 4 discussed how bargaining coordination could be measured. We made a distinction between formal centralization, which has to do with the actual level at which wage contracts are concluded and the existence of parallel union (or employer) organizations, and overall coordination, which could result also from informal (tacit) coordination between independent unions and employers. In the empirical literature, both measures of formal centralization (which we shall denote 'centralization measures') and measures trying to capture coordination in the broader attitudinal sense (which we shall denote 'coordination measures') have been used (OECD, 1997a; Flanagan, 1999). Although the coordination measures conform better to the theoretical aspects one wants to cover, they have the disadvantage of being more subjective and more difficult to compare over time and across countries.

Table 5.1 replicates six different classification schemes, which we find representative of the literature. The first three rankings are from Elmeskov et al. (1998) and are based on work by the OECD; the last three measures are from Nickell and Layard (1999). There is a high correlation between the different

---

[2] Holden (1998) has found support for such nominal rigidities in the Nordic countries. It remains an open question to what extent wage drift can be reduced by avoiding flat wage rate increases that apply to everyone in sectoral agreements. In recent years there has been a tendency in, for example, Sweden to let these agreements determine only the total wage increases in the firms encompassed, and then to give the local union and the firm complete freedom to distribute this total among the individual employees (Elvander, 1999).

Table 5.1. *Coordination of wage bargaining in the 1980s and 1990s*

Country	Centralization (Elmeskov et al.) (1)	Coordination (Elmeskov et al.) (2)	Summary measure of centralization/ cooperation (Elmeskov et al.) (3)	Union coordination (Nickell and Layard) (4)	Employer coordination (Nickell and Layard) (5)	Overall bargaining coordination (Nickell and Layard) (6)
Australia	2; 1 since 1988	2; 1 since 1988	2; 1 since 1988	2	1	1.5
Austria	2	3	3	3	3	3
Belgium	2	2	2	2	2	2
Canada	1	1	1	1	1	1
Denmark	3; gradually 2	3	3	3	3	3
Finland	3; gradually to 2	2	3; gradually to 2	2	3	2.5
France	2	2	2	2	2	2
Germany	2	3	3	2	3	2.5
Ireland	2	2; 3 since 1988	2; 3 since 1988	1	2	1
Italy	1; 3 since 1992	2; 3 since 1992	1; 3 since 1992	2	1	2
Japan	1	3	1	2	2	2
Netherlands	2	2; 3 since 1982	2; 3 since 1982	2	2	2
New Zealand	2; 1 since 1991	1	2; 1 since 1991	1	1	1
Norway	3	3	3	3	3	3
Portugal	2	2	2	2	2	2
Spain	2	3; 2 since 1987	3; 2 since 1986	2	1	1.5
Sweden	3; gradually 2	3; gradually 1 in the 1980s and back to 2 in 1991–95	3; gradually 2	3	3	3
Switzerland				1	3	2
UK	2; gradually to 1	1	2; gradually to 1	1	1	1
USA	1	1	1	1	1	1

Notes: 1 is low coordination/decentralization (wage-setting at the level of the firm); 2 is intermediate coordination/centralization (wage-setting at the industry level); 3 is high coordination/centralization (wage-setting at the economy-wide level). Column (6) is the average of columns (4) and (5).

Sources: Elmeskov *et al.* (1998) and Nickell and Layard (1999).

measures (as is usually the case). However, several countries are considered more highly coordinated according to the coordination measures than according to the centralization measures. Comparing columns (1) and (2) (from Elmeskov *et al.*, 1998), this holds for Austria, Germany, and Japan for the whole period, and for Denmark, Ireland, Italy, and the Netherlands for part of the period. A comparison of column (6) (from Nickell and Layard, 1999) and column (1) (from Elmskov *et al.*) gives a similar picture. The Nickell–Layard classification serves to emphasize that bargaining coordination in some cases appears to be higher if the employer side as well as the union side is taken into account: Finland, Germany, and Switzerland are examples of this.

A consistent finding in the empirical studies is that the choice of measure of bargaining coordination matters. When broader coordination measures are used, there is support for a monotonic negative relationship between the degree of coordination and unemployment, with higher coordination leading to lower unemployment, as illustrated by line I in Figure 5.1. When centralization measures are used, one tends instead to find a hump-shaped relationship like curve II in Figure 5.1.

Table 5.2 gives a summary picture of estimated effects in those studies that have found the degree of bargaining coordination to be important.[3] The studies have been ordered according to whether they show a monotonic relationship or a hump-shaped one. Column (3) shows the estimated difference in unemployment between a bargaining system with intermediate coordination and a bargaining system with low coordination when other factors are controlled for. Similarly, column (4) shows the estimated unemployment difference between a system with high coordination and one with low coordination. Unemployment is on average 3.2 percentage points *lower* under intermediate than under decentralized bargaining in the studies showing a monotonic relationship, whereas it is on average 1.9 percentage points *higher* in the studies showing a hump shape. In both types of study the estimated difference between high and low coordination is very large. In the studies finding a monotonic relationship, unemployment is on average 6.8 percentage points lower under high than under low coordination. The average difference is almost as large—4.9 percentage points—in the studies finding a hump shape. So, although the studies disagree on the effects of intermediate bargaining, they agree that high coordination seems *ceteris paribus* to produce lower unemployment than low coordination. The results from the two sets of studies are illustrated in Figure 5.3.

It is interesting to compare the results on bargaining coordination with those on union density and coverage of collective agreements in the studies surveyed.

---

[3] A study not included in the table is OECD (1997*a*), which had problems coming up with any significant relationships. It found only some weak evidence in favour of a monotonic relationship (and some weak evidence in favour of the hypothesis that more foreign trade will lead to lower unemployment in countries with intermediate coordination).

Table 5.2. *Unemployment under various bargaining regimes* (ceteris paribus *differences from uncoordinated/decentralized systems) in various studies*[a]

	Study	Intermediate bargaining (1)	Coordinated bargaining (2)	Dependent variable (3)	Coordination measure (4)
1	Layard et al. (1991)	−4.7	−10.4	Unemployment	Coordination
2	Zetterberg (1995)[b]	−0.4	−2.4	Unemployment	Centralization
3	Scarpetta (1996)[c]	−6.2	−12.3	Unemployment	Coordination
4	Bleaney (1996)[d]	−2.0	−3.9	Unemployment	Coordination
5	Elmeskov et al. (1998)[e]	−0.8	−5.7	Unemployment	Coordination
6	Nickell and Layard (1999)	−4.6	−6.0	Unemployment[f]	Coordination
7	Nickell and Layard (1999)	−9.5	−19.0	Non-employment	Coordination
8	Zetterberg (1995)[g]	2.6	−1.5	Unemployment	Centralization
9	Bleaney (1996)[h]	3.5	−2.1	Unemployment	Centralization/ coordination
10	Scarpetta (1996)[i]	0.9	−12.0	Unemployment	Centralization
11	Elmeskov et al. (1998)[j]	1.3	−2.4	Unemployment	Centralization
12	Elmeskov et al. (1998)[k]	1.2	−4.4	Unemployment	Centralization/ coordination
13	Nicoletti et al. (2001)	3.6	−2.2	Non-employment	Centralization/ coordination
	Average with monotonic relationship (rows 1–6)	−3.2	−6.8	Unemployment	Coordination
	Average with hump shape (rows 8–12)	1.9	−4.9	Unemployment	Centralization/ coordination

[a]The table shows how the unemployment rate under intermediate and high coordination differs from that under low coordination when other factors are controlled for.

[b]Equation (3) in table 4.14. We have classified the countries ranked 1–5 as highly coordinated, the countries ranked 6–10 as intermediately coordinated, and the countries ranked 11–17 as uncoordinated.

[c]Equation (2) in table 1.

[d]Equation (1) in table 5.

[e]Equation (1) in table 2.

[f]The equation explains the log of unemployment rate. In the calculation of the effect on the unemployment rate, we have assumed that unemployment under decentralization is equal to the averge rate of unemployment among the countries studied during the estimation period.

[g]Equation (5) in table 4.14. We have classified the countries ranked 1–3 and 7–9 as centralized, the countries ranked 13–17 as intermediately centralized and the countries ranked 4–6 and 10–12 as decentralized.

[h]Equation (4) in table 5. Bleaney distinguishes between highly centralized systems, highly decentralized systems, moderately centralized systems with a high degree of corporatism, and moderately centralized systems with a low degree of corporatism. In our table the last two categories have been amalgamated.

[i]Equation (8) in table 1. The entry for intermediate centralization refers to the country ranked 14 and the entry for coordination to the country ranked 1. The comparison is with the country ranked 17.

[j]Equation (2) in table 2.

[k]Equation (4) in table 2.

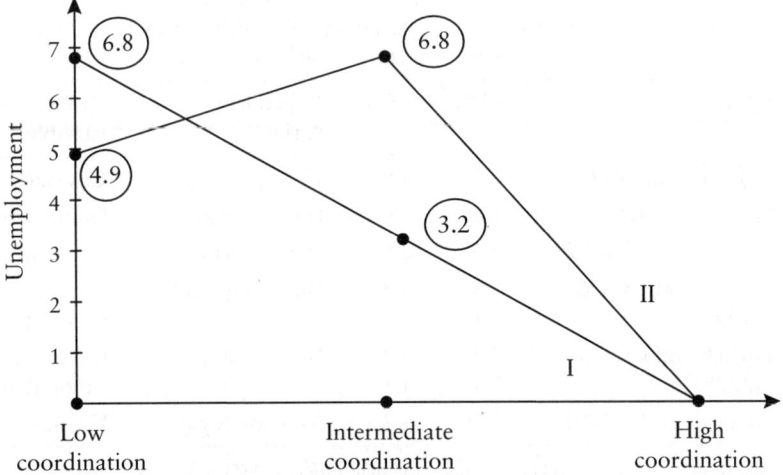

Figure 5.3. *The relationship between bargaining coordination and unemployment in empirical studies*

Notes: The diagram shows the average estimated differences in unemployment between, on the one hand, low and intermediate coordination and, on the other hand, high coordination.
 I: Average monotonic relationship according to Table 5.2
II: Average hump-shaped relationship according to Table 5.2

In general, these latter variables seem to have lower explanatory power than bargaining coordination. In Zetterberg (1995) and Bleaney (1996), union density and coverage have not been included at all. Estimated effects in the other studies are summarized in Table 5.3. It shows how much higher unemployment is at intermediate (45%) and high rates (75%) of density or coverage compared with low rates (15%). The rates have been chosen to capture the existing span of differences between OECD countries. The majority of the studies suggest that the difference between high and low density/coverage accounts for a smaller difference in unemployment than the difference between high and low coordination.[4]

If one takes the reported results at face value, they would seem to imply that changes in bargaining coordination may be more important for macroeconomic outcomes than changes in union membership and coverage of union contracts. But it is not clear, of course, that one can treat density/coverage and bargaining coordination as independent of one another. It might be more relevant to compare the unemployment effects of systems characterized by both low density/coverage and low coordination with systems characterized by both

---

[4] The exceptions are the unemployment equations estimated by Nickell and Layard (1999) and Nicoletti *et al.* (2001).

Table 5.3. *Unemployment under various rates of union density and coverage of collective agreements* (ceteris paribus *differences from 15% union density or coverage*) *in different studies*[a]

	Study	45%	75%	Dependent variable	Explanatory variable
1	Layard et al. (1991)	2.5	4.9	Unemployment	Coverage
2	Scarpetta (1996)[b]	1.8	3.6	Unemployment	Union density
3	Elmeskov et al. (1998)	0.3[c]	0.6[c]	Unemployment	Union density
4	Nickell and Layard (1999)	2.8 3.7	6.5 9.0	Unemployment[d]	Coverage Union density[d]
5	Nickell and Layard (1999)	0.4[c] 2.4	0.8[c] 4.8	Non-employment	Coverage Union density
6	Nicoletti et al. (2001)	2.1	4.2	Non-employment	Union density

[a]The table shows how much higher the unemployment rate is at 45% and 75% density or coverage rates compared with 15% rates when other factors are controlled for.
[b]Equation (2) in table 2.
[c]Not significant.
[d]The explanatory variable is the log of the unemployment rate. In the calculation of the effect on the unemployment rate, we have assumed that unemployment at 15% density and coverage rates is equal to the average rate of unemployment among the countries studied during the estimation period.

high density/coverage and high coordination. One reason is that there appears to be a correlation across countries between unionization and bargaining coordination, as we discussed in Section 2.7. Another reason is the recent tendency towards both decentralization and deunionization in some countries, as discussed in Chapters 2 and 4. Theory also predicts that it should be easier to achieve high coordination in the union sector, the higher is the coverage of collective agreements, as the benefits of coordination become larger the more employees that are encompassed (Holden and Raaum, 1991).

The estimates seem to suggest that the employment performance of an economy with both high bargaining coordination and high unionization is, *ceteris paribus*, superior to that of an economy with low coordination and low unionization. The results with respect to countries with intermediate bargaining coordination and intermediate levels of unionization are more ambiguous: here the studies finding a hump-shaped relationship between coordination and unemployment suggest that decentralization and deunionization would both tend to reduce unemployment, whereas most of the studies finding a monotonic relationship indicate that such simultaneous moves would tend to raise unemployment.

The conclusion that the combination of high coordination and high unionization may be superior to the combination of low coordination and low unionization is subject to several caveats.

1. It may not be correct to enter density/coverage variables and bargaining coordination as separate variables that do not interact with each other. One could argue that higher union coverage might reduce the aggregate wage and unemployment levels at a high degree of coordination within the union sector, because the extent of internalization becomes larger. But the effect might be reversed at a low degree of coordination, because wages in union contracts are higher than in other contracts and internalization effects are then small anyway. OECD (1997*a*) found some evidence in favour of this hypothesis.

2. High unionization and bargaining coordination may go hand in hand with factors such as generous unemployment insurance, high taxes, and high employment protection that tend to raise unemployment.[5] It may therefore be misleading to control for these variables, as has been done in the studies surveyed, when trying to assess the impact of bargaining coordination and unionization.

3. As discussed in Section 5.1.3, centralized systems with multi-level bargaining may perform worse during periods of low inflation because nominal wage rigidities can then make it impossible for central negotiators to exercise real wage restraint. This may not be captured by empirical studies encompassing periods of high inflation.

4. An obvious drawback of the empirical studies is the limited variability in the variables that measure the degree of bargaining coordination. This is obvious when only cross-country variations among around twenty OECD countries are examined. But most of the problem remains in the panel studies too, because there is little variation over time in each country: typically, changes in bargaining structure occur very slowly and infrequently. For example, in the rankings by Elmeskov *et al.* (1998) there are only between seven and nine changes in the bargaining systems within nineteen OECD countries over the 1980–95 period (the exact number depending on the measure being used; see Table 5.1).

These caveats notwithstanding, the empirical studies still suggest that, in the absence of accompanying policy changes, a development towards decentralization and deunionization could entail a risk of worse long-term employment performance than would otherwise occur for those countries that are today characterized by high bargaining coordination. The chance that such a development will promote employment appears greater for countries that start out with an intermediate degree of coordination.

---

[5] This is to some extent the topic of Part II below. Note, however, that countries with high bargaining coordination and high unionization tend to have more active labour market policies, which, according to many of the studies surveyed, tends to reduce unemployment.

5.2. THE INTERACTION BETWEEN BARGAINING STRUCTURE AND ECONOMIC POLICY

According to the conventional analysis, the degree of coordination of wage-setting may have a direct impact on real wages and employment. Another possibility is that bargaining structure has an effect because it interacts with other factors. This section considers the interaction with two types of policy: tax and monetary policy.

5.2.1. *The interaction with tax policy*

It is a controversial issue in itself whether or not higher labour taxes raise real wage costs and unemployment. The outcome depends on the extent to which taxes are shifted on to employees. Here, different theoretical assumptions give different results. Empirical studies of wage-setting and unemployment have also produced differing results (see Nickell and Layard, 1999; Calmfors and Holmlund, 2000).

If there is an 'income' from being unemployed that is independent of taxes (a fixed after-tax real unemployment compensation, income from household production that is not taxed, or simply the value of leisure) and bargaining is decentralized, then the real after-tax consumption wage will, under stylized assumptions (constant–elastic labour demand and risk-neutral workers), be a constant mark-up on the real income of the unemployed (see e.g. Alesina and Perotti, 1997; Daveri and Tabellini, 2000). In this case, an increase in the income tax rate will lead to a higher pre-tax wage. And a higher payroll tax is not shifted on to employees in the form of a lower wage. So both types of tax increase raise the labour cost to employers and thus also unemployment.

Internalization of the government budget constraint is one mechanism through which bargaining coordination may influence the impact of taxes on wages and employment: with coordinated wage bargaining, wage-setters will realize that their own wage decisions, by affecting total wage income, also affect total tax revenues and therefore the amount of transfers from the government they get back. Suppose, for example, that all income taxes go back to union members in the form of transfers. Then, the real disposable income of union members is independent of the tax rate. As a consequence, if there were complete coordination of wage-setting, then the wage decision would not be affected by the tax rate. So under these extreme assumptions, one would expect a zero wage response to a change in the tax rate (Alesina and Perotti, 1997). In general, such internalization provides an argument for why high taxes should lead to less adverse wage and employment effects, the higher the degree of bargaining coordination.

However, according to an argument by Alesina and Perotti (1997) the degree of bargaining cooperation may also affect the impact of taxes through another channel. This argument has to do with the fact that consumers substitute away from goods whose prices rise. Such substitution reduces the effect on the aggregate price level of a wage rise and thus tends to lead to less wage moderation. The amount of substitution will in general be larger, the larger is the mass of products affected by the wage rise. As a consequence, there exists also a mechanism according to which high taxes will have a larger effect on the wage, the higher is the degree of bargaining coordination. Alesina and Perotti have argued that this effect dominates at low levels of coordination, but it is overtaken by the internalization effect discussed above at high levels of coordination. The upshot is that the interaction between taxes and wages may also produce a hump-shaped relationship between the extent of bargaining coordination and unemployment.

There are only a few empirical studies of the interaction between taxes and bargaining structure. Summers *et al.* (1993) found that the total number of hours worked responded less to taxes, the higher was the degree of bargaining coordination (measured by a centralization indicator). They used this finding as an explanation of why countries with more coordinated bargaining seem to have opted for higher government expenditures than other countries. Similarly, Phelps (1994), using a coordination measure, found that unemployment responds less to changes in tax pressure when wage-setting is more coordinated. In contrast, Elmeskov *et al.* (1998), and Daveri and Tabellini (2000) found support for a hump-shaped relationship between the impact of taxes on unemployment and bargaining coordination. Daveri and Tabellini then distinguished between Anglo-Saxon countries (with decentralized bargaining), continental European countries (with an intermediate degree of coordination), and the Scandinavian countries (with a high degree of coordination), whereas Elmeskov *et al.* used a coordination measure giving a large weight to centralization (see Table 5.1 above). Alesina and Perotti (1997) found evidence of a hump-shaped relationship between the impact of taxes on the relative unit labour cost of a country and the degree of coordination.

The estimated interaction effects in the studies indicating a hump-shaped relationship are given in Table 5.4. Like the estimated direct effects in Table 5.2, the estimated interaction effects are also large.[6] The findings of Daveri and Tabellini and Elmeskov *et al.* are consistent with the picture from the direct effects in Table 5.2, that high coordination leads to a more favourable employment outcome than low coordination. Alesina and Perotti, however, find the interaction effects to be insignificant for both high-coordination and low-coordination countries. An important difference from Table 5.2 is that the adverse effects of intermediate coordination appear to be much larger here. In none of the studies of interaction effects do union density or coverage appear as significant explanatory variables.

---

[6] The Summers *et al.* (1993) study deviates from this picture, however. There, the difference in the total number of hours worked between high and low coordination countries is only around 0.2% at the average level of taxes during the estimation period.

Table 5.4 *Macroeconomic outcomes of tax–wage interactions under various bargaining regimes (ceteris paribus differences from uncoordinated/decentralized systems) in various studies*[a]

	Study	Intermediate bargaining	Coordinated bargaining	Dependent variable	Coordination measure
1	Elmeskov *et al.* (1998)[b]	6.9	− 4.6 (2.3)[c]	Unemployment	Coordination
2	Daveri and Tabellini (2000)[d]	5.8	− 7.2 (4.9)[c]	Unemployment	Geographical[e]
3	Alesina and Perotti (1997)[f]	18.8 (17.8)	0 (4)[c]	Relative unit labour cost	Centralization

[a]The table shows how much the value of the dependent variable under intermediate and high coordination differs from that under low coordination when other factors are controlled for.
[b]Equation (4) in table 4. The effects are evaluated at the average tax ratio for the sample period (1983–95).
[c]The figure within parentheses gives the insignificant point estimate.
[d]Equation (5) in table 9. The effects are evaluated at the same tax ratio as in Elmeskov *et al.*
[e]This study associates the Scandinavian countries with high coordination, the European continental countries with intermediate coordination, and the Anglo-Saxon countries with low coordination.
[f]Equation (3) in table 2. The effects are evaluated at the average tax ratio for the sample period (1965–90).

5.2.2. *The interaction with monetary policy*

Another interaction between bargaining structure and policy concerns monetary policy. Recent literature emphasizes this aspect. The hypothesis is that coordinated unions will act strategically and take the anticipated monetary policy reactions of central banks to wage settlements into account. These monetary policy responses are in turn assumed to be related to the degree of central bank independence.

The interaction between unions and central banks have been analysed in two ways. The first approach focuses on the existence of an inflation bias for monetary policy, which coordinated unions might want to influence. The second approach analyses instead how central bank responses are likely to affect the employment costs of wage increases.

An inflation bias argument for wage restraint

Recently, Skott (1997), Cukierman and Lippi (1999), and Velasco and Guzzo (1999) have argued that there exists an inflation bias argument for why coordinated bargaining should promote real wage moderation.[7] The starting point is Barro and Gordon's (1983) analysis of an inflation bias in monetary policy. Their argument was that, when discretionary policy is possible, policy-makers

---

[7] These analyses were preceded by Yashiv (1989), Cubbitt (1992, 1995), and Agell and Ysander (1993).

concerned with both inflation and unemployment have an incentive to pursue inflationary policies when equilibrium unemployment is higher than their unemployment goal. But because wage-setters learn to anticipate this behaviour, all attempts to reduce unemployment below its equilibrium level will fail, and the economy gets locked into an equilibrium with socially inefficient inflation. This inflation bias is larger the higher is the equilibrium rate of unemployment, as this is associated with a stronger temptation to pursue inflationary policies.

The argument is now that coordinated unions will realize that they can influence the inflation bias of monetary policy through their real wage decisions, as these affect equilibrium unemployment. So if unions are concerned about inflation (in addition to real wages and employment), they have an incentive to compromise on their real wage objectives in order to reduce equilibrium unemployment, because this will induce the central bank to pursue a policy that will lead to lower inflation. The interaction between coordinated unions and the central bank will thus add a motive for real wage restraint. This analysis leads to the conclusion that making the central bank more conservative, in the sense that a higher priority is given to price stability, implies higher equilibrium unemployment in a setting with high bargaining coordination. The incentives for coordinated unions to restrain wages in order to hold down inflation become weaker with a conservative central bank, which will anyway keep down inflation, than with a liberal central bank, which is prone to pursue inflationary policies if unemployment is high.

How reasonable is the inflation bias argument for wage restraint? On the face of it, the argument might seem to provide an explanation of the macroeconomic experiences of, for example, the Scandinavian countries in the second half of the 1970s and the 1980s. A characteristic feature of these economies then was the combination of high inflation and real wage restraint (Calmfors, 1993*b*; Layard *et al.*, 1991). Still, it appears implausible to us that concerns about inflation would play an important role for union behaviour. If this were true, one should have seen unions urging central banks to tighten monetary policy in order to lower inflation, as this would reduce the need for them to compromise on real wage objectives. But this was certainly not the case in the Scandinavian countries even in the 1970s and 1980s, when dependent central banks resorted to a policy of devaluation and inflation. On the contrary, unions usually argued against attempts to pursue less accommodative policies. This appears to have been the case in most other countries, too.

The central bank as a deterrent to wage increases

An alternative approach emphasizes the role of the central bank as a deterrent to wage increases (Hall and Franzese, 1998; Soskice and Iversen, 1998, 2000; Bratsiotis and Martin, 1999; Corricelli *et al.*, 2000). According to this argument, unions set wages by trading off real wages against employment without caring about inflation *per se*. Central bank behaviour will then be important to the extent that it affects this trade-off.

The reasoning is as follows. Consider a large union which contemplates a money wage rise. The benefit of this is a real wage gain. If there is a neutral monetary policy (a constant money supply), the real wage gain would simply be traded off against the employment loss that arises because the relative price of the products produced by the union members rises, and because the wage rise induces an increase in the general price level which reduces the real money supply. But if monetary policy is not neutral, the reactions of the central bank must also be taken into account. If the central bank gives a high priority to price stability, it will respond to the wage rise with a contractionary monetary policy. This policy response reduces the nominal money supply and thus exacerbates the fall in the real money supply. As a consequence, the perceived elasticity of labour demand increases. So a given money wage rise is associated with a larger employment loss than would otherwise be the case. This provides an extra incentive for wage restraint.

This argument reverses the inflation bias argument. The more inflation-averse the central bank, the stronger the incentives of unions to show restraint in order not to trigger a policy response that adds to the employment losses of a wage rise. With this reasoning, conservative (independent) central banks are thus conducive to high employment, because they deter high wages in an effective way.

The deterrence effect is likely to be most effective at intermediate levels of bargaining. At very decentralized levels, wage-setters are too small to count on any central bank reactions to their wage decisions. And at very high levels of coordination, central bank behaviour may not matter much either, because the incentives for real wage restraint may then be very strong anyway. The latter argument is easy to see if one assumes: (1) a closed economy; (2) constant returns to scale, so that the output price of each firm equals the wage; and (3) that the demand for each sector's output depends on the relative price (the relative wage) and the real aggregate money supply (Soskice and Iversen, 2000). With intermediate coordination, unions will trade off the real wage gain (the relative wage increase) that follows from a higher money wage against the employment loss that follows from a higher relative price and a lower real money supply. But with *complete* coordination across the economy, wage-setters will realize that they cannot affect real (and relative) wages: all that a money wage increase can do is to reduce the real money supply and hence real aggregate demand and employment. So the best strategy under complete coordination is to set the money wage so that there is full employment. This logic holds independently of how the central bank responds to wage increases.

The threat that the Bundesbank might react to high wage settlements has been pointed to as a moderating influence on earlier wage bargaining in Germany, which is usually considered to have an intermediate degree of coordination of wage-setting (Hall and Franzese, 1998; Soskice and Iversen, 1998). Cukierman *et al.* (1998) have also found empirical evidence that money supply growth in countries with a high degree of central bank independence, like Germany and Austria, tends systematically to be reduced when nominal wage growth increases.

A similar argument to the one for Germany has been made for Sweden, which in 1992 moved to an inflation target regime. Calmfors (2000) has pointed to how the union confederation for blue-collar workers (LO) has run a large internal campaign among its officials to convince them of the need for wage moderation in order to avoid interest rate reactions from the central bank.

The analysis here emphasizes that the relationship between bargaining structure and macroeconomic performance may depend on the monetary regime. But the monetary regime might also influence the bargaining structure. Our discussion suggests that non-accommodating monetary policy and coordination of wage bargaining could to some extent be substitutes, because a non-accommodating monetary policy strengthens the incentives for wage moderation under intermediate bargaining coordination. But with a more accommodating policy the macroeconomic outcomes will be worse, as the incentives for wage restraint become weaker. This has led Holden (2000) to suggest that there may be a stronger motive for unions (and employers) to coordinate wage bargaining, the more accommodating the monetary regime. This could help explain why accommodating monetary policy and a high degree of coordination of wage bargaining coexisted for a long time in the Nordic countries.

Empirical research

There are only a few empirical studies of the interaction between monetary regime and bargaining structure. Soskice and Iversen (2000) observed that unemployment was lower in countries with an intermediate level of coordination when central banks had a high degree of independence. This observation survives in the regressions by Iversen (1998*a,b*), who studied the interaction between monetary regime and a centralization measure of coordination, controlling for a number of other factors. He found that a less accommodating monetary policy reduced unemployment substantially with intermediate centralization, whereas it raised it with high centralization.

Cukierman and Lippi (1999) found that higher central bank independence reduced unemployment in intermediate systems, but raised it in decentralized ones. The conclusion of Hall and Franzese (1998), who used a coordination measure, was that higher central bank independence led to higher unemployment at low levels of coordination, but that this effect became smaller at higher levels of coordination (and was possibly reversed at very high levels).[8]

---

[8] This literature also makes inferences on the relationship between the extent of bargaining coordination and unemployment, but here the results are very diverse. For example, Cukierman and Lippi found a hump-shaped relationship at low levels of central bank independence and a monotonic one at high levels of independence, whereas Iversen found a U-shaped relationship at high levels of independence and a monotonic one at low levels of independence.

The empirical results are obviously not very robust. This is not surprising in view of the limited number of observations of different combinations of bargaining structure and central bank independence. The most that can be said probably is that there is *some* support for the hypothesis that a non-accommodating monetary regime has worked well under intermediate coordination of bargaining, that is under the conditions that have prevailed in most Western European countries. This conclusion does not seem to depend on how coordination is measured. We shall return to these arguments in our discussion in Section 5.4 of how the EMU might affect wage-setting.

5.3. BARGAINING STRUCTURE AND MACROECONOMIC SHOCKS

Bargaining structure may also interact with macroeconomic shocks. This section considers such interaction with both macroeconomic shocks in general and nominal demand shocks in particular.

5.3.1. *Macroeconomic shocks in general*

The implicit assumption in most of the literature on bargaining structure, wage-setting and unemployment is that there are stable relationships between, on the one hand, labour market institutions and, on the other hand, real wage levels and (equilibrium) unemployment, at least during the time period studied. In general, institutional variables do a good job of explaining cross-country variation in unemployment in the 1980s and 1990s and to some extent also variation over time during these periods. But it is equally clear that institutional variables cannot explain the evolution of unemployment in Western Europe over a longer time period: most of the labour market institutions that have been held responsible for recently high unemployment already existed in the 1960s, when unemployment was generally low.

These observations make it natural to study the interaction between macroeconomic shocks and labour market institutions such as bargaining structure. The hypothesis is then that labour market institutions have affected macroeconomic performance mainly because of their influence on the response to the macroeconomic shocks that have occurred: the productivity slowdown and the oil price increases in the 1970s, and disinflation and high real interest rates in the 1980s and early 1990s. Bargaining structure is important in this context because it may influence the flexibility of both nominal and real wages.

A recent contribution is Blanchard and Wolfers (2000). According to this study, the responses to negative unemployment shocks have been larger in economies with less coordinated wage-setting and higher union density and coverage of collective agreements. One suggested interpretation is that it may be easier to slow down real wage growth in response to, say, a reduction in productivity growth if it can be done in a coordinated way across unions. The preferences of outsiders in the labour market may also be taken into account to a larger extent under coordinated than under uncoordinated bargaining.

As in the earlier studies we have surveyed, differences in the extent of bargaining coordination account for large unemployment differences in the Blanchard–Wolfers study: comparing the post-1995 period with the 1960–4 period, the estimated increase in unemployment in their baseline regression is 8.9 percentage points smaller with high coordination than with low coordination (and 4.4 percentage points smaller with intermediate coordination). These differences are again much larger than the differences stemming from different degrees of unionization (see Section 5.1.4).[9] Similar results to those of Blanchard and Wolfers were obtained by Phelps (1994) and Nicoletti *et al.* (2001). All three studies used coordination measures (see Section 5.1.4).

The evidence thus seems to suggest that a higher degree of coordination leads to smaller unemployment responses in the case of adverse shocks. However, it is also the case that these results have not been subjected to much testing of how robust they are to different measures of the degree of coordination.

5.3.2. *Bargaining structure and nominal wage flexibility*

The extent of nominal wage flexibility is an important determinant of how the economy responds to nominal demand shocks.[10] This section discusses how the degree of bargaining coordination is likely to affect nominal wage flexibility. Three aspects are considered: (1) the length of wage contracts; (2) coordination failures; and (3) social norms.

The length of wage contracts

Long-term wage contracts are one reason for nominal wage rigidity. Theories of contract length emphasize the costs of wage negotiations: bargaining consumes scarce time of both firm managers and union officials, it may upset labour–management relations, and there is the ultimate risk of a costly labour market conflict. The optimal choice of contract length involves a trade-off between these costs and the costs in terms of additional variations in output, employment, and profits that arise when wages cannot be adjusted to unanticipated events during the contract period (Ball, 1987; Ball *et al.*, 1988; Calmfors and Johansson, 2000).

In systems with decentralized and unsynchronized wage setting, contract length may be chosen in a socially inefficient way (Ball, 1987). Most notably, there exists an *aggregate-demand externality*: wage-setters in an individual bargaining area do not take into account that a long-term wage contract on

---

[9] The quoted effects have been calculated from eqn (1) in table 1 in Blanchand and Wolfers (2000). At 75% and 45% union densities, unemployment is estimated to have risen by 3.9 and 2.0 percentage points more, respectively, than at a density of 15%.

[10] As is well known, the effects on employment variability of nominal wage rigidity are exacerbated by *real* wage rigidity (see e.g. Romer, 1996), but we neglect this aspect here.

their part will contribute to aggregate demand fluctuations in the economy. The reason is that money wage stickiness in a part of the economy means lower flexibility of the aggregate price level in the case of nominal shocks. If decisions on the length of wage contracts are taken at a centralized level, wage-setters have an incentive to internalize this externality. This effect should work in the direction of shorter wage contracts with centralized decisions on the length of wage contracts.[11]

Another aspect concerns negotiation costs. It is not clear how these are affected by the degree of coordination/centralization. On the one hand, the delegation of bargaining to higher-level organizations in a centralized system could be a way for both unions and employers to economize on resources, by reducing the number of negotiations that need to be undertaken. This was discussed in Chapter 4. A similar argument could apply when bargaining is not delegated, but wage-setters can more or less copy the contracts struck in a key bargain. These mechanisms should tend to make contract periods shorter when bargaining is more coordinated. But on the other hand, coordination in itself involves costs when various unions and employers are to agree on a common stand (Groth and Johansson, 2000). In addition, because of the association of the union and employer sides with different political groupings, labour market conflicts at industry or national level may be seen to involve political costs, which there may be strong incentives to avoid. These forces should work in the opposite direction of longer wage contracts when bargaining is more coordinated/centralized.

Coordination failures

Another explanation of nominal wage rigidity emphasizes the need for coordination if nominal wage growth (or the nominal wage level) is to be cut. A widely quoted argument is due to Keynes (1936). He argued that the concerns of employees over relative wages would make them oppose money wage reductions, unless all wages were cut simultaneously, so as to preserve existing wage differentials. Keynes's conjecture has been questioned for the United States on the ground that employees seem to have 'little systematic knowledge of pay rates at other firms' (Bewley, 1998). In contrast, evidence for Sweden indicates that inter-firm comparisons do play an important role (Agell and Lundborg, 1995, 1999). This may reflect the higher degree of unionization, as a major function of unions is to disseminate information on pay across firms.

One obvious explanation of the difficulty of adjusting money wages in a decentralized bargaining system is that pay deals may be unsynchronized. It is well known that long and overlapping wage contracts may cause severe rigidities. The reason is that the money wages negotiated in new contracts

---

[11] Ball (1987) also points to another externality when the choice of contract length is decentralized. It arises because each wage-setter will then not take into account that an increase in contract length will contribute to lower real wage variability in other bargaining areas, which will tend to increase welfare there.

are then to a large extent tied down by a desire to avoid large deviations from wages in already existing contracts (J.B. Taylor, 1980; Jackman, 1985; Blanchard, 1986).

Coordinated bargaining has the obvious advantage that contract periods can be synchronized. This is, of course, the outcome when different firms or sectors delegate bargaining to peak-level organizations. But also when the formal contracts are concluded at a lower level, synchronization can be achieved through more informal mechanisms of coordination. Japan is such an example: there, contracts are concluded at the level of the firm, but contract periods are still highly synchronized. Another example is Sweden, where the attempts to coordinate contract periods between sectors were also successful after nationwide bargaining was abandoned in the early 1980s (Calmfors *et al.*, 1997). This synchronization has been achieved mainly by the unions them-selves, but there have also been government pressures in this direction: the contracts for 1991–2 stand out especially in this respect, because a government team of mediators was then appointed with the double task of scaling down wage increases and synchronizing contract periods. In 1997 there was also an agreement on the framework for future bargaining between a number of unions and employers' organizations at mainly the industry level, which is likely to have such a synchronization effect (Elvander, 1999).

One version of the coordination failure argument in decentralized systems has been advanced by Ball and Romer (1991). They stressed how the benefit of changing the wage (and thus the price) in an individual firm depends on whether other firms do the same, because of product demand interrelation-ships. With small demand shocks, adjustment costs may make it unprofitable for each firm to change the wage independently of what happens in other firms. With very large shocks, it will always pay to adjust the wage even if others do not. But for shocks of intermediate size, the individual wage-setter may gain from adjusting the wage only if others do the same. This gives rise to *multiple equilibria*: which one materializes will depend on the expectations of what other wage-setters will do. Coordination of wage bargaining is a way of removing this indeterminacy and ensuring that the economy ends up in a good equilibrium in which wages adjust.

Social norms and downward money wage rigidity

Another line of argument stresses how money wage cuts (and, possibly, also very low rates of money wage growth) may conflict with social norms about fairness. Firms do not want to cut money wages because this would have a negative impact on morale and would reduce productivity (Solow, 1979; Akerlof and Yellen, 1990). One can only speculate about how such social norms are affected by the degree of coordination of wage-setting. To the extent that the norms reflect concerns about relative wages, we are essentially back to the argument in the preceding section. However, if they represent something more intrinsic, we have a much weaker basis for the analysis.

We know from survey studies of the attitudes to wage cuts that these are sometimes accepted at the level of the firm when shocks have been so large that the survival of the firm is at stake (Agell and Lundborg, 1995, 1999; Bewley, 1998). There are a number of examples of such concession bargaining in various countries. In the case of a severe macroeconomic shock, one could, under decentralization, conceive of such concession bargaining in those firms that are hit the hardest, whereas this may be more difficult to achieve in a more centralized setting. There are many examples from countries like Germany and Sweden of how industry unions have tried actively to prevent such local amendments to sectoral collective agreements (Hege, 1999).

One could also argue that decentralized bargaining is more conducive to performance-related pay in the individual firms, and that such schemes could facilitate downward pay adjustments in recessions. But the contribution to macroeconomic stability depends on how these pay schemes are constructed. For example, profit sharing à la Weitzman (1985), where the normal fixed nominal wage is replaced by a combination of a lower fixed base wage and a profit share, is not likely to reduce employment variations in the case of price shocks. Such profit-sharing substitutes the condition that the price × the marginal product = the base wage for the usual profit maximization condition that the price × the marginal product = the normal wage. If the base wage is set lower than the normal wage, profit-sharing then obviously raises employment. But there is no reason to expect variations in the price to produce smaller variations in employment around its (higher) average.[12]

Conclusions on bargaining structure and nominal wage flexibility
There is not much systematic empirical evidence on how nominal wage flexibility is affected by the degree of bargaining coordination. This variable has usually not been included in studies of nominal wage flexibility. Alogoskoufis and Manning (1988), however, found a negative association between the degree of centralization and the responsiveness of wages to prices. In preliminary work, Groth and Johansson (2000) have found a U-shaped relationship between the degree of centralization and contract length. This suggests that both high centralization and decentralization are associated with more nominal rigidity than an intermediate degree of centralization. But according to their study, an increase in the degree of centralization leads to shorter wage contracts in the majority of countries.

As discussed in Chapter 4, social pacts, establishing norms of low nominal wage growth, came about in several of the EU countries that in the 1980s or the 1990s opted for non-accommodating monetary regimes by trying to maintain

---

[12] If the employment variations are to be reduced, the base wage must be set so low that there is normally excess demand for labour, in which case price variations would lead only to variations in the amount of excess demand. This was Weitzman's original idea, but it does not appear a likely outcome in unionized markets.

fixed exchange rates within the ERM and later for membership in the EMU. The Netherlands, Ireland, Finland, Italy, and Portugal (and to some extent Belgium and Spain) are all such examples (Elmeskov *et al.*, 1998; Pochet, 1999*a,b,c*). A probable explanation is that strong incentives for such coordination were created when it became apparent that reductions of the high unemployment necessitated downward real wage adjustments, and that in the prevailing monetary regime these could be accomplished only through money wage restraint. Norway in the early 1990s is another example where reductions of money wage growth were achieved through a centralized social contract (Holden, 1996).

An interesting case is provided by Finland, where the central labour market organizations came very close to an agreement on across-the-board nominal wage cuts in the deep recession of 1991 (Calmfors *et al.*, 1997). The agreement was an attempt to adjust to rapidly increasing unemployment—it rose from 3.5% in 1990 to 18.4% in 1993—in a situation in which the central bank tried to avoid a currency depreciation. However, the wage cuts were never implemented, because speculation against the Finnish markka triggered a depreciation when one of the major trade unions began to voice concerns over the agreement. One way of reading this experience is that a coordinated wage-setting system might indeed be capable of delivering nominal wage reductions in a non-accommodating monetary regime that is credible enough (which the Finnish regime obviously was not at the time).

To summarize, there are strong *theoretical* reasons for expecting coordinated wage bargaining to make nominal wages more flexible. More coordinated bargaining has also been adopted in recent years by several European countries which have achieved real wage reductions through low money wage increases. But there does not exist direct systematic empirical evidence in favour of a positive relationship between bargaining coordination and nominal wage flexibility, although the findings in Section 5.3.1 that macroeconomic shocks have less pervasive employment effects under coordination might perhaps be seen as indirect evidence.

5.4. BARGAINING STRUCTURE AND THE EMU

The EMU represents a fundamental change in the European macroeconomic environment. An important question is how this will affect union behaviour and wage-setting. As above, we shall distinguish between the effects on equilibrium real wage and unemployment levels on the one hand, and on nominal wage flexibility on the other.

5.4.1. *Real wage restraint and bargaining structure*

The common currency is likely to reinforce the tendencies towards stronger product market integration that are the result of deregulations, the single market, the IT development, etc. (Burda, 1999). As was discussed in Chapter 3, whether or not this will increase competitive pressures is not self-evident. But to the extent that it does, one can think of more product market integration as increasing the elasticity of product demand. Then labour demand also becomes more elastic. This would strengthen the incentive for real wage moderation in general, but, as elaborated in Section 5.1.2, the largest restraining effect on wages should be expected in bargaining systems with an intermediate degree of coordination. Because this type of bargaining is common in Western Europe, there might therefore be a substantial effect on equilibrium unemployment. But one should probably expect this to happen gradually over time.

A factor that may be more important in the short and medium run is the change in the interaction between monetary policy and wage bargaining that the EMU entails. This change will affect the EU countries in different ways depending on their earlier monetary regimes.

In the earlier ERM system, the monetary policy stance was determined by the German Bundesbank. Monetary policy in Germany was pursued with the main aim of achieving price stability in that country. The other ERM countries then had to adjust their monetary policies to maintain a fixed exchange rate against the German mark. This asymmetry may have had important consequences for wage-setting. As we discussed in Section 5.2.2, the threat of monetary policy reactions is likely to have acted as a strong deterrent to wage increases in Germany. This mechanism did not work in the other ERM countries, which had their monetary policies tied down by the fixed exchange rate, so that the central banks could not react to wage increases. However, low German wage increases helped keep down wage increases in the other ERM countries as well, because their producers were competing with German ones. Such considerations may have played a role for unions especially in Austria, Belgium, and the Netherlands, where wage comparisons with Germany have been important (Hochreiter and Winckler, 1995; Visser, 1998*b,c*; Pochet, 1999*a,b*).[13]

With monetary policy now being determined by the European Central Bank (ECB), the relationship between monetary policy and wage-setting has changed character (Hall and Franzese, 1998; Soskice and Iversen, 1998). For Germany, EMU membership can be regarded as an effective decentralization of wage-setting in the sense that wage bargainers become too small relative to the central bank responsible for monetary policy to make strategic considerations. German trade unions need no longer fear that large wage increases will trigger a monetary policy response that adds to unemployment. The common monetary policy thus means a lower perceived elasticity of labour demand with respect to wages, which should work in the direction of higher wages and lower employment in Germany. This effect will be absent in the other European

[13] In the case of Belgium, the Competitive Acts of 1989 and 1996 even stipulated formally that wage bargaining must be based on the judgements of the Central Economic Council (an advisory body) of the development of wage competitiveness relative to the major trading partners (Germany, France, and the Netherlands, according to the 1996 Act).

countries that were members of the ERM system, as monetary policy there could not earlier play the role it did in Germany. These countries will, however, be affected to the extent that higher wages in Germany mean less competitive pressures to hold back their own wages.

A similar argument to the one for Germany may apply to Sweden, where the bargaining structure in recent years has moved closer to the German model with an emphasis on the industry level. After a number of devaluations in 1976–92, the Swedish central bank has successfully established a credible inflation target regime. This has from 1999 been underpinned by an increase in the degree of independence of the central bank. Swedish membership in the EMU could therefore eliminate the threat of interest rate reactions to wage increases that Swedish unions seem to perceive today (Calmfors, 2000). This reasoning builds on the assumption that the inflation target regime is indeed credible. If the alternative to EMU membership is a monetary policy where the central bank is expected ultimately to react to inflationary wage increases by an accommodating policy, the argument is reversed. EMU membership then creates stronger incentives for wage discipline. Such an argument might perhaps fit the Italian picture, but it has also been put forward for Finland, which has a long history of devaluations in the postwar period.

To the extent that the EMU means less wage restraint and higher unemployment, because monetary policy becomes a less effective deterrent to wage increases, the functioning of bargaining systems with an intermediate degree of coordination will deteriorate. This factor might very well dominate in the medium term. So in this time perspective alternative bargaining arrangements could become more attractive. This could work in the direction of either more decentralization or more coordination. The recent moves in the direction of greater coordination in Germany (Bündnis für Arbeit) might be interpreted in this vein as an attempt to substitute a more cooperative wage-setting system for the earlier policy game between the Bundesbank and the unions.

5.4.2. *Nominal wage flexibility in the EMU*

Another issue is how the EMU will affect nominal wage flexibility under current bargaining institutions. Here there are differing perspectives. One common view is that the common currency increases the demand for nominal wage flexibility, because there is a need for alternative adjustment mechanisms when there is no longer a domestic monetary policy. The argument rests either on the risk of asymmetric shocks (see e.g. Calmfors *et al.*, 1997; Obstfeld, 1998) or on the risk that a common monetary policy could affect the various economies differently (Dornbusch *et al.*, 1998). An alternative view is that exchange rate variations arising from monetary or financial disturbances are the most important source of macroeconomic instability (Canzoneri *et al.*, 1996; Vinals and Jimeno, 1998; Buiter, 2000). With this view, a common currency would tend to reduce the need for nominal wage flexibility.

A third possibility is that an own monetary policy works mainly as an insurance against very large shocks that occur only infrequently (Calmfors *et al.*, 1997; Mélitz, 1997). Even if exchange rate flexibility does not contribute to macroeconomic stability in normal times, it may do so at specific occasions when it really matters. Examples are German unification and the deep recessions in Finland, Sweden, and the UK in the early 1990s, when large stabilizing exchange rate changes did occur.

It is thus not self-evident whether the EMU will lead to larger macroeconomic variability. But we shall ask the conditional question: *if* this were to happen, will nominal wages become more flexible? As discussed in Section 5.3.2, one can look at the issue from two perspectives: contract length and social norms. If long contract periods are the main reason for nominal wage stickiness, one could, on the one hand, argue that an increase in macroeconomic variability in the EMU would work in the direction of shorter contract periods. But on the other hand, lower inflation than earlier would work in the opposite direction (Calmfors, 1998).

If one regards social norms against wage cuts as the main obstacle to nominal wage flexibility, then the relevant question is how these norms are likely to change with EMU membership. An interesting perspective on this is given by two recent studies by Agell and Lundborg (1995, 1999). The two studies asked Swedish personnel managers similar questions in 1991 and 1998 about their judgements concerning the acceptability of wage cuts. Although Sweden between these years moved from stable low unemployment to high unemployment and from high inflation to a credible low-inflation regime, there was no change in attitudes between the two studies. This suggests that even very large macroeconomic regime shifts may be insufficient to change the attitudes to wage cuts in unionized labour markets.

Our conclusion is that the EMU in itself is not very likely to lead to more nominal wage flexibility *under present bargaining conditions*, even if this were to be required. But a crucial issue is to what extent a perceived need for more nominal wage flexibility could lead to changes in the bargaining structure. This is discussed in Chapter 6.

5.5. CONCLUSIONS

This chapter has surveyed theoretical and empirical research on the relationship between bargaining structure and macroeconomic performance. The discussion has been used as a basis for considering the effects of the EMU on collective bargaining.

An important caveat is that the stability of bargaining institutions over time provides a serious limitation to empirical research. We do not have the variability in the data that we normally require in order to make statistical inferences. A consequence is that empirical results become very sensitive to how the degree of bargaining coordination is measured. However, if we take results at face value, they can be summarized as follows.

1. There is ample empirical support for the theoretical proposition that highly coordinated wage bargaining promotes real wage moderation and low unemployment. This holds both when the degree of bargaining coordination is assumed to have a direct effect and when it is assumed to interact with tax pressures and macroeconomic shocks.

2. It is less clear how an intermediate degree of bargaining coordination (industry bargaining) and decentralized bargaining at the firm level perform relative to each other. Here, the theoretical conclusions are ambiguous. There is about as much empirical support for the hypothesis that decentralized bargaining performs better than an intermediate degree of bargaining coordination as there is for the reverse hypothesis.

3. There is a theoretical case for why a non-accommodating monetary policy regime should promote wage restraint, and thus employment, in bargaining systems with an intermediate degree of coordination. There is *some* empirical support for this hypothesis.

4. There is a lack of direct empirical evidence on how nominal wage flexibility is affected by the degree of bargaining coordination. But theoretical considerations suggest strongly that nominal wages should be more flexible with a high degree of coordination. The finding that macroeconomic shocks tend to have less adverse employment shocks under coordinated bargaining can perhaps be interpreted as indirect support for this hypothesis.

5. If increasing product market integration in Europe leads to more competitive pressures (which may require a successful European industrial and competition policy), then a consequence is likely to be more wage restraint, especially in countries with industry bargaining. But in the short and medium run, the change in the game between unions and central banks, which is implied by the EMU, may dominate. In the earlier ERM system, wage settlements in Germany—and thus in the whole euro area—may have been held back because unions feared the monetary policy responses of the Bundesbank. This restraining force does not exist in the EMU, where each union will be too small relative to the ECB to make strategic considerations.

The empirical studies suggest that, everything else equal, unemployment may be substantially lower under high bargaining coordination than under low (even if low coordination may possibly lead to lower unemployment than intermediate coordination). This effect appears to be stronger than the unemployment-reducing effect of lower union density and coverage. If this is correct, then there is a risk that the combined effect on employment of a long-run trend towards both lower bargaining coordination and deunionization could be negative in countries such as Austria, Belgium, Denmark, Finland, Ireland, the Netherlands, Norway, and Sweden, which have traditionally had high coordination. To avoid such a development, accompanying policy changes may be required. The chances that a combination of lower unionization and decentralization will improve employment performance are greater in economies that are today characterized by an intermediate degree of bargaining coordination. The most favourable scenario from an employment point of view, however, might be one that combines high coordination with lower unionization, although it might not represent a feasible scenario in the long run. These alternative possibilities are discussed in Chapter 6.

6

The Future Prospects for Trade Unions in Europe

In the preceding chapters we have discussed a number of aspects of union presence. Chapter 2 analysed the determinants of union membership and charted the recent decline that has occurred in most West European countries. Chapter 3 discussed how the ability of unions to raise wages depends on the existence of product market rents as well as on the bargaining power of unions. The focus was on the impact of increased international, i.e. European product market, integration. Chapter 4 tried to give a comprehensive picture of what unions do—in addition to bargaining with employers about the division of the joint surplus—and looked more closely at other crucial aspects of union influence than membership: the structure of bargaining, the coverage of collective agreements, and union presence in works councils. Finally, Chapter 5 analysed the macroeconomic outcomes of different bargaining structures in terms of both average unemployment over the business cycle and cyclical employment variability.

This chapter takes the earlier chapters as an input and asks, what is likely to happen to union power and presence in the future? We discuss three major issues: (1) future membership trends; (2) the future development of bargaining structures; and (3) possible future union strategies.

6.1. PROSPECTS FOR UNION MEMBERSHIP

It is probable that union density will continue to fall. According to our econometric models of union density, reported in Chapter 2, increased participation rates are likely to bring into the labour market individuals who are less likely to unionize, mainly because they will find more precarious jobs (in terms of both contract length and stability of the occupation) and jobs in sectors and firms where unions are not established or visible (e.g. commercial and personal services, and small firms). There is little scope for expansion of membership in the traditional core sectors of unionization: manufacturing and the public sector. In fact, as the unionized generation of workers in these sectors retires, union membership tends to decline. Typically, losses in the core sectors will most likely fail to be balanced by membership increases in the growing new, mostly tertiary, sectors; here density rates are low in nearly all countries, and employment growth is difficult to translate into union growth.

For these structural reasons, we expect union density to continue to decline. But a fall in unemployment is likely to work in the opposite direction in most European countries, as we showed in Chapter 2. (The exception is the countries where unions administer the unemployment insurance according to the so-called Ghent system—Denmark, Finland, Sweden, and Belgium—and where union density may be positively linked to unemployment, but these countries represent only a small percentage of the population of Western Europe.) However, we do not believe that a return to lower unemployment in Western Europe will be a strong enough force to reverse the trend towards lower unionization. A main reason is that our econometric analysis in Section 2.8 above indicated that the response to changes in unemployment may be very slow. So, as we argued, it is likely that the rise in unemployment in the 1980s has exerted only part of its adverse effect on unionization. A development where unemployment falls below recent levels, but still stays above the pre-1980 level, might therefore represent only a weak countervailing force.

The possibility of multiple equilibria with respect to union membership, which was discussed in Section 2.3, also makes a return to earlier membership rates less probable. The decision to join a union may depend on social norms that have changed once membership rates have gone down. Past rises in unemployment could therefore have persistent effects.

Another main finding in Chapter 2 is that institutions matter a great deal for the unions' capacity to recruit members, and that these institutions, which by their nature are relatively invariant over time, show a wide variation across countries. We have shown the relevance for union organizing of three major institutional conditions: union access to the workplace, union involvement in the provision and administration of unemployment insurance, and centralization of collective bargaining. Where all three of these institutions are (or were) present (as in Denmark, Finland, and Sweden, and to a large degree in Belgium), unions will have a greater likelihood of fighting off the negative influence on membership growth caused by structural change. On the other hand, centralization alone, or workplace access by itself, may not be enough to prevent union membership decline.

We have not been able to establish the influence of mandatory provisions of minimum wages, maximum working hours, employee benefits (e.g. rights to paid leave and holidays), or information and consultation rights in firms (works councils) on the propensity of workers to join trade unions. Such mandatory provisions, both direct and through extension of collective agreements, as discussed in Chapter 4, vary across countries, as they are based on national labour law. In the 1990s, some minimum rights (e.g. maximum working hours, information and consultation rights in multinational firms, entitlement to parental leave, minimum rights of part-time employees and those on atypical employment contracts) have been established on the basis of EU legislation, creating a new floor of rights in some

EU member states without prior legislation in these areas (e.g. the UK and Portugal).

It is conceivable that some of the EU Directives may undercut unions' attempts to expand into areas with non-standard work arrangements, since the directives provide protection that unions might otherwise have supplied. Mandatory provisions and institutions like works councils may also compete with the unions for members in standard employment, in the sense that they take away the need to seek insurance of working conditions through membership. Competition between unions and works councils may increase under conditions of decentralized and transnational bargaining within large firms (see below). On the other hand, the European Directive on works councils may strengthen union membership at the local level. Mandatory statutes, applying on a European scale, may also help trade unions to the extent that they attenuate the competition from the non-union sector.

We recall from Chapter 4 that unionization rates among works council members, elected by the entire workforce, including those that are not union members, are usually between 65% and 100%, even in firms where union density rates among the electing workers are no higher than 20%–40% (Rogers and Streeck, 1995; Klandermans and Visser, 1995). Especially in countries with low unionization rates (e.g. France, the Netherlands, and Spain), works council elections give unions a presence and legitimacy that they otherwise would not have. Mandatory works councils, representing the entire workforce with a brief to monitor and implement collective agreements to all workers, may be thought of as an 'extension mechanism' for these agreements. A mandatory statute establishing information and consultation rights does away with the need for trade unions to fight for recognition and membership on a firm-by-firm basis (as is the case in the USA and under new UK legislation), and gives the unions some influence even in firms where membership is low.

Unions across different EU countries might react to declining membership in a variety of ways, in order to fight current trends. They may be able to attract non-standard workers with innovative new organizing strategies. In addition, collection of dues and organization may be easier with the new information and communication technologies. Moreover, on an individual basis unions will have different growth trajectories, and unions organizing in expanding sectors may still grow in absolute size if they can muster the methods and resources that are needed. We will discuss these issues—possible future union strategies or 'what can unions do to survive?'—in the final Section 6.3.

However, as we have emphasized throughout this report, union membership is just one facet of union influence. And while we believe that, on the basis of current trends, union membership in Western Europe will continue to decline, the prospects for overall union influence are considerably less clear. For this reason, we now sketch out a number of possible scenarios for the future of collective bargaining in Western Europe.

6.2. FOUR SCENARIOS FOR COLLECTIVE BARGAINING IN THE FUTURE

Although union membership in most European countries has declined, there is no clearly identifiable concomitant trend in the 1990s in the other important indicators of union influence—coverage, coordination, and centralization—as we have discussed in Chapter 4. While in many countries we have seen a tendency towards more decentralization of the level at which formal bargaining takes place, at the same time we have also observed more 'informal coordination' in connection with social pacts. It is too early as yet to be able to observe the full impact on the level of collective bargaining of the Europeanization of monetary policy and product market integration. However, in this section we provide our views about various likely scenarios for the next decade or so. We also give at the end an opinion—based on our judgements as to relative probabilities—about which scenario is most likely to occur.

We distinguish four different possibilities for the future evolution of collective bargaining in Europe. These are: (1) a continued trend towards more decentralization of bargaining to firm and local levels; (2) a development where tensions in the monetary union promote national coordination attempts very much along the lines of the social pacts of recent years in some countries; (3) a movement towards high-level transnational coordination of bargaining; and (4) a development where decentralization to the firm level is combined with transnational cooperation within large transnational firms—a kind of transnational coordination from below.

6.2.1. *Decentralization of collective bargaining*

In Chapter 4 we documented a trend towards more decentralization of actual bargaining to firm and local levels. Our first scenario encompasses a continuation of that trend in the countries where it has already started, as well as a shift in this direction in the few countries where it has not yet occurred. A possible development is that such decentralization becomes the dominant pattern across the countries of Western Europe. One can point to a number of factors motivating this.

The main driving force behind further decentralization is likely to be, as in past years, pressure from the employers. It is obvious that bargaining at the local level can confer a number of advantages to firms. One important factor is the reorganization of modern working life: standardized tasks and hierarchical 'Tayloristic' organizations seem increasingly to be replaced by more flexible tasks ('multi-tasking') and flatter hierarchies, allowing greater decentralization of decision-making within firms. It has been claimed that this development increases the efficiency cost of centralized wage bargaining, which usually entails pay according to very standardized principles as well as pay compression. The argument is that the ongoing changes of the character of work requires an increased use of wage-setting at the local level as an incentive device with pay differentiation as a likely consequence (Lindbeck and Snower, forthcoming). Incentive schemes that are based on individual output, or on the output of workplace-based teams, are best designed at the local level where knowledge of local production conditions is greatest. Systems that make employee pay contingent on company performance are also easier to implement at the local level than at higher bargaining levels, because such schemes can then be coordinated with basic pay schedules. In general, decentralized bargaining makes it possible for individual firms to find the pay levels, pay systems, working-time arrangements, training schemes, and other productivity-enhancing measures that are most suited to the specific conditions they meet. This is likely to be more important the more heterogeneous firms become (Ramaswamy and Rowthorn, 1993).

The preference of employers for decentralized bargaining may also have to do with the devolution of 'operational and financial responsibility' to 'quasi-autonomous business units' within large corporations. This is made easier the more cost components—including wage rates—are under the direct control of management (Marginson and Sisson, 1998).

Traditionally, a benefit of sectoral (and national) wage agreements for employers has been that they have provided a level playing field by preventing undercutting, owing to lower wages, by domestic competitors. Increased international competition makes this aspect less relevant. Instead, it becomes more important for internationally competing firms to have the flexibility to react unilaterally to wage competition from foreign firms (Marginson and Sisson, 1998; Crouch, 2000*b*).

Another advantage of decentralized bargaining for employers relates to its potential to limit union power to the workplace. A smaller role for sectoral unions and national union confederations in wage bargaining is likely to reduce their political weight as well. Indeed, the new UK recognition machinery is a manifestation of the political desire not only to impart worker democracy and give unions a role and accountability, but also to limit their overall power.[1] In Sweden, the motivation for the decision of employers to abandon national bargaining in the early 1980s was mainly a desire to reduce the political clout of the trade union movement, which lobbied very succesfully for a number of new labour market regulations in the 1970s (Elvander, 1988).

It is more difficult to forecast how an increasing importance of small and medium-sized firms—not least in the service sector—will affect the extent of centralization. On the one hand, it is usually large corporations that have broken out of sectoral wage agreements (see Visser, 1992; Crouch, 2000*b*, and the discussion in Chapter 4). This may be related to the fact that large firms are

---

[1] The new UK recognition machinery, introduced by the Labour Party in its 1999 Employment Relations Bill and loosely based on US representation elections, may lead to even greater decentralization of bargaining in that country.

more exposed to international competition than small firms, as we argued above. Another explanation is that large firms can more easily bear some of the fixed costs associated with wage bargaining, whereas it may be more efficient for smaller firms to 'buy' these services from employers' associations. On the other hand, the coordination costs may become very high in sectors where small firms are very differentiated; this may prevent new firms from entering employers' associations.

Just as the wage level is the outcome of bargaining, the level at which bargaining occurs could be seen as the outcome of a bargaining process, too, where employers and employees have different interests. The choice of bargaining level will then reflect the relative bargaining strength of employers and labour. A trend towards decentralization could then be viewed as a shift in bargaining power away from unions and towards firms, who try to pick the bargaining level that affords them the most 'surplus' net of labour costs. However, where such changes in the locus of collective bargaining are the result of negotiations between higher-level unions and employers' organizations at the industry or national levels, these organizations may retain some bargaining prerogatives. This is, for instance, the case in the central and industry agreements that introduced further decentralization in Denmark (1987–91), the Netherlands (1993), and Italy (1993, 1998). These are typical cases of 'centralized', 'organized', or 'controlled' decentralization (Due *et al.*, 1994; Traxler, 1996; Visser, 1998*b,c*). As we have seen in Chapter 4, single-level bargaining is quite rare in Europe. (Britain is now the most prominent example.) It is easy to conceive of areas where efficiency considerations speak in favour of retaining industry agreements even when wage bargaining is shifted to the level of the firm. One such area is training: here it may be important to take decisions at the industry level in order to avoid under-provision of training, which could occur when decisions are taken at the company level because of the incentive to engage in 'cherry picking' from competitors (see e.g. Booth *et al.*, 1999).

One possible reason for increasing the relative bargaining strength of employers is increasing capital mobility, which has rendered the threat of moving production abroad more credible. Another possible reason why unions may have to give in to employer demands for more decentralized wage bargaining is that falling union density weakens the power of unions. The wide divergence between union density and coverage found in some countries—what was termed 'excess coverage' in Chapter 4—means that union presence and coverage must be maintained by *erga omnes* institutions. Continuing falls in membership will mean that these are being run by fewer and fewer individuals, threatening the credibility and democratic legitimacy of unions in these countries, and weakening their bargaining position. As a consequence, firms might face less opposition in shifting to their own preferred bargaining structure.

In addition, if the trend towards lower rates of unionization is accompanied by a trend towards less coverage of union contracts, this will reduce the benefits of coordination to unions as well. As discussed in Chapter 5, the gains from bargaining coordination between unions at sectoral or multi-sectoral levels are larger the more employees are encompassed (Holden and Raaum, 1991); so lower union coverage means that there will be smaller benefits of coordination against which coordination costs can be offset.

If decentralization occurs as a response to pressure from employers, it might seem natural to conclude that it is bad only for employees. But this conclusion is not self-evident. Decentralized bargaining will facilitate adaptability to local labour demand and supply conditions, which is a benefit for everyone. Sometimes the goals of employers may coincide with bargaining arrangements and sharing rules that also work in favour of labour, for example where union involvement actually leads to an increase in the available surplus, a possibility raised in Chapter 4. For example, it is easier for management to empower workers to make decisions when bargaining is local, as suggested above. And there is a well established trend in both the UK and the USA towards a form of 'shared capitalism', whereby both workers and management share financial risk as well as rewards and decision-making authority (Freeman, 2000). Local bargaining and individual choice in collective agreements, as in some *à la carte* agreements that have been negotiated in the Netherlands, may also give individual workers more choice over their working hours, holidays, and leave arrangements, and may better reflect differences in preferences for leisure or income within a more heterogeneous workforce.

Moreover, from the viewpoint of aggregate wage and employment levels, local bargaining may have a less deleterious effect than intermediate-level bargaining, as we discussed in Chapter 5. Finally, local bargaining might also encourage union executives to make procedures more democratic and responsive to the wishes of the rank-and-file membership—a goal that the democratic countries of Europe must surely applaud. Such a development might also help restore disaffected members to trade unions.

6.2.2. *National coordination through social pacts*

As we have discussed, coordination through social pacts and consensual norms has been an important feature of wage bargaining in several EU countries in the runup to the EMU. This has occurred despite falls in unionization and despite a tendency to conclude formal wage contracts at more decentralized levels. According to our second scenario, this pattern would continue in the coming years. This scenario would be very much linked to monetary unification. There may be a perceived need to make up for the loss of domestic monetary policy autonomy and find a substitute for domestic currency depreciation in the EMU by making nominal wages more flexible (Calmfors *et al.*, 1997). As discussed in Sections 5.3 and 5.4, bargaining coordination may be seen as an appropriate means of achieving this. With the forces working in the direction of actual bargaining taking place at decentralized levels, which we described in Scenario 1, such coordination is not likely to take the form of formal contracts concluded at centralized levels. Instead, the looser form of coordination in recent social pacts, setting guidelines and working via moral suasion, is the most probable outcome in such a scenario. Judging from the European experiences of recent years, this type of coordination is likely to focus mainly on the achievement of macroeconomic objectives. Unlike earlier formal centralization, the social pacts of recent years have not included attempts at compressing the wage structure (OECD, 1997*a*; Wallerstein, 1999; Crouch, 2000*a*). We expect such redistributive motives to be largely absent also from future coordination attempts of this type, as they would seem to require a much stronger bargaining authority of peak-level organizations than is implied by voluntary cooperation in social pacts.

The incentives to enter into such social pacts will differ between actors. Governments should be the actors most interested in finding a substitute for lost policy instruments. Employers may be less interested, as they are likely to see decentralization/low coordination as the first-best option for the reasons described in the preceding scenario. But at the same time, they may see the benefits of achieving wage moderation through coordination rather than through a lengthy and uncertain process of labour market reforms involving serious political conflicts. For unions, the exercise of nominal wage restraint means a lot of stress, but in a situation where they are losing ground they may have an incentive to demonstrate their ability as a social actor by being a partner to social pacts (Crouch, 2000*a*).

The strength of the incentives for bargaining coordination and social pacts will depend on actual macroeconomic developments. If cyclical developments turn out to diverge strongly among the euro countries, and if—as we expect—fiscal policy proves to be an insufficient stabilization policy tool in this situation, then it is likely that wage restraint through coordinated action may come to be seen as a necessary means of stabilizing a recession-struck economy. However, also in the absence of *actual* macroeconomic imbalances, there will be incentives in this direction. There is a widespread fear that giving up domestic monetary policy as an instrument is potentially dangerous. The mere uncertainty about the macroeconomic consequences of the EMU—and the risk of very large imbalances at specific occasions—may provide a precautionary motive for this type of coordination.[2] It will be much easier to achieve coordinated wage restraint, when it is needed, if there is a degree of coordination also in more normal times. Since such coordination efforts have already been undertaken in several countries in recent years, it may therefore be perceived as natural—and efficient—to continue these as a stand-by measure for the future. Other countries may want to enter into similar procedures. The agreement in Sweden in 1997 of a new framework for

---

[2] See also Visser (1998*c*). The reasoning has some similarities with the precautionary motive for labour market reform advanced by Calmfors (2001).

bargaining within industry with the aim of securing international competitiveness (the Industrial Agreement) could perhaps be interpreted as a
preparation for future EMU membership (Elvander, 1999). So could the
establishment of a government mediation institute in 2000, as it coincides with
a decision in principle of the governing Social Democratic Party that Sweden
should join the EMU.

An interesting example of how a specific type of bargaining coordination can
be used as a 'stand-by facility' is provided by Finland. It was widely conceived
there that EMU membership entails a macroeconomic risk. As a response to
this, so-called *buffer funds* have been set up.[3] The background is a system
where unemployment insurance and pensions are financed to a large extent
by employer contributions that have been negotiated between unions and
employers' organizations. The idea is to raise these negotiated employers'
contributions above the disbursements for unemployment benefits and pensions in business cycle upswings. The additional proceeds are put into buffer
funds which are to be spent in recessions in order to prevent contributions from
then having to be raised. The buffer funds are controlled by the central labour
market organizations.

The Finnish system has been devised to smooth fluctuations in wage costs
over the business cycle. A more ambitious system could instead aim at lowering
wage costs in deep downswings (Calmfors, 1998, 2000). This would amount to
establishing an *ex ante* machinery for cuts in money wage costs without having
to cut money wages. For such a system to work best, it should probably be
reserved for extreme recessions, in which ordinary wage adjustments cannot be
expected to be large enough: if the system is used regularly in the case of normal
business cycle fluctuations, there is the risk that it has little effect because the
incentives for normal variations in money wage growth are reduced.

Another incentive for national bargaining coordination is that the common
monetary policy in the EMU may not work as an effective deterrent to excessive
wage increases, as we discussed in Section 5.4.1. Trade unions in individual
EMU countries will not restrain wages because of any fear that wage increases
on their part will trigger interest rate reactions by the ECB: they will all be
too small to affect the behaviour of the common monetary policy. For this
reason, there may be an incentive for national coordination in one form or
another as an alternative way of promoting wage restraint, as has been argued
by Holden (2000).

Finally, it has been argued that more international integration will increase
the exposure to shocks and therefore lead to a higher demand for 'social
insurance' in general (Rodrik, 1998; Agell, 1999). As discussed in Chapter 4, a
reduction of wage dispersion associated with centralized and/or coordinated
bargaining could be seen as one such form of insurance. It has also been noted

---

[3] The system is described in Boldt (1998), Holm *et al.* (1999), and Pochet (1999*b*).

that a higher degree of openness of the economy has in the past been correlated with more bargaining coordination (Cameron, 1978; Agell, 1999).

In the scenario we have sketched, there will be large built-in tensions. On the one hand, unions may see coordination through social pacts as a way of obtaining legitimacy in a situation where their influence is threatened by membership losses. On the other hand, to the extent that there is continued decentralization of actual bargaining levels, coordination costs will increase. And with a continued trend towards lower unionization unions may not have enough legitimacy to fight off employers' attempts at achieving more decentralization, and the legitimacy of moderating agreements struck by unions among members may be weakened. In addition, to the extent that the coverage of union contracts also starts to fall, it will become more difficult to maintain a high degree of coordination, as coordination will produce less favourable results the fewer employees are included (Holden and Raaum, 1991).

Another long-term threat to national coordination is likely to be provided by the internationalization of product and labour markets, which tends to liberate companies from their historical national roots. As a consequence, national governments will have less leverage to cajole companies into accepting a joint policy. Increasingly, national frames of reference—as in a national wage policy that is developed for the sake of the national interest or social solidarity—may lose their economic, political, and moral relevance for the strongest players in the economy, that is, firms that are already strongly internationalized. This puts greater strains on the central organizations of employers and unions when they try to define national guidelines for policy.

Moreover, to the extent that a common currency makes cross-national differences in wages and labour costs more transparent, there may emerge new comparability ('equal pay for equal work') pressures on union leaders, which will complicate their task of legitimizing wage policies inspired by notions of national interest and social solidarity. The greatest pressure will probably be felt among workers in similar occupations and firms in neighbouring countries (with the lowest barriers of language and the smallest travel distances). Will union leaders be willing and able to prevent their members, especially those employed in multinational companies, from insisting on equal pay—in the much more comparable common currency—with workers in high-wage and high-productivity economies? In a longer-term perspective, this may also make national coordination of wage bargaining much more difficult.

Our discussion suggests that bargaining coordination through social pacts and consensual norms may work only up to a point. Such coordination may represent an unstable equilibrium, which may easily break down once the levels of unionization and coverage of collective agreements fall below a critical level. Another way of phrasing the conclusion is that wage moderation through coordination may increasingly come to require government interventions. These could range from threats if employers and unions cannot agree to more traditional incomes policy attempts to regulate wage increases at the level of the firm, of the type employed in Belgium during the 1990s (Pochet, 1999*b*). But also, such interventions are likely to be incompatible with decentralization and deunionization in the long run. They are moreover likely to be ineffective, as they tend to impose relative wage rigidities in parts of the economy at the same time as they cannot be enforced in other parts.

6.2.3. *Bargaining coordination at the European level*

Our analysis leads naturally to a discussion of the possibilities of increasing the coordination of wage bargaining at the European level. This represents our third scenario. One can point to a number of factors that could influence such a development.

A first factor is product market integration. As was emphasized in Chapter 3, product market integration may have complex effects. There may be forces working in the direction of both more and less competition. To the extent that more competition between firms in different EU countries is promoted, the incentives for unions to cooperate transnationally are strengthened. Such transnational coordination will serve to increase the possibilities of unions to capture existing rents, as it will reduce the risk that wage increases will lead to large losses of market shares and thus of jobs. This would be the same driving force that has led to industry-level bargaining within nations (see Chapter 3). The argument seems to play a role especially among German trade unions (Bispinck and Schulten, 1998). There appears to be a worry that national attempts to achieve wage competitiveness will lead to a reduction in labour's share of national income. Some small steps in the direction of developing a European strategy for wage bargaining (a joint code of conduct) have also been taken within the European Metalworkers' Federation (Hege, 1999). Moreover, since 1999 officials from the metalworkers' unions from North Rhineland Westphalia, Belgium, Luxembourg, and the Netherlands have participated in each other's bargaining rounds on a regional level. A development in this direction could lead to higher real wages than would otherwise occur and could be detrimental to employment for the reasons discussed in Section 5.2.

Another factor working in the direction of more European bargaining coordination is related to the EU as an actor. EU decision-making provides a general incentive for both national union confederations and employers' associations in different member states to coordinate their views on various policy issues so as to enable them to exercise maximum influence. This could over time make also coordination of wage bargaining more natural, as the costs of such coordination are reduced if procedures for forming common views already exist in other fields. The Maastricht and Amsterdam Treaties have squarely placed Europe's social partners—unions and employers—on the list of EU institutions (Falkner, 1998). With the Social Protocol and the agreement on social policy of the Maastricht Treaty (1993), the EU member states established a new institutional framework for consultation and coordination, with two important features (Keller and Sorries, 1999). First, employers and labour—the 'social partners'—were given the right not only to be consulted, but also to negotiate and sign framework agreements at the European level which can become binding under EU law (by the Commission adopting a Directive embodying the agreement). Second, the EU's remit was extended to include matters such as working conditions, and qualified voting was introduced in certain areas (such as health and safety, information, and consultation of workers) instead of unanimity. The Social Protocol later became, with little change, the Social Section of the Amsterdam Treaty (1997), which now included the UK following that country's decision to end its 'opt-out' policy.

One could argue that the 'social partnership' at the European level has served to restore some of the legitimacy to unions that they may have been losing nationally. There are obvious driving forces. European politicians want to enhance the legitimacy of the EU project and EU institutions. One way of achieving this is to engage broad organizations such as trade unions in consultations and decisions at the European level. And it is in the self-interest of unions to respond to this to enhance their own legitimacy. So EU institutions and trade unions at the European level can offer each other legitimacy by cooperating (Crouch, 2000a).

A third factor that might encourage unions to coordinate collective bargaining across national borders is the Europeanization of monetary policy. Chapter 5 stressed how the earlier policy game between the Bundesbank and unions in Germany is likely to have contributed to wage restraint in the whole ERM area, and described how this restraining force may disappear in the EMU. Put differently, the *de facto* decentralization of wage bargaining relative to monetary policy means that central bank reactions to wage settlements will no longer be internalized. This may provide an incentive for unions to try to re-establish the earlier game at the European level by coordinating their wage settlements. Such a development might be stimulated by the so-called Macroeconomic Dialogue within the framework of the Employment Pact, which was established by the EU in 1999. The dialogue provides an arena where European-level union and employer representatives will regularly meet with the ECB (and the Commission and EU ministers of finance) to discuss macroeconomic issues. Transnational bargaining coordination would make unions a more 'equal' partner to the ECB in this context.

There are thus factors working in favour of greater coordination among unions at the European level. But we still find it unlikely that there will be a far-reaching development in this direction within the foreseeable future. Below, we shall discuss in more detail the prospects for (1) a central unified system of industrial relations at the EU level; (2) coordination with respect to specific issues that are subject to decision-making at the EU level; (3) transnational coordination at the industry level; and (4) more informal coordination via pattern bargaining.

Prospects for a central unified system of industrial relations
Looking first at the possibility of a central unified system of industrial relations within the EU, with a pan-European union organization responsible for actual bargaining over wages and other substantive conditions of work, or for coordinating bargaining in different countries, we find this highly improbable. The existing union and employers' confederations at the European level do not today have the bargaining authority for such a system to work. The employers' side, which in most countries has been working in favour of a decentralization of bargaining, is strongly opposed to any development in this direction. It is clear that the coordination costs would be huge. Moreover, these costs are likely to increase in the medium term as membership of the European Union is expanded to include more countries, which will increase the diversity of membership. A further obstacle is that trade unions play a significant role in many European countries in managing heterogeneous national social insurance systems (see Part II of this volume).

Prospects for coordination with respect to specific labour market issues that are subject to decision-making at the EU level
It is more probable that there could be coordination when it comes to specific labour market issues. The European Commission has tried to obtain the cooperation of the social partners and supranational institutions to widen the applicability of the legal provisions of first the Social Protocol of the Maastricht Treaty and then the Social Section of the Amsterdam Treaty. Three framework agreements have also been signed between the social partners at the European level (ETUC—the European Trade Union Confederation, UNICE—the private-sector employers' confederation, and CEEP—the peak public enterprise employers' confederation): on parental leave (1995), part-time employment contracts (1997), and fixed-term employment contracts (1999). These agreements have established certain minimum provisions (Marginson and Sisson, 1998; CEC, 2000).

Even if employers would in principle be opposed to such agreements at the European level, they may in practice have strong incentives to enter into them. To the extent that specific labour market issues are put on the agenda by the European Commission or the Council of Ministers, the alternative to agreements between the social partners may be legislated regulations that are more rigid. So employers may be dragged into this form of European-wide bargaining on specific issues as a 'lesser evil' than the alternative. Although this is far from coordination of pay at the European level, it may still have important implications for wage costs.

Prospects for transnational coordination at the industry level
Another possibility is transnational coordination only across industry unions in sectors that are exposed to strong intra-EU competition, such as the metal industry. The prospects for this may be greater than for more large-scale

coordination, but the obstacles will be very large here, too. First, there is the opposition from employers, and in some sectors, such as the metal industry, there does not exist any European confederation of employers. Second, bargaining institutions in various countries have developed over very long time periods and in diverse ways, and are characterized by a large amount of inertia. Third, the costs of transnational coordination will be very substantial at the industry level, too. Union–employer relations, bargaining arrangements, the norms that guide wage demands and settlements, the structure of unions and employers' organizations, traditions of government involvement, and procedures for dispute settlement differ fundamentally between countries. As pointed out by Pochet (1999c), the main effect of more transnational exchanges between unions is likely to be a growing awareness of how different they are. Fourth, unions have been lagging far behind other areas in the internationalization process. One reason could be that knowledge on industrial relations is very country-specific. Insufficient knowledge of foreign languages among (especially blue-collar) union representatives is also likely to be an important obstacle for many years to come. Fifth, the gains from transnational coordination at the industry level in the EU will be reduced to the extent that competition comes from outside the EU.

Prospects for more informal coordination via pattern bargaining
A final possibility is transnational coordination through a system of pattern bargaining. This will involve much lower coordination costs than formal cooperation. But there are important obstacles here, too. One obstacle is the need to agree on a wage leader. A German union—namely IG Metall—is the natural candidate, and it appears to be striving for such a role (Hege, 1999). Such German wage leadership might be natural for unions in Austria, Belgium, and the Netherlands to accept, where comparisons with German wage developments have traditionally played an important role; but unions in France, Spain, and Italy—not to mention the UK—may oppose domination by German unions (Burda, 1999). And German unions themselves may have great difficulty convincing their rank-and-file membership that they should take into account European rather than national conditions when formulating their wage demands. Furthermore, the declining importance of the traditional manufacturing sector with its strong unions also makes it much more difficult for a union such as IG Metall to take on the role of wage leader.

Our overall conclusion is that the obstacles for coordination of wage bargaining at a European level seem very great. This certainly applies to a pan-European system of bargaining, but we also find it hard to believe that transnational coordination at the industry level or a system of pattern bargaining at the European level will develop within the foreseeable future. There may be coordination with respect to specific issues relating to EU decision-making, but otherwise we expect transnational union coordination over at least the coming decade to be confined more to non-committing declarations and exchange of experiences than to actual bargaining behaviour.

6.2.4. *Decentralization and transnational coordination within multinational firms*

A fourth possible scenario represents a combination of the first and third scenarios, in which decentralization to firm level is combined with transnational coordination of wage-setting within large multinational firms.

We can see two ways through which such a scenario might come about (see also Chapter 4). The first is related to the strengthening of firms' bargaining power relative to employees, which follows from having production units in different countries, among which production can be relocated. In this case there is an incentive for local unions in production units in different countries to coordinate their wage bargaining in order to defend themselves. The incentive is stronger, the more the employers make use of threats to relocate production.

The other way through which more transnational bargaining coordination within multinational firms could come about is when production is vertically integrated. Then it is in the interest of the employer to have coordinated bargaining in order to see to it that unions internalize input externalities (see Section 5.1.1) and avoid the possibility that work stoppages at one site block production at other sites (so that employers have to 'divide the pie' several times with labour, as discussed in Section 3.1).

One could argue that the prospects for transnational bargaining coordination among local unions within multinational corporations are considerably greater than among national sectoral unions or national union confederations in different countries. The argument would rest on costs of coordination being substantially smaller within multinational firms. There are several reasons for this. Similarities in production could mean that units in different countries are exposed to similar supply-side as well as demand-side shocks. Similarities in production might also lead to similarities in systems of pay and in other working conditions. Moreover, such a tendency is likely to be strengthened by employers' desires to run the units in different countries according to the same management principles. Finally, coordination on the union side will be facilitated by the fact that employees in different countries will interact regularly in their normal work.

As noted in Section 4.3, the European works councils (EWCs) may play an important role in this context. The EWCs are the result of a Commission Directive in 1994, which required multinational firms in the EU above a minimum size to establish EWCs either according to a statutory model or through a negotiated agreement with unions in the firm. Although the EWCs usually have formal rights concerning information and consultation only, they represent standardized and institutionalized networks of employees across borders, where local union representatives are likely to meet on a regular basis.

This may provide a basis for coordination of bargaining (Marginson and Sisson, 1998). However, we do not believe that collective agreements encompassing production units in different countries within multinational firms or other more formal types of bargaining coordination will develop in the near future. But it is possible that common norms on pay-setting may develop within these firms or that some production units may come to act as pattern-setters for the rest.

A development in the direction of more transnational wage-setting coordination within multinational firms will contribute to the diversity of national bargaining systems. To the extent that firms in service sectors remain largely national in character, wage-setting there will be influenced only by local conditions, whereas transnational considerations will play a role in multinational companies. Heterogeneity of firms is then likely to translate into heterogeneity of bargaining considerations.

6.2.5. *The most likely development*

Our discussion of possible scenarios has made it clear that future industrial relations systems in the European economies will be the outcome of a complex set of influences. As there are conflicting forces at work, it is not evident how the future bargaining system will evolve. So it is quite risky to try to forecast future developments.

However, our assesment is that the forces working in the direction of decentralized bargaining at the level of the firm or workplace are very strong. In our view, such a continued trend towards more decentralized bargaining can be expected to dominate in the long run. The development in a medium-term perspective is more difficult to judge. As we have argued, monetary unification in Europe creates incentives for more national coordination as a means of substituting nominal wage flexibility for monetary policy autonomy. In a setting where the levels at which formal bargaining occurs are being decentralized, such coordination is likely to be of a more informal character, within social pacts of the type that have occurred in several European countries in recent years. The extent of such national coordination efforts will depend on actual macroeconomic developments over the coming years: the more asymmetric are macroeconomic developments, the greater will be the incentives for social pacts.

In the end, however, there will be strong contradictions between any such attempts at national coordination and the likely development towards lower unionization, less coverage of union contracts, and decentralization of formal bargaining levels. This will probably mean the end to national coordination attempts. But it is hard to predict how smooth the transition will be. One possibility is that the attempts at national coordination become less and less effective and gradually 'fade away'. Another possibility is that the long-run transition to decentralization becomes a 'bumpy ride', where the failure of unions to deliver coordinated wage restraint in times of macroeconomic crisis provoke governments in some countries to take more drastic action, for example in the form of more traditional incomes policies, actually legislating about wage changes (as has occurred in recent years in Belgium, and sometimes in Denmark and Norway, where there are institutions for compulsory mediation). Although European integration could provide another challenge to national coordination by weakening the national ties of both unions and employers, we do see formidable obstacles to a more formal coordination of wage bargaining at the European level involving national industry unions or national union confederations. In contrast, one should expect to see transnational coordination with respect to specific issues where decision-making is taking place at the EU level.

To the extent that transnational bargaining coordination develops, it is most likely to occur *within* multinational firms. Such a development is consistent with the trend towards decentralization that we have identified. However, it is possible that bargaining coordination within transnational firms could in time also improve the prospects for transnational union coordination at higher levels, especially at the sectoral level. It may be more realistic to build such cooperation from the bottom up than from the top down. If there were to be a development in the direction of transnational bargaining, i.e. coordination among national union confederations or national industry unions, this is the most likely way in which it might come about. Still, we do not find this very probable.

Our basic long-run prediction is thus that there will be more decentralized wage bargaining at the level of the—possibly multinational—firm, and that national coordination will no longer be possible to achieve. How should one judge the macroeconomic consequences of this?

The reason why employers favour changes in this direction is that they are likely to have positive effects on productive efficiency by allowing greater adaptability to local conditions and greater possibilities of designing effective incentive systems. But our survey of the literature on bargaining coordination and unemployment in Chapter 5 shows that there are also risks. How such risks should be judged depends on the degree of national coordination that prevails today. A move from an intermediate degree of coordination (sectoral bargaining) to decentralized bargaining at the firm level together with a trend towards lower unionization may promote high employment. But the empirical results seem also to suggest that simultaneous moves from a high degree of bargaining coordination—as has prevailed in countries like Austria, Belgium, Denmark, Finland, Ireland, the Netherlands, Norway, and Sweden—to decentralization and lower unionization could, *everything else equal*, lead to higher aggregate real wages, and thus could have adverse employment effects. It is difficult to interpret these results, as everything else will not be equal. To some extent, the decentralization and deunionization trends may be driven by factors that may themselves tend to raise employment, such as increased product market competition and more flexible and non-standard employment contracts, or (as in the British case) legislation that weakens union bargaining power. It may also be the case that the same underlying causes—such as a reduced demand for 'social insurance'—lead to both lower taxation, which may promote employment, and lower degrees of unionization and bargaining coordination.

The empirical research seems to point to the importance of ensuring that a lower degree of bargaining coordination is associated with other labour market institutions that serve to guarantee high employment. Apart from the factors already discussed, these institutions could include unemployment insurance systems generating stronger incentives for employment and wage moderation (either through benefit levels or through the creation of a link between employee contributions to finance unemployment insurance and unemployment in individual bargaining areas, as suggested in Part II of this book); a more efficient and active labour market policy; and education systems that better match labour supply and demand.

6.3. POSSIBLE UNION STRATEGIES

The diversity in trends of union presence in different countries suggests that the strategies chosen by unions to cope with the new challenges will be an important determinant of their future role. Unions typically are not passive agents: they are organizations that respond and adapt to change. So an analysis of the future role of unions in Europe must assess the likely future union strategies. (See e.g. Hyman, 1994, for an interesting attempt to sketch out the implications of various 'models of trade unionism'.)

Our assessment is that future union strategies, at least in most continental European countries, will represent some mix between being: (1) a provider of services; (2) a bargaining agent in wage-setting in the individual company (and in a lesser way, in industries); (3) a partner to the company in local 'productivity coalitions'; and (4) a social and political movement at the national level. An obvious role would seem to be to strike a reasonable balance between employer demands for productive efficiency and the legitimate desires of employees to cope with the stresses of modern working life associated not least with a two-gender workforce, increasing complexity of jobs, the need for a rapid adjustment to new conditions, and more stringent training requirements. This is a task that can be performed at both local and industry levels in actual bargaining with employers, and at the national level by influencing political decision-making on basic labour market institutions. In response to decentralization of collective bargaining and greater involvement of local representatives and works councils in negotiating and implementing agreements, unions may also specialize in training and selecting local representatives, and providing professional support to works councils. The development of European works councils may be an important new task for the unions and give them an opportunity to build and reinforce transnational union networks.

The future of unions as political organizations, so prominent in Europe's history of the twentieth century, is more uncertain. Like the central employers' federations, trade unions have traditionally been invited to serve as members of national joint councils and advisory committees. Within the context of the EU decision-making on social and employment policy, the European federations of employers and unions have in recent years gained a role as co-legislators. However, this privileged position is not uncontested, for instance from the side of members of parliaments or interest groups representing potentially conflicting interests (e.g. consumers, environmentalists, and pensioners).

As we argued in Section 6.2, it may be attractive for trade unions in a situation of declining membership to seek extra support and legitimacy from being a social partner that is consulted by governments and can conclude agreements with them affecting the welfare of union members. But this entails a risk when lower unionization and a decentralization of bargaining reduce the credibility of unions as a social actor. There is a difference, however, between the ability of unions to help coordinate national wage bargaining and the possibility of their exerting continuing influence on political issues. The latter possibilities are probably greater. To be able to deliver coordinated wage restraint, it is union influence in absolute terms that matters. But when it comes to exerting a general political influence, the issue is one of relative strength: in a situation when membership and engagement in all types of organizations, including political parties, are faltering, unions may very well continue to wield an important influence if they do no worse than others.

In recent years, and in response to membership decline, many European trade unions have engaged in organizational restructuring, especially through mergers and takeovers, as we discussed in Section 2.9 (see also Streeck and Visser, 1998). In a situation with structural shifts in employment and with growing pressure to attend to the needs of more heterogeneous constituencies under increasingly decentralized labour–management relations, trade unions must adapt their internal operation and external representation. In the process, sectoral and occupational boundaries are becoming increasingly unimportant for union organization. It is not irrelevant to note, however, that union mergers have thus far stayed within national borders. The absence of international union mergers is a further testimony of the deeply national roots of European trade unions, even after decades of European integration.

Union mergers can be seen as a method to exploit economies of scale, and this way alleviate the cost pressures that result from decentralization, costlier services to members that become more demanding, and stagnating or declining membership levels. One possible strategy of 'old' unions is to move out of declining and into expanding areas. To this end, mergers between industrial unions, with a declining potential membership but with rich endowments from the past, and unions in services, usually too poor to organize effective recruitment drives in their expanding membership markets, can be expected to take place. However, such 'conglomerate unions' will be internally very diverse and will face difficult pressures with regard to the management of this diversity. Organizational restructuring could be expected to result both in centralized service provision for cost-cutting reasons and in decentralized collective bargaining for the reasons we discussed in Section 6.2.

As a final point, we want to stress once more the difficulties of predicting the future role of trade unions in Europe. The role of unions is shaped by a complex set of interrelated factors involving, *inter alia*, politics, history, social policy and economics. At any point in history, conditions may be more or less favourable to unions, and their fortunes have therefore varied over time. A corollary of this argument is that there is no simple determinant of union influence, and changing conditions might very well affect the trends that we have identified. We do, however, believe that continued membership decline and a continued trend towards decentralization of wage bargaining are the most likely long-run outcomes. Ultimately, this is likely to weaken attempts at coordinated wage bargaining at the national level. National coordination is not likely to be replaced by high-level coordination at the European level, except with respect to specific labour market issues placed on the EU agenda. But increasing product market integration at the European level could gradually lead to new patterns of union behaviour, with transnational cooperation within trans-European firms at the micro level, which could bring new international dimensions to union policy. Since this implies that large firms will conduct their own bargaining, the disintegration of bargaining and coordination at the national level could be hastened.

Comments

VILLY BERGSTRÖM

The scope of this report is impressive. Theoretical and empirical research on trade unions is discussed from almost every conceivable point of view. In fact, the content of the report is more extensive than the title indicates. It will probably become a standard work on the economic theory of trade unions for many years to come.

The problem is that the report is so rich that it lacks clear theses about the present situation as well as about development trends. This is a natural result of its covering many countries with reviews of experiences and empirical data on trade union problems specific to particular countries, relating to microeconomics and allocation as well as to macroeconomics and stabilization policy.

The starting point is the trend towards reduced union density since the early 1980s in most countries. The authors discuss a number of explanatory factors, such as the state of the labour market, structural changes in the economy, and the increased flexibility in the labour market.

However, the decline in union membership is perhaps primarily related to a general phenomenon that Robert D. Putnam calls loss of 'social capital' in his recently published book *Bowling Alone*: The Collapse and Revival of American Community (2000). This concerns the reduced participation in political parties, churches, sports clubs, and other social associations during recent decades. It is clear that this reduction is age-related. Younger people take part much less in social organizations than do older people. The same applies to trade union membership.

So the reasons discussed in this report for the decline in union density as a result of union problems or economic problems may be secondary, and the main reason may be a general decline in social associations with a common cause, not necessarily connected to unions themselves.

The authors ask whether reduced union membership leads to reduced influence for unions. I believe that the influence and importance of the trade unions has fallen independently of the fall in membership. For ten to fifteen years, legislation in many countries has consistently reduced union privileges and rights. Trade unions are on the defensive in many countries, in direct contrast to conditions during the build-up of the welfare state.

I can give a few examples from Sweden, which I think may be relevant also for other countries. My comments will be on macroeconomic issues.

That unions are on the defensive is exemplified by the trade unions' now frequent demands for referendums on various political proposals such as entry to the EMU. When the trade union movement was on the offensive, the conservative parties' demands for referendums were often rejected. It is now the selfsame parties that distrust referendums, as these often tend to preserve the status quo and check the deregulation, internationalization, and liberalization of the economy.

Other signs of the reduced power of the trade union movement are particularly clear in Sweden but also evident in other countries. When the large union confederations held a press conference fifteen years ago on any political proposal, it was covered by all television stations as well as the radio and newspapers; now, such trade union press conferences are sometimes attended only by their own organizational press. Instead, there are crowds of cameramen and journalists at central bank press conferences as soon as the banks publish a report. Every day the daily papers' financial pages contain articles and analyses of central bank policy. Interest has shifted away from the trade unions to the central banks, reflecting a shift of power between these institutions.

Why is this so? The answers are indicated in the above report. When there was full employment with a monetary policy regime of fixed exchange rates, the trade unions had real power. 'Guaranteed' full employment under Keynesianism gave them security. In many countries, inflation was more or less a residual in the stabilization policy regime that guaranteed full employment. Given a fixed exchange rate, the trade unions could—within reasonable limits and at least in the short run, say a year or two—nibble at business profits by an aggressive wage policy.

Together with the objective of wage equalization, the 'wage policy loyal to undercompensated groups' was successful in many countries, at least up to the early and mid-1980s. This approach to economic policy had the advantage that wage-earners could adopt a positive attitude to rationalization, structural change, and efficiency improvements in production: they had the security of being able to obtain new jobs at approximately the same pay if the old disappeared. So when the supply side of the economy changed, labour adjusted with less resistance, although there were fewer incentives to respond to demand changes on the labour market.

A moderate cost pressure from wage policy also contributed at times to rationalization and efficiency improvements in production. The scope for wage increases was not completely fixed but could be created to some extent by pay policy with its focus on lifting the levels of compensation for low paid work.

Deregulation and the liberalization of labour market legislation have changed all this. The labour market is now more similar to other markets—less of a 'social institution', to use a concept from Robert Solow's book, *The Labour Market as a Social Institution* (1990).

The change in the monetary policy regime in many countries that have introduced inflation targets and a floating exchange rate is an autonomous reason for the reduction of trade union power, particularly in small open economies. The trade unions cannot, as in the case of a fixed exchange rate, affect the distribution between profits and wages. The inflation target, if it is credible, spells out the trade-off between wage policy and employment.

In my country the Swedish trade union confederation, LO, the blue-collar union confederation, has carried out an extensive campaign among its members to clarify this correlation, not because the trade union leadership has any warm feelings for the new stabilization policy regime, but because wage-earners have to adapt. The inflation target with a floating exchange rate and free capital movements sets the conditions for unions. It is clear to the trade union movement that nominal pay increases must be restricted by the growth of productivity and the inflation target. Pay increases in excess of this are at the expense of employment. Central banks will see to that.

I believe that a regime with inflation targets is concrete and easy to comprehend, that the implications of a credible inflation target are understood in a different way from the implications for wage policy and employment of the more abstract objective of a 'fixed exchange rate'. The goal conflicts between unemployment and inflation are made clear. The monetary policy regime with inflation targets is understood and acknowledged by broad groups in the population as well as by the trade union movement (although under protest), which was not the case to the same extent for the fixed exchange rate.

Also relevant here is the increased independence of the central banks under the Maastricht conditions. Many central banks have responded to this independence with an openness about goals and means and by communication with the public in a way that was not previously the case.

Does this apply within EMU?

It is possible that the discipline that the new monetary policy regime creates in many countries will be lost in EMU. To date the new regime seems to have functioned well in small open economies, with low inflation and increased employment resulting.

Unfortunately, there is still mass unemployment in Europe so the new regime has not been properly put to the test under conditions of full employment. However, the Swedish trade union movement, for instance, will not experience the trade-off between pay policy and employment in the same way under EMU as under the present regime. ECB interest rate policy will in general not be affected by Swedish pay policy and inflation.

Entry into EMU for many countries will more resemble a return to a fixed exchange rate regime, even for many trade unions in big countries such as Germany (perhaps not for the leading union IG Metall, whose pay policy to some extent sets the norm for the whole of Germany).

Can flexible pay policy and fiscal policy replace the loss of interest rate policy of the individual countries to stabilize the price level and the real economy? Many European trade unions were in favour of entering the EMU and some Swedish trade unions wanted to join. These unions must therefore have thought through the consequences of joining for collective agreements and fixed wages.

Unions may regard the spread of bonus wages, profit-sharing and a 'thirteenth monthly wage'—premiums that usually total up to 10% of the annual wage—as the flexible part they are prepared to play with for adaptation in their own country when monetary and exchange rate policy are centralized in Brussels and Frankfurt. These extra payments are spreading to large parts of the private business sector in Sweden, at the same time as 15%–20% of the labour force no longer has permanent employment but temporary posts, project employment, or other time-limited arrangements. This leads to increased flexibility in the labour market, which will probably be pursued to an increasingly great extent in EMU. It is not clear what this means for union organization. Will insecurity push people back to the unions again?

Fiscal policy then? The issue is whether fiscal policy can be adjusted sufficiently quickly, bearing in mind the inertia of the political process and the built-in distribution conflicts in every tax and budget decision. What is happening in Ireland, where inflation is now over 5% and real growth 8%, arouses concern about the prospects of fiscal policy. Ireland has had a year and a half to tighten policy without succeeding.

I have even heard government ministers express a longing for EMU because fiscal policy in EMU would be relieved of the constraint that is now felt through the inflation target at the smallest loss of credibility of government finances. A small country can neglect its budget discipline at least to some extent without the EMU interest rate being affected.

A solution to the problem of the inertia of the political process concerning parliamentary decisions and political conflicts would be to delegate limited, specific measures within tax and budget policy for the government to decide. This might for instance concern VAT (value-added tax) and/or employers' payroll tax so that 'internal appreciation' or 'depreciation' could replace the loss of the country's own currency. This would resemble the delegation of monetary policy to independent central banks, although I realize that such a procedure would raise concerns from the point of view of democracy and would be even more controversial than the control of monetary policy by experts.

Let me end by congratulating the authors on an excellent report, and one that will become a reference work on the economics of unions in years to come.

ROBERT J. FLANAGAN

This is an admirable, wide-ranging report that succeeds in integrating the findings of the most recent theoretical and empirical research. The authors manage to maintain a sharp focus on the evidence in a subject area in which ideological predilections and nostalgia for past institutions often influence discussion. The scenarios sketched in the final chapter are particularly notable for their balanced consideration of opposing forces bearing on the future fortunes of European labour unions. I will focus on a short list of issues that could benefit from further attention from the research community.

Union density discussion

The modelling and prediction of changes in union density has always been a challenging research area, reflecting both weak theoretical guidance and the difficulty of 'doing numbers' to judge the importance of some of the most interesting hypotheses. Economists and industrial relations specialists have not generally predicted the major changes in union representation, such as the decline in union density in Europe (and elsewhere), that are documented in the report.

Understanding the relationship between government activity and union strength is of central importance—probably more so in Europe than in North America—and at the end of an ambitious empirical analysis of union density, the report signals this by stressing that union membership appears to be influenced most consistently by cyclical influences and the 'political game' (not otherwise defined). The authors try to capture political influences by a variable (*GOVN*) representing the political orientation of the executive government in office (ranging from conservative to pro-labour). In the regression results, however, the sign on this 'political climate' variable changes from country to country, indicating that pro-labour governments appear to enhance union membership in some countries and detract from it in others. At first glance the results seem puzzling, but in fact variables representing the general political climate of a government are likely to be less helpful in understanding trends in union membership than variables that capture the exact *mechanisms* through which government actions influence union fortunes.

Consider two ways in which a pro-labour government might try to assist workers. First, it might pass legislation influencing collective bargaining procedures (collective bargaining coverage, union recognition, and the like). The report reviews research (mainly for the United Kingdom) indicating that such changes in procedures can clearly influence membership and other labour relations outcomes.

Alternatively, the government might pass legislation providing additional benefits for workers, such as dismissal protection, pension benefits, health and safety regulation, etc. When this mechanism is adopted, unions may have increased difficulty in differentiating their product, because working conditions that used to be unique to union contracts have increasingly been provided via legislation to all workers, irrespective of union status. Indeed, unions through their legislative efforts have supported many of the legislative developments that may have reduced their distinctiveness to potential members. This hypothesis is consistent with the findings cited in the report of cohort effects in declining union membership. It also fits with the finding that union membership is stronger and may increase with unemployment in countries with a Ghent system of unemployment insurance. This perspective inverts the title of the other conference report (Part II). An increasingly important question may be: *What does the welfare state do to unions?*

The main point is that the effect of a pro-labour government on union membership will depend on the specific policies that it chooses to assist workers. Explanations of changes in union membership based on the general orientation of a government are likely to be much less revealing than explanations based on the particular mechanisms through which a government attempts to influence the welfare of workers.

There is a rather different question, concerning the relationship between governments and unions, that has received little consideration in the research community or in the report: Why (how) do European (and US) unions maintain *political* influence despite waning economic influence? In all countries outside of Scandinavia, unions represent less than half of all employees and a much smaller fraction of the electorate. It is not surprising that unions try to substitute political for collective bargaining action when their economic power diminishes. Why political systems respond to such efforts is less well understood.

Transnational company discussion
This is a very interesting topic, which raises the provocative possibility that greater European integration may reduce product market competition. Part of the argument rests on a possible growth of large multinational corporations (MNCs), which might generate significant economic rents that unions might organize to capture.

The potential role of MNCs in the product and labour markets deserves more attention than it has received, but there are several points that may be raised about the ability of MNCs to undermine competition in national markets. First, to gain market share, MNCs would presumably have to set prices below those charged by national firms. Moreover, the prices subsequently charged by MNCs would be disciplined by threat of potential entry by national firms.

Second, even if a growing presence by MNCs produced less competitive product markets, this would not necessarily be a good thing for unions, as these firms have special tactical advantages, such as production switching across national borders in the event of labour disputes. I agree with the authors that labour relations considerations are unlikely to determine plant location, but labour market strategy need not dominate plant location decisions for MNCs to acquire a 'divide-and-rule' capability. Moreover, efforts by unions to develop transnational cooperation to counter these tactical advantages have not been notably successful over the past thirty years. One would need to see reasons why such efforts by unions might be more successful in the future before putting significant weight on this aspect of the rent-capture argument.

Third, while the report documents the significant flows of foreign investment among European countries, the crucial factor for unions (and the rent-capture argument) would seem to be the proportion of employment that is found in

MNCs in each country. The British Workplace Employment Survey of 1998 reports that 9%–10% of employment is in foreign-owned firms. If this is typical of other European countries, it seems like a slim reed on which to base a resurgence of unionization.

Bargaining structure and economic outcomes
In general, the report provides a fine summary of a large and complex literature on the interrelationships between bargaining arrangements and economic outcomes. However, one should ask if there is not a paradox or contradiction in concluding that coordinated bargaining is best at a time when (as data in the report show) many countries are moving towards more decentralized bargaining. (One should not overgeneralize from single observations, but I shall note that the United States, with perhaps the most uncoordinated, decentralized wage-setting arrangements found among industrialized nations, has experienced unemployment rates of around 4% after a remarkably long expansion during the 1990s.)

In fact, there is some evidence that *correlations* between institutional structure and macroeconomic outcomes have weakened over time. While institutions change slowly and infrequently, the environment in which they operate can change rapidly in the wake of trade agreements and the like. On the one hand, the theory that is reviewed in the report suggests that one should expect weaker correlations between institutions and outcomes if trade or the size of the non-union sector increases (as it does, subject to coverage practices, with declining union density). On the other hand, the empirical studies reviewed in the report have not been set up to test the effects of these changes in the economic environment on the relationship between bargaining structure and macroeconomic outcomes. There is a danger of drawing conclusions that would not apply to an integrated European economy.

Scenarios for the future
The discussion of possible future scenarios at the end of the report reflects a tension between two views about how institutions are determined. A 'survival of the fittest' hypothesis predicts that market forces will produce a convergence in labour market institutions over time. At present it is fair to say that students of comparative labour market institutions conclude that this hypothesis is not proved. Research simply does not support the notion that history has produced a single set of equilibrium labour market institutions. But one could take the position that the market forces have not been sufficiently strong historically, and that further efforts at integration may produce more convergence than has been observed in the past. This view appears to assume that unions have common economic interests across countries—a proposition that seems to remain debatable in Europe.

A second view is that the observed variance in labour market institutions is driven by a variance in underlying, country-specific norms. To the extent that there are fundamental differences in interests and expectations about what collective action should yield across countries, unions will indeed have difficulties in developing responses that will limit the erosion of their power.

What the future in fact brings for European labour unions will depend very much on which of these views turns out to be dominant. For now, research provides little guidance on this intriguing question, but the discussion in the final chapter of the report provides as clear an appraisal of the conflicting issues as one is likely to find.

References

Acemoglu, D, Aghion, P, and Violante, G L (2000), 'Deunionisation, Technical Change and Inequality', unpublished paper, University College London.

Agell, J (1999), 'On the Benefits from Rigid Labour Markets: Norms, Market Failures, and Social Insurance', *Economic Journal*, 109.

—— and Lommerud, K E (1992), 'Union Egalitarianism as Income Insurance', *Economica*, 59.

—— and Lundborg, P (1995), 'Theories of Pay and Unemployment: Survey Evidence from Swedish Manufacturing Firms', *Scandinavian Journal of Economics*, 97.

—— and —— (1999), *Survey Evidence on Wage Rigidity and Unemployment: Sweden in the 1990s*, IFAU Working Paper no. 1999: 2.

—— and Ysander, B C (1993), 'Should Governments Learn to Live with Inflation? Comment', *American Economic Review*, 83.

Akerlof, G (1980), 'A Theory of Social Custom, of Which Unemployment May Be One Consequence', *Quarterly Journal of Economics*, 95.

—— and Yellen, J (1990), 'Fairness and Unemployment', *American Economic Review*, 78.

Alesina, A, and Perotti, R (1997), 'The Welfare State and Competitiveness', *American Economic Review*, 87.

Alogoskoufis, G C, and Manning, A (1988), 'On the Persistence of Unemployment', *Economic Policy*, 7.

Ashenfelter, O, and Pencavel, J H (1969), 'American Trade Union Growth, 1900–1960', *Quarterly Journal of Economics*, 88.

Askenazy, P (2000), 'French Laws of Work-Sharing to 35 Hours: A Primer', Paris: CEPREMAP.

Bain, G S, and Elias, P (1985), 'Trade Union Membership in Great Britain: An Individual-Level Analysis', *British Journal of Industrial Relations*, 23.

—— and Elsheikh, F (1976), *Union Growth and the Business Cycle*, Oxford: Blackwell.

—— and Price, R (1980), *Profiles of Union Growth: A Comparative Statistical Portrait of Eight Countries*, Oxford: Blackwell.

Ball, L (1987), 'Externalities from Contract Length', *American Economic Review*, 77.

—— and Romer, D (1991), 'Sticky Prices as Coordination Failure', *American Economic Review*, 81.

—— Mankiw, N G, and Romer, D (1988), 'The New Keynesian Economics and the Output–Inflation Trade-off', *Brookings Papers on Economic Activity*, 1.

Barro, R, and Gordon, D B (1983), 'A Positive Theory of Monetary Policy in a Natural Rate Model', *Journal of Political Economy*, 91.

Barth, E, Raaum, O, and Naylor, R (2000), 'Union Wage Effects: Does Membership Matter?' *Manchester School*, 68.

Bertola, G, Boeri, T, and Nicoletti, G (2001), *Welfare and Employment in a United Europe*, Cambridge, Mass.: MIT Press.

Bewley, T F (1998), 'Why Not Cut Pay?' *European Economic Review*, 42.

Bild, T, Jørgensen, H, Larsen, M, and Madsen, M (1998), 'Do Trade Unions Have a Future? The Case of Denmark', *Acta Sociologica*, 41.

Binmore, K, Rubinstein, A, and Wolinsky, A (1986), 'The Nash Bargaining Solution in Economic Modelling', *Rand Journal of Economics*, 17.

Bispinck, R, and Schulten, T (1998), 'Globalisierung und das deutsche Kollektivvertragssystem', *WSI-Mitteilungen*, 4.

Blanchard, O (1986), 'The Wage–Price Spiral', *Quarterly Journal of Economics*, 101.

—— (1998), 'The Medium Run', *Brooking Papers on Economic Activity*, 1.

—— and Wolfers, J (2000), 'The Role of Shocks and Institutions in the Rise of European Unemployment: The Aggregate Evidence', *Economic Journal*, 110.

Blanchflower, D, and Freeman, R B (1990), 'Going Different Ways: Unionism in the US and Other Advanced OECD Countries', London: LSE Centre for Economic Performance, Discussion Paper no. 5.

Blaschke, S (2000), 'Union Density and European Integration: Diverging Convergence', *European Journal of Industrial Relations*, 6.

Blau, F, and Kahn, L H (1996), 'International Differences in Male Wage Inequality: Institutions versus Market Forces', *Journal of Political Economy*, 104.

Bleaney, M (1996), 'Central Bank Independence, Wage-Bargaining Structure, and Macroeconomic Performance in OECD Countries', *Oxford Economic Papers*, 48.

Boeri, T, and Burda, M (2000), 'Union Membership, Firing Restrictions and Wage Compression in Equilibrium Unemployment', unpublished paper, Bocconi University, Milan, and Humboldt University, Berlin.

—— Börsch-Supan, A, and Tabellini, G (2001), 'Would You Like to Shrink the Welfare State? The Opinions of European Citizens', *Economic Policy*, 32.

Boldt, P J (1998), 'Finnish Social Partner Agreement on Counter-Cyclical EMU Buffers', mimeo, Finnish Confederation of Labour.

Booth, A L (1983), 'A Reconsideration of Trade Union Growth in the United Kingdom', *British Journal of Industrial Relations*, 21.

—— (1984), 'A Public Choice Model of Trade Union Behaviour and Membership', *Economic Journal*, 94.

—— (1985), 'The Free Rider Problem and a Social Custom Theory of Trade Union Membership', *Quarterly Journal of Economics*, 100.

—— (1986), 'Estimating the Probability of Trade Union Membership: A Study of Men and Women in Britain', *Economica*, 53.

—— (1995), *The Economics of the Trade Union*, Cambridge: Cambridge University Press.

—— and Chatterji, M (1995), 'Union Membership and Wage Bargaining when Membership is not Compulsory', *Economic Journal*, 105.

—— Francesconi, M, and Zoega, G (1999), 'Training, Rent-sharing and Unions', London: CEPR Discussion Paper no. 2200.

Bratsiotis, G, and Martin, C (1999), 'Stabilisation, Policy Targets and Unemployment in Imperfectly Competitive Economies', *Scandinavian Journal of Economics*, 101.

Brown, W (ed.) (1981), *The Changing Contours of British Industrial Relations*, Oxford. Basil Blackwell.

—— (1993), 'The Contraction of Collective Bargaining in Britain', *British Journal of Industrial Relations*, 31.

—— Deakin, S, and Ryan, P (1997), 'The Effects of British Industrial Relations Legislation 1979–97', London: NIER, Paper no. 161.

Bruno, M, and Sachs, J (1985), *The Economics of Stagflation*, Cambridge, Mass.: Harvard University Press.

Buiter, W (2000), 'Optimal Currency Areas: Why Does the Exchange Rate Regime Matter? With an Application to UK Membership in EMU', *Scottish Journal of Political Economy*, 47.

Burda, M (1995), 'Unions and Wage Insurance', London: CEPR Discussion Paper no. 1232.

—— (1999), 'European Labour Markets and the Euro: How Much Flexibility Do We Really Need?' London: CEPR Discussion Paper no. 2217.

Calmfors, L (1993a), 'Centralisation of Wage Bargaining and Macroeconomic Performance: A Survey', *OECD Economic Studies*, 21.

—— (1993b), 'Lessons from the Swedish Macroeconomic Experience', *European Journal of Political Economy*, 9.

—— (1998), 'Macroeconomic Policy, Wage Setting, and Employment: What Difference Does the EMU Make?' *Oxford Review of Economic Policy*, 14.

—— (2001), 'Unemployment, Labour-Market Reform and Monetary Union', *Journal of Labor Economics*, 19.

—— (2000), 'EMU och arbetslösheten', *Ekonomisk Debatt*, 2.

—— and Driffill, J (1988), 'Bargaining Structure, Corporatism and Macroeconomic Performance', *Economic Policy*, 6.

—— and Holmlund, B (2000), 'European Unemployment: A Partial Survey', *Swedish Economic Policy Review*, 7.

—— and Johansson, Å (2000), 'Unemployment Benefits, Contract Length and Nominal Wage Flexibility', unpublished paper: Institute for International Economic Studies, Stockholm University.

—— Flam, H, Gottfries, N, Jerneck, M, Lindahl, R, Haaland Matlary, J, Nordh Berntsson, C, Rabinowicz, E, and Vredin, A (1997), *EMU: A Swedish Perspective*, Dordrecht: Kluwer Academic Publishers.

Cameron, D (1978), 'The Expansion of the Public Economy: A Comparative Analysis', *American Political Science Review*, 77.

Canzoneri, M, Valles, J, and Viñals, J (1996), 'Do Exchange Rates Move to Address International Macroeconomic Imbalances?' London: CEPR Discussion Paper no. 1498.

Carruth, A, and Disney, R (1988), 'Where Have Two Million Trade Union Members Gone?' *Economica*, 55.

—— and Schnabel, C (1990), 'Empirical Modelling of Trade Union Growth in Germany, 1956–1986: Traditional versus Cointegration and Error Correction Methods', *Weltwirtschaftliches Archiv*, 126.

CEC (2000), *Industrial Relations in Europe*, Brussels: Commission of the European Community, DGV.

CEPII (1996), 'Intra- versus Inter-industry Trade Flows inside the EU Due to the Internal Market Programme', mimeo, European Commission, Brussels.

CEPS (1996), 'The Determinants of Foreign Direct Investment Flows in Europe and the Impact of the Single Market', mimeo, European Commission, Brussels.

Checchi, D, and Corneo, G (1996), 'Social Custom and Strategic Effects in Trade Union Membership: Italy 1951–1993', Discussion Paper A-526, University of Bonn.

Clegg, H A (1976), *Trade Unionism under Collective Bargaining*, Oxford: Blackwell.

—— (1979), *The Changing System of Industrial Relations in Great Britain*, Oxford: Blackwell.

Cobble, D S (1994), 'Labour Law Reform and Postindustrial Unionism', *Dissent*, Fall.

Commons, J R, *et al.* (1918), *History of Labor in the United States*, New York: Macmillan.

Cook, A H, Lorwin, V R, and Kaplan Davids, A (eds) (1983), *Women and Trade Unions in Eleven Countries*, Philadelphia: Temple University Press.

Corricelli, F, Cukierman, A, and Dalmazzo, A (2000), 'Monetary Institutions, Mono- polistic Competition, Unionized Labor Markets and Economic Performance', unpublished paper, University of Sienna.

——Crouch, C J (1982), *Trade Unions: The Logic of Collective Action*, Glasgow: Fontana.

——(2000*a*), 'The Snakes and Ladders of Twenty-First-Century Trade Unionism', *Oxford Review of Economic Policy*, 16.

——(2000*b*), 'National Wage Determination and European Monetary Union', in C Crouch (ed.), *After the Euro: Shaping Institutions for Governance in the Wake of European Monetary Union*, Oxford: Oxford University Press.

Cubbitt, R P (1992), 'Monetary Policy Games and Private Sector Precommitment', *Oxford Economic Papers*, 44.

——(1995), 'Corporatism, Monetary Policy and Economic Performance: A Simple Game Theoretic Analysis', *Scandinavian Journal of Economics*, 97.

Cukierman, A, and Lippi, F (1999), 'Central Bank Independence, Centralisation of Wage Bargaining, Inflation and Unemployment: Theory and Some Evidence', *European Economic Review*, 43.

——Rodriguez, P, and Webb, S (1998), 'Central Bank Autonomy and Exchange Rate Regimes: Their Effects on Monetary Accommodation and Activism', in S Eijffinger and H Huizinga (eds.), *Positive Political Economy: Theory and Evidence*, Cambridge: Cambridge University Press.

Danthine, J P, and Hunt, J (1994), 'Wage Bargaining Structure, Employment and Economic Integration', *Economic Journal*, 104.

Daveri, F, and Tabellini, G (2000), 'Unemployment, Growth and Taxation in Industrial Countries', *Economic Policy*, 30.

Davis, S, and Henrekson, M (2000), 'Wage Setting Institutions as Industrial Policy', NBER Working Paper no. 7502, January.

Delsen, L (1995), *Atypical Employment: An International Perspective. Causes, Con- sequences and Policy*, Groningen: Wolters-Noordhoff.

Dickens, W, and Leonard, J (1985), 'Accounting for the Decline in Union Membership, 1950–1980', *Industrial and Labor Relations Review*, 38.

Disney, R (1990), 'Explanations of the Decline in Trade Union Density in Britain: An Appraisal', *British Journal of Industrial Relations*, 28.

DIW (1999), *Wochenbericht* 23/99, 27–28/95.

Dornbusch, R, Favero, C, and Giavazzi, F (1998), 'Immediate Challenges for the European Central Bank', *Economic Policy*, 26.

Driffill, J, and Van der Ploeg, F (1993), 'Monopoly Unions and the Liberalisation of International Trade', *Economic Journal*, 103.

Duca, J (1998), 'How Increased Product Market Competition May Be Reshaping America's Labor Markets', *Economic Review of the Federal Reserve Bank of Dallas*, 25 January.

Due, J *et al.* (1994), *The Survival of the Danish Model: A Historical Sociological Analysis of the Danish System of Collective Bargaining*, Copenhagen: DJØF Publishing.

Dufour, C, and Nunes, C (1998), *Enquête auprès des sécretaires de comités d'entreprise*, Paris: IRES/DARES.

Ebbinghaus, B, and Visser, J (1999), 'When Institutions Matter: Union Growth and Decline in Western Europe, 1950–1995', *European Sociological Review*, 15.

—— and —— (2000), *Trade Unions in Western Europe since 1945*, London: Macmillan.

EIRO (2000), *Wage Policy and EMU*, Dublin: European Industrial Relations Observatory (http://www.eiro.eurofound.ie/2000/07/study/TN0007402S.html).

Elias, P (1996), 'Growth and Decline in Trade Union Membership in Great Britain: Evidence from Work Histories', in D Gallie, R Penn, and M Rose (eds.), *Trade Unions in Recession*, Oxford: Oxford University Press.

Elmeskov, J, Martin, J, and Scarpetta, S (1998), 'Key Lessons for Labour Market Reforms: Evidence from OECD Countries' Experiences', *Swedish Economic Policy Review*, 5.

Elvander, N (1988), *Den svenska modellen: Löneförhandlingar och inkomstpolitik 1982–1986*, Stockholm: Publica, Allmänna Förlaget.

—— (1999), *The Industrial Agreement: An Analysis of Its Ideas and Performance*, Sandviken: ALMEGAs förlag.

Esping-Andersen, G, and Regini, M (2000), *Why Deregulate Labour Markets?* Oxford: Oxford University Press.

Faith, R L, and Reid, J D (1987), 'An Agency Theory of Unionism', *Journal of Economic Behavior and Organisation*, 8.

Fajertag, G, and Pochet, P (eds.) (1997), *Social Pacts in Europe*. Brussels: European Trade Union Institute with Observatoire Social Européenne.

—— and —— (eds.) (2000), *Social Pacts in Europe: New Dynamics*, Brussels: European Trade Union Institute with Observatoire Social Européenne.

Falkner, G (1998), *EU Social Policy in the 1990s: Towards a Corporatist Policy Community*. London: Routledge.

Ferrera, M (1996), 'The "Southern Model" of Welfare in Social Europe', *Journal of European Social Policy*, 6.

Flanagan, R (1999), 'Macroeconomic Performance and Collective Bargaining: An International Perspective', *Journal of Economic Literature*, 37.

—— Soskice, D W, and Ulman, L (1983), *Unionism, Economic Stabilization and Incomes Policies: European Experience*, Washington, DC: Brookings Institution.

Flassbeck, H, and Scheremet, W (1995), 'Gleicher Lohn für gleiche Arbeit', *Die Zeit*, no. 19, 5 May.

Flora, P (ed.) (1986), *Growth to Limits: The Western European Welfare States since World War II* (4 Vols.), Berlin: Walter de Gruyter.

Fontagné, L, and Freudenberg, M (1999), 'Marché unique et développement des échanges', *Economie et Statistique*, 6.

Freeman, R B (1986), 'The Effect of the Union Wage Differential on Management Opposition and Union Organising Success', *American Economic Review*, 76.

—— (2000), 'Shared Capitalism or Apartheid Economy', *Centrepiece*, Spring.

—— and Kleiner, M M (1988), 'Employer Behaviour in the Face of Union Organising Drives', NBER Working Paper no. 2805.

—— and Medoff, J (1984), *What Do Unions Do?* New York: Basic Books.

—— and Pelletier, J (1990), 'The Impact of Industrial Relations Legislation on British Union Density', *British Journal of Industrial Relations*, 28.

Gallie, D (1996), 'Trade Union Allegiance and Decline in British Urban Labour Markets', in D Gallie, R Penn, and M Rose (eds.), *Trade Unions in Recession*, Oxford: Oxford University Press.

—— White, M, Cheng, Y, and Tomlinson, M (1998), *Restructuring the Employment Relation*, Oxford: Oxford University Press.

Golden, M A, Wallerstein, M, and Lange, P (1997), 'Postwar Trade-Union Organization and Industrial Relations in Twelve Countries', in H Kitschelt, P Lange, G Marks, and J D Stephens (eds.), *Continuity and Change in Contemporary Capitalism*, Cambridge: Cambridge University Press.

Goldthorpe, J and Hirsch, F (1976), 'The Political Economy of Inflation', Cambridge, Mass.: Harvard University Press.

Green, F (1990), 'Trade Union Availability and Trade Union Membership in Britain', *Manchester School*, 57.

—— (1992), 'Recent Trends in British Trade Union Density: How Much of a Compositional Effect?' *British Journal of Industrial Relations*, 30.

Griffin, L J, Botsko, C, Wahl, A-M, and Isaac, L W (1991), 'Theoretical Generality and Case Particularity: Qualitative Comparative Analysis and Trade Union Growth and Decline', *International Journal of Comparative Sociology*, 32.

Groth, C, and Johansson, Å (2000), *Centralization of Wage Bargaining, Central Bank Independence and the Phillips Curve*, mimeo, Institute for International Economic Studies, Stockholm University.

Grout, P A (1984), 'Investment and Wages in the Absence of Binding Contracts', *Econometrica*, 52.

Guest, D A, and Dewe, P (1988), 'Why Do Workers Belong to a Trade Union? A Social Psychological Study in the UK Electronics Industry', *British Journal of Industrial Relations*, 26.

Hakim, C (1996), *Key Issues in Women's Work: Female Heterogeneity and the Polarisation of Women's Employment*, London: Athlone.

Hall, P A, and Franzese, R J (1998), 'Mixed Signals: Central Bank Independence, Coordinated Wage-Bargaining, and European Monetary Union', *International Organization*, 52.

Hamermesh, D (1993), *Labour Demand*, Princeton: Princeton University Press.

Hancké, B (1993), 'Trade Union Membership in Europe 1960–90: Rediscovering Local Unions', *British Journal of Industrial Relations*, 31.

Hassel, A (1999), 'Bündnisse für Arbeit: nationale Handlungsfähigkeit im Europäischen Regimewettbewerb', MPIfG Discussion Paper no. 99/5.

Hege, A (1999), 'Collective Bargaining in Germany in the Age of Monetary Union', in P Pochet (ed.), *Monetary Union and Collective Bargaining in Europe*, 'Work and Society' series, no. 22, Brussels: PIE–Peter Lang.

Hibbs, D A, and Locking, H (1996), 'Wage Compression, Wage Drift and Wage Inflation in Sweden', *Labour Economics*, 3.

Hirschman, A (1970), *Exit, Voice and Loyalty*, Cambridge, Mass.: Harvard University Press.

Hochreiter, E, and Winckler, G (1995), 'The Advantages of Tying Austria's Hands: The Success of the Hard Currency Strategy', *European Journal of Political Economy*, 11.

Holden, S (1988), 'Local and Central Wage Bargaining', *Scandinavian Journal of Economics*, 90.

—— (1990*a*), 'Wage Drift and Bargaining: Evidence from Norway', *Economica*, 56.

—— (1990*b*), 'Wage Drift in Norway: A Bargaining Approach', in L Calmfors (ed.), *Wage Formation and Macroeconomic Policy in the Nordic Countries*, Oxford: SNS and Oxford University Press.

—— (1996), 'The Unemployment Problem: A Norwegian Perspective', unpublished paper, Department of Economics, University of Oslo.

—— (1998), 'Wage Drift and the Relevance of Centralised Wage Setting', *Scandinavian Journal of Economics*, 100.

—— (2000), 'Monetary Regime and the Co-ordination of Wage Setting', unpublished paper, University of Oslo.

—— and Raaum, O (1991), 'Wage Moderation and Union Structure', *Oxford Economic Papers*, 43.

Holm, P, Kiander, J, and Tossavainen, P (1999), 'Social Security Funds, Payroll Tax Adjustment and Real Exchange Rate: the Finnish Model', VATT, Government Institute for Economic Research, Discussion Paper no. 198, Helsinki.

Holmlund, B, and Lundborg, P (1999), 'Wage Bargaining, Union Membership, and the Organization of Unemployment Insurance', *Labour Economics*, 6.

—— and Skedinger, P (1990), 'Wage Bargaining and Wage Drift: Evidence from the Swedish Wood Industry', in L Calmfors (ed.), *Wage Formation and Macroeconomic Policy in the Nordic Countries*, Oxford: SNS and Oxford University Press.

Horn, H, and Wolinsky, A (1988), 'Worker Substitutability and Patterns of Unionisation', *Economic Journal*, 98.

Hyman, R (1994), 'Changing Trade Union Identities and Strategies', in R Hyman, and A Ferner (eds.), *New Frontiers in European Industrial Relations*, Oxford: Blackwell.

ILO (1955), *Unemployment Insurance Schemes,* Geneva: International Labour Office.

—— (1997), *World Labour Report 1997–1998: Industrial Relations, Democracy and Social Stability*, Geneva: International Labour Office.

Inglehart, R (1977), *The Silent Revolution: Changing Values and Political Styles among Western Publics*, Princeton: Princeton University Press.

Iversen, T (1998*a*), 'Wage Bargaining, Central Bank Independence, and the Real Effects of Money', *International Organization*, 52.

—— (1998*b*), 'Wage Bargaining, Hard Money and Economic Performance: Theory and Evidence for Organized Market Economies', *British Journal of Political Science*, 28.

—— (1999), *Contested Economic Institutions*, Cambridge: Cambridge University Press.

Jackman, R (1985), 'Counterinflationary Policy in a Unionised Economy with Non-synchronised Wage Setting', *Scandinavian Journal of Economics*, 87.

Jacobson, D, and Andreosso-O'Callaghan, B (1996), *Industrial Economics and Organisation*, Maidenhead, Berks: McGraw-Hill.

Jacquemin, A, Buiges, P, and Ilkovitz, F (1989), 'Horizontal Mergers and Competition Policy in the European Community', *European Economy*, 40.

Jowell, R, Witherspoon, S, Brook, L, and Taylor, B (eds.) (1990), *British Social Attitudes: The 7th Report*, Aldershot, Hants: Gower.

Keller, B, and Sorries, B (1999), 'Sectoral Social Dialogues: New Opportunities or More Impasses?' *Industrial Relations Journal*, 30.

Keynes, J M (1936), *The General Theory of Employment, Interest, and Money.* London: Macmillan.

Kjellberg, A (1997), *Fackliga organisationer och medlemmar i dagens Sverige*, Lund: Arkiv förlag.

Klandermans, P G (1984), 'Mobilization and Participation: Social–Psychological Expansions of Resource Mobilization Theory', *American Sociological Review*, 49.

——and Visser, J (1995), *De vakbeweging na de welvaartsstaat*, Assen: van Gorcum.

Kohaut, S, and Bellman, L (1997), 'Betriebliche Determinanten der Tarifbindung: Eine empirische Analyse auf der Basis des IAB-Betriebspanels 1997', *Industrielle Beziehungen*, 4.

——and Schnabel, C (1999), 'Tarifbindung im Wandel', *IW-Trends*, 26.

Korpi, W, and Shalev, M (1979), 'Strikes, Industrial Relations and Class Conflicts in Capitalist Societies', *British Journal of Sociology*, 30.

Layard, R, Nickell, S, and Jackman, R (1991), *Unemployment: Macroeconomic Performance and the Labour Market*, Oxford: Oxford University Press.

Lester, R (1958), *As Unions Mature*, Princeton: Princeton University Press.

Lindbeck, A, and Snower, D J (1988), *The Insider–Outsider Theory of Employment and Unemployment*, Cambridge, Mass.: MIT Press.

——and—— (forthcoming), 'Centralized Bargaining and Reorganized Work: Are They Compatible?' *European Economic Review*.

Lynch, L (ed.) (1994), *Training and the Private Sector: International Comparisons*, 'Comparative Labor Market' series, Chicago: University of Chicago Press.

Machin, S (2000), 'Union Decline in Britain', London: Centre for Economic Performance Discussion Paper no. 455, April.

——Stewart, M, and van Reenan, J (1993), 'The Economic Effects of Multiple Unionism: Evidence from the 1984 Workplace Industrial Relations Survey', *Scandinavian Journal of Economics*, 95.

Marginson, P, and Sisson, K (1998), 'European Collective Bargaining: A Virtual Prospect?' *Journal of Common Market Studies*, 36.

Martens, A (1985), 'Vakbondsgroei en vakbondsmacht in België', *Tijdschrift voor Arbeidsvraagstukken*, 1.

Marwell, G, and Oliver, P (1993), *The Critical Mass in Collective Action: A Micro-Social Theory*, Cambridge: Cambridge University Press.

Mélitz, J (1997), 'The Evidence about the Costs and Benefits of the EMU', *Swedish Economic Policy Review*, 4.

Metcalf, D (1993), 'Industrial Relations and Economic Performance', *British Journal of Industrial Relations*, 31.

——and Stewart, M (1992), 'Closed Shops and Relative Pay: Institutional Arrangements or High Density?' *Oxford Bulletin of Economics and Statistics*, 54.

——Hansen, K, and Charlwood, A (2000), 'Unions and the Sword of Justice: Unions and Pay Systems, Pay Inequality, Pay Discrimination and Low Pay', London: Centre for Economic Performance Discussion Paper no. 452, April.

Millward, N (1990), 'The State of the Unions', in R Jowell, S Witherspoon, L Brook, and B Taylor (eds.), *British Social Attitudes: The 7th Report*, Aldershot, Hants: Gower.

Milner, S (1995), 'The Coverage of Collective Pay-setting Institutions in Britain, 1895–1990', *British Journal of Industrial Relations*, 33.

Moene, K-O (1988), 'Unions' Threats and Wage Determination', *Economic Journal*, 98.

—— and Wallerstein, M (1992), 'The Process of Creative Destruction and the Scope of Collective Bargaining', unpublished paper, Department of Economics, University of Oslo.

—— —— and Hoel, M (1993), 'Bargaining Structure and Economic Performance', in R Flanagan, K-O Moene, and M Wallerstein (eds.), *Trade Union Behaviour, Pay Bargaining and Economic Performance*, FIEF 'Studies in Labour Markets and Economic Policy', Oxford: Clarendon Press.

Naylor, R A (1989), 'Strikes, Free Riders and Social Customs', *Quarterly Journal of Economics*, 104.

—— (1990), 'A Social Custom Model of Collective Action', *European Journal of Political Economy*, 6.

—— (1995), 'On the Economic Effects of Multiple Unionism', *Scandinavian Journal of Economics*, 97.

—— (1998), 'International Trade and Economic Integration when Labour Markets Are Generally Unionised', *European Economic Review*, 42.

—— (1999), 'Union Wage Strategies and International Trade', *Economic Journal*, 109.

—— and Cripps, M W (1993), 'An Economic Theory of the Open Shop Trade Union', *European Economic Review*, 37.

—— and Raaum, O (1993), 'The Open Shop Union, Wages and Management Opposition', *Oxford Economic Papers*, 45.

Neven, D, Roller, L-H, and Zhang, Z (1998), 'Union Power and Product Market Competition: Evidence from the Airline Industry', London: CEPR Discussion Paper no. 1912.

Nickell, S J (1999), 'Product Markets and Labour Markets', *Labour Economics*, 6.

—— and Layard, R (1999), 'Labor Market Institutions and Economic Performance', in O Ashenfelter and D Card (eds.), *Handbook of Labor Economics*, iii, Amsterdam: North-Holland.

—— and Van Ours, J (2000), 'The Netherlands and the United Kingdom: A European Unemployment Miracle?' *Economic Policy*, 30.

Nicoletti, G, Haffner, R, Nickell, S, Scarpetta, S, and Zoegi, G (2001), 'European Integration, Liberalization and Labour Market Performance', in G Bertola, T Boeri, and G Nicoletti, *Welfare and Employment in a United Europe*, Cambridge, Mass.: MIT Press.

Obstfeld, M (1998), *EMU: Ready or Not?* 'Essays in International Finance' no. 209, Princeton: Department of Economics, Princeton University.

OECD (1991), *Employment Outlook*, Paris: OECD.

—— (1994a), *The OECD Jobs Study*, Paris: OECD.

—— (1994b), *The OECD Jobs Study*, Part II, *The Adjustment Potential of the Labour Market*, Paris: OECD.

—— (1997a), *Employment Outlook*, Paris: OECD.

—— (1997b), *Implementing the OECD Jobs Strategy: Lessons from Member Countries' Experience*, Paris: OECD.

Olson, M (1965), *The Logic of Collective Action: Public Goods and the Theory of Groups*, Cambridge, Mass.: Harvard University Press.

—— (1982), *The Rise and Decline of Nations: Economic Growth, Stagflation, and Social Rigidities*, New Haven: Yale University Press.

Osborne, M J (1984), 'Capitalist–Worker Conflict and Involuntary Unemployment', *Review of Economic Studies*, 51.

Pedersen, P J (1982), 'Union Growth in Denmark, 1911–1939', *Scandinavian Journal of Economics*, 84.

Peoples, J (1998), 'Deregulation and the Labour Market', *Journal of Economic Perspectives*, 12.

Phelps, E (1994), *Structural Slumps: The Modern Equilibrium Theory of Unemployment, Interest, and Assets*, Cambridge, Mass.: Harvard University Press.

Phelphs Brown, H (1959), *The Growth of British Industrial Relations*, London, Macmillan.

—— (1986), *The Origins of Trade Union Power*, Oxford: Oxford University Press.

Pizzorno, A (1978), 'Le Due logiche dell'azione di classe', in A Pizzorno, E Reyneri, and M Regini, *Lotte operaie e sindacato: Il ciclo 1968–72 in Italia*, Bologna: Il Mulino.

Pochet, P (1999a), 'Monetary Union and Collective Bargaining in Europe: An Overview', in P Pochet (ed.), *Monetary Union and Collective Bargaining in Europe*, 'Work and Society' series, no. 22, Brussels: PIE–Peter Lang.

—— (1999b), 'Monetary Union and Collective Bargaining in Belgium', in P Pochet (ed.), *Monetary Union and Collective Bargaining in Europe*, 'Work and Society' series, no. 22, Brussels: PIE–Peter Lang.

—— (1999c), 'Monetary Union and Collective Bargaining in Finland', in P Pochet, (ed.), *Monetary Union and Collective Bargaining in Europe*, 'Work and Society' series, no. 22, Brussels: PIE–Peter Lang.

—— (1999d), 'Conclusions and Perspectives', in P Pochet (ed.), *Monetary Union and Collective Bargaining in Europe*, 'Work and Society' series, no. 22, Brussels: PIE–Peter Lang.

—— and Vanhercke, B (1998), *Social Challenges of Economic and Monetary Union*, Brussels: European University Press.

Ramaswamy, R, and Rowthorn, R (1993), 'Centralised Bargaining, Efficiency Wages and Flexibility', IMF Working Paper no. WP/93/25.

Putnam, R D (2000), *Bowling Alone: The Collapse and Revival of the American Community*, New York: Simon & Schuster.

Regini, M (1991), *Confini mobili: la costruzione dell'economia fra politica e società*, Bologna: Il Mulino.

—— (1997), 'Still Engaging in Corporatism? Recent Italian Experience in Comparative Perspective', *European Journal of Industrial Relations*, 3.

Richards, A, and García de Polavieja, J (1997), 'Trade Unions, Unemployment and Working Class Fragmentation in Spain', Madrid: Istituto Juan March de Estudios e Investigaciones, Working Paper no. 1997/112.

Roche, W K, and Larragy, J (1990), 'Cyclical and Institutional Determinants of Annual Trade Union Growth in Ireland: Evidence from the DUES Data Series', *European Sociological Review*, 6.

Rodrik, D (1998), 'Why Do More Open Economies Have Bigger Governments?' *Journal of Political Economy*, 106.

Rödseth, A, and Holden, S (1990), 'Wage Formation in Norway', in L Calmfors (ed.), *Wage Formation and Macroeconomic Policy in the Nordic Countries*, Oxford: SNS and Oxford University Press.

Rogers, J, and Streeck, W (1995), *Works Councils: Consultation, Representation and Cooperation in Industrial Relations*, Chicago: University of Chicago Press.

Romer, D (1996), *Advanced Macroeconomics*, New York: McGraw-Hill.

Rothstein, B (1992), 'Labour Market Institutions and Working-Class Strength', in S Steinmo, K Thelen, and F Longstreth (eds.), *Structuring Politics: Historical Institutionalism in Comparative Analysis*, Cambridge: Cambridge University Press.

Scarpetta, S (1996), 'Assessing the Role of Labour Market Policies and Institutional Settings on Unemployment: A Cross-Country Study', *OECD Economic Studies*, 26.

Scharpf, F W (1991), *Crisis and Choice in European Social Democracy*, Ithaca, NY: Cornell University Press.

—— and Smith, V A (eds.) (2000), *Globalization and the Adjustment of National Welfare States*, Oxford: Oxford University Press.

Schelling, T C (1978), *The Micromotives of Macrobehaviour*, New York: W.W. Norton.

Scheuer, S (1984), *Hvorfor stiger den faglige organisering?* Copenhagen: Nyt fra Samfundsvidenskaberne.

—— (1992), 'Denmark: Return to Decentralization', in A Ferner and R Hyman (eds.), *Industrial Relations in the New Europe*, Oxford: Blackwell.

Schippers, J J (1986), 'Determinanten van vakbondslidmaatschap', *Sociaal Maandblad Arbeid*, 41.

Schnabel, C (1999), 'Die Arbeitsmarkt und beschäftigungspolitische Herausforderung in Ostdeutschland' in E. Wiedemann *et al.* (eds.), *Beiträge zur Arbeitsmarkt- und Berufsforschung*, BeitrAB 223, Nürnberg: Institut für Arbeitsmarkt und Berufsforschung.

Schulten, T (1996), 'European Works Councils: Prospects for a New System of European Industrial Relations', *European Journal of Industrial Relations*, 2.

Shalev, M (1992), 'The Resurgence of Labour Quiescence', in M Regini (ed.), *The Future of Labour Movements*, London: Sage.

Shister, J (1967), 'The Direction of Unionism: Thrust or Drift?' *Industrial and Labour Relations Review*, 20.

Sinclair, D M (1995), 'The Importance of Sex for the Propensity to Unionize', *British Journal of Industrial Relations*, 33.

Sisson, K (1987), *The Management of Collective Bargaining: An International Comparison*, Oxford: Blackwell.

Skott, P (1997), 'Stagflationary Consequences of Prudent Monetary Policy in a Unionized Economy', *Oxford Economic Papers*, 49.

Slichter, S (1950), 'Notes on the Structure of Wages', *Review of Economics and Statistics*, 32.

——Healy, J, and Livernash, R (1960), *The Impact of Collective Bargaining on Management*, Washingon DC: Brookings Institution.

Solow, R M (1979), 'Another Possible Source of Wage Stickiness', *Journal of Macroeconomics*, 1.

Solow, R (1990), *The Labour Market as a Social Institution*, Oxford: Basil Blackwell.

Soskice, D, and Iversen, T (1998), 'Multiple Wage-Bargaining Systems in the Single European Currency Area', *Oxford Review of Economic Policy*, 14.

—— and —— (2000), 'The Nonneutrality of Monetary Policy with Large Price or Wage Setters', *Quarterly Journal of Economics*, 114.

SOU (1998: 141), *Medling och lönebildning*, Slutbetänkande från utredningen om ett förstärkt förlikningsmannainstitut, Stockholm: Fritzes.

Spilsbury, M, Hoskins, M, Ashton, D N, and Maguire, M J (1987), 'A Note on the Trade Union Membership Patterns of Young Adults', *British Journal of Industrial Relations*, 25.

Stewart, M B (1987), 'Collective Bargaining Arrangements, Closed Shops and Relative Pay', *Economic Journal*, 97.

——(1990), 'Union Wage Differentials, Product Market Influences and the Division of Rents', *Economic Journal*, 100.

Streeck, W (1981), *Organisationsprobleme in der sozialstaatlichen Demokratie*, Königstein: Athenäum.

——(1998), 'The Internationalization of Industrial Relations in Europe', Cologne: Max Planck Institute for the Study of Societies, MPIfG Discussion Paper no. 98/2.

——and Visser, J (1997), 'The Rise of the Conglomerate Union', *European Journal of Industrial Relations*, 3.

——and ——(1998), 'An Evolutionary Dynamic of Union Organization', Cologne: Max Planck Institute for the Study of Societies, Discussion Paper no. 98/4.

Summers, L, Gruber, J, and Vergara, R (1993), 'Taxation and Structure of Labor Markets: The Case of Corporatism', *Quarterly Journal of Economics*, 108.

Taylor, A (1989), *Trade Unions and Politics: A Comparative Introduction*, London: Macmillan.

Taylor, J B (1980), 'Aggregate Dynamics and Staggered Contracts', *Journal of Political Economy*, 88.

Traxler, F (1994), 'Collective Bargaining: Levels and Coverage', *Employment Outlook 1994*, Paris: OECD.

——(1996), 'Collective Bargaining in the OECD: Developments, Preconditions and Effects', *European Journal of Industrial Relations*, 4.

Van den Berg, A (1996), 'Vakbeweging, economische conjunctuur en institutionele verandering in Nederland: Een tijdreeksstudie van tachtig jaar ledenontwikkeling', *Mens en Maatschappij*, 71, special issue.

——and Grift, Y (1998), 'Dutch Trade Union Membership 1979–1995', paper presented at the 1998 EALE conference, Blackenberg.

Van de Vall, M (1970), *Labor Organizations: A Macro- and Micro-Sociological Analysis on a Comparative Basis*, Cambridge: Cambridge University Press.

Van Ours, J C (1991), 'Union Growth in the Netherlands 1961–1989'. Amsterdam: Vrije Universiteit, ALERT research memorandum no. 1991–33.

Velasco, A, and Guzzo, V (1999), 'The Case for a Populist Central Banker', *European Economic Review*, 43.

Viñals, J, and Jimeno, J (1998), 'The Impact of EMU on European Unemployment', Oesterreichische Nationalbank, Working Paper 34.

Visser, J (1986), 'Die Mitgliederentwicklung der westeuropäischen Gewerkschaften. Trends und Konjunkturen', *Journal für Sozialforschung*, 26.

——(1989), *European Trade Unions in Figures*, Deventer and Boston: Kluwer.

——(1990), *In Search of Inclusive Unionism*, Boston and Deventer: Kluwer.

——(1991), 'Trends in Union Membership', *Employment Outlook 1991*, Paris: OECD.

—— (1992), 'The Strength of Union Movements in Advanced Capitalist Democracies: Social and Organizational Variations', in M Regini (ed.), *The Future of Labour Movements*, London: Sage.

—— (1993), 'Union Organisation: Why Countries Differ', *International Journal of Comparative Labour Law and Industrial Relations*, 9.

—— (1994), 'Trade Union Membership Database: OECD Countries, 1890–1990', Amsterdam: University of Amsterdam/Sociology of Organization Research Unit, unpublished datafile.

—— (1996), 'Trends and Variations in European Industrial Relations', Amsterdam: University of Amsterdam, CESAR Research Paper no. 4/96.

—— (1998*a*), 'European Trade Unions in the mid-1990s', in B Towers and M Terry (eds.), *Industrial Relations Journal, European Annual Review 1997*.

—— (1998*b*), 'Two Cheers for Corporatism, One for the Market', *British Journal of Industrial Relations*, 36.

—— (1998*c*), 'Concertation: The Art of Making Social Pacts', in *National Social Pacts, Assessment and Future Prospects*, Paris: Notre Europe.

—— (2000), 'A Combined Indicator of Union Centralisation and Coordination', Amsterdam: Amsterdam Institute for Advanced Labour Studies, Working Paper no. 00/3.

—— and Van Rij, C (1999), *Vakbeweging en flexibiliteit*, Amsterdam: Welboom-Elsevier.

Waddington, J, and Whitston, C (1997), 'Why Do People Join Unions in a Period of Membership Decline?' *British Journal of Industrial Relations*, 35.

Wallerstein, M (1989), 'Union Organization in Advanced Industrial Democracies', *American Political Science Review*, 83.

—— (1991), 'Reply to Stephens', *American Political Science Review*, 85.

—— (1999), 'Wage-Setting Institutions and Pay Inequality in Advanced Industrial Societies', *American Journal of Political Science*, 43.

Webb, S, and Webb, B (1894), *The History of Trade Unionism*, London: Longmans, Green, 1920 edn.

Weitzman, M L (1985), 'The Simple Macroeconomics of Profit Sharing', *American Economic Review*, 75.

Western, B (1997), *Between Capital and Class: Postwar Unionization in the Capitalist Democracies*, Princeton: Princeton University Press.

Willman *et al.* (1993), *Union Business: Trade Union Organisation and Financial Reform in the Thatcher Years*, Cambridge: Cambridge University Press.

Yashiv, E (1989), 'Inflation and the Role of Money under Discretion and Rules'. Working Paper no. 8–89, PSIE, Massachusetts Institute of Technology, November.

Zetterberg, J (1995), 'Unemployment, Labour Market Policy and the Wage Bargaining System', in J Johannesson and E Wadensjö (eds.), *Labour Market Policy at the Crossroads*, Stockholm: EFA, Ministry of Labour.

PART II

WHAT DO UNIONS DO TO THE WELFARE STATES?

Agar Brugiavini, Bernhard Ebbinghaus, Richard Freeman,
Pietro Garibaldi, Bertil Holmlund, Martin Schludi,
and Thierry Verdier

We wish to thank Tito Boeri and Giorgio Brunello for helpful discussions throughout the development of this part of the volume. Gilles Saint-Paul and Michele Salviati made many constructive comments. Giacomo De Giorgi and Mattia Makovec have provided excellent research assistance.

Despite their significance, the forms of dialogue used and the routes followed by the reform process are generally not well known. In a way they are the hidden face of recent pension reforms. Most of the work, especially international comparisons, has concentrated on the purely technical aspects... The decision-making aspects have largely been left in the shadows, yet they are a major factor in the implementation of reforms and the long-term viability of systems.

Reynaud (2000: 2)

1

Introduction

The quotation from Reynaud (2000) provides the motivation for the research described in this part of the volume. In the economic, sociological, and political analysis of welfare systems and their reforms, little emphasis has been traditionally given to the decision-making process, and on the specific roles of the various actors in implementing reforms. This part of the volume partially fills in this gap, and investigates the interactions between trade unions, welfare systems, and welfare reforms.

Historically, trade unions have played a prominent role in the provision of insurance to workers and their families. Indeed, the function of protecting employees against social risks has often anticipated the role of unions as workers' representatives in bargaining over wages and work conditions. While unions have a long established role as an institution that provides voice and protection to workers, the economic literature has shown that these activities can be efficiency-enhancing, inasmuch as insurance markets are imperfect and/or incomplete, and non-competitive forces in the product markets are sizeable. Further, trade unions have also shown concern for wage inequality, and have promoted redistribution policies in ways that go well beyond the traditional 'wage compression' paradigm.

Nevertheless, unions enjoy a monopoly position in particular labour markets, and, without appropriate incentives and countervailing forces, their activities may adversely affect the economic performance of a country. Thus, union involvement in the welfare state may simply reflect the monopolistic face of trade unions, and consist of lobbying for generous policies to the exclusive advantage of union members. The use of selective incentive may be implemented under different formats of the organization of labour—entailing different degrees of union coverage and union fragmentation—and may be prominent when unions are involved in self-administration of welfare benefits, and/or when they play a key political role in welfare policy decision-making. Trade unions seem affected by a 'seniority bias' both in their wage bargaining and in their choices over social welfare policies. This seniority bias may, in turn, have negative effects on employment, and ultimately on the membership structure of unions themselves.

This part of the volume discusses some policy issues that arise in this context. The overall theme is the policy dilemma created by the many different activities of trade unions in the field of welfare provision, notably pension policies and unemployment protection. Throughout the following chapters, a tension emerges between the role of unions as insurance providers, as institutions that facilitate agreements between different parties, and as rent-seeking monopolists. By making use of an interdisciplinary approach, involving economic theory, political science, and statistical analysis, we are able to rationalize a set of distinct features of the interaction between union activities and union structure on the one hand, and welfare arrangements and welfare developments on the other.

To our knowledge, this is the first attempt to lay out a comprehensive description of the possible effects of trade unions on welfare regimes and social expenditure trends. We build on uneven foundations, since there exist few contributions that bring together the industrial relations and economic literature. Nevertheless, we believe that we show that the benefits of cross-fertilization far outweigh the costs of bringing different methodological approaches together when dealing with this topic.

Indeed, this part of the volume uncovers aspects of union behaviour that seem to have been overlooked by models depicting trade unions concerned only with industrial relations outcomes. In particular, we establish a new important link between the traditional rent-seeking activities of unions and some 'political economic activities', such as taking direct responsibility for the provision and administration of insurance, or taking long-term commitment in welfare policies involving intergenerational transfers.

While unions may exhibit a 'static-efficiency' role in providing insurance, they are likely to feature a 'dynamic inefficiency' role, in the sense of treating differently different generations of workers. The activities of unions that best conform to this view are the implementation of 'soft landing plans' in public pension systems, widely observed in Europe. More generally, unions tend to preserve the status quo when it comes to cutting pension benefits or reducing the generosity of pension provisions, or when a retrenchment process of welfare spending is to be implemented. The cost of these dynamic inefficiencies may be accepted by younger generations as long as an intergenerational contract can be enforced, whereby unions guarantee that the status quo will be preserved, and are credible in their commitment. In this intergenerationally implicit pact the unions could play a key role because they are long-lived agents, certainly lasting longer than many governments.

In the light of the recent trends in population ageing, most OECD member countries are under pressure to reform their social policies in order to stabilize welfare costs. Winning the support of unions in welfare reforms may be the first step towards achieving this goal. But such a role also requires that the trade unions become aware of the costs of social protection expenditure for the whole economy and of the potential inefficiencies and distortions that may result from their actions at a microeconomic level in the labour market.

This part is organized as follows. *Chapter 2* shows that there are important correlations between the unions' strength and activities and their welfare outcomes. The attempt is made to provide a taxonomy of the large differences across countries in union strength and social expenditure, by making use simultaneously of both labour relations and political economy categories as well as welfare categories and social spending measures. One dimension of our analysis provides four clusters of groups of countries, which share common features in terms of union strength and bargaining traditions and in terms of welfare arrangements. At one extreme we place Nordic countries, which have a longstanding tradition of universal protection and high union density, while at the other extreme a cluster of Anglo-Saxon countries emerges as characterized by low social protection expenditure and low union density. Continental countries and southern European countries lie somewhere in between. This classification is by no means exhaustive or complete, and important differences emerge both within each group and in other dimensions of union activities, particularly in their role as market institutions. We cannot explain cross-country variability without referring to the industrial model that each state has adopted and, most importantly, to the different routes through which unions influence welfare policies.

Chapter 3 develops the relationship between union actions and welfare outcomes. It gives an economist's perspective, and presents an abstract economic model that offers an analytical framework for investigating the behaviour of unions in the welfare state. Further, it presents real-world counterparts to the empirical implications emerging from the model. In light of the stylized facts presented in Chapter 2, which confirm the involvement of unions in pension arrangements along several dimensions, Chapter 3 takes the provision of old-age insurance as a natural example. Economic theory stresses the role of unions as insurance providers, and looks at a full bargaining setup where unions have influence on current wages, pensions, and employment outcomes. A novel feature of the description of union behaviour is that it also accounts for heterogeneity of union members, by distinguishing senior workers from junior workers. This clearly brings out the effects of the seniority bias affecting union decisions in wage bargaining, and also in pressing for generous pension policies. A review of the existing literature on unions and pensions based on microeconomic empirical research is provided, along with some fresh evidence on the interaction between unions and welfare at a macro level.

Chapter 4 provides a detailed account of the position of unions over pension reforms. We regard this aspect of union activities as a major indicator establishing whether unions have a truly solidaristic approach in negotiating reforms, or appear to be driven mainly by internal membership considerations and by a strong seniority bias. We provide examples both of situations where unions oppose welfare-restructuring reforms by effectively preventing their implementation and of those where they negotiate over policy changes by taking a long-term view.

Chapter 5 explores the involvement of unions in the provision of unemployment insurance. We present theoretical considerations, policy arguments, and empirical evidence in light of a particular unemployment insurance arrangement known as the 'Ghent regime'. This form of unemployment provision is adopted in some Nordic countries, and it is an interesting example of self-administered insurance by the trade unions in contrast with a compulsory universal system. It is an interesting economic case because the provision of unemployment insurance in a Ghent regime has the nature of an 'exclusive service', but this is usually coupled with a subsidy by the government financed through general taxation. Hence the policy questions we ask in the introduction to this chapter, related to the traditional trade-off of union activities, can be addressed in this context. Is the Ghent unemployment arrangement efficient in the sense of providing the correct incentives to job search? Do unions internalize the cost of the negative effects that financing the scheme may entail?

Chapter 6 concludes with a summary of the main findings of this part of the report: that seniority bias in unions leads to economic outcomes that are more favourable to older than to younger workers, which itself can harm union growth, and the ways in which unions can counteract this tendency and choose policies that benefit both young and older workers.

2

Unions' Involvement in the Welfare State

Trade unions have been a major social force in the development of modern welfare states, and even today they often assume multiple roles in shaping and administering social insurance. Historically, the unions developed mutual insurance as part of associational self-help to compensate for the lack of private insurance or public social protection. At the same time, they mobilized, together with allied political parties, for the expansion of social rights. Increasingly, many of the protective functions that unions provided as selective incentives to their members came to be taken over by the state or at least regulated by public policy. In some publicly mandated schemes, unions (or worker representatives) gained an institutionalized administrative role in return for their co-financing of social insurance. In some rare instances unions were able to maintain the control over voluntary insurance funds while receiving state subsidies. This is still the case for unemployment insurance in some Nordic countries (see Chapter 5). Furthermore, in addition to publicly mandated social security, unions have often negotiated supplementary occupational benefits. In particular, they have an interest in private schemes if public benefits are provided only for a basic level of income security.

The role of unions in welfare policy-making and implementation varies across countries, reflecting different political traditions and institutional legacies. On the Continent, many welfare states followed the *Bismarckian* principle: social insurance was based not only on payroll contributions paid by employers and employees, but also on their representation in the self-governing social insurance scheme. On the other hand, in the *Beveridge* tradition of state-provided social assistance to the needy, unions would not be directly involved in the administration of the basic pension and other welfare schemes. This latter broad set of countries provides an interesting variation, not only in terms of union influence in the welfare state, but also in terms of welfare regimes (Esping-Andersen 1990, 1999).

Following the classification of welfare regimes applied by Bertola *et al.* (2001), our set of countries represents the whole spectrum of European welfare regimes: namely *Nordic* (Sweden, Finland, Denmark, Norway), *Continental* (Austria, Belgium, France, Germany, the Netherlands), *Anglo-Saxon* (UK and

Ireland), and *Southern* (Greece, Italy, Portugal, Spain).[1] In order to capture these pronounced cross-national differences, in this chapter we focus on a specific group of European countries: namely, Austria, Denmark, France, Germany, Italy, the Netherlands, Sweden, and the United Kingdom. However, whenever possible a wider set of countries is considered, including the United States, Canada, and Japan.

This chapter aims at mapping union involvement in public and private social protection across different welfare regimes. We will first analyse the relationship between union movements and welfare states, comparing the different welfare regimes and industrial relations traditions. Not only these institutional legacies and organizational differences, but also the membership structure of unions has an impact on union strategies and influence in social policy. We will then study the involvement of unions in welfare states, focusing here on two social protection functions: old-age insurance and unemployment insurance. In the case of old-age insurance, we review both publicly (mandated) and private (voluntary) insurance, since unions may play a role in shaping policy-making and in participating in the administration of both. In particular, we will distinguish among the following four dimensions of union influence: (1) unions as political movements, (2) unions and self-administration in public schemes, (3) unions and private pensions, and (4) institutional participation and political veto points.

2.1. UNIONS AND WELFARE STATE DEVELOPMENT

When studying the development and scope of modern welfare states, social expenditures are commonly used as the best overall indicator for the economic resources committed to social protection.[2] The common socio-economic explanations for the long-term increase and the cross-national variations are related to three main factors: demographic structure, the labour market, and the level of economic resources (Peracchi, 1999). Thus, pension (and health) expenditures are expected to rise with an ageing population. Also, expenditures on unemployment and early retirement have increased with aggravated labour market conditions. And on a global scale, one can find that the more wealthy a nation, the higher is social spending as more economic resources are available for (re)distribution. Yet these exogenous factors can explain only a part of the long-term growth, and even less of the cross-national variations in social protection. A number of historical contingencies, institutional legacies, and

---

[1] This classification was based on each country's position in its ability to: help the poor, reduce inequality, and increase rewards from labour market participation (see Bertola *et al.*, 2001).

[2] According to Eurostat (1996), social protection is social intervention from public or private bodies to relieve households and individuals of various social risks, provided that it is mandatory and does not take place under individual arrangements. OECD and ILO social expenditure statistics differ from Eurostat owing to differences in the inclusion of private insurances, transfers from reserves, and administrative costs.

socio-political factors have led to historically developed differences in social protection, which go beyond the size of the welfare state and include societal choices about who provides social protection and under what conditions (Esping-Andersen 1990, 1999).

A fundamental difference in welfare regimes derives from the choice between two distinct principles of social protection: (1) the maintenance of living standards, i.e. income protection in case of a social risk, as first introduced in Bismarck Germany, and (2) the eradication of poverty, i.e. the guarantee of a minimum income to those with no or insufficient income from work, as pioneered by the Beveridge reforms in Great Britain. While income protection is based on distribution within a social risk pool and reproduces earnings inequality, the anti-poverty policy is based on redistribution of resources from the better-off to the poor. The Bismarckian view corresponds broadly to the provision of earnings-related benefits (typically characterized by relatively high average replacement rates), while the Beveridge tradition places more emphasis on the safety net aspect and typically adopts flat-rate benefits. These were traditionally means-tested but have become more and more general citizenship rights (also for long-term resident aliens).

The continental welfare states, including to some extent the Southern countries, conform to the Bismarckian approach, at least with respect to pension policies. The Nordic welfare states and typically the Anglo-Saxon countries conform more to the Beveridge basic pension idea, whereby coverage is universal, including all retirees, and is not related primarily to labour market activities. However, in these universal welfare systems, supplementary earnings-related pensions coexist, as voluntary occupational pensions and/or mandatory state superannuation schemes. Therefore, in practice the replacement rate of supplementary pensions on top of the Beveridge basic pension may also vary according to contributions in the Nordic and Anglo-Saxon countries, as in the case of Bismarckian social insurance. On the other hand, in the postwar period the Continental and Southern European Bismarckian welfare states have added in some cases minimum or social pension credits or even (in the Netherlands) basic pensions.

A first glance at some general indicators on welfare state regimes (see Table 2.1) indicates some clustering across Europe, though there are also significant deviations within a cluster. Esping-Andersen's (1990) measure of decommodification for the 1980s summarizes the generosity and comprehensiveness of social security for three social risks (old age, sickness, and unemployment), and serves as the basis for his clustering of countries.[3] With the exception of Finland, all Nordic universalistic welfare states show—as expected—the highest scores. They are followed at a distance by the 'Christian

---

[3] Decommodification is the extent to which individuals uphold a socially acceptable standard of living independently of market participation. It is essentially a measure of the generosity of the safety net available to non-employed individuals.

Table 2.1. *Welfare states in Western Europe, 1990s*

	Decommo-dification, 1980s[a]	Social expenditure ratio 1997[b]	Social expenditure receipts (%) 1997[c] from				Share in social expenditure (%) 1996	
			Workers	Firms	State	Others	Old-age/disability[d]	Unemployment
	(1)	(2)	(3)	(4)	(5)	(6)	(7)	(8)
North								
Denmark	38.1	31.4	17.5	8.5	67.8	6.2	49.6	13.8
Finland	29.2	29.9	13.3	35.1	44.8	6.8	48.5	13.9
Norway	38.3	28.5	14.3	23.5	61.2	1.0	48.8	5.7
Sweden	39.1	33.7	6.8	40.0	45.3	7.9	50.9	10.3
Centre								
Austria	31.1	28.8	27.1	37.7	34.6	0.6	56.6	5.7
Belgium	32.4	28.5	25.9	44.5	20.4	9.2	49.4	14.5
Germany	27.7	29.9	28.9	38.6	30.1	2.4	48.4	9.6
Netherlands	32.4	30.3	46.4	22.6	15.6	15.3	53.7	12
South								
France	27.5	30.8	27.9	49.9	20.2	1.9	49.6	8.1
Greece	—	23.6	23.4	38.0	30.3	8.3	57.6	4.3
Italy	24.1	25.9	18.0	49.3	29.6	3.1	72.9	1.9
Portugal	—	22.5	16.8	26.0	42.2	15.0	54.9	5.8
Spain	—	21.4	17.5	52.2	27.1	3.3	53.1	14.5
Anglo-Saxon								
Great Britain	23.4	26.8	15.2	25.0	47.9	11.9	52.3	5.8
Ireland	23.3	17.5	13.8	21.4	63.9	0.9	30.9	16.7
EU average	—	28.2	23.7	39.2	31.9	5.2	53.1	8.4

[a]Decommodification index (1980): combined additive measure of benefit quality, coverage, and conditions for pension, sickness, and unemployment benefits (see Esping-Andersen 1990: 54).
[b]Gross social expenditure ratio (% GDP).
[c]Or latest year available.
[d]Including survivors and disability.

Sources: (1) Esping-Andersen (1990: 52); (2)–(8) Eurostat (2000: 246 ff.); own calculations.

democratic' social insurance states of Austria, Belgium, Germany, and the Netherlands. The Anglo-Saxon liberal welfare states (Britain and Ireland) are at the bottom of the index, as Esping-Andersen's regime analysis assumes. Also, the Southern welfare states, Italy, and probably Portugal and Spain (for which no data on decommodification are given), have a lower degree of decommodification as occupational schemes and familist traditions play a role (Ferrera, 1997). Borderline cases are Finland, which is a latecomer among Nordic welfare states, and France, which is partly a Bismarckian social insurance state and a more familist Southern welfare state.

Comparing Eurostat social expenditure (as a percentage of GDP) for 1997, we find a similar pattern: social spending is highest in the Nordic and Continental welfare states (including France), while the Anglo-Saxon and Southern countries lag behind. Cross-national variations can also be found with respect to the form of financing and the expenditure structure. The relatively extensive Nordic welfare states are financed largely by general taxation, with some social insurance contributions from employees and especially employers. In the leaner Anglo-Saxon welfare states too, a relatively small share of social expenditure is financed by mandatory employment-related contributions. In contrast, the Continental social insurance states follow the Bismarckian model more closely—more than half of current expenditures are financed by payroll taxes. Yet not everywhere are the burdens shouldered equally by the two sides of industry. (The Dutch workers and the Belgian employers contribute more than their counterparts.) Finally, in the Southern and Continental welfare states social insurance contributions are also important, especially in France. As in Belgium, mandatory employer contributions exceed the share of workers in payroll taxes (see Table 2.1).

Comprehensive and efficient insurance against social risks rarely provided by private insurance markets; thus, the state has intervened by making social insurance compulsory. According to economic theory, this market failure is due to informational problems affecting the contracts that each worker should sign with a private insurance company. Unions, in particular encompassing union movements and general unions that organize unskilled and semi-skilled workers, see advantages in a mandatory social insurance. In contrast to voluntary programmes, a mandatory programme provides comprehensive coverage, thereby leading to a larger risk pool and covering also those who might not be capable of supporting themselves or who would be adversely selected under private arrangements. Once publicly mandated programmes are installed, they are likely to crowd out private arrangements, at least for the basic benefits provided under the state plan. Moreover, redistribution can be enforced under publicly mandated schemes, while in a truly voluntary scheme those that are net payers may leave when they perceive that they are subsidizing the social benefits granted to others. Thus, particularistic social groups, for instance high-level white-collar workers with market power or civil servants with political power, could gain from occupational pensions that would not redistribute resources across groups.

There are also reasons for unions to consider occupational pensions, at least as supplements to state provision. Union-run insurance could be a selected incentive for union membership. However, the odds against mutual self-help through union-provided insurance are usually high: the risk pool might be too small for union movements with low union density, membership fluctuation is often too large, and the risk is too cyclical (e.g. unemployment). Occupational private benefits could be a second-best (if not the best) solution if unions are strong enough to negotiate such schemes on a comprehensive basis. When unions have a say in running pension funds, they can influence investment decisions and secure administrative posts for their activists. However, when fringe benefits are provided unilaterally and voluntarily by employers, unions have no say at all. Moreover, when labour is weak and cannot force employers to provide comprehensive coverage, voluntary occupational benefits may lead to substantial inequality. Thus, the role and strategy of unions is contingent not only on the institutional legacy of welfare states, but also on their organizational characteristics. The organization of labour in general, as well as the character of employer–union relations, shape the opportunity structure for unions to influence social protection, whether in the form of publicly mandated, collectively negotiated, or unilateral voluntarist schemes.

A comparison of western European industrial relations systems according to qualitative and quantitative indicators reveals some clustering into four regimes similar to the welfare regimes (see Table 2.2 and Part I above). First, in terms of the organization of labour, we find systematic differences with respect to cleavage structures and mobilization patterns. When we look at the number of main confederations, and the nature of splits within the labour movement, we find substantial differences. The Nordic countries all have one social democratic labour confederation that organizes the blue-collar workers (largely in industrial unions) in particular, while white-collar workers have founded rival or separate peak organizations. The British and Irish (Anglo-Saxon) union confederations, on the other hand, are the only peak associations, though it is a relatively weak umbrella for a mixture of craft, general, and industrial unions (some of which are affiliated to the Labour Party). Political and religious splits are particularly pronounced in the Latin (Southern) labour movements. But these cleavages also have some residual importance in the Benelux countries and Switzerland, while postwar Austrian and German non-partisan unitary confederations have largely overcome these splits.

With respect to the level of unionization, measured by union density, Scandinavian (Nordic) countries are leading the ranks with constantly high unionization levels, while the Latin (Southern) labour movement reveals more cyclical patterns of political mobilization. The Continental labour movements have a medium level of membership mobilization—Belgium and Austria rank higher than Germany, the Netherlands, and Switzerland. Britain and Ireland (Anglo-Saxon) had somewhat higher levels in the past, but Britain in particular has witnessed a dramatic decline in unionization since the Thatcher government introduced new labour legislation in the 1980s.

Partly as a consequence of the concentration or fragmentation and strength or weakness of unions, important differences exist in respect to strike propensity and the volume of industrial conflicts: polarized Latin (Southern) and Anglo-Saxon labour relations, but also more recently Scandinavian (Nordic) countries, display a higher level of strikes and lockouts compared with the Continental social partnership countries.

On the side of capital, we also find considerable differences in organization, although for less political reasons. Some countries, in particular Germany and Sweden, have specialized employers' peak associations that are relatively centralized and well organized, whereas in other countries general business

Table 2.2. *Industrial relations in Western Europe, 1990s*

Country	Union movement			Employers		Collective bargaining		
	No. of peaks[a] (1)	Cleavages[b] (2)	Density[c] (3)	Peak[d] (4)	Coverage[e] (5)	Main level[f] (6)	Coverage[g] (7)	State extension[h] (8)
North								
Denmark	1.7	Collarline	75.9	EA	90–100	Sector	>80	Voluntary
Finland	2.0	Collarline	78.8	BA ind.	60–70	National	95	Mandatory
Norway	1.8	Collarline	52.5	EA	70–80	National	75	Voluntary
Sweden	2.0	Collarline	87.5	EA ind.	90–100	Sector	83	Voluntary
Centre								
Austria	1.0	—	38.9	BA	100	Sector	98	Mandatory
Belgium	2.2	Religion	59.8	BA	80–90	Nat./sector	90	Mandatory
Germany	1.4	Collarline	26.5	EA	80–90	Sector	W. 90	Mandatory
Netherlands	2.3	Collar/rel.	22.9	BA	70–80	Sector	81	Mandatory
Switzerland	2.5	Collar/rel.	22.2	EA	ca. 50	Sector	53	Mandatory
West								
Great Britain	1.4	(Pol. affil.)	32.0	BA	20–30	Firm	47	None
Ireland	1.2	(Pol. affil.)	44.4	BA	30–40	Nat./firm	>70	Mandatory
South								
France	4.2	Political	8.6	BA ind.	30–40	Sector/firm	82	Mandatory
Italy	2.5	Political	32.4	BA	70–80	Sector	70	None
Portugal	2.0	Political	31.8	BA ind.	30–40	Sector	79	Mandatory
Spain	2.3	Political	12.5	BA	60–70	Sector/firm	>70	Mandatory

[a]Number of main confederations (weighted by share) in 1990.
[b]Cleavages: religious, political and/or collarline (white vs blue-collar).
[c]Density (net): active union members as percentage of dependent labour force 1995.
[d]Major peak employer association: Ind. = industry only; EA = employer association proper, BA = business association (employer and trade association).
[e]Coverage: percentage of employees in organized firms.
[f]Level: main level of collective bargaining.
[g]Coverage: share of employees covered by collective agreements.
[h]Extension: *erga omnes* extension of collective agreements, mandatory for all firms or voluntary.

Source: Ebbinghaus and Visser (1997), Ebbinghaus and Visser (2000).

associations combine labour market and producer interests within their ranks. A low level of membership, weak centralization, and often paternalistic union opposition are particularly pronounced in the Anglo-Saxon and Latin (Southern) industrial relations systems. As a consequence, collective bargaining covers fewer workers, especially in Britain. While in the Scandinavian countries both employers and unions are well organized and therefore can enforce voluntary collective agreements throughout the economy, thus hardly needing state intervention, this is not the case elsewhere. Particularly in Latin (Southern) industrial relations, such state intervention can be crucial in extending collective agreements that have been negotiated by relatively less well organized and unrepresentative bargaining partners to larger parts of the economy. In Britain, however, no legal extension mechanisms are at the unions' disposal—which is particularly harmful given the increased decentralization of collective bargaining and the lessening recognition of unions at the workplace level.

One aspect of the relationship between welfare regimes and labour relations can be explored by looking at the correlation of unionization and welfare state indicators. Historical accounts and time-series models have found that strong union movements and the expansion of the welfare state have indeed gone together (Esping-Andersen 1990, 1999). This can also be seen from Figures 2.1 and 2.2, which plot net union density with welfare state indicators across

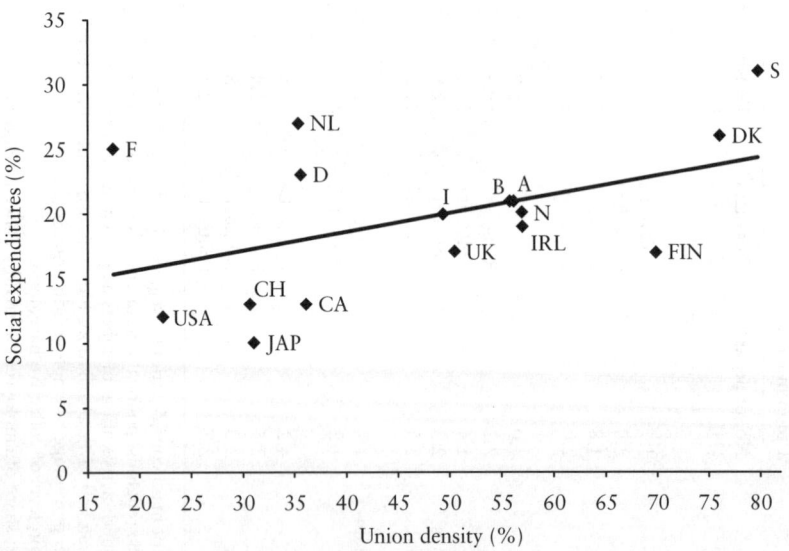

Figure 2.1. *Union density and social expenditure, 1980*

Source: Ebbinghaus and Visser (2000), Huber and Stephens (1999), OECD (1994).

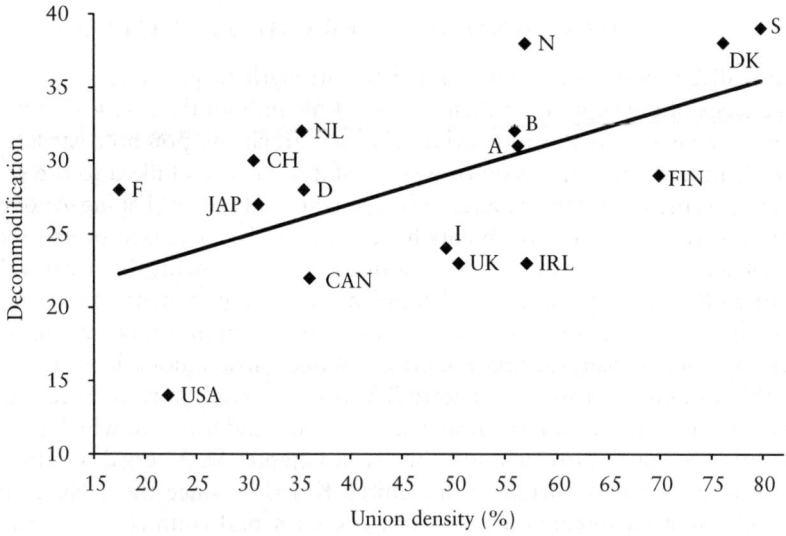

Figure 2.2. *Union density and decommodification, 1980*

Source: Ebbinghaus and Visser (2000), Esping-Andersen (1990), Huber and Stephens (1999), OECD (1994).

OECD countries for 1980. For many countries, 1980 is the year for which Esping-Andersen (1990) provides his decommodification indicator and welfare states had reached their growth limits (Flora, 1986); but it marks also a turning point in postwar union density (Ebbinghaus and Visser, 2000). When looking at social expenditure (OECD data) and decommodification cross-nationally, we can find some relationship between union density and welfare state development. The Nordic high-density countries (Sweden and Denmark) are also the highest welfare spenders, while the low-density country (the USA) is also the worst performer. Yet the relationship is not that clear-cut, as some countries, like France, have well developed welfare states, while union density in the 1980s is much lower there than would be expected. In these cases there seem to be other historical, political, etc., factors that account for the particular welfare regime. Thus, institutional factors intervene; for instance, despite low unionization, bargaining coverage is relatively comprehensive in France because of the intervention of the state via the *erga omnes* extension of collective agreements. Such state extension has made collectively negotiated occupational pensions mandatory for French employees, something the weak and divided French unions would not have been able to achieve by themselves. Moreover, it provides the unions, together with the employers, with an additional institutionalized role in the administration of these social insurance funds.

2.2. UNIONS AND MEMBERSHIP STRUCTURE

Historically, union movements gained the strength to promote social rights on the basis of the support of their rank-and-file in both the political arena (as potential voters) and the industrial relations arena (as potential strike supporters). Indeed, the expansion of welfare states has been linked to the rise of labour movements and their increased organizational power (Esping-Andersen, 1990). However, union movements have come under increased pressure over the 1980s and 1990s with the onset of mass unemployment, the decentralization of collective bargaining, the flexibilization of employment contracts, and social changes. Thus, over recent decades there has been an increasing divergence in union density across countries. While most unions have lost considerably in union density (see Figure 2.3), there is an important exception in the case of the Nordic countries, such as Denmark and Sweden, which profited from union-led unemployment insurance (see Chapter 5). A very dramatic drop in unionization has occurred in the United Kingdom since the 1980s, but in addition union movements in some of the continental countries, for instance the Netherlands, have shown a long-term decline. While about four out of five Scandinavian workers are unionized, this is the case only for every third Italian and British worker, every fourth German and Dutch worker, and every eleventh French worker (Ebbinghaus and Visser, 2000).

Indeed, it is noteworthy that four Nordic countries—Denmark, Finland, Iceland, and Sweden—had the highest unionization rates in the early 1990s. These countries had membership rates exceeding 70%, with Sweden ranking top with a density of over 80%. On the other hand, union density in Norway, where unemployment insurance is now compulsory and state-run, is only around 55%, a remarkable difference from Sweden, given the similarities between the two countries in other dimensions. The four countries with the highest membership rates organize their unemployment insurance systems through trade union affiliated funds with voluntary membership. These funds are generously supported by the government. The practice of organizing unemployment insurance through government-subsidized but union-administered unemployment funds is often referred to as the 'Ghent system', after the Belgian town where it was first introduced in 1901 (Western, 1997). Unemployment insurance in most other OECD countries is based on compulsory rather than voluntary systems. Belgium practises an intermediate system with compulsory unemployment insurance but union involvement in the benefit administration, which provides a similar selective incentive for joining a union. The large difference between union density in Belgium and the Netherlands can be explained partly by the involvement of unions in Belgian unemployment insurance.

While most union movements find it difficult to organize the unemployed and young people, they retain increasingly more and more non-actives, especially pensioners. This trend is most pronounced among Southern European

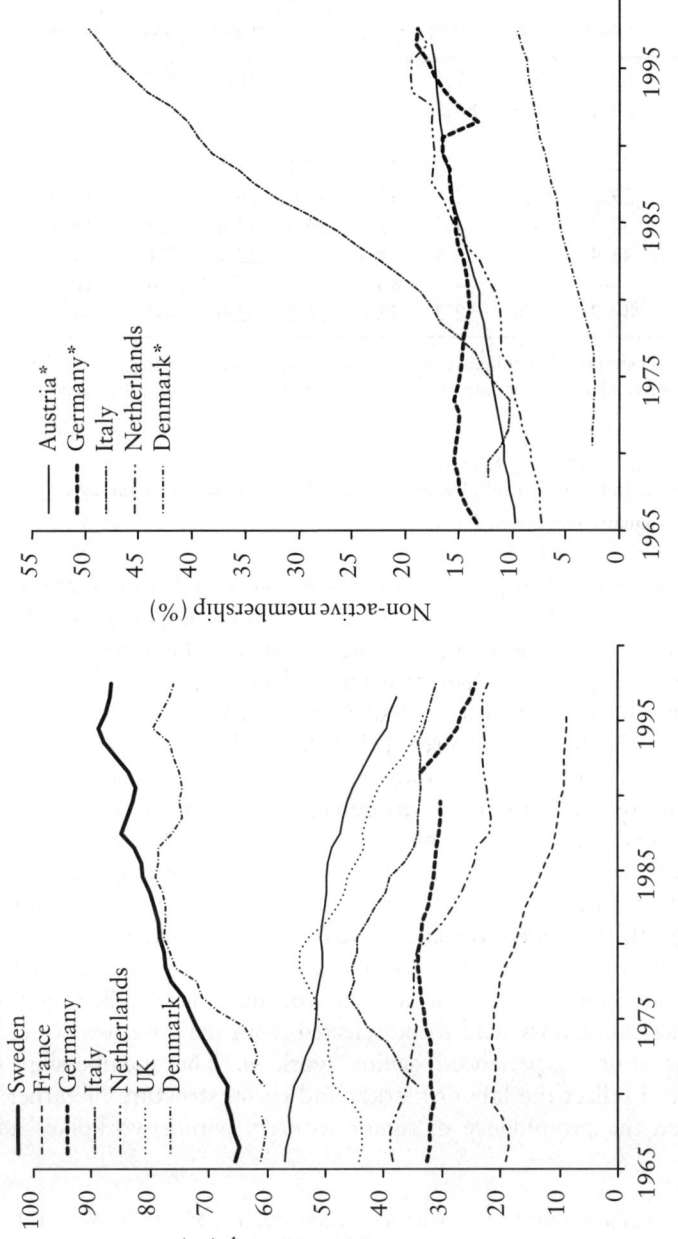

Figure 2.3. *Net union density and non-active membership (%)*

Table 2.3. *Union density and non-active members in Western Europe*

	Gross density (%)			Net density (%)			Non-active members (%)		
	1965	1980	1995	1965	1980	1995	1965	1980	1995
Austria	63.0	58.4	47.1	56.9	50.8	38.9	9.7	13.1	17.2[e]
Denmark	61.1	80.6	85.5	—	77.5	75.9	—	3.8	8.7[e]
									[~15.0]
France	—	—	—	19.1	17.1	8.6	—	—	[~25.0][x]
Germany	37.7	39.1	32.3	32.7	33.6	26.5	13.3	14.0	17.9[e]
Italy	32.7	54.5	61.5	28.7	44.4	32.4	12.2	18.5	47.4[r]
Netherlands	41.4	36.6	28.4	38.4	32.4	22.9	7.1	11.6	19.3[r]
Sweden	—	—	—	65.4	78.2	87.5	[6.4]	[10.9]	[15.3][x]
UK	44.2	52.8	32.2	42.6	52.2	32.0	—	—	—[m]

Notes: Net density: total members (excluding non-actives) as a percentage of the dependent labour force; non-active members include (in some cases) students, conscripts, and unemployed.
[e] Estimated.
[r] Reported.
[x] Not included in membership figures.
[m] Minimal rate, Italy 1965, 1968; UK net density, 1995, Labour Force Survey.

Source: Ebbinghaus and Visser, 2000.

union movements. Unique in Europe is the very high representation of non-actives in Italy: half of all members are not in employment (see Table 2.3).[4] Also across Continental and Nordic countries, the rates of 'non-actives' (including groups other than pensioners) have risen over time: most union movements have reached a level of between 15% and 25%, still markedly lower than the Italian rate (see Table 2.3), whereas in Britain and Ireland unions traditionally organize only the gainfully employed. Most frequently, pensioners remain organized in public-sector unions, especially railways and civil service grades. For instance, in Austria (1994) 40% of members in the railway workers' union, nearly 30% in the postal workers' union, and around 20% in the other public sector unions are retirees (Ebbinghaus and Visser, 2000). Union movements have increasingly encountered problems in attempting to organize the younger workers, so the membership structure has become increasingly aged. But also, at workplace level union shop stewards and works councillors tend to be selected from the core workforce, and are often the more experienced senior workers. The membership structure does indeed reflect the labour market and social structure of earlier decades, and, given the prominence of senior workers within workplace and union

---

[4] Within the three main Italian union movements (CGIL: 55%, CISL: 50%, UIL: 27% non-actives in 1997), the pensioner unions (SPI, FNP, UILP respectively) are, at least since the 1980s, the largest affiliates. In the other countries, information on pensioners is less readily available as these members remain with their union after retirement and often are not explicitly reported, even if they pay reduced union dues.

decision-making structures, union movements face a severe *seniority bias*, not only in interest representation but also in their policies, as will be argued later.

2.3 UNIONS AS A POLITICAL MOVEMENT

Union movements have been major advocates for welfare state expansion. They have used not only classic pressure group lobbyism, but also links with allied political parties to advance labour and social rights. Early examples include the British unions, which founded the Trades Union Congress as a platform in order to influence Parliament in its labour and social policy legislation as early as the 1860s. The British unions also sponsored the campaign of selected members of Parliament, and at the turn of century founded the Labour Party, which they have supported and dominated through collective affiliation for most of its existence. In many Continental and Nordic countries it was the social democratic party that promoted the foundation of a union confederation. Political party and trade unions were two wings within the same socialist labour movement. In Britain and Scandinavia, the links between the (blue-collar) unions and the Labour or Social Democratic Parties remained institutionalized for most of the postwar period. This certainly brought advantages when the Left was in government, but disadvantages when they were not, most notably under Thatcher's Conservative government. In recent years, the British Labour Party and the Scandinavian political parties have attempted to de-emphasize their formal union links. In particular, New Labour has been reluctant to make campaign promises to unions before elections; indeed, once in power the Blair government reversed Conservative anti-union legislation only partly, departing from the traditional repeal of a former Tory government's acts.

In some Continental countries religious union movements have emerged and maintained links with Christian democratic parties. However, in France and Southern countries syndicalist union movements rejected the parliamentary parties and electoral avenue, but were later replaced by union movements that came to be dominated by communists and maintained close ties to the communist party, while other religious–political movements competed with them for worker allegiance. These different political legacies still play a role with respect to the fragmentation of labour movements and party–union ties, although there has been some, at times significant, change. Most notably, the postwar German union confederation (DGB) was founded as a unitary movement, abandoning the formal ties with the Social Democratic Party. The Austrian union confederation (ÖGB) also encompasses different political movements, but allows these to organize along party political lines and to maintain close ties with the respective parties. In the Netherlands, the initially very pillorized organizational landscape was remodelled when the socialist and Catholic union movements merged in the 1980s, with the new Dutch union confederation (FNV) maintaining a more distant relationship with former political allies (Labour Party and the newly merged Christian Democratic Party).

In three continental countries (Austria, Germany, and the Netherlands), union members play an important role in both party families, and labour interests thus have a means of influencing at least one ruling party at any time. In Austria since 1970 the Social Democrats governed alone or in coalition (partly with the Christian Democrats) until 1999, providing the unions with close ties to the government. In Germany, the Kohl government within its own coalition often had to balance the welfare retrenchment position[5] of its liberal coalition partner and the status quo defending social unionist wing within the Christian Democratic Party. Moreover, German pension reforms have been traditionally an interparty compromise, though finding a consensus between incumbent and opposition parties became more difficult in the 1990s. By the same token, the inclusion of union-friendly left-wing parties may also facilitate blame avoidance (Pierson, 1994). Thus, the Dutch Christian Democrats were able to push through unpopular reforms when they brought the Labour Party into a coalition government from 1989 to 1994. But this does not necessarily mean that incumbent parties can easily influence union politics; indeed, government efforts towards welfare retrenchment have come under criticism by unions.

In the Latin countries with their contentious Southern labour relations, political cleavages have led to political union pluralism, which often increases competition among unions and hampers unity. In France, the Left was excluded from governing for most of the postwar period until Socialist Mitterand's presidency. The Socialist Party has some (informal) support from the CFDT (Confédération Française Democratique du Travail), while the CGT (Confédération Générale du Travail) is closely allied with the Communist Party and the other union movements are not linked to particular parties. In Italy the Social Democrats and Socialists governed in coalitions with the Christian Democrats until 1992, giving the non-communist union movements some influence in government circles, although the Communist Party, and indirectly its ally, the largest union movement (CGIL), remained excluded from power. With the political crisis and realignment of the party system in the 1990s, the three Italian union movements have grown closer together and have consorted with centre–left governments (see Chapter 4).

Party–union ties are important not only with respect to the influence of unions on allied political parties, but also in the reverse direction. Thus, incumbent parties may seek to gain support from their allied unions, for instance in terms of wage moderation or to gain their acquiescence *vis-à-vis* unpopular welfare reforms. Yet French left-wing governments most of the time found only the CFDT to be a willing cooperative partner, as the communist and

---

[5] A position in favour of welfare cuts aimed at reducing or stabilizing social expenditure.

other unions tended to take a more hostile approach to reform plans. In Italy, however, the participation of the reformed ex-communist party (PDS) in the centre–left governments of the 1990s provided a more favourable environment for CGIL's cooperation and paved the way for concentration supported by all three union movements and the government.

In light of the changes in the membership structure outlined above, it is no surprise that unions have lobbied for the interests of current pensioners or those workers close to retirement. In the past, organized labour and allied political parties have mobilized for the expansion of welfare benefits. Especially in countries with social democratic governments that had close ties with the labour movements, most notably in Scandinavia, social security and public services were expanded over the postwar period (Esping-Andersen, 1990). But Christian democratic governments, sometimes in coalition with social democrats, also expanded social transfers, following Christian democratic social teaching and demands by its worker wings (Kersbergen, 1995). At the same time, status division among the workforce has been reflected in union structures. For instance, separate organizations for white-collar workers have been linked to different social rights manipulated by divide-and-rule strategies by employers and the state. Similarly, public employees have been given special pension rights in return for loyalty to the state, and special interest organizations defend these status differences.

2.4. UNIONS AND SOCIAL INSURANCE ADMINISTRATION

While unemployment insurance in most countries is provided via mandatory state schemes, in some countries unions assume a role in the self-administration of these funds and also in labour market administration (see Table 2.4). In Germany the unions are represented on the tripartite boards of the Labour Office, which is in charge of unemployment insurance and employment services. In Italy the unemployment schemes are run by the Social Insurance Institute, which is governed by a tripartite board. In the Netherlands the bipartite sector schemes have recently become controlled by a tripartite institute. In France unemployment insurance has been run by the social partners (hence not by individual unions, as under the Ghent system) following a collective agreement in 1958 and is financed largely by employer contributions. A particular role is also played by unions in labour market administration in Germany, the Netherlands, Denmark, and most importantly Sweden, where extensive active labour market policies helped reduce unemployment and thus benefited union-run unemployment schemes.

In several countries the social partners also play a role in the administration of other branches of social insurance. When the first public social insurance system was introduced in Bismarck Germany in the 1880s, self-administration by employers and workers was introduced in return for their joint financial

Table 2.4. *Governance in unemployment insurance and labour market administration*

	Unemployment insurance	Labour market administration
Austria	Mandatory unemployment insurance (1920) under Ministry of Social Administration, employer and employee contributions, state subsidies for assistance	Local and regional labour offices under Ministry of Social Administration
Denmark	Voluntary union-run unemployment funds (Ghent system, since 1933 state subsidies), supervised by Ministry of Labour	Employment exchange run by local unemployment fund
France	Voluntary unemployment scheme (UNEDIC) run by social partners (since 1958, collective agreement)	ANPE (1967–), national public agency with local offices, administered by Labour Ministry
Germany	Mandatory public insurance scheme (1928–) run by Federal Labour Office (tripartite administration), employer and employee contributions plus state subsidy	Local and regional branches of Federal Labour Office (tripartite administration), state subsidy
Italy	Separate schemes, including industrial redundancy scheme (CIG), administered by INPS (tripartite board)	Local and regional offices of labour
Netherlands	WW (1952–) short-term unemployment insurance: bipartite industrial insurance boards controlled by tripartite Social Insurance Council, since 1995: LISV (tripartite board) WWV (1965–) + RWW long-term unemployment and social assistance: local government, controlled by Social Ministry	Since 1991 tripartite employment boards (replace 1930 labour exchanges)
Sweden	Voluntary union-run unemployment funds (Ghent system, since 1934 state subsidies), supervised by AMS Since 1974 unemployment assistance for the uninsured by county labour market board	Local employment service, supervised by National Labour Market Board (AMS; since 1949, tripartite)
UK	National Insurance Fund (job-seekers' allowance), administered by ministry	Employment offices under Department of Employment administration

Source: Flora (1986: Appendix vol.); MISSOC, database.

contribution and in order to limit the authority of the central state. Such self-administration by the social partners was institutionalized in old-age insurance in continental European countries, while the Scandinavian and British basic pension schemes were initially only tax-financed basic pensions under sole government supervision.

There are also variations among continental European systems (see Table 2.5): they differ in their representativity (tripartite or bipartite, parity or unequal representation) and in their selection of representatives (social elections or nomination by organizations). Union movements, especially in pluralist union systems, can gain legitimization by winning votes in social elections. Even if they have only a low unionization rate, democratic social elections help them to claim representativity for the entire workforce. Moreover, representatives receive compensation for their participation in administrative functions, and this can provide an extra source of income for union officials. For instance, French unionists are heavily financed by the state and social insurance schemes for their participation in self-administrative functions, from vocational training to pension schemes.[6] Thus, by providing reimbursement of expenses, the social insurance boards, sickness funds, or unemployment schemes at national, regional, and local levels finance, at least partly, many positions for full-time union officials. The recent threat by French employers to withdraw from social security boards in retaliation for the 35-hour working week legislation has led to a major debate over the future of self-administration in France.

Nevertheless, self-administration does not necessarily have an impact on policy-making. In many cases the contribution and benefit levels are set by government or parliament. And even when the state has no direct control, governments can increase their influence by providing subsidies and shifting financing towards general taxation. This was the deliberate strategy of the French governments of the 1990s, whether left or right-wing. By financing an increasing share of public pensions out of general taxes, successive French governments sought to get to grips with rising expenditures through tighter state control.

On the other hand, the state may also hold the social partners hostage by shifting costs on to their shoulders. Thus, after German unification, the Kohl government levied some of the social transfers to the East on to the social insurance system, which then called for increases in social contributions and pushed labour costs up. In addition, social insurance contributions were already providing solidarity functions, such as credits for child-rearing or years of education; the new red–green Schröder government, which came into

---

[6] In the words of a French unionist, 'unions need financial assistance... Only 8% of all French workers and only 6% of those in the private sector pay dues to a trade union. Unions cannot continue to exist and defend employees in the workplace on only 1,000 Francs per year, per member'.

Table 2.5. *Governance in social policy-making, public pension schemes, and private occupational pensions*

	Corporatist policy-making	Self-administration in pension scheme	Collective/private occupational schemes
Austria	Statutory Chamber of Labour (elected worker representatives), statutory consultation in policy-making	Tripartite self-administration of seven occupational pension funds[a]	Recently: supplementary private pensions
Denmark	None (occasionally: tripartite royal commissions)	None (public pension scheme supervised by ministry: basic pension administered locally, supplementary pension centrally)	Collectively negotiated and private occupational pension schemes; collective negotiated early retirement pay (efterløn)
France	Statutory Social and Economic Council (worker, employer and general interest representatives), statutory consultation in policy-making	National, regional, and local funds governed by state-nominated director, but bipartite board (social elections)[b]	Supplementary pensions set-up by collective agreements (1947—cadres, 1961—other employees; made compulsory in 1972); two federations of various local funds governed by bipartite boards
Germany	None (Sozialbeirat advisory to ministry)	Bipartite self-administration of regional blue-collar or central white-collar schemes (social elections)[a]	In private sector: voluntary occupational pensions by employers; in public sector: collectively negotiated scheme for non-tenured public employees
Italy	Statutory National Labour Council, consultation role	Public national institute (tripartite board nominated by organizations)[a]	Since 1990s: collectively negotiated sectoral pension funds
Netherlands	Statutory Social–Economic Council (tripartite), consultation in policy-making; voluntary bipartite Labour Foundation makes policy recommendations	Public pension scheme (bipartite self-administration by labour councils, supervised by Social Insurance Council; since 1995, tripartite central supervision)	Sector-wide occupational schemes (bipartite, sometimes *erga omnes* extension); also sector-wide early retirement schemes (VUT, bipartite)
Sweden	None (occasional tripartite royal commissions)	None (public pension scheme supervised by ministry)	Collective negotiated four (two private, two public sector) major occupational pensions (bipartite)
UK	None (royal commissions may include union representatives)	None (public basic and supplementary pension schemes supervised by ministry)	Voluntary private pension trusts sponsored by firm (rarely worker representatives on board), opt-out option of state supplementary pension

[a] Contribution and benefits are set by legislator.
[b] French employers threatened to withdraw from social administration in retaliation to 35-hr law.

Sources: Ebbinghaus and Hassel (2000); Flora (1986: Appendix vol.); EIRR, passim; EIRO, passim; MISSOC, database.

power in 1998, introduced green taxes to subsidize these social benefits and reduce social insurance contributions accordingly. Still, the principle of parity representation and half-and-half cost-sharing, enshrined in postwar German social insurance, was also upheld with the introduction of a new old-age care insurance by the Kohl government in 1995, though at the insistence of employers one former public holiday became a full working day as partial compensation for increasing labour costs at a time of increased competition.

Nevertheless, worker representatives may play an important role in the implementation of policies, as self-administrated schemes, particularly at the local level, may be able to ignore or even counteract policy changes decided by the central state. In the French system, the supplementary pension system is organized by a plethora of national, regional, and local funds run by the social partners and divided according to occupational groups. In such a fragmented system responsibilities are diluted, and changes decided at the centre tend to be unevenly implemented. The Dutch disability insurance is another case in point: the government found it difficult to enforce a tightening of eligibility rules, since the social partners were misusing their supervisory role in the multiple-sector insurance boards. As a consequence, the Dutch government shifted from changing the statutory rules to redesigning the governance system in order to bring about change (Visser and Hemerijck, 1997). Instead of the paralysed phalanx of postwar corporatist institutions, the left–liberal government introduced a new independent body to supervise, and a new tripartite institute to implement, changes in the mid-1990s. Indeed, state intervention to restore public responsibility in a self-administrative governance structure may be a precondition for the effectiveness of welfare reforms in corporatist societies, where social partners have used their institutional role to form coalitions at the expense of the general public.

2.5. UNIONS AND OCCUPATIONAL WELFARE

In addition to the institutionalized role that unions might play in social insurance administration, they might also gain or lose in influence from the increasing importance of private occupational welfare. Today many wage-earners receive private occupational pensions, typically as a supplement to rather than a substitute for public pensions. Significant differences exist as to the coverage, governance, and scope of occupational pensions cross-nationally and also within each country. Occupational pensions when provided voluntarily by employers do not leave much space for union involvement. For instance, British employers are free to decide on occupational pensions, though they have to follow state regulation when opting out of the earnings-related state scheme and in order to profit from favourable tax treatment. However, if occupational pensions are negotiated by the social partners, unions have a direct involvement and private pensions become part of the wage bargaining process. But the state may also help, not so much by regulation as by making collectively negotiated pensions binding to all firms in an industry, as is often the case in the Netherlands.

Among the countries with traditionally employer sponsored schemes are Germany and Britain. In Germany, the earnings-related social insurance provides the largest share of retirement income, yet the coverage of occupational schemes is substantial (most non-tenured public employees and half of all private employees), although, except for higher-paid white-collar employees, it supplements less than 20% of pension income. Many larger German private employers also provide voluntary occupational pensions (via book reserves, insurance plans, or pension funds), yet works councils and workers have only a limited say. Occupational and private pensions play a more important role in Britain, as one can opt out from the public earnings-related scheme. Currently, about two-thirds of employees are covered by private or occupational pension plans, the majority by company plans (Bonoli, 1999). But British pension funds are sponsored by the employer, who also nominates the trustees, while the workers (or their unions) have usually no representation rights. In other countries, such as Austria and Italy, employer-sponsored occupational pensions remained until recently relatively unimportant, and unions were in favour of extending state rather than private pensions.

Unions are much more involved in other cases, where occupational pensions are negotiated. In Sweden, coverage by collective occupational schemes is nearly universal through comprehensive collective agreements.[7] These private pensions have thus far only supplemented (by about 10%) the basic and earnings-related public pension, though their importance will increase in the future. In France, occupational pension was made mandatory by state legislation for most workers, so coverage is virtually universal.[8] Since public pensions typically provide not more than 50% of final pay, the occupational pension makes a significant contribution to maintaining the standard of living, especially for higher earning employees. In the Dutch pension system, occupational pensions in both private and public sectors are nearly as widespread, as a result of collective agreements (some extended *erga omnes* by the state). They contribute to a sizeable share of income during old age, since the public scheme provides only a universal flat-rate benefit, regardless of previous employment records. Denmark has a mixture of partly negotiated and partly

---

[7] In Sweden, four major supplementary occupational pension schemes have been established by collective agreements. They are run by the unions in the blue-collar, white-collar, central state, and local state sectors and by the respective employers' associations.

[8] The first supplementary insurance was introduced by the organizations for managerial and professional staff ('*cadres*') in 1947, a collective agreement for other workers was signed in 1961, and supplementary pension was made mandatory in 1972. Two federations, for cadres and for employees, coordinate the many occupational, regional, and local funds that exist and are governed by bipartite boards with employer and union representatives.

individual pension schemes, while in Germany public employees (other than tenured civil servants) have a negotiated occupational pension scheme. Recently the first occupational pensions have been negotiated in Italy.

Thus, traditionally, in countries with a Bismarckian welfare system, public pensions, characterized by earnings-related benefits and by high replacement rates, have tended to crowd out occupational pensions. On the other hand, under a Beveridge system, the basic pension scheme, especially when limited to flat-rate benefits, has generated demand for more substantial 'second-tier', contribution-related pension. Moreover, much depends on who sets up occupational pensions—whether unions can negotiate occupational welfare, or the terms are set unilaterally by employers. In addition, the state may intervene by regulating 'voluntary' private pensions or by extending *erga omnes* collective agreements to the non-organized.

These specific public–private mixes thus establish the opportunity structure for trade unions and influence their strategies. In negotiated systems, employers and unions play a larger role in welfare provision, often filling the gap left by public policy. Thus, cuts in public welfare benefits might be compensated by improvements in collectively negotiated occupational schemes. However, these occupational benefits would have to be negotiated, and thus might require a trade-off with wage growth. Unions would therefore have to find a balance between the short-term interests of their employed members and the long-term interests of current and future pensioners. Independent of the governance, the public–private mix will also determine how much of the overall welfare costs are 'privatized' and thus internalized by employers and/or employees. This might induce a greater cost awareness of pension spending on the side of the unions, while in public schemes unions would have the option to press for a higher state subsidy rather than for larger contributions and/or cuts in benefits.

Thus, rent-seeking is most pronounced in pension arrangements that cover only a small segment of employees but are financed out of general taxation. (For instance, German civil servants' pensions are financed not by contributions but out of the public budget.) Therefore, public-sector unions may have lower incentives to accept benefit cuts than unions with schemes that would lead to higher employee contributions. The more likely it is for pension schemes to become privatized, and for them to be publicly funded, the less possible will rent-seeking be by any particular group at the expense of the general public. But also, the less possible will solidarity (redistribution) be, and the larger the inequalities in coverage and benefits, unless state regulation or strong unions as bargaining partners can raise universal standards.

2.6. INSTITUTIONAL AND POLITICAL VETO POINTS

Pensioners and those of early retirement age make up a sizeable share of the electorate: today in most European countries about one-third of all voters are above 55 (Walker, 1999: 21). Although pensioners' organizations have emerged in most countries, however, unions are still a major pressure group in pension politics and they often have an institutionalized role in social policy decision-making (see Table 2.5). The legislator and governments consult with unions informally, and in some countries consultation of such social partners (unions and employers' associations) is formally institutionalized. As in EU social policy-making, where the European Economic and Social Committee has to be formally consulted, several Continental countries have statutory tripartite councils for social policy consultation, sometimes dating back to state corporatist legacies. Given the relatively heterogeneous and indirect interest representation by these corporatist institutions, the impact on law-making and policy-making is rather limited, though it may shape public debates by voicing the plurality of interests at stake. France's very heterogeneous and divided Economic and Social Council (CES, since 1947) has the broadest statutory consultation role, but it has often been instrumentalized (or just ignored) by governments. The Dutch Social–Economic Council (SER, since 1950) has been influential in the heyday of corporatist consultation, but its more recent reform proposals have been overturned several times by the government. The Italian National Labour Council plays a rather secondary consultation role. The largest influence is granted to the Austrian Chambers (labour, commerce and industry, agriculture), which are formally part of social policy-making (and collective bargaining).[9] Since labour, capital, and agricultural interests are represented separately, approval by all Chambers requires informal compromises struck by the main associations.

Such formal consultation has not been introduced in Germany or Scandinavia, though informal consultation with the social partners does take place and reform commissions include traditionally organizational representatives in addition to experts. In the UK, policy proposals have often been developed by partisan policy institutes, and royal commissions may include individuals connected to particular interest groups. However, the British government has probably the greatest leeway in formulating policy proposals.

In the case of unilateral welfare retrenchment by governments, often collective protests have emerged, ranging from one-day mass demonstrations as in the Netherlands in 1991 to month-long mass strikes as in France in 1995. Despite declining density rates, union movements are still the largest collective mass organizations in modern industrial societies, and so the rather unusual mobilization of their membership to protest a government policy sends a major political signal. When in the summer of 1991 the Dutch left–centre government announced major welfare cuts, the unions mounted the largest postwar demonstration (one million people) ever in the streets of the capital (Visser and Hemerijck, 1997: 117). This struggle also divided the Labour Party, but Kok as

---

[9] The representatives to these statutory Chambers are elected at regional level. (Membership in the Chamber of Commerce and Industry is compulsory for firms; in the Labour Chamber the different political currents stand for election.)

party chairman was able to win a majority vote for the government plan at a special party congress. Yet the next election in 1994 brought major losses in votes for both the Social Democrats and the Christian Democrats. Mass demonstrations have largely a discursive and symbolic function: they voice a protest in the public debate and indicate that more severe political consequences may follow from unilateral state action. Since union movements are still mass organizations, politicians may worry about the electoral consequences, though much depends on the rules of the electoral system and the majority position of the government at the time. Moreover, unions may counteract in the collective bargaining realm what they have lost by changes in the law. A good example is the unsuccessful attempt of Germany's government to reduce sick pay by legislative means from 100% to 80% of the current wage, since unions managed to fill this gap and reinstall the 100% level by collective bargaining (Schludi, 1997).

An even more severe threat than demonstrations may be strike action against the government. The French strike wave in the winter of 1995, following the retrenchment plans by the Conservative government under Juppé, is a case in point. In particular, the efforts to cut the special pension schemes in the public sector (in line with unopposed cuts in the private sector that were introduced by the Balladur government in 1993) led to a massive spontaneous strike by public-sector workers who later were supported by their unions and the general public. The government, after *ad hoc* consultation with the unions, back-tracked, postponing the major cuts in the public-sector pension schemes. A year earlier, major demonstrations and strikes against retrenchment efforts by the Berlusconi government had been successful in bringing down the Conservative government and leading to concertation with the new centre–left Dini government on a consensual welfare reform.

Under Britain's Westminster political system and its centralized social security system, UK governments have more degrees of freedom for unilateral action. In particular, the strategy of the Conservative Thatcher government to 'take the unions on' in the industrial relations realm by removing existing union immunities, regulating strike ballots, and abolishing closed shops successfully weakened British unions. Moreover, the symbolic victory over the miners' strike in 1984/5 provided a further indication of how weak British unions were when facing a government determined to privatize public services. Nevertheless, welfare retrenchment in popular public programmes, especially the National Health Service, remained more limited and gradual. Thus, even where unions do not dispose of formal veto points to block government action, they might cause governments to abstain from welfare cuts by mobilizing public support (Pierson, 1994). Therefore, governments have an incentive to consult and even negotiate with unions (Ebbinghaus and Hassel, 2000). Especially in pension reform, the route of (formal or informal) consultation and negotiation has been preferred in most industrialized countries in recent years (Reynaud 2000); this will be analysed in Chapter 4.

In this chapter we have shown that unions have played an important but varying role in the development and organization of social policy. Not only can we detect different welfare regimes reflecting particular historical and institutional legacies, but also, variations in industrial relations have led to different involvements of unions in policy-making and the implementation of welfare policies. Having looked mainly at pension and unemployment insurance, we found cross-national variations across the union system in political influence, veto power, institutionalized consultation, self-administration, and involvement in occupational welfare. Thus, unions have numerous ways of influencing welfare policies. The question remains, what are their strategies, and whose interests are they representing? A first analysis of union membership and decision-making structures has indicated that unions are prone to have a seniority bias towards senior workers (those close to retirement) and retired workers (pensioners). How this seniority bias might lead to status quo and rent-seeking behaviour will be discussed in the next chapter.

3

Unions and Pensions: Theory, Evidence, and Implications

In our introduction we highlighted that the typical union:

1. engages in wage bargaining and rent-sharing activities in non-(perfectly) competitive product markets; and
2. expresses 'voice' at the workplace and provides directly (or indirectly) social services and social protection to union members.

In both of these areas, what unions do is closely linked to how welfare states operate. Unions will bargain for higher wages when the state provides greater unemployment insurance and social pensions funded out of general revenues, despite potential losses of employment. Union voice in turn can greatly influence social policies. In some cases union policies or stances on public policies can yield welfare state outcomes that create more efficient insurance to workers subject to economic risk. In other cases, however, they may produce inefficient outcomes, biased towards senior members at the cost of workers in general. This chapter examines these issues in the area of pensions. It develops the economic theory of how unions go about setting policies on pensions; presents empirical evidence on their impact on occupational pensions and policies on state pensions and early retirement options; and examines how union activities depend on labour relations institutions.

We do not attempt a close inspection of the normative issues, but rather aim to develop the positive political economy implications of the effects of unions on pension policies and reforms. The principal message is that for a variety of reasons union policies show a seniority bias in policies on pensions, favouring outcomes that reward more senior workers at the expense of younger workers. This policy, however, can harm union membership and power, as it makes unions less attractive to younger and more mobile workers.

3.1. WHAT UNIONS DO TO PENSIONS: ECONOMIC THEORY

In this chapter we lay out a framework to analyse what trade unions do to occupational pensions and their attitude towards state pensions. The basic analysis treats unions as a monopoly agent, able to determine wages and pensions subject to an employment constraint and the need to pay for promised pensions. It shows that union bargaining on pensions is biased towards senior workers, which has inefficient employment consequences, and that the union stance depends on state welfare policies.

We first consider union preferences for occupational pensions versus wages and employment. Occupational pensions are collective insurance schemes for old age offered by employers to employees within a firm or an industry. In Chapter 2 we discussed the involvement of unions in occupational welfare, and in Chapter 4 we document the importance of occupational pensions in many countries and the variation in the public–private pension mix across countries. There are advantages and disadvantages in insuring pensions (1) through a collectively bargained fund of the type we will examine, (2) through a state-run fund, which the social security literature analyses, or (3) through individual arrangements, say with an insurance company or a personal pension contract as in the UK. Collectively bargained pension funds have economies of scale, so that the loading factors on the insurance contract are mitigated. They also allow unions to pressure employers to make a contribution to pensions that might be more difficult if workers bought annuities individually from union-won wage gains. In an economy characterized by uncertainty about future outcomes, there also exists a more general efficiency argument justifying the involvement of unions in private pension provisions, which has been over-looked in the past. Individual contracts between employers and employees cannot be enforced, as employers cannot credibly commit to pay due pensions and promised deferred payments. In fact, employers may be unable to lock up-front the whole intertemporal payment that is actuarially fair to workers in the presence of adverse economic shocks. The role of unions is to help make such a commitment credible. But group insurance often reduces the portability of pension rights, while the back-loaded nature of most defined benefit pensions provides an advantage for employees who stay on at the expense of more mobile workers.

Privately provided pensions, whether set by firm policy or collectively bargained, come at the expense of wages or other potential gains to workers, and thus are best regarded as deferred wages and part of the employment contract. The idea that pensions are fringe benefits and therefore part of union bargaining goes back to Freeman (1981), who argued that unions weighted pensions more heavily in their objective function than they would be weighted in competitive markets. This is because workers who are more attached to the firm generally have more weight within the union; and they tend to be older workers, who benefit more from a given pension plan than younger workers, who are invariably more mobile and may leave before they can gain the benefits of the plan. Even when unions represent the median member, they will give greater weight to the preferences of older workers relative to younger workers than do competitive markets. Unions represent infra-marginal workers, while markets respond to marginal workers. The pensions that unionized firms gain are a substantial part of union seniority advantages.

Consistent with their seniority bias, unions generally favour defined benefit plans rather than defined contribution plans: it is only with defined benefit plans that young workers subsidize the pensions of older workers. Pension funds of a defined benefit form have prevailed in the UK, in the USA, and in the Netherlands. Defined benefits are higher for workers who are loyal to the firm—'stayers'—because they are more likely to fulfil vesting rules and because the amount of a pension often depends on the last few years' earnings. Since pensions are received in the future, and are usually based on years of seniority or final years' pay, a worker who leaves may be unable to claim a defined benefit pension from the original firm or may receive a defined benefit much lower than a 'stayer', other things being equal (Askildsen and Ireland, 1997). For their part, firms often prefer lower vesting of pensions in order to keep workers with them and reduce turnover cost. But this could produce lower overall mobility than would be optimal for the economy more broadly. At the same time, there exists a potential role of commitment by unions on the delivery of long-term benefits when the firm cannot guarantee a credible commitment.

The interaction of unions with government pensions is more complex, since in this case unions do not have to trade off wages or other benefits for pensions as they do in collective bargaining. Public pensions will, after all, be paid through the tax system, so that persons other than union members are likely to foot at least some of the pension bill. It is not surprising then that unions seem to favour public pensions over private arrangements and that they often favour preserving the status quo in public pensions when it comes to a retrenchment on pension policies (see Chapter 4). Moreover, whatever the union role in setting public pensions, the level of those pensions will affect union bargaining for occupational pensions, as the following analysis shows.

3.1.1. *Union behaviour with a homogeneous workforce*

We examine the factors that determine union policies towards pensions with a simple economic model of union behaviour (see the Appendix). In this model, workers are concerned with their current wage and with their expected retirement income, which depends on an occupational pension and a public old-age benefit. Occupational pensions depend on employment status, whereas publicly provided old-age benefits are given to the previously unemployed as well as to previously employed workers. Occupational pensions are part of the employment package, collectively bargained. Public pensions are financed through a payroll tax levied on workers throughout the economy.

In this model workers are either employed, whereby they receive a wage and the promise of an occupational pension, or unemployed. Workers have no access to credit/insurance markets, while the firm has perfect access to these markets, so that unions can improve worker well-being by providing old-age or other forms of insurance. Following Freeman and Medoff (1984), and

Askildsen and Ireland (1997), we assume that workers are uncertain about whether they will receive their pensions since economic conditions may cost them their jobs. The probability that they will remain attached to a firm and thus gain their pension is a key determinant of the utility that workers derive from pensions and thus of union bargaining for pensions. An unemployed worker receives an unemployment benefit when young and the state pension when old, but does not receive any occupational benefit.

The union bargains for wages and pensions. Its goal is to maximize the welfare of the representative member who may be employed or unemployed with given probabilities. The firm has the 'right to manage', and thus determines employment. This means that there is some inefficiency in union rent extraction, but it is generally regarded as the most realistic assumption for an analysis of collective bargaining (Oswald, 1982). The firm sells a product, which generates revenue that is increasing in the employment level, but at a decreasing rate. The firm seeks to maximize profits and determines employment depending on the cost of labour that it negotiates with the union.

In this situation, the union faces a trade-off among three variables: wages, occupational pensions paid to employed members in the future, and the probability of employment for its representative worker. Once it decides on an optimal trade-off between wages and occupational pensions, the union presents the firm with a given expected 'total cost of hiring' (current wage + present expected value of future benefits), which will determine employment, as in the standard analysis of a monopoly trade union. What is critical in this framework is that wages, occupational pensions, and employment all change when other factors that influence employee well-being change, including the level of unemployment benefits, the level of public pensions, and payroll tax rates. The analysis demonstrates that collectively bargained solutions will be affected by welfare state policies.

Consider, for example, what an increase in public pensions will do to union behaviour. On the one hand, at any given level of total labour cost, workers will want to substitute current wages for occupational pensions, as public benefits partially substitute for occupational benefits. Put differently, public pensions will crowd occupational benefits but by less than one for one, so that total long-term pension benefits will increase. But the union will not keep the same labour cost when public pensions rise. Higher public pensions available to unemployed workers as well as employed union members will make unemployment less costly, so the union will shift its bargaining towards raising total compensation, which will reduce the equilibrium level of employment. As long as public pensions do not depend on previous employment status and the payroll tax that funds them comes partly from non-members, the higher the value of public pensions, the less important is employment relative to unemployment for a trade union member.

Whether the union takes the higher compensation in the form of wages or additional occupational pensions is uncertain. The higher total compensation generates an income effect since workers will receive higher lifetime incomes. If this has only a modest effect on the desire for pensions, workers will want less to be spent on occupational pensions and more to go on wages, but if the income effect for pensions is large, workers could want higher occupational pensions as well and may even want lower current wages. On net, we would expect the substitution effect to dominate, so that higher public pensions raise wages, but the only certainty from maximizing behaviour is that total compensation will be higher.

The same sort of argument illuminates how unions are likely to alter pensions in response to changes or differences in other exogenous factors. Compare, for example, worker and thus union desire for pensions when workers have little chance of collecting benefits, because jobs are short-lived owing to technological or competitive conditions, with their desire for pensions when they have near-permanent employment. This difference in the likelihood of receiving a pension will produce a vastly different desire for pensions. As the likelihood of receiving future benefits increases, workers will value these benefits more relative to current wages, and thus will accept lower wages in exchange for this benefit. At the same time, however, the higher probability that workers will obtain a pension increases the effective price of a given amount of occupational benefits to the firm. If actuarial calculations show that a 100 per year pension will cost the firm a present value of 500 when the workers have a 50% chance of staying until retirement, it would cost the firm 1,000 if the workers had a 100% chance of staying. Given these two forces, the total effect of an increase in the probability of getting a pension as a result of an exogenous increase in the probability of remaining with a firm will be to reduce both current wages and the level of occupational benefits.

Finally, consider the effect of an increase in the payroll tax rate. Many union models predict that an increase in the payroll tax will raise labour costs (Alesina and Perotti, 1997). Taking account of the intertemporal nature of the union decision with respect to pensions does not affect this prediction. An increase in the payroll tax will raise labour cost and reduce employment in the union model. But again, the effect on current wages is generally ambiguous. There is a negative substitution effect of an increase in the tax rate on current wages (as opposed to future benefits), but also a positive income effect because of the increase in the total cost of hiring. For occupational pensions, it is likely that they increase as the payroll tax increases.[1]

[1] The basic model can be extended along several dimensions. It readily generalizes to situations where the union bargains with the firm over wages and benefits, while the firm keeps its 'right to manage' on employment decisions. The generalization to bargaining over employment as well the two elements of labour costs, however, yields a qualitatively different solution: a set of optimal contracts in wages and employment govern the relationship between the union and the firm, with more employment than in the 'right to manage' case. The smaller the bargaining power of the union, the lower the labour costs, current wages, and deferred benefits, and the greater will be employment.

3.1.2. *Union behaviour when workers differ by age or seniority*

Treating workers as homogeneous is, of course, unrealistic. Union members will have differing preferences towards pensions and other forms of compensation depending on age, seniority, degree of attachment to the firm, and idiosyncratic personal factors. Since unions take collective decisions along democratic lines, this poses a set of political economy problems for them. A union must reconcile conflicts about pension provision between young and old workers and determine an objective function for collective bargaining to bring to the bargaining table. Like other political decision-makers, it will be influenced by the attitudes of the median person engaged in the political process.

To analyse differences in preferences between young and old workers within a union, consider workers who differ in age in a two-period model. Young workers work in the first period of their life and retire in the second period, when they live on pensions. Older workers are retirees living on pension benefits. At the beginning, the union chooses the current wage rate of young workers and the level of occupational benefits to be paid at retirement. Given this, the firm chooses the employment level. In the last period, benefits are paid to workers previously employed.

One way to analyse this situation is to assume that the union's objective function is determined by young workers, subject to delivering to older workers their promised occupational pension benefits. The union must then bargain for wages and pensions so that the firm generates a large enough surplus to pay retirees their pension. The equilibrium labour cost for young workers will be a decreasing function of the number of retirees, since more retirees puts a greater 'tax' on younger workers to pay their occupational pensions. To be sure, the young workers will also bargain for pensions for themselves when they are older. But the fact that retirees must be paid reduces the surplus that the firm has to pay younger workers. The welfare of a young trade union member is decreasing with the size of old workers in the union.

This has an important implication for the dynamics of union membership. Since young workers gain less income when a firm and union are obligated to pay considerable revenues to retirees, ageing unions with disproportionately many retirees owed occupational pensions will have more difficulties attracting young workers, reducing membership over time. Better to join a new firm (and form a new union) than to take on part of the occupational pension 'debt' to older workers in an established union.

Voting on benefits and wages

The division between workers and retirees examined above is clearly extreme. At any workplace there will be a continuum of workers by age. Indeed, the majority are likely to be middle-aged workers who have intermediate preferences over wages and benefits. These workers are likely to be pivotal in determining the union's bargaining stance. Following Askildsen and Ireland

(1997), we assume that workers inside the union are continuously differentiated according to their likely survival probability in the firm, which can be indexed by their seniority or age. A worker characterized by a survival probability will take into account that probability and the contingency of unemployment in deciding between pensions and wages. If employed, that worker will expect to receive occupational benefits differentially according to his chance of remaining with the firm. Similarly, from the point of view of the firm, the total labour cost of hiring a worker, which is the sum of the current wage and the expected cost of paying an occupational benefit, also depends on attachment. How will the union reconcile the differing preferences of workers and reach a collective decision about the trade-off between pensions and wages?

The answer depends on the political mechanism within the union. Consider first the case where wages and benefits are decided by simple majority voting, with no logrolling. Each union member will have a preferred policy outcome that depends on his attachment probability, the average attachment probability in the union, and other factors. When a voting equilibrium inside the union exists, the equilibrium choice of labour cost, current wages, and deferred benefits will be the one preferred by the trade union member with the median characteristic. In any median voter model, all we have to do to deduce the equilibrium values of current wages, benefits, and employment for the group is to find the preferences of the median voter.

Consider first how an increase in survival probabilities for all other workers affects the preferences of a single worker. For a given employed worker, an exogenous increase in his average chance of remaining with the firm increases the 'price' of occupational benefits paid by the firm. The value of being employed for any given trade union member is reduced, since more of the firm's surplus will go towards paying the pensions of other workers. Since firms with higher survival probabilities will have to spend more to deliver any given occupational benefit to workers, occupational benefits will be more costly to the worker and he will prefer smaller benefits. Unless the increased attachment between workers and firms is accompanied by an increase in productivity (for reasons of human capital formation), the total labour cost of a given wage/pension package will be increased with greater attachment, which implies that the workers must reduce their demand for pensions and/or wages.

Consider now an increase in the attachment probability of the pivotal agent in the union, say because people who are more concerned or more attached to the firm get more political power within the union, while the average attachment of workers is unchanged. In that case, the pivotal agent wants higher long-term benefits. At the same time, because occupational benefits are attached to employment, the pivotal agent also cares more about employment. Consequently, his preferred level of total labour costs (current wage + future occupational benefits as a package) is reduced. Since he knows he has a high chance of getting the pension, he will want to avoid the risk of job loss, and thus will favour a more moderate compensation package that increases employment. In this case, the *seniority bias* of unions, by which we mean the disproportionate impact of more senior workers on union policies, will induce unions to be more concerned with employment. Giving the senior employee a big payoff upon retirement makes him more risk-averse of losing the job because of high current wage or labour cost demands.

3.1.3. *Additional causes of seniority bias in union behaviour*

There are other factors, however, which add to the likely greater role of senior workers in a trade union and reduce their sensitivity to the chance of job loss. Some workers may hold insider positions within the firm and face little risk that the firm will lay them off under bad external conditions. Seniority rules and last-in–first-out conventions discriminate between young workers and senior workers in terms of their risks of being unemployed and their access to occupational benefits. Since senior union members have a greater probability of being employed, they will value more an increase in total lifetime compensation than they would if they were truly at risk of unemployment. In addition to pensions, moreover, 'soft landing' plans such as early retirement plans, long-term unemployment insurance, and disability plans, applied mainly to senior and older workers, make unemployment less costly to such workers, further inducing them to demand more on the labour cost. Getting more protection against the risk of unemployment, the pivotal agent will prefer higher labour costs at the risk of a greater loss of employment for junior workers. The gains in current wages and occupational benefits are paid by the disproportionately high probability of unemployment for young workers.

Reinforcing this is the likelihood that older workers will be more effective at lobbying inside the union than younger workers. Here, we apply the general argument of Mulligan and Salai-i-Martin (1999), on gerontocracy and the comparative advantage in lobbying that senior citizens possess. The argument rests on three elements. (1) The technology of lobbying or political influence is time-intensive rather than money-intensive. (2) Senior workers and retirees have a lower opportunity cost of time than junior and active workers. (3) There is a crucial asymmetry in the sense that old and senior workers cannot be young or junior anymore while, on the contrary, young and junior individuals may reasonably expect to be old and senior in the future. If lobbying by senior members within unions takes place, this then provides an additional channel along which the union's positions will be biased in favour of wages and occupational pensions at the expense of junior workers' employment levels.

In sum, the more realistic one makes the union model, the greater is the likely seniority bias of union decision-making. The prediction for the macro economy is striking: economies in which unions are dominated by older members will be more likely to suffer from high youth unemployment, while workers will enjoy high current wages and occupational pensions.

3.1.4. *Implications for membership*

How will young workers respond to this situation?

Assume that membership in the union is a matter of individual choice: a worker can select a union or non-union workplace and join or not join the union at a given workplace. Workers are indexed by their likely survival in the firm, and they decide to join the union by comparing their expected payoff inside the union to the welfare they might get in some other occupation in the non-unionized sector of the economy. How workers will fare within the union setting depends on the political equilibrium inside the union, which itself depends on the position of the pivotal agent within the union. But of course, the pivotal agent is determined by the type of individuals who decide to join the union (Booth, 1984). Hence an equilibrium with endogenous membership will determine simultaneously the political equilibrium decided within the union, the size of the union, and the nature of the pivotal agent within the union.

There are two potential equilibria in this situation: one in which unions are dominated by older workers with a long-lasting relationship and fail to attract younger workers, and one in which the union is composed mainly of workers with a low attachment probability, which in turn produces a political equilibrium that reflects their preferences. The former seems to characterize unions in advanced countries in Europe today, while the latter may have characterized them during periods of rapid membership growth. To be sure, the division between younger and older workers is not as stark as this analysis suggests. Mobile or young workers eventually become senior workers or insiders over time. This reduces the potential opposition between young workers and more senior ones. Still, the basic problem that this analysis highlights remains: unions dominated by older workers will be less attractive to younger workers, creating a membership problem for the union among the young.

3.2. THE IMPORTANCE OF INSTITUTIONAL SETTING

The analysis thus far has shown that the welfare state and union seniority bias in decision-making can lead to collective bargained packages that disproportionately benefit older workers at the expense of the young, with adverse effects on union membership. But in some European countries the relation between the welfare system and unions is more complex, because the institutional setting induces unions to take account of other factors as well in their bargaining stance. We consider two such settings: systems in which unions are the institution that delivers welfare services; and systems in which unions bargain at a national rather than sectoral or firm level. Both institutional settings mitigate seniority bias in decision-making and make unions more attractive to more junior workers.

3.2.1. *The union's role in providing welfare services*

As an institution providing a public good (bargained wages and labour conditions covering individuals who are not necessarily union members), trade
unions face the usual problem of free-riding with respect to membership and
active unionism. One way for the union to mitigate this problem is to provide
exclusive services or goods to their members. In this respect, it may be of special
importance to unions to be closely involved in the management of pensions,
unemployment insurance, and disability funds. Such activities give the union
privileged access to information on procedures, legal aspects, and conditions
related to the allocation of these benefits. At the worker level, the union can
then provide this information and associated services such as helping and filling
in forms, on a discriminatory basis, for individuals who are entitled to these
benefits in exchange for union membership and participation. Playing a role in
such funds generates positions for the union leadership that can be part of an
incentive mechanism for the promotion and reward of 'good' behaviour inside
the union.

Participation in the management of benefits or pensions funds gives the union
some leverage in public policy-making. In particular, it allows the union to
present itself as a defender and manager of workers' rights in general, and to
partly control the ideological agenda in society. Doing so may stimulate solidarity towards workers outside the union and may change perceptions on the
union's role in society. This in turn may help solve the free-rider problem and
give unions support among workers who are not members.

But participation in benefits fund management may also generate a preference for the status quo situation regarding reform on non-wage policies. Unions
that, under the status quo, are involved in the management of benefits' funds,
will oppose any reform that will reduce their role in this respect. Conversely,
unions that are not yet active in such activities may find here a beneficial
dimension for which they are ready to make concessions on some other front.
But there could be a force in the other direction: union involvement in managing programs or funds, for instance taking responsibility for a private second-
tier pension programme, should make them aware of the burden of financing
old-age protection and of the costs as well as benefits to union members and
workers more broadly.

3.2.2. *Centralization and union policies*

Since generous public pensions directly increase the welfare of a union's
members and improve their outside options and the union's bargaining power
with respect to employers, trade unions have an incentive to promote generous
public pension systems. However, increased public transfers have to be
financed by higher taxes, public borrowing, or monetization and higher inflation. In the present European context, monetization is not possible and the

public borrowing alternative is quite limited. Taxes are therefore the principal way of funding the welfare state. However funded, pay-as-you-go pensions involve the transfer of resources from one group to another, as reflected in the size of the pension budget.

The extent to which trade unions support generous public benefits depends on how far they internalize the budget constraint of the government. In a system of decentralized union bargaining at the sectoral level, sector-specific unions will not rationally internalize the fact that higher public benefits induce higher payroll taxes at the level of the economy with negative consequences on employment and income levels. After all, much of the taxation burden of these transfers will be passed on to other segments of the economy while the gains will be felt directly by union members. Each sector-specific union will therefore impose a negative externality on the other sectors of the economy (Alesina and Perotti, 1997). On the other hand, in a more centralized bargaining setting, unions will necessarily take into account the basic trade-off, at the macro-economic level, between higher public benefits and higher taxes.

The implication is that, all else the same, public benefits systems in countries with more decentralized union structures should be associated with higher total compensation and higher unemployment. By contrast, countries characterized by centralized and encompassing unions will have, everything else being equal, lower unit costs of labour and lower unemployment for the same level of public benefits. If unions had the same political clout in the two settings, the greater recognition of the costs of pensions in the centralized setting would produce lower public pensions and possibly more occupational pensions.

Thus, the relation between unions and the welfare state depends not only on union seniority bias but also on the structure of the national collective bargaining system. This in turn has consequences for union membership: it should be easier to attract young workers and to maintain union density in countries with centralized bargaining systems.

3.3. WHAT UNIONS DO IN PRACTICE: EMPIRICAL EVIDENCE ON UNIONS AND PENSIONS

While there exists a well established literature on the effects of unions on wage growth, wage inequality, and employment, empirical economic research on the effect of unions in a broader bargaining framework is sparse. A notable exception is the work pioneered by Freeman (1981). Here, we briefly review findings on the link between unions and pensions from data on individual workers and firms, then provide new aggregate evidence on the macro link between union density and pension spending.

3.3.1. *Microeconomic evidence on occupational pensions*

Analysis of micro data documents how the presence of unions affects (1) the probability that a worker or firm has a private pension plan and (2) the level of old-age benefits. On the basis of our earlier arguments, we expect that, by raising the total labour compensation, unions will increase the absolute amount spent on pensions. In addition, we expect that, for given total compensation, the seniority bias of unions will raise occupational pensions relative to current wages. For the United States, Freeman (1985) and Gustman and Steinmeier (1986) show that the presence of unions does indeed increase pension coverage. Unions give more weight to the representative worker, whose demand for pensions is higher, than to younger marginal workers. But there is an alternative, or complementary, explanation for the positive union–pension relation to the one that they and we have proposed. This is that unionism increases the probability of attachment to the firm and thus of tenure with the firm (Freeman, 1980), which will make it more likely that a worker will be around long enough to benefit from an occupational pension scheme. By itself, this will increase the union workers' demand for pensions relative to that of non-union workers. Furthermore, unions can monitor the actions of firms in terms of pension policies more than individual workers can do, and it is therefore more likely that unionized plants have occupational pensions in place.

The evidence on the effect of unions on occupational pensions in Europe comes to the same conclusions. Disney and Cameron (1990) use cross-sectional data from the Family Expenditure Survey 1984 and find that in the UK union status raises the probability of occupational pension coverage by between 8 and 35 percentage points, the strongest effect being among manual workers. Calculations based on the British Household Panel Study (BHPS), 1997, wave 7, show that firms with a union are more likely to offer an occupational pension, and that union members are more likely to have an occupational pension within firms that offer them (Table 3.1). Since this analysis does not control for the size of the plant, which is presumably related to both membership and OP provision,[2] the observed relation may exaggerate the union effect. Still, it suggests the importance that unions attach to occupational pension provisions for their members in those European countries where those pension systems are sizeable, and is prima facie evidence of the involvement of unions in the establishment of pension funds.

There are reasons to expect collective bargaining to favour defined benefit plans and reasons to expect collective bargaining to favour defined contribution (DC) plans. Theory is ambiguous, because on the one hand incentive models (Lazear 1979, 1985) suggest that union firms do not need to motivate workers by offering defined benefit plans, as there is already a union premium incentive for workers not to shirk; but on the other hand, the greater protection that unions give members from firing makes those plans more rewarding to them.[3] In fact, as noted earlier, the empirical evidence shows that unions favour

---

[2] Both in the USA and in Europe (Andrietti, 2000) there is evidence that larger plants are more likely to offer occupational pensions and to be unionized.

[3] See Andrietti (2000) for a discussion on this point.

Table 3.1. *Occupational pensions and union membership in the UK*

	Union firm	Non-union firm	Total
Firm with OP	2139 (88.9%)	1311 (41.25%)	3450 (61.78%)
Firm without OP	267 (11.10%)	1867 (58.75%)	2134 (38.22%)
Total	2406 (100.00%)	3178 (100.00%)	5584 (100.00%)

	Union worker	Non-union worker	Total
OP worker	1290 (78.75%)	1296 (32.84%)	2586
Non-OP worker	348 (21.25%)	2650 (67.16%)	2998
Total	1638 (100.00%)	3946 (100.00%)	5584 (100.00%)

Note: Union membership may be a noisy measure, as the question includes staff associations as well as trade unions proper.

Source: Own calculations based on the British Household Panel Survey, 1997.

defined benefit plans. What probably tips the balance is the seniority bias in union policies: defined benefit plans allow unions to redistribute money to older workers, particularly when the union first initiates the pension scheme, in an acceptable manner.

3.3.2. *Unionism and pre-retirement options*

Our analysis suggests that countries with stronger unions and older membership should have more generous public pension systems as a result of (1) a direct positive effect of pensions on the welfare of union members, and (2) the gains for unions from an 'outside option' that increases the bargaining power of the union against the firm. Consistent with this analysis, we saw in Chapter 2 a positive relationship between trends in passive union membership and old-age spending overall. In this chapter we show that this relation goes beyond pensions to include pre-retirement options.

In several countries, governments, facing politically sensitive unemployment problems in declining sectors, have implemented and subsidized various 'soft landing' plans (early retirement, disability, long-term unemployment benefits) to reduce the labour supply. These are restricted to a number of industries, or firms within an industry, that are restructuring. In these cases the eligibility requirements for retirement are less stringent than the general rules: a worker becomes eligible even if he is younger than the normal retirement age and has a lower number of payroll tax payments (in years) than normally required. Workers have a strong incentive to accept the deal, as it is usually quite generous. We call this situation a 'pre-retirement option'.

In some respects pre-retirement is similar to collective redundancies. Both reflect an adverse shock for the industry, and both affect a number of workers at the same time. Pre-retirement options offer older workers a soft landing at a cost to the active population and tax payers. Bridging pensions, paid at rates equivalent to the standard retirement pension, with no penalty, have been used extensively in Austria, Finland, Italy, Sweden, West Germany, and the Netherlands (see OECD, 1992). They are often accompanied by disability pensions. Firms and unions find them appealing because part of the cost falls on the taxpayer. According to Leonard and Van Audenrode (1993), government subsidies to declining industries and government-paid early retirement schemes are larger in Europe than in the United States. Total government aid to declining industries as a percentage of GNP cost 2.2% of GDP in the European Communities during the late 1980s, with Belgium, Italy, and Greece spending substantially over the average.[4]

While displaced workers benefit from the generous treatment provided by bridging pensions, those employees remaining in the same plant bear little or no cost of the policy because the costs are spread over the entire working population. Ebbinghaus (2000) documents the potential collusive behaviour between employers and unions in this case. Our analysis shows that remaining employees could even benefit from the policy, because the bargained wage depends not only on bargaining strength but also on the alternative options available to the parties if the settlement is not reached. The availability of generous bridging pensions clearly strengthens the bargaining position of employed insiders.

3.3.3. *Unionism and early retirement options*

In a similar vein, unions often favour the 'early retirement option'. This is embedded in many social security systems (Italy and Spain) along with private pension plans (e.g. the Netherlands, Sweden, UK). This is a different path for workers to take to exit the labour market into retirement, though it is not restricted to particular industries or firms and is completely voluntary. Gruber and Wise (1999) document how the incentives existing within pension programmes for early retirement are very strong regardless of whether this is of

---

[4] The Italian experience is illuminating. In Italy collective dismissals have been regulated since 1991 by Law 223, which was introduced to meet European guidelines. The Law also regulates early retirement as a result of displacement, which was used intensively during the 1980s by large restructuring firms, with union support. Dismissed workers with at least 30 years of contributions have access to seniority pensions (which usually require 35 years of contribution). Initially there was no cost for firms in implementing this policy, and both the anticipated pensions and the missing social security contributions were borne by the taxpayer. It is only since 1992 that firms bear 50% of these additional costs. Workers aged between 50 and 59 who have less than 30 years of contributions can still enrol in special mobility lists where they can draw substantial benefits (up to 80% of previous pay) for as long as 4 years (in the south of Italy). Their social security contributions are borne by the taxpayer and are measured not as a proportion of unemployment benefits, but as a proportion of pay before dismissal. In practice, the large majority of these workers can stay in the list up to retirement. The procedure for access to these lists is negotiated with the unions. Union approval is important, because applying firms can obtain a rebate on the fixed contribution they have to pay.

a pay-as-you-go financing method or fully funded, though salary-related schemes typically provide stronger incentives.

Precise measures of incentives for early retirement are hard to come by. They depend on the institutional setting and on the number of provisions available to workers in old age. For example, in Italy we observe both pre-pensions granted to older workers in some declining industries in a given time span, and a very generous early retirement option which can be claimed at different ages according to gender and sector of employment.[5] In the Netherlands disability benefits are in practice early retirement provisions, since workers rarely return to employment. In this sense a more reliable measure of the importance of early retirement is the fraction of individuals who are not labour force participants at that age—unused labour capacity (Gruber and Wise, 1999; Blöndal and Scarpetta, 1998). It properly counts beneficiaries of disability benefits as retirees, but it does not adjust for the unemployed and those in part-time work and thus underestimates the extent of early exits from the labour market in some countries. The available data on unused labour capacity suggests that a number of countries (notably Italy, the Netherlands, and Belgium) have high unused capacity. These countries are also relatively high in union strength.

In general, bridging pensions are attractive to dismissed employees and their unions only if pension treatments are generous, at least compared with unemployment benefits. Recall that unemployment benefits are usually phased out after a period of time and often require as a condition active labour market search. Also, they often carry a social stigma that is not associated with retirement.

3.3.4. *Macro consequences of soft landing, pre-retirement and early retirement options*

Generous soft landing provisions have adverse effects on wage formation and on employment growth. Once the government is willing to insure firms against the consequences of business failure, the incentive for unions to moderate wage demands is reduced by the availability of soft landings. (See Calmfors and Horn, 1986, for a more general argument.) Reverse order of seniority in the selection of dismissed employees shelters insiders from temporary and relatively mild negative shocks, but harsher shocks will affect the job security of senior workers as well. Unions subject to seniority bias in policy-making will select adjustment measures that insure senior employees against hard landings. Employers who find this an easy way to restructure and scale back the labour force will also favour such programmes. Because neither employers nor unions

---

[5] The recent (1995) Italian reform of the social security system has somewhat changed this pattern.

internalize the true social costs of these programmes, they are likely to distort the allocation of resources and reduce the growth of the economy.

Such programmes may also create strategic complementarities between economic allocations and political processes (Saint-Paul, 1995). This in turn can lead to multiple equilibria. In one case, such programmes will promote the emergence of even more declining sectors, owing to the macroeconomic distortions they generate, enhancing the political demand for such plans. This will create a 'low' equilibrium with a large number of declining sectors, high political demand for soft landing plans, overuse of those plans, and stagnant growth. On the other hand, such programmes could make firms and workers more willing to accept change and mobility. This will produce a 'high' equilibrium with a small number of declining sectors, a moderate political demand for soft landing plans, a moderate implementation of such plans, and a high macroeconomic growth rate. Multiple equilibria of this sort are more likely in decentralized bargaining structures. This kind of explanation may help, then, to explain the variety of experiences observed by Western welfare states on these issues.

3.3.5. *Public pensions, the pay-as-you-go constraint, and intergenerational effects*

In a pay-as-you-go pension system young workers pay for the pension of retired workers through payroll taxes. The extent to which unions support generous pension plans without suffering negative effects in their membership, and without other compensating devices (Bonoli, 1999), depends on how far they internalize the budget constraint of the government and take account of the tax cost of pensions. In the Italian case, public pensions became more generous at a time when gross wages were also growing, so that the budget constraint was not perceived as binding. Conflict emerged during the late 1980s when a quest for pension reforms developed. The objective was to avoid losing younger generations even though they are not the strong group within unions, but represent potential future membership. These considerations have to do not only with the financing of generous pension policies via current payroll taxes, but also with the intergenerational redistribution that is implicit in a pay-as-you-go system.

Pay-as-you-go funded systems often redistribute income from the young to retirees at a certain point in time. If public pensions are actuarially fair, and provide the same return as the capital market rate of return, workers will receive in present-value terms what they put into the system. However, pension systems are actuarially unfair: earlier cohorts of retirees typically obtain a better deal from the system since programmes provide them with pensions for which they have not been taxed. But the persistence of a bias towards older generations, once all have paid taxes into the system, is often due to the ill-design and generosity of pension benefits, and to a failure to adjust to changing

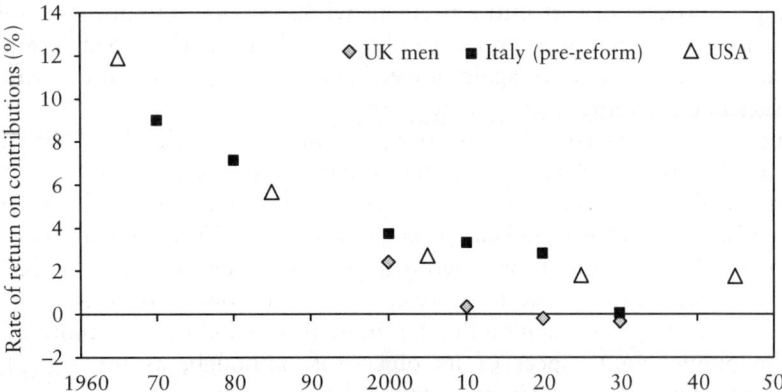

Figure 3.1. *Real rates of returns to PAYG pension programmes, 1960–2050*
Sources: Castellino (1995); Miles and Iben (1998).

demographics. A system that works well with a stable population distribution can become 'unfair' to the young when the population profile shifts towards older persons. As noted earlier, for an occupational pension plan, the ratio of retirees to workers affects the tax that the young must pay for the pensions of the older generation. The final effect of an unchanged pay-as-you-go system in a world of changing real wages and a changing age composition of the population is differential treatment for different cohorts. In many countries, the internal rate of return paid by public schemes has in fact fallen over time (Figure 3.1.)

This redistribution creates tension between generations both at national level and within unions. Guaranteeing the young the same conditions as the old in terms of pension benefits can go only so far in redressing this problem. This could work both in society at large and within unions. As long as there is a certain degree of inertia or commitment concerning the type of contract between the firm and the union, junior workers might accept the pension decisions of their senior fellows since with some probability they might also enjoy part of the gains later. In this case the union will have incentives to maintain the status quo, as this will enhance its capacity to bribe young and junior workers to join without reducing its ability to extract rents through high wages and benefits. In Italy this was made clear explicitly during the 1995 major reform of the public pension system, it was termed the '*acquired right principle*'.[6] When it comes to displaced workers, it is easier for unions to

---

[6] See Chapter 4 on unions and pension reforms. It must be noted that Italian unions played a crucial role in making the 1995 reform possible. However, this result was achieved at the cost of a very gradual transitional phase from the old regime to the new one.

manage a process of exit into retirement while freezing retirement and early retirement rules, than to support spending on labour market policies targeted at the young. Hence, once again, a clear tendency to preserve the status quo emerges in early retirement arrangements.

The more centralized is the wage bargain, and the more closely the union can stick to the promise of permanent pension gains, the easier it is to win young union members to a union policy of generous pension treatments. Hence if, on the one hand, in a centralized bargaining setting the PAYG constraint should be internalized and the quest for generous pensions reduced, on the other hand, a more compact union would be more credible in its commitment. As observed by Visser (1990), a dominant union has more power and will give more weight to the public good aspect of its objectives, although, as we argued, an encompassing union is under more strain when trying to externalize the costs of such objectives.

There could also be another process at work, partly mitigating the harshness of the negative effects on younger generations of workers. Again, the internal age structure of unions may mimic the mechanisms operating in society. If seen as a political equilibrium, the support of generous pay-as-you-go pension systems require a coalition between the old, who draw benefits but are often in a minority, and some other group. According to Tabellini (1992), this coalition involves the old and the poor young (the unemployed). The mechanism works through income redistribution within households. The poor young pay limited taxes to finance current pensions but obtain income from retired parents, who draw generous benefits. This depends both on the preferences of the old and on the presence of extended families in society. While some young active worker will be lucky enough to benefit, many others will not. Hence one can talk of some form of solidarity between retirees and their non-employed children. Even though the high cost of the pension system 'causes' youth unemployment, the fact that part of this generosity is transferred to the unemployed young mitigates their potential opposition to the system. Within family compensation arrangements and labour market institutions, commitment thus helps explain why younger generations will underwrite an intergenerational contract that is to their disadvantage.

3.3.6. *Macroeconomic evidence*

We have seen a variety of results relating the strength of unions to welfare outcomes. Union decision-making over wages, employment, and occupational pensions depends on the generosity of public pensions; while union policies towards public pensions reflects union membership and seniority bias. These relationships cannot be looked at in isolation. According to our analysis, we should find configurations in the cross-country data, with those countries having high passive union membership also evincing high public and private pension spending, high youth unemployment, and limited youth entry into

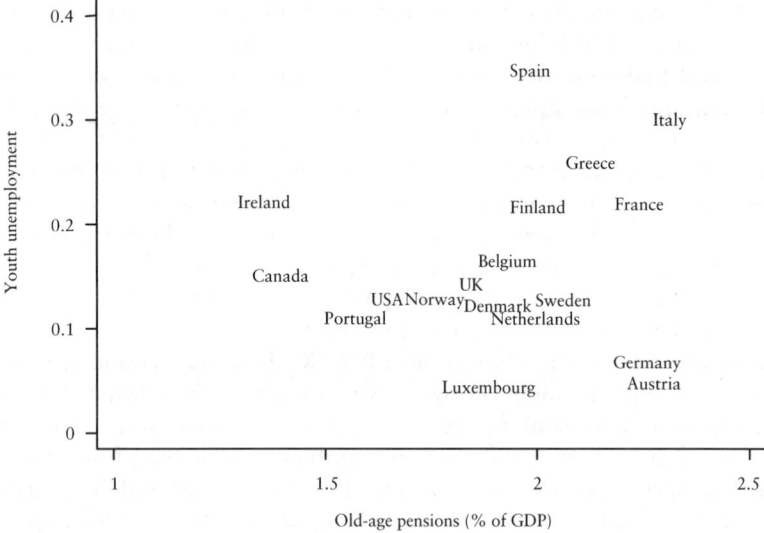

Figure 3.2. *Youth unemployment and generosity of pensions, 1989–1994*

Sources: Old-age spending over GDP is from OECD, Social Expenditure Database, 1998; youth unemployment is from Eurostat (1999).

unions. In fact, Southern countries like Spain, Greece, and Italy, at one extreme, are characterized by high pension spending, high unemployment, and relatively high union coverage, and Anglo-Saxon countries, like Ireland, Canada, and the USA, at the other extreme, have low pension spending, low youth unemployment, and low coverage.

Hence we focus on a simple model, where unionism raises pension expenditure, which in turn may affect youth unemployment (see Figure 3.2). The bottom line of the model is a reduced-form relationship between unionism and youth unemployment, but one that depends, in accordance with our earlier analysis, on the structure of the bargaining system, with more co-ordinated bargaining reducing youth unemployment. Although we do not present a formal model for this, we argue that this effect goes via the tax burden that old-age spending imposes on labour in some countries.[7] Our approach builds on Nickell (1997), where the effects of labour market rigidities on unemployment are analysed.

In a first equation we want to document the idea, stated several times in the text, that variation in pension generosity is explained partly by union

---

[7] On the potential negative effects of taxes (particularly payroll social security taxes) on macroeconomic performance (particularly employment), see e.g. Summers *et al*. (1993); Tyrvainen (1994); Stokey and Rebelo (1995); Nickell (1997); and Daveri and Tabellini (2000).

strength. Since simple diagrams do not allow for a full inspection of the different variables describing union power, we resort to multiple regression analysis and make use of a full set of union measures: union density, union coverage, and union–employer coordination. Here we want to be more specific about which characteristic of unions describes cross-country variation in spending patterns. In turn, variability in the generosity of a pensions system may be reflected in higher youth unemployment. Some authors show that the tax wedge existing between real labour costs and real take-home pay affects unemployment (see ft. 7); we argue that in some countries old-age expenditure is a major determinant of the tax wedge, because variability in the tax wedge is due largely to variability in payroll tax rates.

The results are presented in Table 3.2.2. We base our econometric specifications of old-age spending on two sets of variables: the relevant 'structural' variables, as pointed out by Peracchi (1999) (demographic structure and resources of each country), and union variables, as emerging from the theory (union strength). We use two (averaged) time periods and have data for 16 countries.[8] The first column of the table reports results for old-age spending. We include, as potential determinants of old-age spending, union density and union coverage, while we neglect union–employer coordination. The latter is more relevant in a wage-setting context than in explaining the welfare effects of union activities—and, indeed, did not prove statistically significant in this equation. While union density measures the proportion of trade union members as a percentage of all wage and salary earners, union coverage is an index of the extent to which workers are actually covered by union bargaining through *erga omnes* extensions, regardless of whether or not these workers are union members.[9] The dependency ratio (people older than 55 as a percentage of working-age population) is the relevant demographic variable, while GDP captures variability in the resources of each country.

Table 3.2 suggests that unions have an impact on pension spending, over and above the standard 'pension-spending' determinants. Union coverage has a strong positive effect while union density has a negative effect. The two union variables do not correlate; for example, in Spain and France we observe low union density but very high union coverage. Hence countries where unions have strong bargaining power have high levels of old-age spending, while countries with high density, where presumably a more heterogeneous workforce is actually part of the unions (Scandinavian countries), have lower old-age spending.

In columns (3), (4), and (5) of Table 3.2 we provide regression results for (log) youth unemployment, this is the proportion of unemployed individuals

[8] Hence there is a total of 32 country-time observations. However, we do not have available youth unemployment for Austria in the first time period (reducing the sample to 31 observations). Further, passive membership is available for 8 countries only.

[9] The index takes value 1 for bargaining coverage below 25%, 2 for coverage between 25% and 70%, and 3 for coverage above 70%.

Table 3.2. *Regressions to explain old-age spending and youth unemployment*[a]

	(1) Pension expenditure/ GDP (in logs)	(2) Pension expenditure/ GDP (in logs)	(3) Youth unempl. (in logs)	(4) Youth unempl. (in logs)	(5) Youth unempl. (in logs)
Dependency ratio	2.836* (1.00)	2.739* (1.74)			
Union coverage index (1)–(3)	0.428* (0.15)		0.365* (0.23)	0.314* (0.19)	0.126 (0.18)
Union density (%)	−0.004* (0.002)	−0.014* (0.007)	0.012* (0.006)	0.014* (0.005)	0.012* (0.004)
Co-ordination (union + employer) (2)–(6)			−0.498* (0.108)	−0.450* (0.093)	−0.423* (0.081)
Passive membership (%)		0.009* (0.005)			
Log (pension expenditure/GDP)			1.180* (0.389)	1.423* (0.348)	
Total tax rate					0.037* (0.007)
Log GDP		1.404* (0.86)			
Employment protection			0.016 (0.023)	0.013 (0.019)	0.034 (0.018)
Active labour market policies			−0.016* (0.007)	−0.022* (0.006)	−0.025* (0.006)
UI replacement rate			0.014* (0.006)	0.016* (0.005)	0.010* (0.004)
Change in inflation (% pts p.a.)			−0.219* (0.133)	−0.203* (0.112)	−0.246* (0.106)
Benefit duration (yrs)			−0.110 (0.07)	−0.094 (0.07)	−0.028 (0.04)
Dummy for apprenticeship countries				−0.526* (0.177)	−0.027 (0.025)
N (countries-time)	32	15	31	31	31
R-squared	0.52	0.60	0.71	0.80	0.82

[a]Standard errors in parentheses; asterisks indicate statistically significant estimates.

Sources: We integrate the data set used in Nickell (1997) with old-age expenditure (OECD) as percentage of GDP (*Social Expenditure Database*, 1998). Dependency ratios are own calculations based on population statistics from Eurostat, *Demographic Statistics*, 1998. Following Nickell (1997), the data referring to unions and labour market structure are based on OECD (1994 and 1995)—and from Ebbinghaus-Visser (2000). GDP is in 1990 Euros (and is transformed in logs). Youth unemployment is the unemployment rate for those under 25 (from Eurostat, 1999). Because of a panel element present in the data (2 observations for each country), a GLS procedure is implemented. We treat 'active labour market policies' as endogenous in the youth unemployment equation; this has been instrumented by using policy variables, labour market variables, and demographics. For a discussion on the sources of endogeneity, see the discussion in Nickell (1997).

An auxiliary regression, motivating the inclusion of old-age spending in place of the tax rate, relates the tax wedge (total tax rate inclusive of the payroll tax rate, income, and consumption tax—see Nickell, 1997) to old-age expenditure as follows:

$$Total\ tax\ rate = -15.9 + 29.7(OLDEXP) - 3.5(DEPRATIO) + 0.9(LOGGDP) \\ + UNION\ VARIABLES + LABOUR\ MARKET\ VARIABLES.$$

This gives an R^2 of 0.7 and the only significant explanatory variable is old-age expenditure. Furthermore, an F-test on the joint significance of all explanatory variables (excluding *OLDEXP*) could not reject the null; hence the joint explanatory power of the other variables is negligible.

aged 25 or under as a percentage of the youth labour force. The explanatory variables include all the labour market variables indicated by Nickell (1997), and our results are extremely close to what he found for total unemployment. In particular, there are 'direct rigidities' such as employment protection and generosity of the unemployment insurance system (replacement rate), which have a significant effect on youth unemployment, while active labour market policies tend to reduce youth unemployment. On the union variables, unions tend to raise pay and directly influence unemployment, hence high union density and high union coverage raise youth unemployment. However, the index for union and employer coordination has a significant negative effect on youth unemployment, because when employers and unions coordinate their activities there is less of a tendency to 'leapfrog'.[10] The main difference between Nickell's study and our exercise is that we replace the tax wedge (total tax rate) with old-age spending. In fact, the two variables cannot enter simultaneously as they are highly collinear: we argue that old-age spending can proxy for the total tax rate, given that the tax wedge captures, to a large extent, variability in payroll tax rates. To corroborate our argument, results are presented by using both old-age expenditure (columns (3) and (4)) and the total tax rate (column (5)). Our results confirm that old-age spending has a strong and positive effect on youth unemployment.

Finally, we also include an 'apprenticeship' dummy for countries like Germany, where the schooling system features forms of early entry into the labour market: these countries obviously have lower youth unemployment to start with (columns (4) and (5)). Overall our results suggest that, in line with what has been found by some authors for total unemployment, unions affect youth unemployment directly. But they also have an indirect effect: in those countries where unions favour generous old-age provisions, they tend to impose a tax burden on labour and to cause youth unemployment.

Another aspect we want to describe in more detail is the importance of the age structure of unions for macroeconomic performance. Hence in a further econometric model we relate passive membership to pension generosity. Figure 3.3 is suggestive of a strong positive relationship, but this could be the result of a spurious correlation caused by a few extreme cases (Italy has a remarkably high passive membership and high pension spending). Hence it is useful to control properly for demographics and other union variables in this relationship. Owing to the reduced sample size, when including passive membership in the set of explanatory variables we had to drop a number of variables and select a very parsimonious representation in order to explain old-age expenditure. Furthermore, the same data limitations did not allow us to

---

[10] This is an index going from 1 to 3, where 3 indicates high coordination (e.g. central Europe and the Scandinavian countries). For a full description of how the absence of leapfrogging—the tendency for some unions in decentralized systems to take an earlier pay settlement—can affect unemployment, see Nickell (1997).

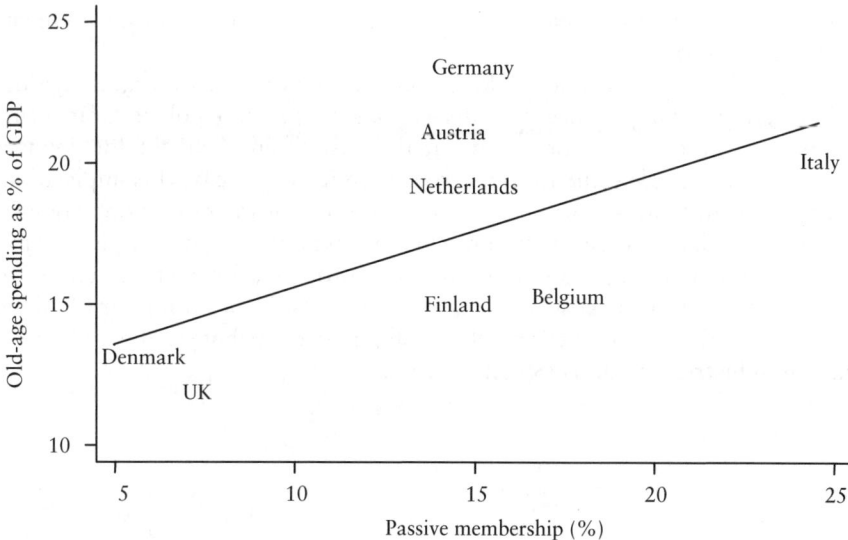

Figure 3.3. *Old-age spending as a percentage of GDP (relative to the dependency ratio) and passive union membership, 1980–1985*

Source: Old-age spending over GDP is from OECD, Social Expenditure Database, 1998; GDP and population statistics are from Eurostat (*Demographic Statistics*, 1998, and ESSPROS, European System of Integrated Social Protection Statistics, 1996); passive membership is from Ebbinghaus and Visser (2000).

analyse youth unemployment as a function of passive membership, along with other explanatory variables. Results for old-age spending are displayed in column (2) of Table 3.2. Even controlling for the dependency ratio and the level of resources in each country/period (as measured by log GDP), passive membership has an overwhelming positive effect on pensions spending. We take this as further evidence of the fact that, where unions have bargaining power (high union coverage) and are seniority-dominated, they push for generous pension policies.

This chapter has shown that unions have a strong interest in pension policies, both at the level of occupational pensions for members and at the national level where state pensions are determined. We have briefly touched upon, but not fully developed, the potential efficiency-enhancing role of unions in setting up occupational pensions. This emerges in economies where, in the presence of uncertainty and imperfect credit markets, firms face a credibility problem in committing to the delivery of future pension benefits through individual contracts signed with their employees, whereas they can commit to trade unions. One could argue that the state is in an even better position than unions to solve this problem, but the state is often vulnerable to more political pressure than labour market organizations. Also, the political time horizon of governments could be too short.

To the extent that senior workers dominate unions, as we argue they do, union actions will produce a seniority bias in pension policies, favouring greater expenditures, in some cases at the cost of employment for younger workers. We provide some fresh macroeconomic evidence on this implication. But the cost to unions from such a policy is a loss of interest among younger workers. We have argued that some institutional arrangements, particularly centralized bargaining, can minimize this problem, by getting unions to internalize some of the costs of their seniority bias. Hence a forward-looking behaviour in the unions–welfare relationship may contribute to the building of trust in industrial relations (Stiglitz, 2000).

4

Learning from Welfare Reforms: The Case of Public Pensions

The tendency, identified in Chapter 3, for unions to have a seniority bias in their policies operates differently across institutional landscapes. We will now examine in more detail the strategies that unions adopt in influencing welfare policies, looking at the current pension reform process across Europe. We have argued so far that unions have tended to defend the status quo of current welfare provisions. As collective organizations of their members' interests, they are opponents to welfare retrenchment, which aims at cutting social benefits in order to control social expenditures; moreover, current pensioners and those who soon expect to become pensioners constitute a sizeable share of the electorate.

As was shown earlier (see Chapter 2), in most European welfare states unions have potential veto points in political decision-making and social policy implementation. Also, they can use the potential threat of massive collective mobilization. In particular, while politicians tend to lower the visibility of benefit cuts by making reforms technically complex, unions can highlight these losses and mobilize against them more effectively than individual voters can (Gillion *et al.*, 2000; Myles and Pierson, forthcoming). Even if unions have not succeeded in blocking legislative changes, they may still be able to render them ineffective when they are participating in self-administration or running private collective schemes. Thus, in systems where social policy-making is shared between the government and social partners, such as in France or the Netherlands, tripartite concerted reform efforts are needed in order to guarantee implementation throughout the fragmented and semi-autonomous systems (Ebbinghaus and Hassel, 2000).

Under these circumstances, governments find it risky to choose unilateral retrenchment. They would gain from negotiating welfare restructuring with the social partners and might be willing to engage in political exchange in order to overcome these veto points. The acquiescence of unions even to painful pension reforms might be achieved by offering appropriate side-payments in the form of concessions in the same or other policy fields. Once the social partners have signed on to reforms, it would be their task to defend the measures *vis-à-vis* their members; the government could thereby avoid or at least deflect part of the blame for unpopular measures.

However, why should unions enter negotiations on welfare retrenchment against the interest of their current members? Indeed, one of the main findings thus far (see Chapter 3) is that unions tend to defend the status quo, and that this can be effective, given multiple veto points (see Chapter 2). Thus, if unions are participating in negotiations over welfare reform, they are first of all interested in defending the acquired social rights of their members, and not in signing them off. However, there are cases when union leaders see the need for, and the long-term positive effects of, reform. While cutting the public deficit might be a primary concern of the government, unions are likely to be concerned about rising social insurance contributions which will reduce take-home pay. They may also be concerned about the high labour costs imposed by social contributions, which has a negative impact on labour demand and thus gives rise to unemployment. Therefore it might well be in the long-term interest of their current and potential future members to support a reduction in welfare costs. For instance, German unions were in favour of the new Schröder government's efforts to cut payroll social contributions by raising green taxes, even if it meant that many members, as car and home-owners, would have to pay higher petrol, gas and oil prices.

Moreover, unions may be willing to negotiate retrenchment measures in order to renegotiate the way in which changes occur and to prevent more severe unilateral welfare cuts. Thus, in the Italian negotiated pension reforms of 1995, the unions were able to bargain for longer transition periods for phasing-in benefit cuts and tightening eligibility criteria. They were also able to maintain some seniority rights for older workers and current pensioners, while agreeing to less favourable conditions for younger workers and job-seekers. In such cases unions in a political exchange may privilege the interest of their core constituency (e.g. senior workers) at the expense of other less represented groups (e.g. younger and unemployed workers). Although the overall outcome of such a reform might still be positive for the public at large, the burden would be placed unequally across groups.

In this chapter we will review some of the main issues and advances in current pension reforms across Europe (see Table 4.1). A major issue is the reform of the relatively generous public pension schemes with their pay-as-you-go financing in most European countries. This has been triggered by the immediate pressure of increased product market competition on labour costs and the rising financial liabilities caused by unfavourable long-term demographic developments. These will require a reform of the pay-as-you-go system in order to maintain the financial and economic viability of the pension schemes, while safeguarding basic income protection. One strategy to reduce labour costs has been to separate the financing of social insurance benefits and that of basic citizenship rights by funding the latter via taxes. Another cause of the explosion of social expenditures, in addition to exogenous demographic shifts, relates to the deliberate policies of shedding labour via early retirement that have dominated continental European welfare states in particular (Esping-Andersen, 1996).

Table 4.1. *Chronology of major old age and disability pension reforms in the 1990s*

Country/ year	Reform	Role and position of unions
Austria		
1996	'Sparpaket' (austerity package: early retirement benefit cuts, benefits frozen)	Grand coalition negotiates with social partners (prior to EMU)
1997	Long-term phasing in of cuts in early retirement pensions and harmonization of public-sector pension provisions with the less generous pensions schemes in the private sector	Grand coalition negotiates 'last minute deal' with social partners
1999/2000	Increase of retirement age, cuts in early retirement (not yet enacted)	Union oppose breakdown of grand coalition, similar plans of right government
Denmark		
1989 +	Establishment of collectively negotiated occupational and earnings-related pensions; pension funds are under supervision of bipartite boards	Unions have changed their opinion in favour of a multi-tier pension system
1994	General income tax on pensions in combination with higher gross pensions	
1999	Cut in early retirement benefits and normal retirement age lowered from 67 to 65; employee contributions to efterløn scheme	Interparty compromise, criticism by general workers' union (SiD), legal guarantee of employee rights demanded
France		
1993	Balladur (private-sector pension) reform: 40 instead of 37.5 years in contribution; 25 instead of 10 best years	Consultation with unions; unions in favour of new state subsidy but most against cuts
1995	Juppé plan: similar cuts in public-sector schemes, ending of favourable early civil service retirement; also budget control by parliament	Unions oppose (fear of changes in self-administration); massive strike wave in defence of status quo, government backtracks except for budget control
1997	Robien law: introduction of private pensions (new Jospin government repeals Act)	Offers in 2000 negotiations on outstanding reforms; most unions are opposed
Germany		
1989	1992 reform (enacted in 1989): shift from gross to net wage indexation, phasing out of early retirement options, increase in retirement age for women (from 60/63 to 65)	Interparty consensus after consultation with social partners
1997	1997 reform: faster phasing in of cuts, introduction of a demographic factor in benefit calculation	Unions end tripartite talks after centre–liberal coalition announces austerity plan in 1996
	Raising the financing share of the state	Limited agreement with opposition
1999	New red–green government annuls demographic factor, but for two years lower pension adjustments, future reform still needed	Unions criticize adjustment (though protest is limited); metalworker union wants wage fund for early retirement at 60 (employers opposed)

Table 4.1. *(Continued)*

Country/ year	Reform	Role and position of unions
Italy		
1992	Amato reform: phased-in increase in retirement age, contribution periods, contribution rates	Consultation with unions
1993	*Ad hoc* measures: freeze of seniority pensions	
1994	Berlusconi plan: faster phasing in, seniority pension freeze, fails with severe cuts	Unions mobilize against cuts; Conservative government loses majority
1995	Dini reform: change to actuarial contribution-defined benefits, phased-in changes to harmonize rules and tighter eligibility, especially of seniority pensions	Agreement with major union movements (confirmed by membership vote but unpopular with workers); employers criticize concessions to unions
1997	Faster phasing in of new benefit formula; seniority pension cuts harmonized (but blue-collar workers are exempted)	Negotiations with social partners; Communist MPs oppose seniority pension cuts, get exemption for blue-collar workers
Netherlands		
1991	Reform of disability pensions and sick pay system	Major demonstration; internal opposition in government parties (grand coalition)
1992	Linking of benefits to active–non-active ratio	(Unions will have to internalize the negative employment effects of wage increases)
1995–97	Early retirement schemes (VUT) become funded; civil servant pension fund privatized	Unions renegotiate VUT agreements to fill in replacement gaps; left–liberal coalition intervenes in governance structure
	Reform of governance system	
Sweden		
1991	End of disability pension for older unemployed	
1996		LO–SAF agreement to change blue-collar occupational pension to funded system
1998	New pension system plan: gradual increase in seniority age, minimum age; benefits based on working life earnings; introduction of funded individual accounts	Interparty consensus (Conservative government and Social Democratic opposition); principal acquiescence from unions
UK		
1988/89	1988: begin of private individual pensions (AVC), diminished benefits of state earnings-related scheme (SERPS); 1989: end of special early retirement scheme	Sharp criticism from unions
1995	Pension Act: minimum solvency standards for private pension funds and compulsory indexation	Public pressures after Maxwell bankruptcy affair

Sources: Compiled from EIRO, EIRR, MISSOC, and various other sources.

As will be shown, it is difficult to reverse the course of early retirement, given the vested interests of unions, employers, and also governments in accommodating labour market pressures.

While these reforms affect the public pension systems, governments have also fostered a shift towards private, in particular funded, pensions. We will analyse two particular aspects of the privatization, and the position of unions on these developments. First, we look at the coverage of occupational pensions and the scope for negotiated occupational pensions. The more successfully unions can negotiate relatively encompassing occupational pensions, the less they may be opposed to a shift towards privatization, while weak or fragmented unions and those facing a tradition of voluntary employer-sponsored plans will be more likely to oppose such privatization. Finally, we will discuss the reasons for governments and unions to seek to act concertedly on pension reform, and the situations in which political or societal consensus has been crucial in assuring long-term reform progress.

4.1. LONG-TERM AND SHORT-TERM REFORM PRESSURES ON PAY-AS-YOU-GO SYSTEMS

Governments are currently pressed to undertake unpopular reforms because today's pension systems face major short-term stresses and long-term challenges. Other things being equal, demographic ageing will force the future working population to finance a rising share of the gross national product for the elderly. Since public pension schemes are typically financed by a pay-as-you-go (PAYG) system,[1] a cut in benefits or a rise in social contributions in order to restore financial soundness in the future will upset intergenerational solidarity. Older workers and those already retired, who have paid into the scheme in the past, see the current benefits as their acquired rights. The increasing demographic imbalance between payers and beneficiaries will make increases in social insurance contribution or general taxes necessary if benefits are to remain at the same level. As was demonstrated (see Chapter 3), the younger cohorts have a much lower, if not negative, rate of return compared with the older cohorts: their parents have paid less into the public schemes than they now receive on average, while their children will get much less in future benefits. Thus, pension reform issues touch fundamental distributional issues that require unions to balance the interests of their older and younger (and potential future) members.

One reform proposal is a shift from pay-as-you-go to a funded system. Yet this poses a double-payer problem: the current active generation would have to pay for the defined benefit pensions of their parents and grandparents, and at the same time make additional savings for their own retirement which

---

[1] Pay-as-you-go (PAYG) systems are based on a direct transfer of payroll taxes from current workers to finance social security benefits of current retirees, with no accumulation of funds.

would be subject to uncertain financial performance. However, some economists (Feldstein, 1998) claim that the double-payer effect for younger cohorts depends on how fast the new system is phased in and to what degree the return on capital in a funded system would outperform the economic growth that is needed to mobilize the necessary resources under a pay-as-you-go system. While a radical system shift does not seem to be viable in democratic systems, a gradual phasing in of additional fully funded supplementary pensions would allow a smoother long-term transition and thus would reduce the double-payer problem. Nevertheless, public PAYG pension systems remain the main source of old-age provision even in countries that have promoted funded pensions. In particular, in order to avoid poverty among those with insufficient savings, some redistribution via state taxes or social insurance contribution will be still needed.

Moreover, current reform plans aim also at increasing the privatization of pensions, thereby forcing employers, unions, and individuals to internalize the costs of old-age protection. Employers might be willing to underwrite the financial risks of a defined benefit (DB) plan in order to attract and retain skilled workers, but more and more private pensions are fully funded under a defined contribution (DC) scheme, where the individual assumes all financial risks (but also benefits in case of exceptional returns). An expansion of the second and third pillar of pension systems (occupational and private pensions) will pose a difficult choice for unions. Occupational pensions might provide new opportunities for unions to negotiate social benefits that have been previously assumed by state initiative, enhancing their role *vis-à-vis* members (and non-members). But when unions are too weak, or if for other reasons they cannot negotiate such collective schemes, a move towards private pensions would undermine comprehensive coverage and solidaristic redistribution, thus reinforcing existing market inequalities.

While it is the long-term implications of an ageing society that make pension reform topical, the time-frame of politics is usually much shorter. The odds against major systemic reforms are relatively high, and when changes are phased in to make them less severe the economic gains take longer to set in. To trigger major reform efforts it often takes more pressing problems, such as current deficits of public pension systems that require bailing out by the state. Such problems constitute a powerful incentive to restore the fiscal soundness by a course of fiscal consolidation. The crises of the European Monetary System in 1992 and 1995, as well as the tight EMU convergence criteria, provided such pressures for reform. Since unions also have a long-term interest in the financial soundness of public pension schemes, their resistance towards benefit cuts is likely to be lower if the financial stability of these schemes is threatened. By the same token, unions might acquiesce to benefit cuts under conditions of pressing economic crisis.

The financing of rising social expenditures is a problem not only for public finances: it has also repercussions on economic competitiveness, if payroll and general taxes increase non-wage labour costs or provide pressure on wages. Thus, unions and employers would have an interest in lowering social expenditures, although they might not be willing to cut those benefits from which they profit most. In fact, all three major actors—the state, employers, and unions—may wish to shift or externalize costs on to others. Thus, in Germany past governments have shifted a part of the financial burdens of unification on to the social insurance system instead of raising general taxes, while the social partners have used the public programmes to finance early retirement in their own interests; both externalization strategies have pushed up non-wage labour costs (Manow and Seils, 2000). In addition to demographic pressures, therefore, the pervasive labour shedding strategy during the 1980s and 1990s increased social expenditures still further. Moreover, this reinforced the Continental dilemma (Scharpf, 1998): social transfers are paid as a result of a slack in labour demand (unemployment and early retirement), yet the financing via social contribution prices labour even further out of the market. The renegotiations of social security financing, in particular old-age provisions, thus becomes a major issue on the reform agenda, and a relatively contentious issue at that.

It should be emphasized that collective wage bargaining might aggravate the dynamics of rising public pension expenditures. Unions have been in favour of linking pension benefits of public pay-as-you-go systems not merely to inflation but also to wage gains; thus, senior workers and current pensioners often receive pension benefits that keep up with rising living standards. In this way, union bargaining policy has consequences for welfare expenditures through the linkage between wages and social benefits (Hassel and Ebbinghaus, 2000). In countries where retired civil servants are not covered by social insurance but receive retirement pay from the public budget (as in France and Germany), public wages determine not only civil servant wages but also their pension benefits. Moreover, these often favourable conditions have reinforced status divisions between civil servants and other public and private employees as well as leading to a high degree of organization which in turn defends their special status. Thus, cuts in the pension system for the private sector may not necessarily be carried out in the public sector as well.

4.2. TAX FINANCING OR PAYROLL CONTRIBUTIONS?

Public pension systems show considerable variation in their financing structures. Broadly speaking, we can distinguish between tax-financed and contribution-financed schemes, though very often the two are mixed (Hansen, 1999). In Denmark the basic pension is financed completely out of general taxation while the small supplementary pension is based on fixed contributions paid by employers and employees. The Dutch general pension, formerly paid by contribution, is since 1990 paid by an earmarked household income tax for which the general basic tax allowance is applied. Swedish basic pensions are financed by employer contributions and more recently also by employee payroll taxes. British basic pensions are financed by employer and employee contributions, though pensions for those without contributions are financed from general taxes. In the other countries the public pensions are financed primarily out of social contributions, though the state subsidizes a considerable share of expenditures, especially solidaristic benefits (e.g. minimum pensions in Austria). In France, in addition to employer and employee contributions, a general contribution covering all sources of income (*contribution sociale généralisée*) was introduced in the 1990s to finance the 'solidarity' repartition and to repay the social debt (see Table 4.2).

Moreover, while payroll-financed schemes differ in how employers and employees share the costs, there have been some major changes over time: in France, Italy, and Sweden the employers have traditionally shouldered the largest share of social contributions.[2] However, Sweden increased the employee contributions in the revised public pension scheme by bringing them into line with employer contributions.

While contribution-financed systems give more voice to organized labour and capital, and while benefits paid from employee contributions are perceived as acquired rights, the pressures for reform are also more eminent, given the direct impact of payroll taxes on labour costs. Generally, in contribution-financed systems unions have pressed to cover the financing of non-contributory benefits (such as credits for schooling and child-rearing) through higher state subsidies (Myles and Pierson, forthcoming). In these systems, unions also have a strong interest in stabilizing the revenue basis by closing loopholes that allow an opting-out of social security coverage. For instance, Austrian, Dutch, and German unions have welcomed recent reforms to make marginal part-time workers and the 'false self-employed' liable to contribution payments.

In France the creation of a new 'old-age solidarity fund' designed to finance non-contributory benefits, was *de facto* a recognition of the state's responsibility for non-contributory benefits. This distinction had been a central request of the labour movement in the previous years (Bonoli, 1999), and serves to guarantee their self-management role in pension insurance schemes. Unions therefore did not resist this reform (despite substantial benefit cuts), since it served their organizational self-interest. By the same token, retrenchment of non-contributory benefits, such as social assistance, usually meets with lower union resistance than is the case for benefits based on contributions, such as social insurance. Thus, in many countries non-contributory benefits (such as credits for schooling) proved to be a primary target for retrenchment of public pensions. In Sweden the universal basic pension, which was not related to individual contribution records, has now been transformed into a minimum

---

[2] Note that employer contributions are not always visible to employees in their payslips, in contrast to their own contributions.

Table 4.2. *Financing of old-age public pension schemes, 1999*

Country	Method of financing		State subsidy	Payroll contribution	
	PAYG	funded		Firm	Employee
Austria	X		23%	12.55% of payroll	10.25% of earnings
Denmark					
Basic pension	X		100%	—	—
Supplementary	X		—	Up to 1,788 kroner (full-time worker)	Up to 894 kroner (full-time worker) +1% of gross income (special pension savings scheme)
France	X		Variable	8.2% of covered earnings + 1.6% of payroll	6.55% of pensionable earnings + 0.1% of all earnings
Germany	X		27%	9.75% of covered earnings	9.75% of covered earnings
Italy	X		28%	23.8% of payroll	8.9% up to 65,280,000 lire per year, 9.9% for earnings exceeding that amount
Netherlands	X	(x)		—	19.3% (of income between 8,800 and 48,175 guilders per year)
Sweden					
Basic pension	X		38%	5.86% of payroll	—
Supplementary	X	(partial)	—	13% of payroll	1% of income
New system	16%[a]	2.5%[a]	—	9.25% of payroll	9.25% of pensionable income
United Kingdom	X		10%–15%	12.2% of employee's earnings over £83 a week[b]	10% between 66 and £500 of weekly earnings

[a] of contributions. [b]According to earnings level.

Source: US Social Security Administration (1999); Verband Deutscher Renteversicherungsträger (VDR) (1999); Kalisch and Tetsuya (1998).

guarantee pension for those who had no or little supplementary (ATP) pension. The two former public schemes became fully integrated into a new pension system that relies on employer and employee contributions (including a portion for an individualized pension fund). The result is a stronger distinction between contribution-related benefits and tax-financed means-tested assistance.

By and large, unions have opposed reforms that shift the financing burden from employers to wage-earners. This has been a major issue in the recent Swedish pension reform, according to which social contributions should be shared equally between wage-earners and employers. As Anderson (1998) points out, this shift was aimed primarily to increase the visibility of pension contributions rather than change the actual amount of contributions paid. Nevertheless, Swedish trade unions feared that not all wage-earners might get full compensation through higher gross wages. In order to assure union acquiescence, the minimum earnings ceiling for income taxes was lifted as part of the reform package, relieving low-wage workers from the shift in social contributions.

4.3. REVERSING EARLY RETIREMENT

The trend towards early retirement can be found in all OECD countries (Ebbinghaus, 2000), but the decline in employment rate among older working people (55–64), especially male workers (see Figure 4.1), varies across welfare regimes. It has been least dramatic in Japan and more moderate in the United States, while most Continental European welfare states show a dramatic decline: today more than every second older man of working age (55–64) has already withdrawn from the labour market. Early retirement in the United Kingdom is less pronounced, partly because of a lack of public income schemes. Sweden has had a relatively high level of employment, thanks to partial pension programmes and better integration of older workers in the workforce, but the recession of the early 1990s has contributed to rising old-age unemployment. The trends in employment for elderly women are less pronounced, given the traditionally lower employment rate among women and the increase in participation rates from cohort to cohort.

In nearly all European countries, unions have been lobbying for policies facilitating early exit from work in order to fight old-age unemployment arising from restructuring and to reduce overall labour supply in times of mass unemployment (Ebbinghaus, 2000). Moreover, worker representatives at the workplace supported early retirement policies to accommodate 'socially acceptable' restructuring and downsizing, and were willing to allow a breach of the seniority principle (in collective agreements and employment protection laws). An example is the German and Swedish practice of agreed dismissal of older workers at age 59 or 57; this allows elderly workers to obtain first long-term unemployment pensions, followed by disability/pre-retirement pensions (at 60), which bridge the time till normal retirement (at 65). Another example of collusion between employers and unions is the Dutch collective

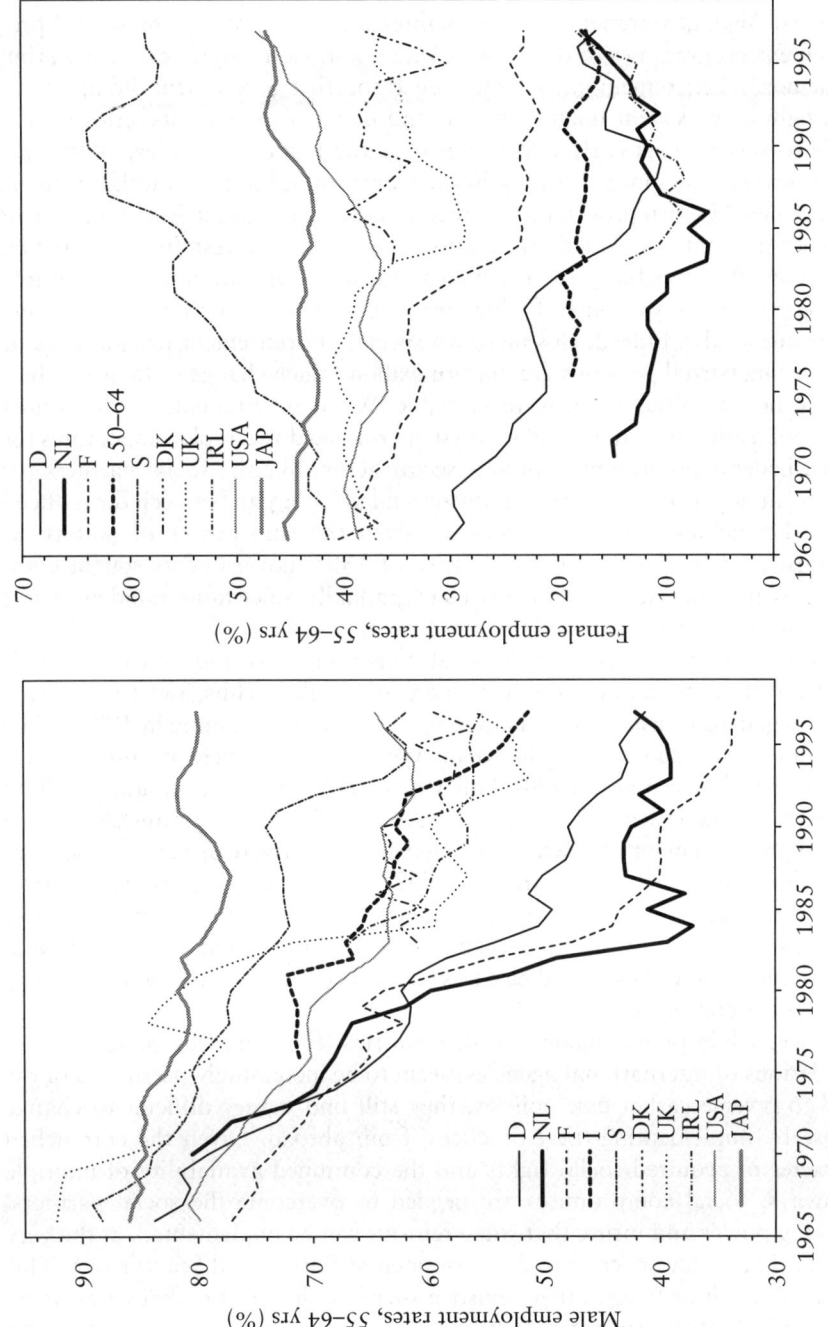

Figure 4.1. *Early retirement across OECD countries, 1965–1996*

Source: OECD, *Labour Force Statistics*, various years, calculations by authors.

pre-retirement insurance (VUT) negotiated at industry level by the social partners. Also, government policies facilitated early retirement by special pre-retirement programmes in the 1980s (Britain and Germany), or by a lowering of the normal retirement age (as the French socialist government did in 1983).

In light of persistent unemployment and financial constraints, efforts were made to reverse past early exit routes over the last two decades. While this policy reversal was most pressing in the Continental European welfare states, the envisaged U-turn proved most difficult in these very countries, in the face of entrenched rights defended by unions, employers' interest in externalizing costs, and the possibility of 'instrument substitution' presented by multiple alternative pathways (some of which were administered by the social partners at various levels). Indeed, closing down special pre-retirement programmes or introducing partial pensions did not bring about much change so long as other, more generous, alternatives were available. When governments (often against fierce opposition by unions) did succeed in bringing down replacement rates for public benefits programmes, private-sector actors like the social partners (or simply employers on their own) frequently filled in the gap between the reduced public benefit and former net wages. Given the veto power of unions, as demonstrated by the French strike wave of 1995, governments sought compromises allowing change to be phased in gradually, since more rapid measures would have adversely affected unemployment.

Higher unemployment and financial constraints also induced the Scandinavian welfare states to put on their emergency brakes. Thus, Sweden departed from its generous disability and gradual retirement programme in 1992, while the Danish government sought to intervene in collectively negotiated pre-retirement schemes in the 1990s. Policy reversal in the liberal-residual welfare states, given the few and limited pathways to early exit, was after closing the special pre-retirement Job Release Scheme in 1988, largely driven by long-term concerns about demographic trends and their financial implications. Reforms were phased in to restore long-term solvency and remove any incentives to quit work early. Indeed, disability benefits were always limited to cases of total incapacitation and thus would be a less common early exit from work pathway than on the continent.

Hence, while policy-makers in all countries (following the policy recommendations of international agencies) seem to be increasingly persuaded of the need to reverse earlier exit policies, they still find it very difficult to change course by implementing 'best practices' from abroad. Given the entrenched character of acquired social rights and the continued availability of multiple pathways, social compromises are needed to overcome the social partners' blocking power and insure that some reforms can be implemented, at the very least in that policy space shared by continental Europe and Scandinavia. This will be difficult as long as there exists a social coalition of early exit between firms (which strive to externalize their restructuring costs and circumvent seniority employment protection) and workers' interests (which perceive an acquired social right to an early retirement, given long working lives, substantial contributions, and a lack of jobs). Hence governments will need to bring the social partners into a reform consensus in order to achieve a reversal. This would require cooperation at several levels (from the national bargaining arena to the workplace) and a coordination of changes across different public, bipartite, and voluntary policies in order to avoid instrument substitution and mere cost shifting from one scheme to another.

4.4. HOW TO CALCULATE BENEFITS FAIRLY

In addition to reversing the trend of early retirement by making the premature drawing of pensions 'actuarially' fair, changing the calculation bases of pension benefits from final salary to contribution history also brings about important savings and provides incentives for accepting longer working lives. Moreover, the harmonization of benefit rules across different sectors and status groups also increases fairness and limits rent-seeking by special interest groups. With regard to these benefit fairness issues, the position of trade unions is shaped largely by the degree of occupational fragmentation. The more universal the coverage and the more harmonious the benefits, the more redistribution can be achieved and the fewer discretionary policies can be carried out—the universal Danish, Dutch, and Swedish basic pension systems, for instance, leave less space for particularistic interests. By contrast, when public and private systems are fragmented along lines of occupational status, there is greater potential for rivalry among unions; Austria, Germany, France, and Italy are cases in point. Certainly, while unions of unskilled workers might press for a harmonization of benefit levels, unions representing skilled workers, white-collar employees, or civil servants are likely to defend the pension privileges of their members. Given the partly diverging interests of unions in a categorically fragmented pension landscape, governments might overcome resistance to pension reform by divide-and-rule strategies; but it might prove difficult to alter the benefits of those groups that have particularly vested interests and are powerful enough to oppose change.

The fragmented French social security system is a case in point. Plans to unify social security failed immediately after the war; the new 'general regime' included only private employees (with further divisions of supplementary pensions into 'cadres' and other employees), while the pre-existing more generous schemes in the public and semi-public sectors remained separate.[3]

---

[3] Over 100 such special schemes cover one-fifth of all employees in France today, the large majority of civil servants and utility workers ('*régimes particuliers*') and semi-public-sector employees ('*régimes spéciaux*') such as railway employees, miners, and central bank employees (Palier, 1997: 87). Moreover, the '*cadres*' (managerial and professional staff) in the private sector signed a collective agreement on supplementary pensions in 1947 to maintain similar standards of living after retirement, while lower-grade white-collar and blue-collar workers only gradually received negotiated occupational pensions, though with more moderate supplementary benefits (on average, one-third of benefits for *cadres*) (Reynaud, 1997: 97).

These fragmented schemes have not only given rise to conflicting interests, but also are amplified by organizational splits and aggravated by political rivalry between union movements. Efforts by French governments to harmonize eligibility criteria and benefits, as well as to enforce 'solidarity' across occupations—that is, financial redistribution among the schemes—have met with fierce resistance by vested interests, particularly public employees, under the special regimes. The reform by the conservative Balladur government in 1993 circumvented the problem of potential resistance from the powerful public-sector unions by confining the welfare cuts to the 'general regime' which affects only private employees (Levy, 2000). On the other hand, the subsequent conservative Juppé government caused major upheavals in the winter of 1995/6 when it announced that it would introduce similar measures for the special and particular regimes in the public sector, such as the increase of the contribution period from 37.5 to 40 years and the abolition of the early retirement at age 55 under the special regimes. These measures were not implemented, and so it is now down to the new left government under Jospin to establish equality between the two sectors. The recent call by Jospin for negotiations of a 'pension pact' that would bring the special regimes into line with the private sector met with resistance from most public-sector unions, which claimed that the government should undo the 1993 reform instead of cutting civil servants' pensions (*Le Monde*, 22–3 March 2000).

Even in universal pension systems without occupational divisions, governments have been attempting to bring about pension reform by divide-and-rule strategies. They might exploit existing interest cleavages within the union camp (for instance between white-collar and blue-collar workers) that emerge from the differential impact of universal benefit calculation for particular occupational groups. Benefit calculations may differ considerably between various pension schemes; they can be anywhere on a wide spectrum stretching from means-tested/universal flat-rate benefits to purely earnings-related/contribution-defined benefit formulas. The choice of benefit calculation has a differential impact on occupational groups: blue-collar workers with a comparatively even distribution of income throughout their working life tend to profit more from benefit calculation based on lifetime income, whereas white-collar employees typically show a steeper and often shorter employment career and thus would gain disproportionally from a benefit formula according to which the reference salary is based on a number of 'best years' (rather than the totality of career earnings), and to which the period needed to qualify for a full pension is comparatively low.

It should not come as a surprise that unions are likely to take different positions concerning the most favourable mix of benefit calculation for their specific rank-and-file. From a 'fairness' point of view, one might expect that more encompassing union confederations, representing the general interests of wage-earners rather than the particular interests of single industries or occupational groups, should opt for a benefit calculation following the principle of lifetime income rather than for one based on a quite arbitrary number of 'best years' or final salary, which often results in perverse redistributive and allocative effects. In this respect, cross-national organizational differences may play out differently: in Nordic countries the peak labour associations are split by collarline differences (blue-collar, white-collar, academics), whereas in some Continental European countries special civil servant federations (Germany, the Netherlands) or autonomous union/strike movements (France, Italy) defend the vested interests of their membership *vis-à-vis* the more encompassing political union movements. Yet, despite the historical institutional and organizational divisions, we do observe a comparatively general convergence towards 'actuarial fairness' in the reform of earnings-related pension schemes, all the more so since this shift is also likely to strengthen work incentives. Thus, the necessity of 'actuarial fairness' within the pension system is a powerful argument for the legitimation of benefit cuts for those who profited from favourable early retirement or defined benefit rules.

4.5. PRIVATIZATION BY MANDATED OR VOLUNTARY OCCUPATIONAL PENSIONS?

Privatization in pension provision has been a major reform trend, though there are important cross-national variations in the importance of private pensions *vis-à-vis* public pensions. As was discussed before (see Chapter 2), in most Nordic and Continental European countries the first, public pillar is by and large the dominant pension system. (Exceptions are the French, Dutch, and more recently Danish private pensions.) In countries with flat-rate basic pensions and insufficient superannuation, occupational and private tiers play a more important role. Thus, in the UK and Japan, those with an adequate private pension can opt out of the earnings-related state pension. The importance of occupational pensions can be seen from coverage rates. Almost all workers in France and the Netherlands are covered by supplementary occupational pensions owing to the state extension of collective agreements (nationwide and sector-wide, respectively), while in other countries (Austria and Italy) the fraction of the workforce contributing to these plans is negligible. The coverage rates are around 40%–50% in the Anglo-Saxon countries (Canada, UK, USA) and also in Japan and Germany. There are important differences in the maturity of these schemes and thus also in the number of beneficiaries, but there are also important differences in the calculation, portability, and indexation of benefits (see Table 4.3).

Occupational pensions are nearly as widespread in Germany as in Britain, although the pension benefits are much less important in Germany, given the still high replacement rate of the state pensions compared with Britain. However, recent plans to lower the replacement rate of old-age insurance by the red–green governments would require a substantial expansion of occupational

Table 4.3. *Occupational pension (OP) coverage and funded pension features, late 1990s*[a]

	Pensioners receiving OP	Labour force covered by OP	Dominant benefit	Maturity of scheme	Portability	Indexation
Canada	54% men, 31% women, 41% total	52% men, 36% women, 45% total	Largely DB	Mature	Vesting after 2 years; little indexation of accrued benefits	Provisions rare; some discretionary increases
Germany	21% men, 9% women	42% total	Largely DB	Immature	Vesting in 10 years; indexation of accrued benefits	Mandatory.
Japan	10% total[b]	38% total	Largely DB (opt-out of earnings-related state pension)	Immature	Vesting graded between 5 and 30 years for voluntary leavers	Rare
Netherlands	76% men, 23% women, 50% total	90% total	DB around 75% of final salary	Mature	Vesting in one year; accrued benefits indexed	Almost universal, though not mandatory
UK	66% total	50% total	Largely DB–final salary (opt-out of SERPS)	Mature	Vesting in 2 years; indexation of accrued benefits	Discretionary, but total or partial indexation quite common
USA	47.5% men, 25.5% women, 35.5% total	44% total	Largely DB–final salary	Mature	Vesting in 5 years; no indexation of accrued benefits	Full indexation rare, discretionary increases common

[a]DB = defined benefit; funded schemes are not all OPs.
[b]Figures on recipients in Japan underestimate pensioner rate owing to common practice of one-time lump-sum benefits.

Source: P. Johnson (1998); Davis (1995); and OECD (1998).

pensions. Some unions, in particular IG Metall, are opposed to such state plans, since these new private pensions would have to be paid by employees alone and would entail financial market risks, so that a part of future negotiated wage gains would be consumed by old-age savings.

Of crucial importance for unions is the question of whether they can co-determine occupational pensions via collective bargaining, or whether these private pensions are voluntary commitments by employers or even just individual private savings plans. Collectively negotiated occupational pensions are now comprehensive in France, but also in most sectors in the Netherlands and Sweden. In Germany occupational pensions for non-tenured public workers are based on a collective agreement dating from the late 1960s. Most recently, in Austria and Italy, collective agreements in several sectors established occupational pensions. Voluntary employer plans play a crucial role in the United Kingdom and in the private sector in Germany.

To the extent that public schemes lose the capacity to fully maintain the standard of living during old age, unions are in favour of compensation through collectively negotiated occupational pensions. This expands the role of unions in wage bargaining as contributions to these schemes become a part of 'deferred wages'. Thus, Dutch wage bargaining in recent years has entailed wage moderation in return for an expansion of occupational benefits. By contrast, voluntary employer plans are a part of 'fringe' benefits and are rarely negotiated, giving unions little influence. Instead, unions have to press for state regulation concerning the vesting and transportability of benefits. They also give preference to collectively negotiated schemes over voluntary employer plans, since the latter typically achieve a much smaller coverage and are often concentrated among white-collar employees in high-income brackets. By contrast, collectively negotiated schemes allow unions to bargain over higher coverage and about substantial rights to their members such as portability and equal treatment of men and women (Hutsebaut, 1999). Nevertheless, even collectively negotiated pensions may reflect different interest structures and power constellations within the trade union camp. For instance, the mandatory French occupational system is based on, and reinforces, the historical division between high replacement schemes for 'cadres' (professional and managerial employees) and other lower skilled employees.

In order to overcome the uneven coverage in voluntary systems, unions have been in favour of making occupational pensions compulsory by legislation where they could not achieve the same by collective bargaining. Thus, recently German unions have demanded that, if the Schröder government wants to promote funded occupational pensions in addition to the public schemes, then such pensions should be made mandatory and be financed by employers. In contrast to mandatory old-age provision on a purely individual basis (an option that is currently under serious discussion in Germany), occupational pensions are typically financed to a large degree by employers. Yet employers insist that occupational pensions should remain as a voluntary fringe benefit.

4.6. TOWARDS MORE FUNDED PRIVATE PENSION SYSTEMS

Occupational pensions have assumed a new importance as governments have become interested in shifting pension provision from public pay-as-you-go systems to private funded schemes. Although traditionally occupational pensions were defined benefit schemes underwritten by employers, recent evidence suggests that there is a definite move in Europe towards the emergence of defined contribution private pension schemes, be it a change from current DB to current DC schemes or the introduction of new DC schemes (Andrietti, 2000). Whether DB or DC, most occupational pension systems are heavily funded, with the exception of systems based on *book reserves*, which are most common among the larger German and Japanese firms. There are still large differences between the assets saved through occupational pensions and through mutual pension funds across countries, although there are significant increases over time resulting from the maturation, appreciation, and expanding coverage of both schemes (see Table 4.4).

In contrast to PAYG public pensions, most occupational schemes are funded, with the exception of the French mandatory supplementary pension, the German public employee scheme, and part of the Swedish collectively negotiated occupational schemes. Some occupational pension funds, for instance in Germany, Britain, and the Netherlands, are defined benefit schemes, where employers underwrite any deficit that may arise from uncovered benefit claims, hence giving rise to hybrid funding. The unfavourable demographic

Table 4.4. *Assets of pension funds as a percentage of GDP in selected countries, 1988 and 1996*

Country	1988	1996	Growth	Country	1988	1996	Growth
Anglo-Saxon				Continental			
Australia	21.1	31.6	+49.8	Austria	0	1.2	—
Canada	26.4	43	+62.9	Belgium	2.4	4.1	+70.8
Ireland	29	45	+55.2	Germany[a]	3.4	5.8	+70.6
UK	58.2	74.7	+28.4	Luxembourg	16.9	19.7	+16.6
USA	36.8	58.2	+58.2	Netherlands	72.7	87.3	20.1
Asian				Switzerland	64.5	117.1	+81.6
Japan[a]	33.7	41.8	+24.0	Southern			
Korea	3.4	3.3	−2.9	France	—	5.6	—
Nordic				Greece	—	12.7	—
Denmark	10.9	23.9	+119.3	Italy	—	3	—
Finland	19.7	40.8	+107.1	Portugal	—	9.9	—
Norway	3.9	7.3	+87.2	Spain	0.1	3.8	+3700
Sweden	30.9	32.6	+5.5				

[a]Not including book reserves, also European Federation for Retirement Provision (1996).
Source: OECD (1998: table V.1).

development is often assumed to be a comparatively limited problem for funded defined contribution schemes, since in these schemes each person builds up savings for their own retirement, and are thus unaffected by a worsening relation between contribution-payers and beneficiaries. (However, there might be secondary effects when all baby boomers cash in their stock market gains at the same time in the future!) Moreover, a rising life expectancy will exert pressure on funded defined benefit schemes as well, especially since individuals who retire will have to buy (relatively costly) annuities out of their life-cycle savings in order to avoid running out of their pension income during their lifetime as a result of longer longevity or financial market problems. Nevertheless, in recent decades funded schemes have been able to realize a higher rate of return than PAYG systems, whether public benefits were linked to wage growth or inflation. On the other hand, private funded schemes clearly entail financial risks and provide only limited leeway for solidaristic redistribution compared with public pay-as-you-go pension schemes. Therefore many unions have voiced criticism about the former.

Moreover, unions fear that the growth of pension funds might strengthen the pressure on firms to raise their rate of return at the expense of wage-earners, for instance by further downsizing or by squeezing wages in relation to profits. Unions are therefore often opposed to a shift from public PAYG systems or DB occupational pensions to private pension funds with only DC benefits. When such schemes are to be installed, unions prefer to have influence over the implementation, the monitoring, and the investment decisions (Hutsebaut, 1999). Pension funds could also be a selective membership incentive, as is the case for union pension funds in the USA, though collective bargaining practice in Continental Europe would make discrimination between union members and non-union members difficult to uphold.

Given the pressure towards private funded pensions, unions are now confronted with such schemes even in countries that have had hardly any experience of them, such as Austria and Italy. In recent years in Austria, Italy, and France funded occupational pensions have been promoted as a safeguard against the demographic problems with publicly mandated PAYG systems. In Italy the social partners negotiated occupational pensions in some branches, partly integrating the end-of-service pay, a deferred wage under many past collective agreements. In Austria tax exemptions are granted only for non-negotiated voluntary employer contributions (that is, they are considered fringe benefits), which has limited the growth potential for negotiated occupational schemes. In France the Conservatives' plans for promoting funded private pensions have been halted by the government change to the left. The Jospin government seems more keen to extend the reserve funds for the current systems than to foster pension funds *à l'anglaise*.

The French and Swedish experiences provide some clue as to how union resistance against pension funds might be circumvented. The French government under Socialist Jospin is reconsidering a reorganization of the new pension funds initially introduced by its Conservative predecessor and currently managed by private companies, proposing instead schemes that would be jointly managed by the social partners. Moreover, in order to counter fears that the establishment of occupational pension funds would erode the financial basis of the public PAYG system, contributions to pension funds will not be deductible from contributions to the public scheme (Levy, 2000). An even more important system change was decided in Sweden in 1998: individual pension accounts on a funded basis are now part of the Swedish public pension (phased in until 2001). The basic and earnings-related pensions will be fully integrated in the new pension scheme, which will be funded jointly by employer and employees (18.5% of wages), and a part of the contribution (2.5% of payroll) will be paid into personal investment funds. While the unions were basically against the individualized pension funds, their acquiescence was assured by the foundation of a state-run pension fund for those unwilling to place their money in a private market fund (Nilsson, 1998).

4.7. UNILATERAL OR NEGOTIATED REFORMS?

Given the long-term nature of pensions and the unpopularity of changes in public pension schemes, political actors have sought to avoid or at least share the blame for retrenchment through concertation with other political actors. By the same token, where governments have tried to curtail pensions unilaterally, the risk of failure has been evident.

The British welfare retrenchment is a remarkable exception to this generalization, since the unilaterally imposed cuts in the pension system *were* implemented successfully. Despite fierce union resistance, the Thatcher government in 1986 introduced in addition to occupational pensions, an option for private pensions involving the contracting-out of the public earnings-related state pension scheme (SERPS). Thus, contrary to the experiences in other European countries, the uncompromising style of policy-making pursued by the Thatcher government, in particular *vis-à-vis* the labour movement, did not result in a failure of the reform, essentially because trade unions were not able to organize resistance to it from a large number of current or future benefit recipients since the earnings-related pension was still relatively new and interests were not particularly vested in it (Bonoli, 1999; Pierson, 1994). Also, the British unions have no direct involvement in public pension policy or in the field of private and occupational pensions, and therefore the government does not need their cooperation for implementation. Most importantly, the political system provides nearly unlimited power to the governing majority in Parliament. At the same time, the weakened Labour Party was unable to present itself as a credible alternative to a Conservative government, and thus failed to take advantage of the pension issue in electoral terms. Nevertheless, even British governments have to listen to concerns of the electorate; thus, the 1995 pension reform was a reaction to the Maxwell scandal concerning the misuse of occupational pension funds. On the other hand, the New Labour government of 1997 has not undone its predecessors' reform but has proposed only limited changes of the private (now labelled 'stakeholder') pension, thereby further limiting the opportunities for unions to influence the government on welfare policies.

At least outside Britain, the unilateral imposition of pension cuts is likely to trigger substantial and often successful opposition from trade unions. Unions not only have more political and economic power in the Nordic welfare states, and to a lesser degree in Continental Europe: they are also considered to be a major proponent of the social insurance system, in which they often play an institutionalized role (see Chapter 2). This suggests that a policy style characterized by concertation clearly helps to strengthen the prospects for the sustainability of effective reforms. Major pension reform attempts that did not have the acquiescence from the trade unions have failed, most notably under the Berlusconi government in Italy in 1994 and under the Juppé government in France in 1995, when the social protests forced these two conservative governments to backtrack in their pension reforms (Ebbinghaus and Hassel, 2000). By contrast, most of the 'successful' pension reforms were more or less peacefully adopted thanks to interparty consensus and/or consultation of the social partners (Austria in 1996 and 1997, France in 1993, Germany in 1989, Italy in 1992, 1995, 1997, Sweden in 1994, 1998, Spain in 1997, and Finland in 1999). These reforms entail various forms of (at least in the long-run) effective expenditure reduction: the link between contributions and benefit was tightened, sharper eligibility rules (especially for early retirement) were introduced, replacement rates were lowered, and the legal retirement age was raised (Baccaro, 2000).

Thus, apart from the exceptional British case, systemic pension reforms in Europe proved difficult *without* a large societal consensus. Since pensions require a long-term perspective, a broad political and social coalition is needed to guarantee that future governments or collective actors will not undo past decisions. Yet there are different ways in which the reforms of the 1990s have taken into account the different societal interests. In some countries social consensus has been achieved primarily through interparty compromise, that is, between governing and opposition parties, though unions could voice their interests within the Left-wing and Christian democratic parties. For instance, the German 1992 pension reform was based on an interparty consensus between the Christian Democrats and the Social Democrats reached in 1989. But this consensus was short-lived as the subsequent German experience shows. A new pension reform, referred to as the 1999-reform, as it should take effect in 1999, was passed in 1997 with a substantial lack of consensus. In fact, after the breakdown of the tripartite Alliance talks in 1995 the 1999-reform was largely opposed by the opposition party in 1997 and was later nullified by the change in power to the Left in 1999. As a result, the reform did not take effect in 1999. In Sweden, after failed efforts of societal committees including the social partners to find a common proposal, the main parties that had supported the initial reform law in 1994 struck a deal in an informal working group, without the social partners and the reform–opposing other parties, which was enacted in 1998 (Wadensjö, 2000). Here the main parliamentary parties were the mediators of the conflicting societal interests, and they were able to find a common consensus that would be difficult for either of the social partners to challenge.

The Italian reform process is instructive for the role that societal concertation can play when the political system is lacking the legitimacy and the capability of reaching a societal consensus. After failed attempts in the 1980s, the Amato government introduced by decree, during a difficult economic crisis, a long-term change in benefit calculations. Only a year later, in midst of the deep crisis of the Italian political system, the technocratic Ciampi government added *ad hoc* measures that remained small incremental steps, not much altering the 'acquired rights', particularly for senior workers. Yet in late 1994 the new centre–right government under Berlusconi 'tried to change unwritten rules of the game that had regulated the Italian social security system' (Regini and Regalia, 1997: 216), provoking widespread protest by the unions, which finally forced the government to backtrack. But in May 1995 the new Dini government, supported by the parliamentary Left, was able to strike a deal with the unions (Ferrera, 1997: 241). While the law introduced important system changes and stood up to incrementalist policy-making traditions, the 'key condition for obtaining trade-union consensus was, in fact, retention of the previous pension system as far as more elderly workers were concerned, with the introduction of a new and more rigorous system for workers with lower seniority' (Regini and Regalia, 1997: 217).

The Austrian case is also illustrative of the advantages of negotiated reform, as it shows how it is possible not only to circumvent blockage but also to avoid blame. In a remarkable break with the long-term tradition of intense concertation with the social partners, the Austrian government unilaterally worked out an austerity plan in 1994. This procedure was heavily criticized by the unions. Since the Social Democrats were dependent on support by the trade unionists in parliament, the government was forced to adopt a watered-down version of the savings package in 1995. By contrast, the second austerity package adopted in 1996, which was negotiated with the social partners, was far more severe than the first one and covered basically all expenditures of the central state. In the area of pensions, the yearly adjustment of pensions was suspended for one year (two years for civil servants' pensions), eligibility criteria for earlier retirement were tightened, and early retirement benefits (also for civil servants' pensions) were lowered. Paradoxically, as Tálos points out, 'the social partners had gone much further than the government would ever have dared' (interview cited in Hemerijck *et al.*, 2000). In 1997 the grand coalition government initially tried to push through the pension reform in the face of massive resistance from the trade unions, but finally struck a last-minute deal with the social partners, which entailed among other things a long-term phasing in of cuts in early retirement pensions and a harmonization of public-sector pension rules with the less generous schemes in the private sector.

To sum up, unions still play a critical role in pension politics. By and large, governments find that concertation with the unions seems a more promising strategy than unilateral retrenchment. To some extent, reaching a consensus in the parliamentary arena might constitute an alternative to negotiating pension deals with the trade unions: at least, interparty compromises might serve as a counterweight to unrealistic union demands. Moreover, pension reform packages might be tailored so as to combine a strategy of overall consolidation with appropriate side-payments to the unions. Empirical evidence suggests that substantial pension reform is difficult, but not impossible, to bring about if a political exchange is possible. The more the union movements are encompassing and have to internalize the welfare effects of their behaviour, the more they will be forward-looking and willing to negotiate employment-friendly welfare reforms that reduce non-wage labour costs and eradicate unfair differences between sectors or social groups.

While some of the pension reform measures will have positive welfare effects, union movements are also worried about potential rising inequalities through uneven coverage, financial market risks, and limited redistribution. A shift towards more private funded schemes may be only the second-best option for many union movements that have profited in the past from expansive public pension systems, but it can also provide a potential new role for unions: negotiating occupational pensions and becoming involved in the administration of pension funds. However, whether this is a possible and acceptable strategy for a union depends not only on the welfare regime, the government regulations, and the reform proposal, but also on the union's organizational cohesion and its strength in the collective bargaining realm.

5

Unions and Unemployment Insurance

We have already noticed that the differences in unionization rates across countries seem to have something to do with how unemployment insurance (UI) is organized in different countries. Here we present a more detailed discussion of the interplay between unemployment insurance and unions. The organization of unemployment insurance affects workers' propensity to join unions and possibly also wage bargaining and the enforcement of the work test in UI. We also explore how the strength of unions may influence UI polices. Finally, we discuss how UI reforms may be designed so as to encourage wage moderation.

5.1. UNEMPLOYMENT INSURANCE AND THE DEMAND FOR UNION MEMBERSHIP

5.1.1. *Theoretical issues*

How would the organization of unemployment insurance affect workers' propensity to join unions? It is useful to distinguish between two effects. The first effect works through the demand for union services, taking the (real) wage as given. We refer to this as the effect on membership demand, or simply the membership effect. The second effect might be referred to as the wage effect: the organization of unemployment insurance may influence real wage outcomes, which in turn might affect workers' decisions to join unions.

We outline a simple framework for thinking about membership demand, drawing on Booth and Chatterji (1995) and Holmlund and Lundborg (1999). We think of an economy with industry-wide wage bargaining and open-shop trade unions. Negotiated contracts are extended to all workers in the industry, irrespective of whether or not they are union members. Workers' membership decisions are taken by comparing the benefits and costs of joining a union, given knowledge of labour demand and thereby the risk of becoming unemployed. The benefits include union services in general, and possibly UI benefits in case of a Ghent system. The costs include regular membership fees as well as UI premiums if a Ghent system is in place.

Why do some workers join unions while others do not? There are a number of conceivable sources of worker heterogeneity that may be of importance. Workers may differ with respect to the valuation they place on regular union services, they may differ with respect to access to income sources while unemployed, or they may face different unemployment risks. To model all these different forms of heterogeneity simultaneously is hardly feasible. We focus on the first mentioned type of heterogeneity; that is, we assume that the valuation of union services varies among the workers. Suppose that the worker compares the expected utility of joining the union with the expected utility of being a non-member. The worker chooses membership as long as the value of membership exceeds the value of being a non-member. Under suitable assumptions, then, there exists a 'marginal' worker who is indifferent between the two options. The identity of the marginal worker varies depending on the economic environment, for example the generosity of benefits, the level of UI premiums, and the risk of becoming unemployed. The indifference condition for the marginal worker allows us to derive a relationship for membership demand with intuitive properties. We focus on three predictions.

1. First and most obvious is the *the organization of UI matters for membership decisions*. If union membership entails unemployment benefits over and above what is available for non-members, there is an incentive to join a union. If the government in a Ghent country takes a step towards a compulsory system by creating a 'basic' unemployment compensation scheme for *all* unemployed, irrespective of union membership status, there is a weaker incentive to join a union.

In practice, Ghent countries have introduced basic UI schemes in the form of benefits for workers who are not members of the UI funds, but with much lower replacement rates than for those who are members. The extreme form of a basic UI scheme is a system with no benefit differentials between members and non-members (effectively a compulsory system); the incentives to join unions will then of course be even weaker.

2. The second prediction concerns the effects of changes in the financing of unemployment insurance. The higher the subsidies to the UI funds are, the lower are the UI premiums for union members and the lower the price of subscribing to such funds. Membership would thus rise as a response to more generous subsidies.

3. The third prediction is that a greater risk of unemployment will raise the demand for union membership in a Ghent system. A greater unemployment risk implies a decline in expected utility for both members and non-members, but the decline is smaller for members because of the availability of UI benefits. The attractiveness of union membership therefore increases. We should therefore expect that union density in a Ghent system will rise if labour market conditions worsen, i.e. if unemployment rises. The direction of the unionization responses to unemployment in compulsory systems is less clear, since there is no obvious reason why a greater unemployment risk should change the relative value of membership relative to non-membership in a particular direction.

The fact that workers can, in fact, join the UI fund directly—without joining the union—complicates the analysis by introducing a third option. Direct membership implies absence of costs as well as benefits associated with regular union services. The choice between taking the direct as opposed to the union-administered route to the UI fund is presumably affected by the relative costs of the options. (The options yield the same insurance benefits.) The direct route can be more expensive, as the UI funds (at least in Sweden) tend to charge higher UI premiums for workers who have chosen direct membership. This premium differentiation may be the result of higher cost of administration for direct membership, and perhaps also a desire to encourage union-mediated membership.

5.1.2. *Empirical evidence*

There is a large empirical literature on the determinants of union density. The role of the organization of unemployment insurance has been examined in some of these studies. For example, Rothstein (1990) and Western (1993, 1994, 1997) use aggregate data for a number of countries and find in their cross-country regressions that union density is substantially higher (13–20 percentage points higher) in Ghent countries. Note that the 'raw' difference between union density in Sweden and Norway is around 25 percentage points.

It is also interesting to note that the relationship between unemployment and union density appears to depend on the prevailing UI system. Western (1993) uses pooled time series on postwar data and finds that a rise in unemployment induces higher union density in Ghent countries, whereas the effect is negative in other countries.[1] Evidence of positive unemployment effects on union density in Ghent countries is also reported in time-series analysis on Finnish data (Pehkonen and Tanninen, 1995) and Danish data (Pedersen, 1990).

Simple 'eyeball econometrics' reveal that similar effects are present also in Sweden. Figure 5.1 plots unionization and aggregate unemployment rates for the period 1987–99. Union density is shown separately for employees on permanent and on temporary contracts. The sharp increase in unemployment in the early 1990s is associated with marked increases in unionization rates. These patterns do not seem to be driven by compositional effects, as they survive if we disaggregate by age, gender, and sector.

The Finnish experience is fairly similar to the Swedish one: the huge increase in unemployment in the early 1990s—from 3.6% in 1990 to almost 18% in 1993—was associated with a substantial increase in union density, which rose from 72% in 1990 to 80% in 1993. Norway is another interesting

---

[1] There is a fairly large empirical literature that exploits time-series data in order to uncover the effects on union density of various macroeconomic variables (unemployment, inflation, etc.). The paper by Ashenfelter and Pencavel (1969) is perhaps the best known early example of this tradition. The microeconomic underpinnings of these empirical models are often weak, however, and the empirical results seem to have been fragile.

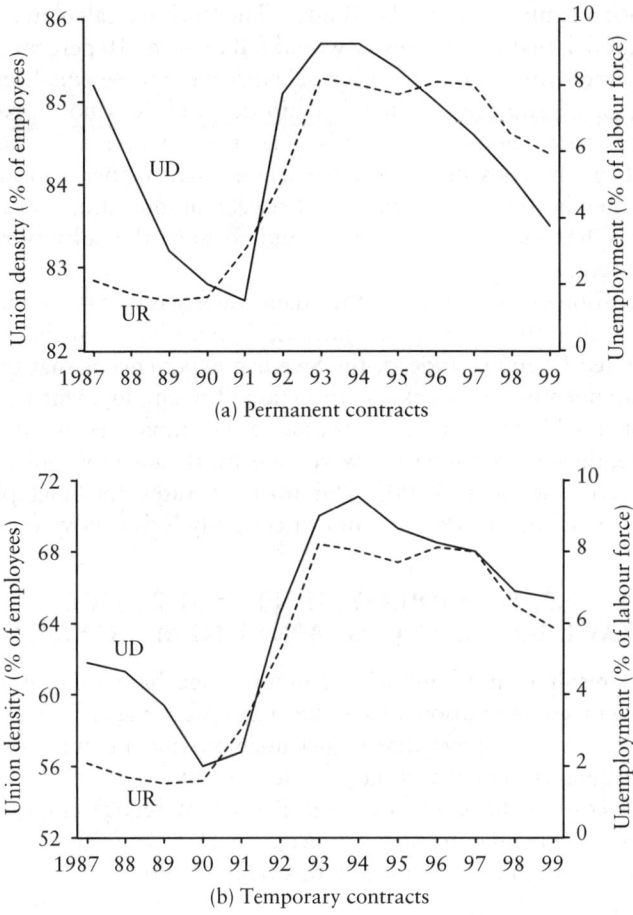

Figure 5.1. *Union density (UD) and unemployment (UR) in Sweden, 1987–1999*
Sources: Statistics Sweden and Kjellberg (2000).

counterfactual. Norway had around 2.5% unemployment in the mid-1980s; by 1992 this was close to 6%. Union density was remarkably stable, however, at 56% in 1985 as well as in 1992.

Changes in the benefit system that affect the relative rewards to union membership in the Ghent system also seem to have effects on unionization rates. The time-series analyses by Pehkonen and Tanninen (1995) for Finland and Pedersen (1990) for Denmark are at least consistent with this claim. A crucial variable in the study by Pehkonen and Tanninen is the relationship between the level of regular benefits (provided by the UI funds run by the unions) and the level of basic unemployment assistance (available for those who are not members of the UI funds). The authors calculate, using their estimated model, that union density would fall by some 10 percentage points if the two unemployment compensation schemes were to be equalized.

The role of UI subsidies in membership demand does not appear to have been subject to econometric analysis. The trend patterns in the data are, however, broadly consistent with the claim that higher subsidies should encourage membership. The difference between unionization rates in Sweden and Norway has increased over time, and so have the subsidy rates in the Swedish system.

An implication of a UI system of the Ghent variety is that it encourages union membership also among the *unemployed*, as benefits are disbursed through union-affiliated UI funds. Indeed, the Swedish experience is that unionization rates among unemployed workers who entered unemployment from employment are at roughly the same level as among the employees at work. In 1998, for example, the membership rates were 77% for the unemployed and 81% for the employed (Kjellberg, 2000). Unionization rates for unemployed new entrants to the labour market are almost certainly lower, however.

5.2. UNEMPLOYMENT INSURANCE, WAGE BARGAINING, AND UNEMPLOYMENT

A standard result in most models of union wage bargaining is that higher unemployment compensation raises the negotiated wage. This rise in wage pressure is driven by the fact that higher unemployment compensation lowers the utility difference between employed and unemployed workers and therefore reduces the cost to the union of wage hikes that reduce employment. The organization of unemployment insurance, as well as the degree of centralization in wage bargaining, may modify this relationship.

The degree of centralization matters because of the induced tax effect of higher benefits and higher wages. Imagine an encompassing union that experiences a rise in benefits. This union will recognize that the higher expenditure on benefits will require higher taxes. It therefore will also recognize that higher wages will require higher taxes, which will moderate wage demands. A similar internalization of the financing of benefits may conceivably take place in a Ghent system, to the extent that the union perceives a direct link between the expenditure of the UI fund and the level of the UI premiums paid by the members of the fund. The connection between expenditure and premiums depends on the subsidy system.

How would more generous subsidies to the UI funds affect wage determination in a Ghent system? There are essentially two effects on incentives in wage-setting, which loosely may be thought of as an income effect and a substitution effect. These effects are similar to those that appear in response to a change in the tax rate on labour earnings. The income effect is due to the fact that higher subsidies allow lower UI premiums and thereby higher disposable income among the employed relative to unemployed workers. This tends to *reduce* wage pressure. The substitution effect arises as higher subsidies reduce the cost to the union of raising the wage, which tends to *increase* wage pressure. The net effect is generally ambiguous, but there is a presumption that the substitution effect dominates, so that wage pressure will in fact increase as a response to higher subsidies (Holmlund and Lundborg, 1999).

There is also an additional effect on wage-setting that is driven by the induced changes in union membership following higher subsidies. The rise in membership is likely to raise the negotiated wage since a larger membership makes it more difficult for the firms to replace striking workers with non-members, should a conflict occur. This effectively weakens the firm's hand in the bargain, and the negotiated wage increases.

A Ghent system thus has several effects on incentives in wage bargaining. A somewhat simplified characterization is as follows. On the one hand, the Ghent system encourages union membership and thus strengthens the union's relative bargaining power; wages are thereby increased and employment is reduced. On the other hand, the Ghent system can help to internalize the costs of wage increases and higher benefits. This would tend to encourage wage moderation and increase employment. A crucial prerequisite for the second effect is that the financing system is such that there exists some relationship between higher unemployment in a particular sector and the costs to union members in the form of higher UI premiums. The important element here is the costs of wage increases at the margin; a policy that makes the financing scheme such that it increases the marginal costs of wage increases will generally be good for employment. The effect is, in fact, analogous to that of higher tax progressivity (cf. Lockwood and Manning, 1993). As is by now well established from a variety of models of non-competitive wage-setting, a rise in tax progressivity is conducive to wage moderation.

There are other aspects of the Ghent system that may also contribute to wage moderation. There is a possible 'enfranchising effect' arising from the fact that the system encourages union membership among the unemployed. This could increase the influence of the unemployed in wage-setting, thus possibly reducing the dominance of employed 'insiders'. Another possible effect relates to an argument made by Holden and Raum (1991). Their argument is that a large union membership can facilitate coordination in wage bargaining. Since the Ghent system encourages union membership, it may also be conducive to coordinated wage agreements.

There is fairly robust evidence from various cross-country regressions that higher union density (or coverage of collective agreements) is associated with higher unemployment (see e.g. Nickell, 1998). The most likely explanation for this relationship is the wage pressure effect. To explore whether the association is modified by a Ghent system, we have estimated a few equations along the lines of Blanchard and Wolfers (2000), using their data set for OECD countries (a maximum of eight five-year periods beginning in 1960). Our baseline model is their first specification where time-invariant measures of institutions are interacted with 'unobservable shocks', the latter represented by time effects. Our specification is as follows:

$$u_{it} = \alpha_i + \beta_t \left[1 + \sum_j (\delta_j + \gamma G) X_{ij} \right] + e_{it},$$

where u_{it} is the unemployment rate in country i in period t (measured as fraction of the labour force), X_{ij} is the value of institution j in country i (taken as fixed over the included time periods), G is a dummy for Ghent countries (Denmark, Finland, Sweden, and Belgium, the latter country assigned a value of 0.5 rather than unity), α_i is the country effect for country i, and β_t is the time effect for period t. The effect of a shock at time t depends on institutions, and the magnitude of the effect is allowed to vary depending on whether or not the Ghent system is in place. The estimate of γ should be negative if strong unions and generous benefit systems have less adverse effects on employment in Ghent countries.

Table 5.1 displays the results. Note that the variables, following Blanchard and Wolfers (2000), are measured in such a way that the expected signs are positive (except for the Ghent variable). Active labour market policy and coordination are therefore multiplied by -1. The first column replicates the results of Blanchard and Wolfers and the remaining columns allow for Ghent

Table 5.1. *Estimated unemployment equations, fixed institutions*

	(1)	(2)	(3)
Time effects	0.073	0.070	0.070
Replacement rate	0.017 (5.1)	0.017 (4.5)	0.017 (4.5)
Benefit length	0.206 (4.9)	0.231 (4.6)	0.201 (4.5)
Active labour market policy × (-1)	0.017 (3.0)	0.024 (1.6)	0.016 (1.5)
Employment protection	0.045 (3.1)	0.057 (3.1)	0.045 (2.7)
Tax wedge	0.018 (3.2)	0.018 (3.0)	0.018 (3.0)
Union coverage	0.098 (0.6)	−0.017 (0.1)	0.107 (0.5)
Union density	0.009 (2.1)	0.010 (1.7)	0.008 (1.5)
Coordination × (-1)	0.304 (5.1)	0.305 (5.2)	0.303 (5.2)
Ghent effect (γ)	–	−0.399 (1.0)	0.492 (0.42)

Notes: The dependent variable is unemployment as a fraction of the labour force. The time effects are the estimated time effect for 1995+ minus the estimated time effect for 1960–5. Column (1) replicates the estimates in Blanchard and Wolfers (2000). The other columns include interactions with institutions and a Ghent dummy: column (2), interactions with all institutions and column (3), only with benefit and union variables (replacement rate, benefit length, union coverage, and union density). Coordination is measured on a scale from 2 to 6 and is the sum of country rankings of coordination among unions and employers. Coverage is a measure of the coverage of collective agreements (1, 2, 3). There are 159 observations from 20 OECD countries. Period dummies and country effects are always included. The data are in the form of 5-year averages. Absolute values of t-statistics are given in parentheses.

effects. There is nothing in these results that suggest that the Ghent organization matters for the unemployment outcomes. The estimated Ghent coefficients are far from significant, and the signs vary depending on the particular specification. These results are perhaps not surprising considering the very high subsidies of the UI funds in the existing Ghent systems. This means that there is in practice little or no relationship between wage increases in a particular sector and the union members' UI premiums.

5.3. HOW DO UNIONS INFLUENCE UNEMPLOYMENT INSURANCE POLICIES?

How do unions influence policies concerning unemployment insurance? One route is through the administration of unemployment insurance and the way the work test is enforced. Another link operates through the political economy of unemployment insurance: rational citizens voting on UI policies would take prevailing wage-setting institutions into account when deciding on their preferred policy. The reason is that these institutions generally affect the employment consequences of a chosen benefit policy.

One can first ask whether there exists an optimal UI policy for a union. Suppose that the benefit level is the only element of the policy, and consider a single union in an economy with decentralized wage bargaining. To a first approximation, the union's preferred policy is to set the benefit level as high as possible. The single union has no incentive to consider the tax consequences of its benefit (and wage) choices, since the overall tax burden is the joint outcome of *all* unions' decisions.

Job search considerations can induce the union to prefer a less generous UI policy, at least to the extent that active job search brings some economic return to the members in terms of lower UI premiums as unemployment is reduced. This can conceivably happen in Ghent systems. A similar 'benefit-moderating' effect can appear if wage bargaining is centralized so that the tax consequences of higher benefits are recognized (analogous to the UI premium effects in Ghent systems).

5.3.1. *The administration of unemployment insurance*

If unions are directly involved in the running of the UI systems, they can influence the actual implementation of the UI policies. The Ghent systems are obvious examples. The enforcement of the work test is here in the hands of the labour market offices in cooperation with the union-administered UI funds. If a job-seeker fails to meet a certain requirement, the labour office should notify the UI fund. It is however the UI fund that takes the final decision about whether a benefit sanction should be imposed (such as a temporary withdrawal of benefits).

A reasonable conjecture is that the strictness of the work test depends on the extent to which prolonged unemployment is financed by the members in the fund or by the taxpayers at large. With current practices, involving very high subsidy rates of the funds (and thus low UI premiums among the members), it is unlikely that the Ghent organization is an instrument that makes the work test more effective than it would otherwise have been. The incentives to encourage search effort by means of benefit sanctions if workers fail to meet the search requirements are weak. Indeed, the measures of strictness of UI eligibility criteria in different countries, constructed by the Danish Ministry of Finance (see OECD, 2000), do not suggest that strictness differs between Ghent countries and the rest.

5.3.2. *Voting behaviour on unemployment insurance*

Wage-setting institutions may influence UI policies through their effect on voters' behaviour. Imagine political decision-making in a world with rational voters (and workers) who understand that higher benefits require higher taxes. Voters also understand the moral hazard features of unemployment insurance: higher benefits will tend to raise unemployment through less intensive search or more aggressive wage demands, or both. The more adverse the incentive effects are, the lower the preferred benefits. These adverse incentive effects of unemployment insurance—the price of UI in addition to the direct tax price—may well depend on the strength and structure of labour market organizations and could therefore affect the choice of UI policies.

The precise relationships between wage-setting systems and UI policies are likely to be model-specific. It seems reasonable, however, to expect less adverse incentive effects from more generous unemployment insurance—and therefore higher replacement rates—in economies with coordinated wage bargaining. This should hold because coordination involves internalization of the tax increases needed to finance higher benefits.

A special case with complete centralization of wage-setting to an encompassing monopoly union can be invoked to illustrate the point. Ignoring job search, the union's wage choice determines employment. One can then regard the decisive worker as making two decisions. The wage is set in the labour market and the replacement rate is chosen through the political process. The choice of replacement rate could then be made without considering the effects on wages and employment (but recognizing the tax consequences). This case would imply close to full insurance, i.e. a replacement rate close to unity.

It is less clear how the choice of UI policies would be affected by the bargaining power of unions in economies with decentralized wage bargaining. Focusing on the adverse incentive effects of higher benefits, the crucial issue is how stronger unions would affect these incentives. In some models, one can find 'policy complementarities'. For example, the effect on unemployment of a rise in the replacement rate is stronger, the stronger is the union's hand in the wage bargain. A popular model, associated with Layard and Nickell and others, can be used to derive an expression for a symmetric-equilibrium unemployment rate of the form

$$u = \frac{\kappa \sigma}{1 - \rho^\sigma},$$

where κ is a measure of the worker's bargaining power in a broad sense, ρ is the replacement rate, and σ, with $\sigma \leq 1$, measures the concavity of the worker's utility function. In this particular example it is clear that a rise in the replacement rate has a bigger effect on the unemployment rate if unions are more powerful ($du/d\rho$ is increasing in the measure of union power).

If such policy complementarities are important, they seem to suggest that the adverse incentive effects of higher benefits should be more severe in economies with strong unions. Rational voters would take these relationships into account in their political behaviour, thus opting for less generous benefit systems so as to moderate the adverse incentive effects.

These arguments hinge on a number of assumptions that may be violated in reality. It remains to be verified whether one can, even in theory, produce a robust relationship between the preferred UI policy and the bargaining strength of unions. Rather than going into further theoretical speculations, we have taken a look at the data (see Table 5.2).[2] The data are those used by Blanchard and Wolfers (2000). The dependent variables are two measures of replacement rates. The first is the OECD summary measure, based on an unweighted mean of eighteen different replacement rates for different duration categories and different family situations (see Martin, 1996). The second measure is the replacement rate for the first year of unemployment used by Blanchard and Wolfers (2000).

The results do not support the idea that coordination in wage bargaining is associated with more generous benefits. The coordination variable is always insignificant once we control for union power by means of an index of the coverage of collective agreements. Union coverage does seem to matter, however; the variable typically enters with significant positive coefficients. The positive signs are at variance with the hypothesis discussed above. The coverage variable varies between 1 and 3, so the estimated coefficients suggest (taken at face values) that up to 25-percentage-point differences in replacement rates can be accounted for by differences in coverage. Note also that the Ghent countries have significantly higher replacement rates than the rest.

In conclusion, we have seen that there are some patterns in the data suggesting that the strength of unions may have some impact on the UI policies. Roughly speaking, the data indicate that countries with more powerful unions also tend to have more generous benefit systems.

---

[2] See Di Tella and MacCulloch (1995) and Saint-Paul (1996) for previous attempts to analyse cross-country variations in benefit generosity.

Table 5.2. *Replacement rates and bargaining structure*

	OECD summary measure (%)				Replacement rate for the first year (%)			
	(1)	(2)	(3)	(4)	(5)	(6)	(7)	(8)
Coordination	1.58	0.26	− 0.97	− 1.43	1.95	1.08	− 0.42	− 1.03
	(2.20)	(0.32)	(1.05)	(1.70)	(1.93)	(0.93)	(0.32)	(0.82)
Coverage		6.61	6.61	8.64		4.38	4.37	6.99
		(3.28)	(3.34)	(4.68)		(1.51)	(1.52)	(2.55)
Ghent			8.31	6.95			10.18	8.42
			(2.63)	(2.40)			(2.22)	(1.96)
Dummy for Italy	No	No	No	Yes	No	No	No	Yes
$\bar{R}^2$		0.147	0.199	0.230	0.357	0.203	0.209	0.230	0.329

Notes: 'Coordination' is measured on a scale from 2 to 6 and is sum of country rankings of coordination among unions and employers. 'Coverage' is a measure of the coverage of collective agreements (1, 2, 3). 'Ghent' is dummy for the Ghent-countries (Denmark, Finland, Sweden and Belgium, where Belgium is assigned the value of 0.5). There are 160 observations from 20 OECD countries. Period dummies are always included. The data are in the form of 5-year averages.

5.4. UNEMPLOYMENT INSURANCE REFORMS

The traditional approach to discussions of UI policies emphasizes the trade-off between insurance and incentives. The insurance motive calls for generous benefits so as to equalize consumption across spells of employment and unemployment. Because of moral hazard, the optimal policy involves less than full coverage of income loss. Moral hazard in the context of unemployment insurance appears in several guises, the most frequently discussed being its effects on search effort and wage-setting. The choice of UI regime may also have important consequences for the degree of unionization.

A UI regime of the Ghent variety can be seen as a device to help unions to overcome the standard free-rider problem. The system effectively encourages union membership. The social benefits and costs of (higher) union density depend crucially on the assumptions made concerning the counterfactual, i.e. the nature of the non-unionized labour market. Whereas unions can only make things worse if they enter into a perfectly competitive labour market, they can conceivably improve outcomes in a monopsonistic labour market. Standard textbook models of monopsony in 'company towns', as well as modern theories of dynamic monopsony, predict that minimum wages over some range can increase employment. A labour legislation that encourages unionism can be regarded as a means to achieve, for example, minimum wages without direct legislation. It is probably not a coincidence that there are no legislated minimum wages in Denmark and Sweden, two countries with very high unionization rates.

There is a reasonable case for the view that a Ghent system under certain conditions can be an attractive institutional arrangement. A crucial condition is that the non-unionized labour market is more likely to have monopsonistic rather than perfectly competitive features. A Ghent system, then, can be seen as an institution that delivers (1) UI benefits as well as incentives that in part mitigate the associated moral hazard problems, and (2) worker bargaining power (and worker 'voice' at the workplace) so as to offset monopsonistic exploitation. A condition for mitigation of moral hazard problems is some degree of worker sharing of the costs of UI expenditure, so as to create a direct link between increases in unemployment and the costs to workers in terms of higher UI premiums. Such a link can moderate wage demands by inducing unions to recognize the costs of wage increases.

There is in addition a possible effect working through the monitoring of search effort and the enforcement of the work test in unemployment insurance. The decisions about whether or not to impose a benefit sanction for failing to meet search requirements, for example failing to show up at a scheduled interview with a prospective employer, are taken by the UI funds on the basis of reports from the employment exchange offices. The more costly longer unemployment spells are to employed union members, the stronger are the incentives for the UI fund to encourage the unemployed to actively search for and accept jobs. As we have emphasized, this effect can hardly be of much importance when the UI systems are as heavily subsidized as they are in existing Ghent countries. UI reforms in Ghent systems should therefore involve lower subsidies, in particular at the margin, so as to establish a link between UI premiums and unemployment in the sector covered by the collective agreement.

The role of unions in a compulsory system is less clear. In this case there is no existing institutional framework that can naturally be used to achieve differentiation of UI premiums across workers, thereby influencing incentives in wage-setting and search. One might, however, consider the US-style 'experience rating', which serves to establish a connection between a firm's contribution to layoffs and its contributions to the financing of unemployment insurance. The literature on implicit contracts, pioneered by Feldstein (1976) and others, has explored the role of unemployment insurance with respect to both the level and the financing of benefits. The model features a firm with a pool of 'attached' workers facing uncertain product demand. The firm and its workforce have to agree on a contract that specifies employment, wages, and perhaps work-hours for every possible realization of demand. The number of laid-off workers in each state of demand is given by the difference between the number of attached and employed workers. The model is useful for investigating the role of experience rating in unemployment insurance. In broad conformity with the system practised in the United States, Feldstein assumed that firms that lay workers off have to finance part of the UI benefits to which their workers are eligible. The model implies that a rise in the UI subsidy—a decline in experience rating—causes a reduction in employment.

The general validity of Feldstein's result has been questioned. For example, Burdett and Wright (1989) have relaxed the assumption of a fixed pool of workers attached to the firm and allowed the firm to choose the number of workers. This modification has important implications. It turns out that higher experience rating does reduce layoff rates, but also the number of attached workers. The intuitive explanation is that higher experience rating increases labour costs, which is bound to reduce the number of workers that the firm is willing to hire. The effect on average employment is ambiguous in general, and may plausibly be negative. Finally, it can be noted that simulations undertaken by Mortensen (1994), using the Mortensen–Pissarides (1994) equilibrium model of job creation and destruction, suggest that a fully experienced rated UI tax would increase unemployment, a result driven by the fact that experience rating effectively discourages job creation by making layoffs more costly to firms. The initial claim that experience rating always reduces unemployment has thus not survived a later elaboration of the theory.

On the empirical side, Topel (1983) measured the extent of UI subsidiza-tion across different states in the United States and found that incomplete experience rating accounted for around 30% of all spells of temporary layoff unemployment. Non-subsidized benefits appear to have a negligible impact on layoffs.

There are, of course, good insurance arguments for some cross-industry subsidies in the UI system. An industry-specific shock should not be financed exclusively by workers and employers in the exposed sector. But there are reasonable arguments against current European practices with *no* direct con-nection between increases in unemployment in a sector and the taxes (or fees) that are used to finance the increase in paid-out benefits. There is a case for increasing wage-setters' awareness of the employment consequences of their decisions. Reforms of the financing of unemployment insurance should attempt to establish a direct connection between the costs of unemployment and the taxes (or social security contributions) that are raised to cover the costs of higher unemployment.

UI reforms involving some degree of experience rating raise a number of practical issues. Although it is conceptually straightforward to link employee (or employer) contributions to sectoral unemployment, it may be difficult to do so in practice. Bargaining areas typically coincide with industries, but unemploy-ment rates by industry are not well defined concepts (and data are often lacking). The most practical approach is probably to make use of information on benefit receivers and their previous employers, as in the US system of experience rating. The contribution to UI financing—from employers and/or employees—would then be linked to the firm's contribution to UI expenditures. This would clearly increase the cost of job destruction. However, it is import-ant to provide incentives for job creation as well. This can be achieved by making the contributions dependent on the duration of benefit receipt. On the firm side, this implies incentives to rehire unemployed workers. On the union side, it also implies incentives to promote job-finding activities among the unemployed, thereby reducing the employees' contributions to unemployment support. UI reforms that involve some experience rating can alert union members and union leaders to the social costs of excessive wage increases and insufficient job search.

5.5. HOW COULD A GHENT SYSTEM HELP OTHER EUROPEAN COUNTRIES?

The analysis of this chapter has not provided evidence that a union-administered UI scheme is correlated with higher unemployment (Table 5.1). Further, we have observed that 'Ghent countries' tend to be characterized by significantly high replacement rates (Table 5.2), which, in turn, are positively correlated with unemployment (Table 5.1). These findings suggest that the introduction of a Ghent–UI system should not *per se* be responsible for a growth in unemployment. However, we have highlighted the problems existing in the implementation of a Ghent system, in particular the difficulty in keeping the UI replacement rate under control. If, on the one hand, we cannot draw conclusions on the net effect of a Ghent system on unemployment, on the other hand, this chapter shows that Ghent systems could play other important roles. Such roles refer to the unions' ability to organize workers covered by temporary contracts, and their ability to impose benefit sanctions on unemployed workers who reject job offers.

While it would be hard to assess the ultimate effects of union-managed benefit sanctions on search behaviour, one could argue that the existence of Ghent systems might prevent the emergence of a dual economy, a phenomenon typical of Southern European countries. In France, Spain, and Italy we observe a growing proportion of workers employed in jobs whose terms are regulated by a temporary contract. Clearly, the interests of this growing fraction of workers are not easily represented by the trade unions, and the conflicting goals between the protected insiders and the unprotected outsiders represents an important challenge for Southern European unions, whose actions appear often in conflict with the interest of workers employed in the secondary labour market. Further, the workers employed through such temporary contracts tend to be younger workers, further amplifying the intergenerational conflict in the area of welfare reforms. The evidence presented suggests that in Sweden union membership is high not only among regular workers, but also among workers whose employment contract is temporary in nature (Figure 5.1). Thus, it may well be that a union-administered UI scheme is a way to establish an institutional contact between unions and temporary contracts, since the latter workers are the most likely beneficiaries of the UI benefits.

6

Conclusions

6.1. DO UNIONS INTERACT WITH THE WELFARE STATE? HOW DO THEY DO IT?

This Report has documented the wide differences and often divergent trends in unionization rates and welfare policies among industrialized countries and has argued that these are interdependent patterns. Unions affect the welfare state; and the welfare state affects unions.

The pattern of union development and the way in which unions interact with the welfare state depends critically on both the organization of labour within a country and the employer–union and government–union relationships existing in each country—what is commonly called the *national labour relations system*. During the 1980s union density fell sharply in a number of countries, whereas it remained stable or increased in other countries. By 1990 union density had dropped to 15% in the United States and to 10% in France, though this had very different consequences for collective bargaining in the two countries, owing to the different modes of employer–union relations. By contrast, union density increased by 10–20 percentage points in all Nordic countries except Norway. On average, union density among OECD countries stood at 43% in 1970 and had increased to 47% in 1980; by 1990 it had fallen back to 41% (OECD, 1994). The differing pattern of union growth across countries had a substantial impact on the composition of union members, particularly by age, with potentially large consequences for union policies towards the welfare state.

The design of welfare policy and social protection spending also differs greatly across countries, as do efforts to reform welfare states. Social protection expenditure is high in countries like Sweden and Finland (33.7 percentage points of GDP in Sweden in 1997), while countries like Ireland spend just 17.5% of their GDP. Old-age benefits are a prominent share of total expenditure in Italy and Austria (in comparison to the EU average), while Nordic countries place a stronger emphasis on active labour market policies and social services than on old-age cash benefits. These differences in spending patterns cannot be explained solely in terms of differences in the age distributions of populations, aggregate welfare spending, or labour market shocks affecting these countries. They are at least partly due to differences in policies.

To organize the cross-country data and show the relation between the pattern of unionism and welfare state policies, we distinguish four regimes of labour relations and welfare regimes: namely *Nordic* countries (Sweden, Finland, Denmark); *Continental* countries (Austria, Belgium, France, the Netherlands, Germany); *Anglo-Saxon* countries (UK, Ireland); and *Southern* countries (Greece, Italy, Portugal, Spain). This taxonomy allows us to better understand the patterns in union characteristics and welfare spending, though some countries are hybrid cases (e.g. France and the Netherlands). With respect to unionization, qualitative and quantitative indicators show that the Nordic countries have the highest unionization levels in terms of union density, and the greatest union influence on policies. In these countries unions represent a very heterogeneous workforce in terms of both age and employment status of their members. By contrast, Anglo-Saxon countries are at the other extreme. The rest of the countries are somewhere in between these two polar cases and have experienced diverse patterns of unionization and changes in labour relations. With respect to the welfare state, the Nordic countries tend to have the most comprehensive social expenditure systems, followed by the Continental countries, while the Southern countries and the Anglo-Saxon welfare states are the least generous and the least comprehensive. This taxonomy shows a positive relationship between union strength and the expansion of the welfare states, particularly in the 1980s and early 1990s. Yet the relationship is not one-to-one. Some countries have well developed welfare states and low union density, pointing to additional institutional factors affecting this relationship.

We direct attention to two additional factors that help explain the link between unionization and welfare state outcomes. First is the position of unions in the political system. Trade unions often overlap with political movements, and different political legacies affect the actions of labour movements and their influence on welfare policies. The more closely tied unions are to social democratic parties, the more likely will there be a strong link between union density and welfare state generosity. More broadly, when trade unions have an institutionalized role in political decision-making, the position of unions helps shape public debate or even initiate collective actions. Political parties of all stripes will listen more to union views when unions are a major player in national politics.

Second is the institutional way in which trade unions influence welfare policies. In some countries, trade unions administer some social policies. They then affect policy implementation, especially when benefits are provided in a fragmented and corporatist fashion. This interaction of institutional settings, industrial relations, and welfare outcomes can be seen in the provision of old-age insurance. Unions are typically involved in the establishment of occupational pensions through collective agreements. In these cases, and in general when a funded component of pension provision is relevant, there is a direct link between members' contributions and benefits. Unions cannot charge society at large for generous pensions policies as readily as they might when pensions are funded by the state (though even in these cases negotiated pensions may benefit from preferential tax treatment). At the same time, unions may use their economic strength to obtain greater *monopoly* rents from individual employers the more fragmented is the pension programme and the larger is the number of public or private funds in the economy.

The interaction of institutions, labour relations, and welfare outcomes can also be seen in the role of unions in the provision of unemployment insurance, which we review in Section 6.3.

6.2. WHAT EXPLAINS UNION POLICIES TOWARDS WELFARE OUTCOMES?

On the basis of these stylized facts, we present a model of union policies towards welfare state activities that recognizes the importance of the internal seniority structure of unions and the concern for membership. The model treats pensions as part of the compensation package, which unions can affect through their monopoly power, and also recognizes the insurance role of unions in a broad bargaining agenda. This sets the basis for us to look at the way in which unions affect the welfare state and the labour market through both microeconomic and macroeconomic factors.

We find that union policies towards welfare benefits mitigate the effects on the wellbeing of workers of market failures that result from imperfect insurance and credit markets. From this perspective, union policies towards welfare outcomes can be significantly welfare-improving. In economies where financial market and insurance market imperfections prevail, pension contracts cannot be signed between firms and employees on an individual basis. There are potential efficiency gains stemming from union policies in setting up or bargaining for occupational pensions. The role of unions would be to provide credibility to collective agreements whereby employers commit to the delivery of future pension benefits to their workforce. At the same time, however, the political economy of unions suggests that they act more in the interests of senior workers than of younger workers and that, in a strong welfare state, this will bias them towards preserving the status quo. When senior workers dominate union objective function, unions will be more favourable to generous pension arrangements and soft landing plans for older workers, such as well funded early retirement programmes, at the expense of younger generations. This position may entail important dynamic inefficiencies when economic or demographic conditions necessitate changes in policy that operate against older workers. Such 'seniority bias' is more likely to occur when unions are less encompassing and less representative of the general working population. It is also more likely to occur when unions (and governments) do not face clear commitments on future policy outcomes. But such a seniority bias can cost unions over the long run, both in terms of attracting younger workers and in terms of adverse macroeconomic and growth out-comes that produce higher unemployment and lower membership than would otherwise be attained.

Consistent with this argument, our macroeconomic evidence suggests that economies that spend more on old-age provision have greater youth unemployment. Unions that impose high costs on labour through their support of generous public pensions may thus indirectly contribute to the youth unemployment problem.

6.3. WHICH INSTITUTIONAL STRUCTURE BEST INCREASES UNION WELFARE-ENHANCING ACTIVITIES RELATIVE TO RENT-SEEKING ACTIVITIES?

We looked at a unique situation being carried out in Belgium and some of the Nordic countries in the provision of unemployment insurance—a Ghent UI regime. The Ghent UI system is government-subsidized but union-administered, so that it gives unions direct involvement in the management of insurance against labour market risks. Since the unemployed in Ghent-system countries tend to join unions in order to make it easier for them to receive unemployment benefits, this gives unions a strong preference for this type of exclusive arrangement. But it also encourages them to consider the budget constraint implicit in the financing of unemployment benefits. Even though funds come from the state, the administering trade unions necessarily perceive the link between the spending on unemployment benefits and the funding of these expenditures. This increased responsibility may lead to moderation in wage bargaining and in determining unemployment benefits, which in turn can make job creation easier.

An additional positive effect may come from the influence unions can exert on unemployment benefit recipients. Unions may help in reducing the typical moral hazard problem affecting these provisions through the monitoring of search efforts. Naturally, these beneficial effects will be smaller, the more the unemployment system is subsidized from external finances. Reforms that establish a closer connection between unemployment insurance expenditures and the taxes (or social security contributions) that are raised to cover those costs should lead unions to consider the broad consequences of collective bargaining decisions that can adversely affect employment. Union policies towards occupational pensions, discussed earlier, provide another example in which an increase in the role of unions in administering welfare state benefits and funding them directly from members' contributions is likely to lead to more welfare-enhancing levels of programmes.

Further, our Report argues that the Ghent system may counteract the emergence of a dual economy, whereby a growing number of workers employed in temporary contracts become insulated from union influence and from the insurance schemes provided by the welfare states. The evidence presented suggests that in Ghent countries union membership is high not only among regular workers, but also among workers covered by temporary contracts. Thus, a Ghent system may be a way to establish an institutional contact between unions and temporary workers, since the latter are likely to be very interested in unemployment insurance schemes. This, in turn, would help address one of the main challenges faced by unions in Southern Europe.

More generally, it may be useful to consider the institutional design of industrial relationships in terms of optimal governance structure and the allocation of rights of decision-making between workers, employers, and the government. In this respect economic reasoning suggests that the responsibility for decisions should be given to those agents most directly affected by the outcomes, and to those who have more weight in determining the outcomes of these decisions. In particular, the more responsibility unions have for welfare state programmes, the more responsible they are likely to be towards the funding of those programmes and to the economic consequences thereof. A corollary of this is that we would expect unions to be more favourable to reforming welfare policies under these circumstances, when they are convinced that those reforms can improve economic outcomes.

6.4. CAN UNIONS CONTRIBUTE TO A REFORM OF WELFARE SYSTEMS?

Like other economic decision-makers, unions learn from experience. Indeed, as the 1990s developed, unions became more aware of the economic need to tighten public spending budgets and of the potentially harmful consequences of financing generous social protection expenditures when a population is ageing and the pensioner-to-worker ratio is rising sharply. Moreover, as long-lived institutions with an explicit need to recruit young workers to survive, unions may take a longer perspective on economic and social policies than a particular parliamentary government, whose survival often depends upon short-term considerations. Indeed, we note that there are cases in which unions have adopted a forward-looking behaviour that puts the long-term benefits to the economy over the benefits to senior members. For example, in the year 2000 German unions favoured government's efforts to cut payroll social taxes; in 1996 in Austria unions accepted a temporary freeze in pension benefits as part of the 'austerity package' designed to meet the Maastricht convergence criteria.

But at the same time, our analysis has stressed that unions are prone to seniority bias, not only in wage-setting activities but also in the interaction with welfare policy. This has often led them to seek to preserve the status quo and defend acquired social rights, under conditions in which change could be welfare-enhancing. When unions are directly involved in negotiating reforms with a government this seems to be the norm, though unions may accept welfare retrenchment as part of a broader political arrangement that benefits members in other policies. In Italy unions played a key role in the benefit-reducing and expenditure-stabilizing reform that allowed the country to meet the Maastricht criterion at the onset of European monetary integration. The prospects of monetary integration provided credibility to the tightness of the government budget constraint, generating realistic union expectations on the dynamic evolution of the status quo point. Still, unions bargained to maintain some seniority rights for older workers and retirees at the expense of less represented groups.

There are three potential benefits to unions from taking a more reformist or progressive stance towards reforming welfare state policies. First, they may become more attractive to young workers and thus win back their membership and loyalty; this is critical if unions are to maintain a major role in society in the future. Second, they can help set the reformist agenda in ways that minimize the cost to existing members and maintain redistributive policies that favour workers. Of course, they can also do this by opposing reforms and then bargaining tough on reforms. Third, they invariably gain from economic expansion and growth, which affords greater opportunity for wage increases as well as improved employment. While our analysis shows that unions are more likely to favour broadly socially beneficial policies, despite seniority bias, when they are directly involved in the administration of unemployment insurance and in the growth and management of second-tier occupational pension plans, there are still important forces pushing them towards a reformist agenda: survival and growth. Yes, unions *can* contribute to a reform of welfare systems, but it will require dynamic leadership and convincing economic analysis.

Appendix

Unions and Benefits:
A Simple Analytical Framework

A1. A MODEL OF TRADE UNIONS AND
LONG-TERM BENEFITS

This Appendix presents a formal analysis of the theoretical arguments developed in the non-technical discussion of the main text of Part II.

We start with a monopoly trade union with 'right to manage'. There are two periods, 1 and 2. In period 1 the trade union sets optimally, given its objective function, the level of wages and the long-term benefits to be paid in period 2. The firm then decides its optimal level of employment in order to maximize its intertemporal profit. At the end of period 1 production takes place. In period 2 only a fraction of previously employed workers are still attached to the firm and receive therefore their promised long-term benefits as chosen by the union in the first period.[1]

More precisely, consider a union with a total pool of M identical workers. Each worker cares about consumption over the two periods and has the following preferences:

$$u_1(c_1) + \delta u_2(c_2)$$

where $u_i(\cdot)$ is the intratemporal utility function of period i with standard properties, and is increasing concave with $u_i(0) = 0$; c_1 and c_2 are consumption levels in periods 1 and 2; and δ is the discount rate.

Following Aoki Ildoon and Ireland (1997), we assume that there is some basic uncertainty concerning the future attachment of the worker to the firm in period 2. This may reflect the existence of a stochastic element affecting the worker's likelihood to stay in the firm in the next period.[2] Given such uncertainty, a worker will be concerned about the expected utility of

---

[1] Hence benefits are of a defined benefits (DB) type rather than a defined contribution (DC) type.

[2] Alternatively, if we consider in this two-period setting that workers work in period 1 and retire in period 2, the second-period uncertainty may capture the uncertain longevity of the retired worker.

consumption $Eu_2(c_2)$ in period 2. In period 1 each worker who is employed receives a current wage rate w. This same worker gets the promise of a future occupational pension s paid out in period 2. This specification therefore captures in a simple way the idea that workers may be more risk-averse about uncertain benefits paid in the long term than about current wages paid today when $u_2(\cdot)$ is more concave than $u_1(\cdot)$.

An unemployed worker in period 1 receives an intertemporal utility payoff of V^R. Besides occupational benefits, we assume that there is a first-tier public benefit system through which, independently from the employment status in period 1, an agent receives a transfer T in the second period of his life. This public system is financed in the economy by a payroll or income tax τ. Finally, in period 1 an unemployed worker receives an unemployment benefit b. Formally, we may write down the discounted expected utility of a union member when employed and when unemployed as:

$$U(w(1-\tau),s,T) = u_1(w(1-\tau)) + \delta[qu_2(s+T) + (1-q)u_2(T)]$$

and

$$V^R(b,T) = u_1(b) + \delta u_2(T)$$

where q is the exogenous probability of attachment of the worker to the firm in the second period.

We take the standard view that, given a pool of workers M, the union wants to maximize the expected utility of the representative member, which can be written as

$$V(L,w,s,\tau,T,b) = \frac{L}{M}U(w(1-\tau),s,T) + \left(1 - \frac{L}{M}\right)V^R(b,T)$$

where L is the number of employed workers in period 1.

We consider that the firm sells a product which generates a revenue function in period 1, $R(L)$ increasing concave with $R(0)=0$. Hence, given that only a fraction q of workers will remain attached to the firm in period 2, the firm's discounted expected profits can be written as

$$R(L) - wL - \frac{1}{1+r}sqL$$

with $1/(1+r)$ the discount factor. Finally, let π^R be the reservation level of profits of the firm in order to be part of the relationship with the union.

In the 'right to manage' model, the firm takes as given the current wage rate w and the long-term benefit s and chooses its employment level in order to maximize profits. This provides a demand function for labour $L^D(W)$

decreasing in $W = w + [1/(1+r)]sq$, the total expected discounted cost to hire a worker.

A1.1. The determinants of the trade-off between current wages and deferred benefits

The problem of the monopoly trade union is then written as

$$\text{Max}_{w,L,s} \, V(L, w, s, \tau, T, b)$$
$$L = L^D(W)$$
$$W = w + \frac{1}{1+r}sq$$

This problem is easily decomposed into two steps. First, we may solve the optimal mix between current wages w and deferred payments s for a typical employed worker, given a fixed expected discounted cost of hiring W for the firm. Second, we may determine the trade union's optimal expected discounted labour cost.

Optimal trade-off between current wages and deferred benefits
The first step can be written as the following problem:

$$\text{Max}_{w,s} \, u_1(w(1-\tau)) + \delta[qu_2(s+T) + (1-q)u_2(T)]$$
$$w + \frac{1}{1+r}sq = W$$

which, after a change of variable $w' = w(1-\tau)$ and $s' = s + T$, is rewritten as

$$\text{Max}_{w,s} \, u_1(w') + \delta[qu_2(s') + (1-q)u_2(T)]$$
$$\frac{1}{1-\tau}w' + \frac{1}{1+r}s'q = W + \frac{1}{1+r}qT$$

The optimal wage and long-term benefits are given by the standard marginal condition

$$\frac{u_1'(w')}{u_2'(s')} = \frac{\delta(1+r)}{1-\tau} \tag{1}$$

and the budget constraint. From this we find the net wage $w' = w(1-\tau) = w^*(q, W, \tau, T)$, total benefits $s' = s + T = s^*(q, W, \tau, T)$, and the indirect utility function of an employed worker $U(w^*, s^*) = U^*(q, W, \tau, T)$.

The solution of this problem is illustrated in Figure A1. In the plane (w', s') of after-tax current wages, $w' = w(1-\tau)$ and total long-term benefits $s' = s + T$,

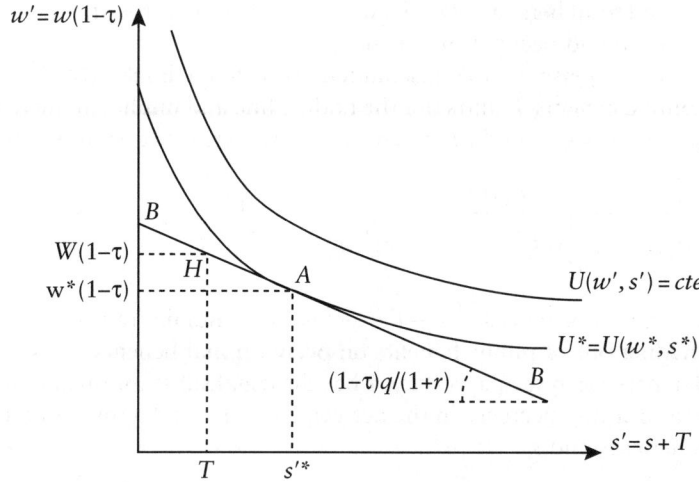

Figure A1

iso-utility curves $u(w', s') = u_1(w') + \delta q u_2(s') = cst$ are drawn with the usual decreasing convex shape. The 'budget line' BB under which the employed worker's expected utility is maximized is given by the expression $[1/(1 - \tau)]w' + [1/(1 + r)]s'q = W + [1/(1 + r)]qT$. It goes through point $H(W(1 - \tau), T)$ with a slope $[(1 - \tau)/(1 + r)]q$. The optimal allocation (w'^*, s'^*) of after-tax current wages and total long-term benefits is given at point A, where the budget line BB is tangent to the optimal iso-utility curve $U^* = U(w^*, s^*) = U^*(q, W, \tau, T)$.

An increase in q induces a clockwise rotation around point B of the budget line (see Figure A2). At the same time, it makes the iso-utility curves of the worker steeper. In general, the rotation of the budget line has three effects on (w'^*, s'^*). First, there are the traditional substitution and income effects coming from the fact that a change in the probability q can be interpreted as a change in the 'relative price' $[(1 - \tau)/(1 + r)]q$ of occupational benefits s'. Second, there is an additional 'wealth' effect emanating from the term $[1/(1 + r)]qT$ in the budget constraint BB. The substitution effect tends to increase w'^* and to reduce s'^*. Under standard 'normality' assumptions on current and future consumption, the income effect tends to reduce both w'^* and s'^*. The wealth effect, on the contrary, induces an increase in w'^* and s'^*. The fact that the utility curves become steeper as a result of an increase in q, on the other hand, induces a decrease in w'^* and an increase in s'^* as future consumption is more valued by the worker.

It is easy to see that the substitution effect and steeper utility slope effects cancel out for total benefits and that the rotation around point H of the budget line leads along the locus determined by equation (1) to a decrease in the net wage rate w' and total benefit s' (see Figure A2). Obviously, the effect is similar for gross wages w and occupational benefits s.

Similarly, an increase in the discounted expected labour cost W or an increase in public benefits T shifts out the budget line and implies an increase in both net and gross wages and total benefits. However, it is easy to see that

$$\frac{\partial s'}{\partial T} = \frac{u_1''(w')}{u_1''(w') + \dfrac{\delta}{q}((1+r)^2/(1-\tau)^2)u_2''(s')} \leq 1$$

Hence occupational benefits $s = s'-T$ decrease with public transfers T. There is some crowding out of public benefits on occupational benefits.

Finally, an increase in the payroll tax τ has the usual substitution and income effects with a resulting decrease in the net wage rate w' and a total ambiguous effect on benefits s' and s.

The quasi-linear case An interesting tractable case is the quasi-linear case, where $u_1(c_1) = c_1$ and $u_2(c_2) = u(c_2)$. It is easy to get

$$w^* = w^*(q, W, \tau, T) = W - \frac{1}{1+r} q\left[u'^{-1}\left(\frac{1-\tau}{\delta(1+r)}\right) - T \right]$$

and

$$s^* = u'^{-1}\left(\frac{1-\tau}{\delta(1+r)}\right) - T$$

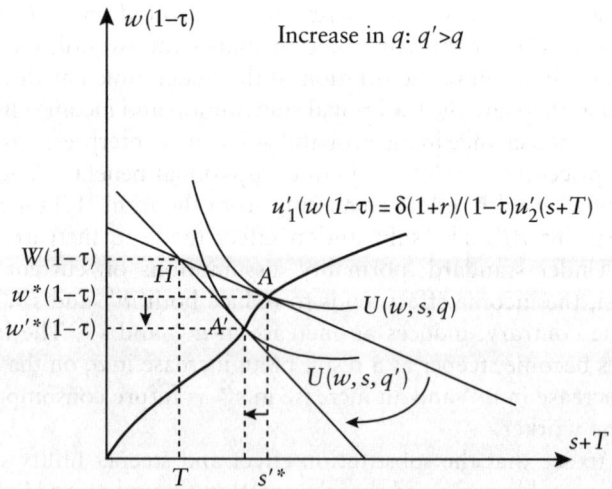

Figure A2

and the indirect utility function of an employed worker $U(w^*, s^*) = U^*(q, W, \tau, T)$ is

$$U^*(q, W, \tau, T) = W(1 - \tau) + \frac{1}{1+r} qT(1 - \tau)$$

$$- \frac{1-\tau}{1+r} q \left[u'^{-1}\left(\frac{1-\tau}{\delta(1+r)}\right) \right] + \delta q u \left[u'^{-1}\left(\frac{1-\tau}{\delta(1+r)}\right) \right]$$

In the simple quasi-linear specification, as income and wealth effects fall entirely on w'^*, there is no net effect of q or W on total benefits s'^*.

Employment and labour costs
The second step of the union problem can be written as

$$\text{Max}_W V(W, q, \tau, T, b) = \frac{L^D(W)}{M} U^*(q, W, \tau, T) + \left(1 - \frac{L^D(W)}{M}\right)$$

$$\times V^R(b, T) R(L^D(W)) - W L^D(W) \geq \pi^R$$

which collapses to the fairly standard problem of the monopoly trade union. Given that there is a participation constraint of the firm, the total labour cost solution is given by $W = W^* = \text{Min}(\tilde{W}(q, \tau, T, b), \bar{W}(\pi^R))$ where $\tilde{W}(q, \tau, T, b)$ is the interior solution of the first-order condition

$$\frac{dL^D(W)}{dW} [U^*(q, W, \tau, T) - V^R(b, T)] + L^D(W) \frac{dU^*(q, W, \tau, T)}{dW} = 0 \quad (2)$$

and $\bar{W}(\pi^R)$ is the labour cost level which makes the firm's participation constraint binding:

$$R(L^D(\bar{W}(\pi^R))) - \bar{W}(\pi^R) L^D(\bar{W}(\pi^R)) = \pi^R$$

From this, it is straightforward to recover wages, benefits, and employment:

$$w = w^*(q, W^*, \tau, T)/(1 - \tau)$$
$$s = s^*(q, W^*, \tau, T) - T$$
$$L = L^D(W^*)$$

The solution is depicted in Figure A3 in the space (W, L) of total expected labour cost W and employment level L. The iso-utility curves of the trade union are depicted by the curve V while the labour demand $L = L^D(W)$ is the locus of vertical tangents of the iso-profit curves π and π^* of the firm. Given that there is a participation constraint of the firm, the labour cost solution is given by $W = W^* = \text{Min}(\tilde{W}(q, \tau, T, b), \bar{W}(\pi^R))$, where $\tilde{W}(q, \tau, T, b)$ is associated with the 'monopoly trade union equilibrium' point E, at which the optimal

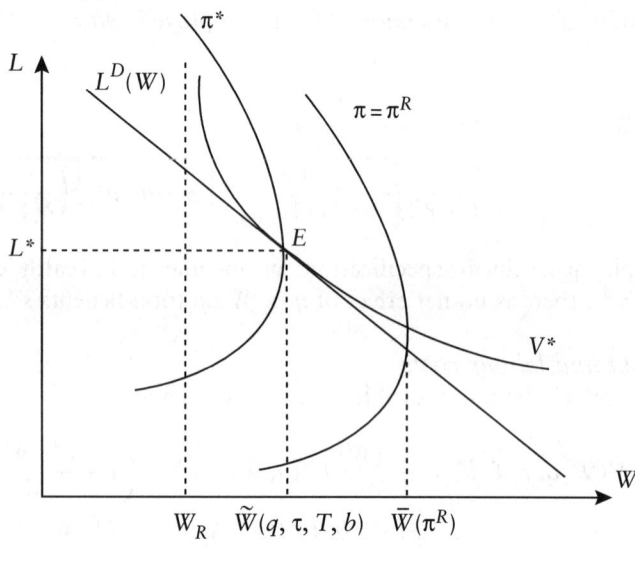

Figure A3

iso-utility curve of the union is tangent to the labour demand curve, and $\bar{W}(\pi^R)$ is the labour cost level at which the firm's participation constraint is binding.

Comparative statics
It is interesting to see how, in this simple framework, wages, occupational pensions and employment change with the probability of attachment to the firm (or concern for long-term benefits) q, unemployment benefits b, reservation profit level π^R, public pensions T, and payroll tax rates τ.

An increase in unemployment benefits b implies, in a standard fashion, an increase in the equilibrium intertemporal labour cost W^* (at least, so long as the participation constraint of the firm is not binding). This, in turn, is associated with an outward shift of equilibrium wages w and a reduction in employment L. Similarly, a positive change in the firm's reservation profit level π^R implies a decrease in W^* (when the firm's participation constraint is binding) with a reduction in w and an increase in employment L.

The impact of a change in q is less straightforward (see Figure A4). Getting back to the definition of the indirect intertemporal utility $U^*(q, W, \tau, T)$ of an employed worker and the intertemporal payoff $V^R(b, q, T)$ of an unemployed worker, it can be seen that an increase in q will induce flatter iso-utility curves for the trade union. A higher probability of future attachment to the firm increases the worker's value to be employed today by the firm, reducing therefore the union's incentive to choose a high total labour cost W. Under reasonable concavity assumptions, this implies that the new tangency point at E' between the labour demand curve and the union's iso-utility is in the

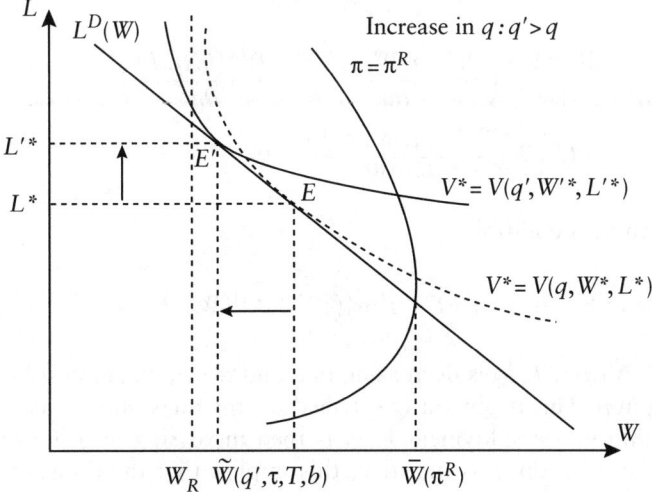

Figure A4

north-west direction of the initial equilibrium point E. This is associated with a lower expected cost of labour $\tilde{W}(q, \tau, T, b)$ and a higher employment level. Given that the direct impact of q on w is negative, this implies that the total impact of an increase in q is to reduce current wages.

Formally, differentiation of the indirect intertemporal utility of an employed worker and an unemployed worker provides

$$\frac{\partial U^*(q, W, \tau, T)}{\partial q} - \frac{\partial V^R(b, q, T)}{\partial q} = \frac{\partial U^*(q, W, \tau, T)}{\partial q}$$
$$= \delta[u_2(s') - u_2(T) + (T - s')u_2'(s')] > 0$$

and

$$\frac{\partial^2 U^*(q, W, \tau, T)}{\partial q \partial W} = \delta(T - s')u_2''(s')\frac{ds'}{dW} > 0$$

as workers are risk-averse (i.e. $u_2''(s) < 0$). Therefore, when the union problem is well behaved (i.e. $\partial^2 V/\partial W^2 < 0$), differentiation of the first-order condition (2) provides

$$\frac{\partial \tilde{W}(q, \tau, T, b)}{\partial q} = -\frac{\partial^2 V/\partial W \partial q}{\partial^2 V/\partial W^2} < 0$$

with

$$\frac{\partial^2 V}{\partial W \partial q} = \frac{dL^D(W)}{dW}\left(\frac{\partial U^*(q, W, \tau, T)}{\partial q} - \frac{\partial V^R(b, q, T)}{\partial q}\right)$$
$$+ L^D(W)\frac{\partial^2 U^*(q, W, \tau, T)}{\partial q \partial W} < 0$$

Hence when the condition

$$\frac{dL^D(W)}{dW}[u_2(s') - u_2(T) + (T - s')u_2'(s')] + L^D(W)(T - s')u_2''(s')\frac{ds'}{dW} > 0$$

is satisfied, $\tilde{W}(q, \tau, T, b)$ is decreasing in q and the trade union solution W^* is decreasing in q. This is obviously satisfied for the quasi-linear case.

The equilibrium employment level is then increasing in q. Given that the direct impact of q on w is negative, this implies that the total impact of an increase in q is to reduce current wages.

Similarly, it can be seen that an increase in public pensions T will induce steeper trade union iso-utility curves (see Figure A5). The intuition is the fact that, as public transfers are not conditional on the employment status, they tend to reduce the relative value for a worker to be employed in period 1. This, in turn, increases the union's incentive to choose a high total labour cost W with an associated lower employment level. Hence $\tilde{W}(q, \tau, T, b)$ is increasing in T, implying that the equilibrium intertemporal labour cost W^* is also weakly increasing in T.

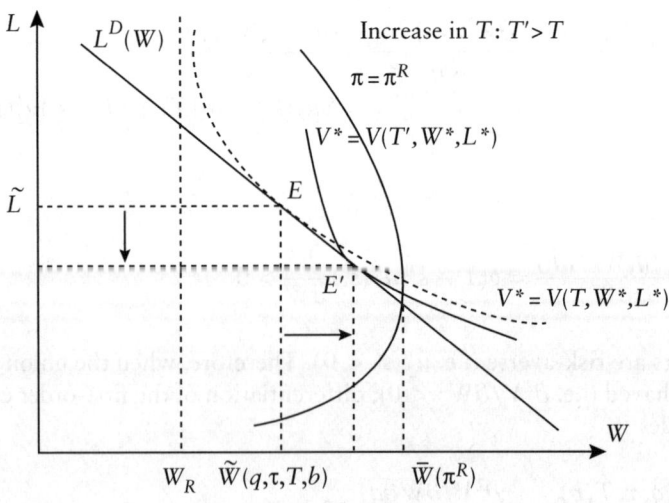

Figure A5

Formally, the effect of an increase in public pensions T on labour costs W will have the sign of $\partial^2 V/\partial W \partial T$:

$$\frac{\partial^2 V}{\partial W \partial T} = \frac{dL^D(W)}{dW}\left(\frac{\partial U^*(q, W, \tau, T)}{\partial T} - \frac{\partial V^R(b, q, T)}{\partial T}\right)$$
$$+ L^D(W)\frac{\partial^2 U^*(q, W, \tau, T)}{\partial T \partial W}$$

But

$$\frac{\partial U^*(q, W, \tau, T)}{\partial T} - \frac{\partial V^R(b, q, T)}{\partial T} = q\delta[u'(s') - u'(T)] < 0$$

and

$$\frac{\partial^2 U^*(q, W, \tau, T)}{\partial T \partial W} = q\delta u''(s')\frac{ds'}{dW} < 0$$

Hence $\tilde{W}(q, \tau, T, b)$ is increasing in T when

$$\frac{dL^D(W)}{dW}[u'(s') - u'(T)] + L^D(W)u''(s')\frac{ds'}{dW} > 0$$

which is again satisfied for the quasi-linear case. This implies that the equilibrium intertemporal labour cost W^* is also weakly increasing in T. Gross and net current wages will consequently also increase with T.

In the general case (when preferences are not quasi-linear), total pensions s' are likely to increase. Occupational pensions are partially crowded out by public pensions through the direct effect of T. At the same time, there is an additional income effect coming from the fact that the equilibrium intertemporal labour cost W^* does increase. The whole effect of public pensions on occupational pensions is therefore on a priori grounds ambiguous. When the impact of public pensions on wages and labour costs is strong enough (resp. weak enough), the second effect is likely to dominate (resp. be dominated) and there is a complementarity (substitutability) between public pensions and occupational pensions.

Finally, let us close this section by investigating the effect of an increase in the payroll tax rate τ. As is straigtforward to see, the indirect utility of an employed worker $U^*(q, W, \tau, T)$ is obviously negatively related to the payroll tax rate. This implies the standard result (Alesina and Perotti, 1997) that the union passes to the employer some fraction of the fiscal burden and that the union-determined discounted labour cost $\tilde{W}(q, \tau, T, b)$ is increasing in τ. Thus, an increase in the payroll tax, everything else being equal, has a negative impact on employment L. The effect on current wages is generally ambiguous. The direct impact of an increase in τ is negative but there is an additional positive income effect coming from the increase in W. For occupational pensions, the positive substitution effect and the induced income effect through the increase in W imply that, in general, they are increasing in the payroll tax τ.

A2. BARGAINING

The simple model of the previous section can be extended along several dimensions. First, one may generalize the analysis to situations where the union bargains with the firm on wages and benefits, while the firm keeps its 'right to manage' on employment decisions. Figure A6 reflects such a situation in the plane (W, L) of discounted expected labour cost and employment. The downward-sloping demand curve of the firm is represented by $L^D(W)$ while typical iso-profit curves π^* and π^R and trade union iso-utility curves V^* are also shown. A bargaining game on wages and benefits with 'right to manage' will essentially pick a point on the labour demand curve between the reservation level curve of the firm $\pi^R\pi^R$ and the reservation discounted labour cost of the union W^R corresponding to its reservation value V^R. Once such a solution (W_B, L_B) is found, it is easy to recover wages and benefits as $w^B = w^*(q, W_B)$ and $s^B = s^*(q, W_B)$. It should be clear by then that all the previous comparative-static results on b, π^R, q τ, T are qualitatively the same as in the monopoly model of the trade union.

In a similar fashion, one can consider the situation of full bargaining between the firm and the union on the three dimensions of current wages, occupational pensions, and employment (w, s, L). This too is represented in Figure A6. The main difference between this and the previous case is simply that now the

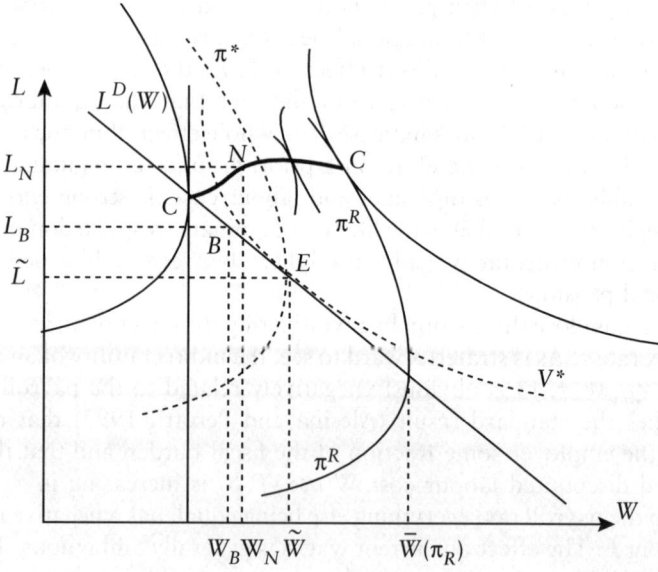

Figure A6

optimal point has to be picked up on the 'contract' curve CC of efficient allocations (W, L) between the union and the firm with an outcome implying more employment L_N, lower expected discounted labour costs W_N, and lower wages and benefits than in the 'right to manage' case. Again, one gets the same qualitative comparative statics as in the case of the monopoly union model.

A3. POLITICAL ECONOMY CONSIDERATIONS WITHIN THE UNION

So far we have considered a framework in which all workers are identical. Obviously, one of the important features of non-wage and benefit policies for unions is the fact that they do not affect all workers the same way. In this section we introduce some heterogeneity across workers' preferences with respect to long-term benefits and employment. Various dimensions may be captured by such differentiation: age, seniority, or degree of attachment to the firm. As long as unions can be viewed as groups taking collective decisions along more or less democratic rules, this introduces a number of interesting political economy issues within the union. What are the points of conflict or convergence between young and old workers inside the union? What kind of preferences of the various workers are represented in the objective function of the union? What is the effect of workers' heterogeneity on wages, pensions, employment, membership? To these questions we now turn.

A3.1. *Introducing young and old workers*

We start first by amending our preceding two-period framework and allowing for the fact that there are young and old workers in the union. Young workers may work in the first period (period 1) of their life and retire in the second period (period 2) (if still alive). Old workers, in fixed number L_0, are retirees and live only in period 1. They do not work and receive benefits s_0 in that period. At the beginning of period 1, the 'monopoly' union chooses the current wage rate of young workers w_y, their future occupational benefits s_y to be paid in period 2. Given this, the firm chooses the employment level L_y. In period 2, benefits s_y are paid to the workers who were previously employed.

We will first assume that the structure of political representation within the union is such that the union's objective function will be the expected discounted utility of young workers in period 1, given some veto power of the old workers to receive what they were promised to receive, namely their benefits s_0.

Given this, and noting $W_y = w_y + [1/(1 + r)]s_y q$, the discounted labour cost of a young worker in period 1, the problem of the union can be written as

$$\text{Max}_W \frac{L^D(W_y)}{M} U^*(q, W_y, \tau, T) + \left(1 - \frac{L^D(W_y)}{M}\right) V^R(q, b, T)$$

$$R(L^D(W_y)) - W_y L^D(W_y) - s_0 L_0 \geq \pi^R$$

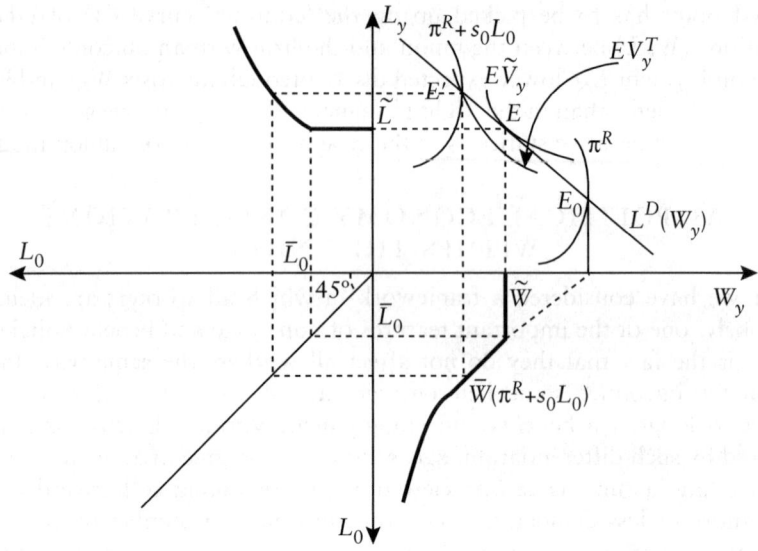

Figure A7

With our assumptions, the only difference between this and the previous section is the fact that the firm now has to generate a large enough surplus to be sure that benefits to old workers can be paid in period 1. Hence the minimum surplus that has to be left over for the firm and old workers is $\pi^R + s_0 L_0$. Obviously, the solution of this problem is simply (with the same notation as before) $W_y = W_y^* = \text{Min}(\tilde{W}(q, \tau, T, b), \bar{W}(\pi^R + s_0 L_0))$.

This is represented in Figure A7. The first quadrant represents the, by now, usual monopoly union equilibrium in terms of the young worker employment level L_y and the discounted labour cost W_y. The iso-utility curve of the young worker EV_y is tangent to the demand function at the point $\tilde{W}(q, \tau, T, b)$. The second quadrant plots the labour cost $\bar{W}(\pi^R + s_0 L_0)$ such that the participation constraint of the firm is binding, as a function of the size L_0 of old workers in the union. This is a downward-sloping relationship, as a larger current surplus and a lower associated labour cost W is necessary to accommodate higher expenditures of the firm on occupational pensions of old workers. The equilibrium-discounted labour cost of young workers W_y^* is then also depicted by a thicker line. When the size of old workers L_0 increases, the minimum 'reservation surplus' to be satisfied, $\pi^R + s_0 L_0$, moves up the labour demand curve $L^D(W_y)$ from point E_0 to some point E'. It follows immediately from this that, as long as the surplus constraint is not binding, the equilibrium labour cost of young workers W_y^* is first fixed at the level $\tilde{W}(q, \tau, T, b)$; then, after some threshold $\bar{L}_0$, the surplus constraint binds, and the equilibrium labour cost is driven by $\bar{W}(\pi^R + s_0 L_0)$ and is consequently decreasing with L_0.

From this it is easy to see that, after the threshold level $\bar{L}_0$, employment of young workers L_y is positively related to the number of old workers in the union. The intuition is simple. A larger volume of occupational pensions paid to old workers induces the union to moderate its demand on labour costs W for the next generation of workers in order to generate a high enough firm's surplus. This, in turn, is associated with a larger fraction of employed workers in period 1.

Nevertheless, it should be noted that such a situation is not in the interest of the young workers. As can be seen in Figure A7, when L_0 becomes larger than $\bar{L}_0$, the equilibrium expected discounted utility EV_y^T of a young worker is decreasing with the number of old workers in the union. Obviously, this aspect has interesting implications for the dynamics of membership inside the union. Consider for instance that trade union membership M is now endogenous and that young workers will enter the union when their expected discounted utility in the union is larger than some reservation level $\bar{V}$. The preceding discussion implies that young workers will be less likely to enter the union, the larger is the number of retired old workers.

A3.2. *Voting on benefits and wages*

In the preceding framework, the decision-making process within the union on current wages and occupational pensions was quite simple. The objective function of the union represented the preferences of the young workers under the constraint of veto power of the old retired union members. Following Askildsen and Ireland (1997), we assume now that workers inside the union are continuously differentiated according to their relative attachment to the firm or, more broadly, their relative evaluation between current wages and long-term benefits, and that they vote to decide the union position on wages, benefits, and employment.

Indeed, suppose that the parameter q is distributed in the union along a distribution, $f(\cdot)$ with mean $\bar{q}$ and median q^m. We abstract, for simplicity, from taxes and denote public benefits to the previously unemployed retirees as T_b. Also, we restrict ourselves to the case of quasi-linear preferences:

$$U(w, s, q) = w + \delta qu(s) \qquad \text{and} \qquad V^R(b, q) = b + \delta qu(T_b)$$

The expected utility of a worker with attachment q can then be written as: $(L/M)U(w, s, q) + (1 - L/M)V^R(b, q)$. The firms's average profit in such a context can be written as

$$E\pi = R(L) - wL - \frac{1}{1+r}s\bar{q}L$$

implying an average discounted labour cost for each hired worker of $W = w + [1/(1+r)]s\bar{q}$.

As we now have some degree of heterogeneity across workers, we need to model the political mechanism by which collective decisions will be taken within the union. Let us consider first the case where wages and benefits are decided by simple majority voting. A typical technical problem in terms of the determination of the political equilibrium is the fact that voting has to be on two dimensions (w, s). In order to alleviate this issue, assume further that there is sequential voting. First, union members vote on the discounted labour cost W faced by firms (or, equivalently, on the employment level $L = L^D(W)$ in the 'right to manage' specification) and then they vote on how to allocate this cost W between current wages and future benefits. We solve the game, as usual, by backward induction.

Let us look therefore at the second stage of this collective decision mechanism. For a given $L = L^D(W)$ and $W = w + [1/(1 + r)]s\bar{q}$, the typical problem of a worker of type q is now written as

$$\text{Max}_{w,s}\, w + \delta q u(s)$$

$$w + \frac{1}{1 + r} s\bar{q} = W$$

The solution of this problem is illustrated in Figure A8 at the tangency point of the iso-utility curve UUq of a typical worker and the budget line $BB\bar{q}$, providing the optimal current wage $w = w^*(q/\bar{q}, \bar{q}, W)$ and benefits $s = s^*(q/\bar{q})$ and the indirect utility function of an employed worker $U(w^*, s^*, q) = U^*(q, \bar{q}, W)$ (see Section A5). An increase in q induces steeper indifferences curves for the worker without changing the budget line. This in

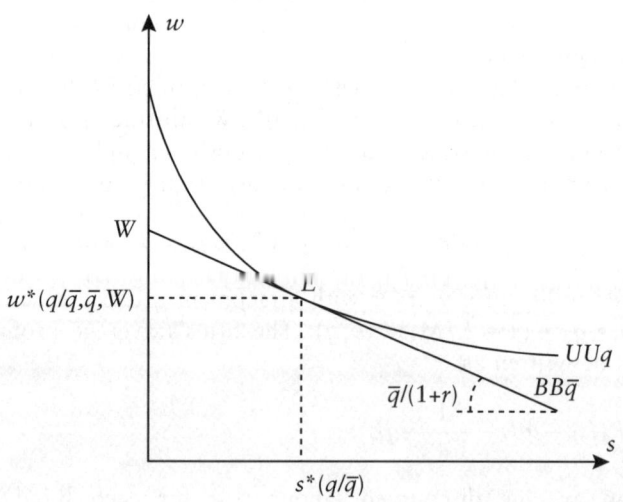

Figure A8

turn leads to a lower current wage w^* and a higher longer-term benefit s^* at the optimal tangency point. Obviously, the indirect utility of an employed worker of type q is increasing in q. An increase in the average value $\bar{q}$ induces a clockwise rotation of the budget line around point W. Because of conflicting substitution and income effects, the impact of such a change on current wages w is ambiguous. In the quasi-linear specification, an increase in $\bar{q}$ has a negative substitution effect only on benefits s. The indirect utility of an employed worker of type q is clearly decreasing in $\bar{q}$. As preferences are single-peaked, the voting equilibrium will be the preferred allocation of the median $w^m = w^*(q^m/\bar{q}, \bar{q}, W)$, and $s^m = s^*(q^m/\bar{q})$. The indirect utility level of an employed worker at this political equilibrium outcome can be written as $U^*(q, \bar{q}, W, q^m) = w^m + \delta q u(s^m)$.

Getting back to the first stage of the voting game, the preferred labour cost value W of a worker of type q will be the solution of the following problem:

$$\text{Max}_W \frac{L^D(W)}{M} U^*(q, \bar{q}, W, q^m) + \left(1 - \frac{L^D(W)}{M}\right) V^R(b, q)$$

$$R(L^D(W)) - WL^D(W) \geq \pi^R$$

Assuming that the participation constraint of the firm is always non-binding, we easily get the solution for the optimal labour cost $\tilde{W}(q, \bar{q}, q^m)$ at the tangency point E^m of the iso-utility of the union member and the labour demand curve $L^D(W)$ (Figure A9). An increase in q induces flatter iso-utility curves of the trade union member as long as public benefits after unemployment T_b are

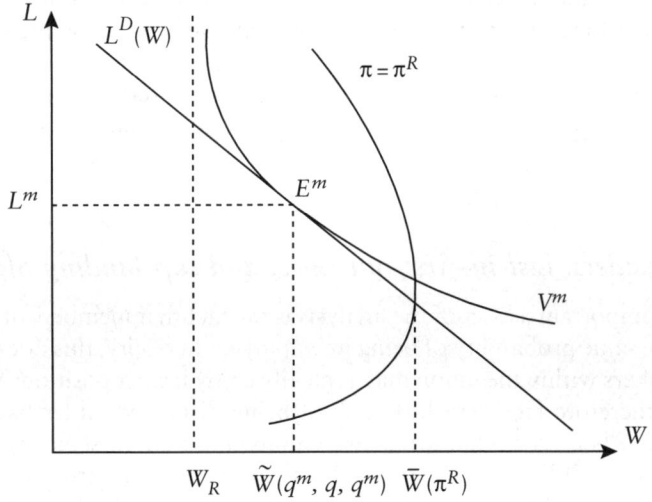

Figure A9

less than occupational benefits s. Indeed, in such a situation the relative value of being employed for a worker increases with his type q. Hence he is more ready to trade off a lower expected labour cost W for a higher probability of being employed. Consequently the cost of labour $\tilde{W}(q, \bar{q}, q^m)$ and the employment level preferred by a union member of type q are, respectively, decreasing and increasing in q.

From this and the single-peakedness of the expected utility function of a typical union member in W, it follows that the majority voting equilibrium in the union in the first stage will again be the one chosen by the median voter of the union q^m. The equilibrium labour cost is $W^m = \tilde{W}(q^m, \bar{q}, q^m)$, out of which we deduce the employment level $L^m = L^D(W^m)$, the current wage $w^m = w^*(q^m/\bar{q}, \bar{q}, W^m)$, and benefits $s^m = s^*(q^m/\bar{q})$.

Out of this analysis, one may investigate how changes, within the union, in the distribution of concerns for benefits $F(q)$ affect the equilibrium values of current wages, benefits, and employment. Consider first that on average unions' members are more attached to the firm (i.e. $\bar{q}$ increases). As the value of being employed decreases with $\bar{q}$, the slope of the iso-utility curves of the median member in Figure A9 becomes steeper, leading to a higher expected cost of labour W^m picked up by the union and lower employment L^m. Holding q^m constant, the impact on benefits $s = s^m$ is unambiguously negative, for occupational benefits are now, *ceteris paribus*, more costly to the firm. The effect on current wages w^m is a priori ambiguous but is likely to be positive if the income effect through W^m is large enough.

Consider now an increase in the pivotal agent q^m. This may be interpreted as due to the fact that the distribution $F(\cdot)$ is more skewed towards concerns for benefits or that people more attached to the firm get more political leverage within the union. In that case, the pivotal agent in the union obviously wants higher long-term benefits s^m. At the same time, as in the present framework occupational benefits are attached to employment, the pivotal agent also cares more about employment. Consequently, his preferred level of labour costs W^m is reduced, current wages w^m are reduced, and employment L^m is increased.

A3.3. *Insiders, last-in–first-out rules, and soft landing plans*

So far, an important aspect of the analysis is the fact that members of the union all face the same probability of being unemployed. In reality, this does not hold. Some workers within the union may typically enjoy insider positions within the firm and therefore face very little risk of being dismissed under bad external conditions. Also, very often firms and unions subscribe to seniority rules and last-in–first-out (LIFO) conventions. These mechanisms discriminate between young workers and more senior workers in terms of their risks of being made unemployed and their access to occupational benefits. Another dimension of implicit employment discrimination across workers is the use of 'soft landing' plans, such as early retirement plans, long-term unemployment insurance, and disability plans, to mitigate unemployment problems. As these plans are applied mainly to senior and older workers, they induce a differential outside payoff according to age or length of service should the firm have to dismiss a worker. This in turn affects differentially the preferred labour package that the worker would wish to vote for in the union.

One can capture the above features in our framework in the following way. First, consider that, for a given employment cost W, the probability of a worker of type q being employed is simply a function $\Phi(q, W)$, such that

$$\int \Phi(q, W) f(q) \, dq = L^D(W)$$

and satisfying the following conditions:

$$\text{(i)} \quad \frac{\partial \Phi(q, W)}{\partial W} \leq 0, \qquad \text{(ii)} \quad \frac{\partial \Phi(q, W)}{\partial q} \geq 0 \qquad \text{(iii)} \quad \frac{\partial^2 \Phi(q, W)}{\partial W \partial q} \geq 0$$

Condition (i) simply states that the probability of being employed decreases with the expected labour cost of the firm. Condition (ii) captures the idea of seniority rules and last-in–first-out (LIFO) conventions in the sense that longer-serving workers (or senior workers) have a higher probability of keeping their jobs than more mobile or younger workers. Finally condition (iii) states that the sensitivity to labour costs of being employed decreases (in absolute value) with the length of attachment of the worker to the firm. This captures in a certain way the idea that longer serving or older workers are more likely to be insiders; therefore their employment status is less sensitive to wages than that of junior (mobile) workers. Obviously, the specification includes the special case of a uniform probability of employment $L^D(W)/M$ when $\Phi(q, W)$ is independent of q.

The 'soft landing' idea applied to senior workers can be captured by simply supposing that the intertemporal payoff of an unemployed worker V^R is designed to be a fraction of what an employed worker of type q would receive in equilibrium $V^*(q)$ (i.e., $V^R = k(q)V^*(q)$ where the fraction $k(q)$ is increasing in q). The cost difference between V^R and what the unemployed worker would receive without a 'soft landing' is 'externalized', i.e. financed outside the firm by general taxation on the rest of the economy.

Given this setting, one may look once more at the voting equilibrium on wages, benefits, and employment inside the union. Again, one can solve the problem in two stages. The second stage provides, as before, for a given labour cost W, the optimal mix preferred by the pivotal agent q^m between current wages $w^m = w^*(q^m/\bar{q}, \bar{q}, W)$ and benefits $s^m = s^*(q^m/\bar{q})$. In the first stage, the determination of the preferred labour cost W for a worker of type q is given by the solution of the amended following maximization problem:

$$\text{Max}_W \; \Phi(q, W)U^*(q, \bar{q}, W, q^m) + (1 - \Phi(q, W))V^R$$
$$R(L^D(W)) - WL^D(W) \geq \pi^R$$
$$\int \Phi(q, W)f(q)\,dq = L^D(W)$$

Assuming again that the participation constraint of the firm never binds, we easily get the labour cost $\tilde{W}(q, \bar{q}, q^m)$ of a worker of type q.

Interestingly now, this labour cost $\tilde{W}(q, \bar{q}, q^m)$ need not be decreasing in q. On the contrary, because of seniority rules, more attached workers (with a higher q) have a higher probability of being employed and therefore value an increase in W more than without such rules. Since their probability of employment is less sensitive to W, they are also less concerned about the impact of an increase in the labour cost W on their change of employment status. Finally, because of the possibility of 'soft landing' plans, their reservation payoff level in the contingency of unemployment is increased, inducing them to demand higher total labour compensations.

For all these reasons, it is very likely that workers more attached to the firm (larger q) will have higher preferred costs of labour $\tilde{W}(q, \bar{q}, q^m)$. Under single-peakedness of the expected utility function of a union member in W, the majority voting equilibrium will be again the one chosen by the median voter of the union q^m and the equilibrium discounted labour cost will be $W^m = \tilde{W}(q^m, \bar{q}, q^m)$ associated with an employment level $L^m = L^D(W^m)$, current wage $w^m = w^*(q^m/\bar{q}, \bar{q}, W^m)$, and benefits $s^m = s^*(q^m/\bar{q})$.

The main difference between this and the previous section is in terms of the impact of a change in the distribution of characteristics of union workers. Consider for instance an increase in the pivotal agent q^m. As the pivotal agent in the union becomes more attached to the firm, he also gets more protection against the risk of unemployment through the seniority rules, FILO conventions, and 'soft landing' plans. Hence his preferred labour cost $W^m = \tilde{W}(q^m, \bar{q}, q^m)$ increases and the employment level $L^m = L^D(W^m)$ decreases. Current wages w^m and benefits are now both increased. The cost of such a strategy is obviously paid by junior workers, who have a disproportionately high probability of unemployment.

From the previous discussion, it follows that the more likely seniority rules, LIFO conventions, and 'soft landing' plans are to be implemented in the economy, the more likely will ageing and shifts in the distribution of characteristics of unions towards senior workers imply higher labour costs, higher unemployment, and larger occupational benefits. Going one step further, we might also expect the seniority rules, FILO conventions, and 'soft landing' plans themselves to be partly endogenous and to be influenced by the unions' activities. As these mechanisms are generally protecting the old or long-serving workers rather than the young workers, one may suspect that the same shift in the distribution towards seniority will make these rules more likely to be implemented, thereby reinforcing the conditions under which one will obtain high labour costs, high unemployment (especially among the young or less attached workers), and greater occupational benefits.

A4. ENDOGENOUS MEMBERSHIP

A4.1. *Endogenous membership and political economy considerations within unions*

Another interesting issue concerns the membership evolution of the union. So far, this has been fixed to a given size, M. Suppose now that it is endogenous. Workers are indexed by the characteristic q distributed uniformly on $[0, 1]$ and decide to join the union, comparing their expected payoff inside the union with the reservation payoff V^0 which they might get in some other non-unionized sector of the economy with $V^0 > V^R(0)$. Clearly, in order to decide whether or not to join the union, each worker has to anticipate the political equilibrium (W^m, L^m, w^m, s^m) within the union. This obviously depends on the position of the pivotal agent within the union, which in turn is determined by the type of individuals who decide to join the union (Booth, 1984). Hence an equilibrium with endogenous membership should determine jointly the political equilibrium decided within the union, the size of the union, and the nature of the pivotal agent within the union.

More precisely, an individual of type q may expect to get a payoff

$$V^*(q) = \Phi(q, W^m)U^*(q, \bar{q}, W^m, q^m) + [1 - \Phi(q, W^m)]V^R(q)$$

by joining the union. For given $\bar{q}$, and q^m, this payoff is increasing in q. Hence, *ceteris paribus*, if an individual of type q decides to join the union, all individuals of type $q' > q$ will also join the union. Define therefore by q_{min} the lowest level such that all workers with a characteristic $q > q_{min}$ decide to join the union. Hence, for given $\bar{q}, W^m, q^m, q_{min}$ is determined by

$$\Phi(q_{min}, W^m)U^*(q_{min}, \bar{q}, W^m, q^m) + [1 - \Phi(q_{min}, W^m)]V^R(q_{min}) = V^0$$

When seniority rules, LIFO conventions, and 'soft landing' plans are applied within the union, it is quite likely that q_{min} is increasing in $\bar{q}$ and q^m. The more, on average, the union is constituted of workers with a high attachment or seniority characteristic q (i.e. a high $\bar{q}$) and reflects the political interest of senior workers (i.e. has a high q^m), the less interesting it is for a mobile or young worker with a low q to join that union and the higher will be the threshold level q_{min} above which workers will decide to be members of the

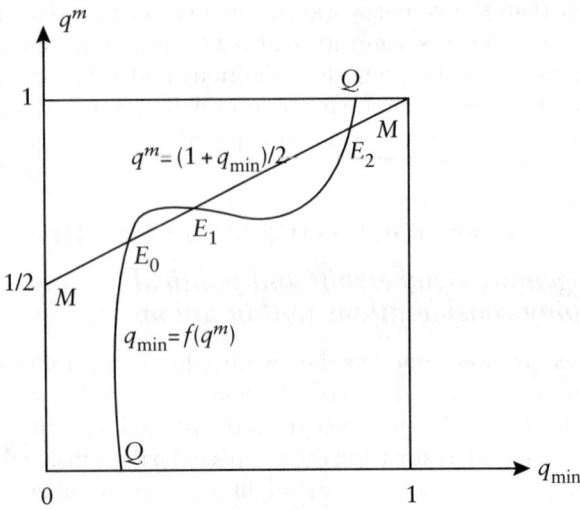

Figure A10

union. (See Section A5 for a formal derivation.) At the same time, given that q is uniformly distributed on $[0, 1]$, we have

$$q^m = \bar{q} = \frac{1 + q_{min}}{2}$$

The resulting union equilibrium with endogenous membership is then described in Figure A10 at the intersection of the curve QQ, which describes the positive relationship between q_{min} and q^m, and the line MM, which describes the relationship $q^m = (1 + q_{min})/2$. As is plotted on the diagram, the two curves may intersect more than once, implying that there may be multiple equilibria in union membership, wages, and benefits. The intuition for such a possibility is quite simple. When the union is composed mainly of workers with a low q, the political equilibrium within the union is more likely to reflect the preferences of these workers with high employment, relatively low wages, and low benefits. Anticipating this, more workers of these types will join the union in the first place. At the same time, however, one may have another equilibrium, at which the union is composed mainly of senior workers with high values of q and protected from unemployment by seniority and LIFO rules. In this case the political pivotal worker within the union is more likely to reflect the preferences of these workers with high wages and benefits, at the cost of a high probability of unemployment for workers with a low q. This, in turn, obviously discourages union membership of the latter and supports a structure of union membership biased towards senior workers.

A5. PROOFS

A5.1. *Political equilibrium inside the union*

Consider first the second voting stage of this collective decision mechanism. For a given $L = L^D(W)$ and $W = w + [1/(1+r)]s\bar{q}$, the typical problem of a worker of type q is now written as

$$\text{Max}_{w,s}\ w + \delta q u(s)$$

$$w + \frac{1}{1+r}s\bar{q} = W$$

The optimal wage and long-term benefit are given by the standard marginal condition

$$u'(s) = \frac{1}{\delta(1+r)}\frac{\bar{q}}{q} \tag{3}$$

and the budget constraint. From this we find the current wage

$$w = w^*\left(\frac{q}{\bar{q}}, \bar{q}, W\right) = W - \frac{1}{1+r}\bar{q}u'^{-1}\left(\frac{1}{\delta(1+r)}\frac{\bar{q}}{q}\right)$$

and benefits

$$s = s^* = u'^{-1}\left(\frac{1}{\delta(1+r)}\frac{\bar{q}}{q}\right)$$

and the indirect utility function of an employed worker $U(w^*, s^*, q) = U^*(q, \bar{q}, W)$. An increase in q induces a downward shift in the first-order condition (3). This in turn leads to a lower current wage w^* and a higher longer-term benefit s^*. Obviously, the indirect utility of an employed worker of type q is increasing in q. An increase in the average value $\bar{q}$ has an ambiguous effect on the current wage and a negative impact on benefits s. The indirect utility of an employed worker of type q is then decreasing in $\bar{q}$.

As preferences are single-peaked, the voting equilibrium will be the preferred allocation of the median, namely

$$w^m = w^*\left(\frac{q^m}{\bar{q}}, \bar{q}, W\right) = W - \frac{1}{1+r}\bar{q}u'^{-1}\left(\frac{1}{\delta(1+r)}\frac{\bar{q}}{q^m}\right)$$

and

$$s^m = s^*\left(\frac{q^m}{\bar{q}}\right) = u'^{-1}\left(\frac{1}{\delta(1+r)}\frac{\bar{q}}{q^m}\right)$$

The indirect utility level of a employed worker at this political equilibrium outcome can be written as

$$U^*(q, \bar{q}, W, q^m) = w^m + \delta q u(s^m)$$

$$= W - \frac{1}{1+r} \bar{q} u'^{-1} \left(\frac{1}{\delta(1+r)} \frac{\bar{q}}{q^m} \right) + \delta q u \left[u'^{-1} \left(\frac{1}{\delta(1+r)} \frac{\bar{q}}{q^m} \right) \right]$$

Getting back to the first stage of the voting game, the preferred labour cost value W of a worker of type q will be the solution of the following problem:

$$\text{Max}_W \ \frac{L^D(W)}{M} U^*(q, \bar{q}, W, q^m) + \left(1 - \frac{L^D(W)}{M} \right) V^R(q)$$

$$R(L^D(W)) - W L^D(W) \geq \pi^R$$

Assuming that the participation constraint of the firm never binds, we get the solution for the optimal labour cost $\tilde{W}(q, \bar{q}, q^m)$ for a worker of type q by the following first-order condition:

$$\frac{dL^D(W)}{dW} [U^*(q, \bar{q}, W, q^m) - V^R(q)] + L^D(W) = 0 \tag{4}$$

Simple differentiation of this condition gives that $\tilde{W}(q, \bar{q}, q^m)$ is decreasing in q as long as public benefits after unemployment T_b are less than occupational benefits s. It is increasing in $\bar{q}$ and increasing (resp. decreasing) in q^m when $q \geq q^m$ (resp. $q \leq q^m$). From this and the single-peakedness of the expected utility function of a typical union member in W, the majority voting equilibrium in the union in the first stage is again the one chosen by the median voter of the union q^m, and the equilibrium discounted labour cost is $W^m = \tilde{W}(q^m, \bar{q}, q^m)$, from which we deduce the employment level $L^m = L^D(W^m)$, and then the current wage

$$w^m = W^m - \frac{1}{1+r} \bar{q} u'^{-1} \left(\frac{1}{\delta(1+r)} \frac{\bar{q}}{q^m} \right)$$

and benefits

$$s^m = u'^{-1} \left(\frac{1}{\delta(1+r)} \frac{\bar{q}}{q^m} \right). \qquad \blacksquare$$

A5.2. Endogenous membership

q_{min} is determined by:

$$V(q_{min}, \bar{q}, W^m, q^m) = \Phi(q_{min}, W^m) U^*(q_{min}, \bar{q}, W^m, q^m)$$

$$+ [1 - \Phi(q_{min}, W^m)] V^R(q_{min}) = V^0$$

Differentiation provides

$$V'_{q_{\min}} dq_{\min} = -V'_{\bar{q}} d\bar{q} - V_{q^m} dq^m - V'_{W^m} \left(\frac{\partial W^m}{\partial q^m} dq^m + \frac{\partial W^m}{\partial \bar{q}} d\bar{q} \right)$$

At the same time,

$$V'_{\bar{q}} = \Phi(q_{\min}, W^m) \frac{\partial U^*(q_{\min}, \bar{q}, W^m, q^m)}{\partial \bar{q}} < 0$$

$$V_{q^m} = \Phi(q_{\min}, W^m) \frac{\partial U^*(q_{\min}, \bar{q}, W^m, q^m)}{\partial q^m} < 0 \qquad \text{for } q_{\min} < q^m$$

Also, as $q_{\min} < q^m$ and $\tilde{W}(q_{\min}, \bar{q}, q^m) < \tilde{W}(q^m, \bar{q}, q^m)$,

$$V'_{W^m} = \frac{\partial V(q_{\min}, \bar{q}, W^m, q^m)}{\partial W^m} < 0$$

From this and the fact that under seniority rules $W^m = \tilde{W}(q^m, \tilde{q}, q^m)$ is increasing in q^m and $\bar{q}$, we have

$$\frac{\partial q_{\min}}{\partial \bar{q}} > 0 \qquad \text{and} \qquad \frac{\partial q_{\min}}{\partial q^m} > 0 \qquad \blacksquare$$

Comments

GILLES SAINT-PAUL

Economists typically believe that unions are cartels which, by artificially restricting the supply of labour, manage to increase wages beyond their market-clearing level, to the benefit of their employed members. They also generally consider that, among heterogeneous members, unions typically represent prime-age males with a stable job and a continuing attachment to the workforce.

This Report shows that unions are in fact involved in many other activities, especially in Western Europe. It characterizes these activities and lays the foundations for their economic analysis, which has been much neglected up to now. It is centred on the effect of unions on the welfare state, a crucial issue, given the size of the welfare states in the European Union and the problems that it will face in the coming decades.

The typical activities of unions beyond the direct negotiation of wages include: direct lobbying for specific policies at the central level, through strikes, demonstrations, party endorsements, etc.; co-provision of fringe benefits at the firm level, along with the employer, which often results from legal provisions; and active participation in the management of key welfare institutions, such as unemployment benefits, health insurance, and pensions.

The existence of such activities raises two important questions. First, why is it in the interest of unions to diversify their activities in such a way rather than concentrate on wage negotiations? Second, is it efficient for society at large that they do so, or should these tasks be disconnected from the labour movement?

From an historical perspective, there is nothing surprising in the involvement of unions in the welfare state. Unions existed before the welfare state and, given their size, they quite naturally provided their workers with insurance and pensions, since they were clearly better at pooling risks and cohorts than the extended family. By now, however, both the state and the market are more efficient at doing that, and accordingly unions have largely retreated from providing social insurance. Nevertheless, as the Report makes clear, in many European countries they retain a big say in the management of such insurance, and most reforms must be negotiated with them in order to be implemented.

The persistence of unions' involvement in the welfare state remains puzzling in the sense that, if financial markets work well, any non-wage benefit provided to workers can be obtained in the form of wages. So, why don't unions try to achieve the highest possible wage for their workers and let them spend these wages as they want, including on contributions to pension and unemployment insurance schemes?

I can think of three reasons.

First, as pointed out by Olson (1965), the union may offer 'selective incentives' for workers who decide to join. These incentives solve the free-rider problem in collective action, which comes from the fact that any wage increase achieved by the union will also benefit those who are not union members. By extending its activities beyond wage-setting, the union increases the scope for selective incentives. For example, it can provide its members with better information about their pensions and promotions, training opportunities, and so on and, to a limited extent, can enforce some discrimination against non-members in the provision of welfare state benefits and other fringe benefits.

Second, as is pointed out in the Report, the union may try to influence the economic environment in which wages are set, so as to enable them to achieve higher wages in future. For example, unemployment insurance, pre-retirement schemes, and the regulation of fixed-term contracts all have the effect of reducing (to some extent) competition from 'outsiders', thus putting union members in a more comfortable position at the time of negotiating wages.[1]

Third, union officials may obtain personal rents from being influential in policy-making. The sums transferred by the welfare state are huge, and by controlling them they may obtain considerable influence and indirect material benefits, just like a cabinet minister or the president of a large firm.

We now turn to the other important question: namely, to what extent do these activities harm or benefit society?

In a perfectly competitive world, such involvement of unions in the welfare state would probably be useless from the perspective of achieving social efficiency. However, we do not live in such a world, but instead in an economy in which some employees command rents. These employees may stand to lose from many policy changes, to the extent that such changes reduce their rents. Governments may have to face violent opposition and/or lose an election if they try to implement a given reform while ignoring the losses it generates. The active participation of unions in the management of the welfare state and of other aspects of labour market regulation may help to identify which policies are feasible, i.e. which trade-offs incumbent employees are willing to accept. In other words, unions' participation may help to reveal to the policy-maker useful information about their members' preferences, and therefore about possible gains and losses from reform. Such information might be quite costly to obtain in the absence of unions.

While governments have often failed when trying to impose labour market reforms, we have seen episodes where substantial progress has been made by direct negotiation between employers' and employees' unions. For example, in Spain in 1997 labour unions and employers agreed on a reduction of dismissal

[1] This line of reasoning leads to the 'political insider' theory of labour market institutions (see Saint-Paul, 2000).

costs for some categories of workers with permanent contracts, in exchange for a reduction in the (widespread) use of temporary contracts. In France, in June 2000 the *patronat* signed an agreement with two leading labour unions that introduces tough conditionality requirements in the payment of unemployment benefits: namely, benefits can now be discontinued if there is evidence that a worker has turned down a number of adequate job offers. At the time of writing (26 June 2000) it remains to be seen whether the government and other unions will allow this arrangement to proceed.

These two examples illustrate the potential role that unions may play in identifying margins of manoeuvre in the realm of labour market policy. This argument also suggests that there exists some optimal partitioning of the workforce into different unions that yields the most efficient aggregation of information. Too few unions would fail to transmit the diversity of workers' situations, while too many would make negotiations very costly. Therefore, there exists some intermediate number of unions that will achieve the best trade-off between complexity and representativeness. Calmfors and Driffill (1988) have argued that the lowest rates of unemployment are obtained with either complete centralization or complete decentralization of wage negotiations, i.e. with either a single encompassing union or a large number of competing unions. The above argument about informational efficiency, however, suggests that there may be some virtues to intermediate situations, despite their costs in employment terms.

Let us now turn to the costs of unions' involvement in a wide range of activities.

The first shortcoming I want to point out is that excess union involvement may lead to a disproportionate representation of union members in public decision-making, i.e. to a *democratic deficit*. For example, in a country like France there is systematic extension to a whole sector of wage agreements signed by unions that represent very few people. It is true, as correctly pointed out by the authors of the report, that this practice in itself reduces the value of joining the union. Nevertheless, many aspects of working conditions, wages, and fringe benefits are decided by some 10% of the workforce. Similarly, the lack of involvement of the unemployed, retirees, capital owners, and non-unionized employees in the management of social security is problematic. In many Western European countries, the scope of policies that are determined by social partners rather than voters is quite wide.

Second, social partners have an interest in shifting costs to third parties, in particular taxpayers. Therefore they fail to fully internalize the social costs of the policies they are choosing. One prominent example is pre-retirement, which allows firms to get rid of their older workers with a large government subsidy, to the benefit of those other workers in the firm who keep their jobs, and of the firms themselves, but at the expense of society at large—which on the other hand is having a hard time trying to save its pension system from a financial crisis!

Third, excess union involvement artificially ties the provision of some goods to the firm, in a way that may be inefficient. Using France again as an illustration, examples range from the purely anecdotal union-run summer camps, where children are induced to spend their holidays with their parents' colleagues' children; to the more significant legally mandated training that firms have to provide for their employees, which costs up to 4% of the wage bill and which workers could as well purchase on the market; to the serious issue of pension funds, which many people (including those on the employers' side) want to be managed by employers and unions at the firm level, and to imply a significant participation of employees in their own firm's capital; such a scheme certainly has a poor performance in terms of portability and risk-sharing, and it is better that pension funds be financial products that any worker can freely purchase on the market independently of his employer and his union affiliation.

This leads us to the fourth shortcoming of unions' participation in the management of the welfare state: namely, that the design of the welfare state will chiefly represent dominant workers within unions, i.e. workers with a stable, lifetime job and a strong attachement to the workforce. This will reduce the scope for portability and proportionality of welfare benefits, thus leading to a rigid labour market with inefficiently low levels of mobility, part-time work, and so forth.

It is clear that all these drawbacks could be considerably alleviated if unions were made more 'encompassing', i.e. if they reflected the interests of a larger fraction of the population, which may include 'outsiders', the unemployed, pensioners (as in Italy), and so on. This is indeed what the authors of the Report recommend. An encompassing union is more democratic, and less likely to reflect special interests and to shift costs to third parties. Scandinavian unions are believed to be encompassing, which may explain the good employment performance of these countries in the last few decades. I am sceptical, however, about the prospects for moving towards such a model. After all, existing unions are engaged in redistributive activities that benefit their members at the expense of other people; therefore they have no incentive to transform themselves so as also to represent these other people. The best one can hope for is that those who are not represented may organize themselves in their own unions. Indeed, some recent theoretical literature (e.g. Grossman and Helpman, 1994) has shown that, if a very large share of the population is organized into competing lobbies, policy outcomes will be more efficient than if a smaller share of the population is organized.

MICHELE SALVATI

I presume that my role as a discussant is more that of a politician than an economist—or, better, that it is the role of a translator, of somebody who stays between the two communities and tries to help them to understand each other. Not a comfortable role, neither in a general nor in this particular case, since frames of minds, objectives, and constraints of social scientists and politicians could not be more different, as Max Weber taught us a long time ago.

Let me first state that I see this Report as an important achievement: path-breaking and understandingly incomplete, but important. The researchers who wrote it are mainly economists, and the Report clearly bears their imprint. Now, welfare arrangements in general (the analysis, however, is limited to two kinds of welfare provision: pensions and unemployment benefits) are very complex, institutionally and culturally specific social constructions. Even if mainstream political economists have long explored social institutions far removed from their traditional concerns—from the family to criminal law—it is understandable that they are more at ease on a turf where cross-national and cross-cultural differences are less prominent and rational choice motivations can be followed in their consequences on an institutional ground presumed to be constant and taken for granted. Just to give an example, the two more formal chapters of the Report—there is a model or more models in both, though the chapters contain only a verbal description—concern occupational pensions (Chapter 3) and the Ghent system of unemployment insurance (Chapter 5). None of the specific conclusions reached in these chapters can be simply extended to Italy, in which a system of occupational, funded pensions is only now taking shape and where a system of universal, or union-negotiated, unemployment insurance with a decent replacement ratio is simply non-existent. Of course, the gist of those conclusions has some value for Italy, too, if we are willing to stretch the analogy a bit; but in order to achieve more reliable results we would need to draft completely different models.

Since I mentioned two chapters of the Report, let me briefly survey the other two: Chapter 2 on the typology of welfare states, and Chapter 4 on public (basically, pay-as-you-go) pensions. These are more descriptive chapters, with no formal models, but are no less useful for that. Chapter 2 builds on a famous typology of Gosta Esping-Andersen (presented in the early 1990s and recently reworked in his *Social Transformations of Post-industrial Economies* (1999). The typology is further detailed in this chapter and fresh data on unions and welfare arrangements in the fields of pensions and unemployment insurance are added. Chapter 4, on public pensions, is also mainly descriptive, and the role of unions in shaping (helping or obstructing) the reforms of the 1990s is sensibly analysed through examples taken from the recent experience of many European countries. For both demographic and economic reasons, the financially unsustainable promises made from the 1960s to the 1980s had to be repealed and the entire public pension system had to be reshaped in many countries. This process is still under way, since the present state of affairs in many countries is a long way from (1) being financially sustainable in the long run, (2) being incentive-compatible, and (3) conforming to acceptable criteria of equity. And this has proved, and is proving, a politically painful process, with the unions very much dragging their feet, to put it mildly. Despite this conservative bias, however, almost everywhere the unions have an important role to play in such a process, the big exception in Europe being Britain. A fair number of cases are analysed and the factors that may explain national differences are well identified, very much as political scientists would do.

This is the shortest description that can be given of the structure of the Report. What are its main questions and answers?

1. The first is preliminary but also fundamental. *Do unions interact with the welfare state?* Yes, they do, and the evidence provided is convincing. *And how do they do it?* Again, the descriptive evidence shows the main ways very clearly: through the bargaining system, through their influence on political parties and the political system, through a direct organizational involvement, as in the Ghent system of unemployment insurance. In a short report, it is difficult to answer these preliminary questions any more fully.

2. *What are the effects of unions on welfare outcomes?* This question is framed in the Report in a very general way, but the answer is based largely on the analysis and the models of occupational pensions, tailored on a rather specific institutional context, as I have already said. The main conclusion—that unions may mitigate market failures' effects on workers arising from imperfect insurance and credit markets, but that they may bias the reform process towards the status quo and possibly at the expense of the younger generation—is supported both by the models on occupational pensions and by the more descriptive evidence provided by Chapter 4 on public pensions. Whether myopic behaviour on the part of unions may have contributed, via old-age spending and spending on pre-pensions and other soft landing schemes, to a negative performance of the economy in terms of growth and employment is a more debatable conclusion, and no hard evidence is given.

3. *Which model of the union better resolves the trade-off between welfare-enhancing and rent-seeking activities?* Again, this question is very general, but the answer depends on the analysis of the Ghent experience of unemployment insurance. So far as it goes, I find the answer convincing: this system may encourage workers to internalize the budget constraint implicit in the financing of unemployment benefits, and it may better control the search effort of benefit recipients. There is also a suggestion, slightly more than an aside, which is very important for Italy and would deserve a closer scrutiny: a Ghent system may be a way of establishing a stronger institutional contact between unions and temporary workers. It actually works in this way in some countries of northern Europe, and if it can be transferred to southern Europe, where temporary work and atypical labour contracts are very widespread, it might meet a big challenge that unions are facing.

4. *Is it possible to win the support of unions in reforming welfare states?* This question is tackled not so much on the basis of a specific analysis, but as a summing-up question, answered on the basis of the entire evidence of the Report. The answer is reasonable. True, unions show a clear seniority bias, not

only in their usual wage-setting activity, but also in their interaction with welfare policies. And this is bad, for both employment and equity reasons. But there are examples, especially for big, encompassing unions, engaged in a political exchange with governments, in which unions have adopted forward-looking behaviour and have recognized the long-term benefit for the economy at large of welfare restructuring.

The Report stops here, implicitly raising a big question: *In which conditions, through which strategies, can these forward-looking aspects of unions' behaviour be strengthened and their more corporatist and organizational interests correspondingly weakened?* This is a question that can hardly be answered in a general way, since the specific interplay between unions, employers' organizations, and the political and welfare systems, as it exists in different countries, must be set out in great detail. There is, however, a general factor on which the search for a welfare-enhancing strategy, for a positive involvement of unions, has to be focused, and this is trust. Trust is an aspect of social capital that is essential for tipping the balance of unions' involvement in favour of welfare-enhancing developments. And trust is not something that is or is not simply there, but is something that may be, and has to be, patiently constructed and may easily be destroyed: since the interests of all the actors are inevitably in a short-term conflict, a welfare-enhancing solution can be found only if a long-run, forward-looking view is taken. And this is why trust is essential: because any single actor has to bet on a behaviour of all the others projected in a rather distant future, having very limited possibilities of sanctioning a violation of the implicit agreement.

A couple of examples may give a better idea of what I have in mind. It is very difficult for trust to develop when governments are weak and subject to frequent political and policy changes: since governments are involved in neo-corporatist agreements (or 'concertation', as we say in Italy, where the word 'corporatism' still brings with it unpleasant fascist memories), the temporal stability of the government strategy is an essential condition for such agreements, which go well beyond the credibility of any specific side-payments that the government may have promised. Again, it is difficult to build relations of trust when other divisions interfere with the basic, short-run conflict of interest of industrial relations. The potential sources of conflict multiply and so does the number of actors involved. In this case the possibility of taking a forward-looking view based on mutual trust is correspondingly reduced.

I come now to my role as a 'translator', and my last two points are addressed to economists, in so far as they deal with that subject of research and try to establish a bridge of mutual understanding with union leaders and activists. Obviously, economists tackle this subject of research like any other subject, with the help of their tools and their paradigms. This is what they should do, and it is why I appreciated this Report so much. But when discussing the pros and cons of a union or non-union solution from the point of view of an economic objective (growth, employment, price stability, etc.), they should always bear in mind that unions are institutions that play a much wider role in the texture of a democratic state. Joseph Stiglitz gave a beautiful keynote address at the Boston meeting of the Industrial Relations Research Association (Stiglitz, 2000), in which this wider role was explicitly recognized. I would make this address compulsory reading in the training of young labour economists.

When talking as an economist to union leaders, I usually stress the negative consequences for employment of an increase in wages (or payroll taxes, or unemployment insurance). This is one of our staple arguments, and is variously elaborated upon in the above Report. The immediate reaction was: if we had listened to the economists, we would still have a 60-hour work-week or a $1 hourly wage. Of course we can rebuke this objection. My advice is to take it seriously, since it asks economists to think in a wider framework than we usually do. Even if we stick to our guns, as we certainly should do, we should at least think in terms of dynamic, general equilibrium models, in which we may trace the influence of unions and industrial relations on such variables as investment, productivity, and technical progress. More generally, we should take into account those dynamic processes that may soften or even reverse the neat trade-offs that appear in the static, partial equilibrium models we normally use. Higher wages and cooperative industrial relations may work—up to a point and in certain circumstances—as a stimulus, more than an obstacle. Like the governments and the unions that they praise, economists too should take a more encompassing, long-run view.

References

Alesina, A, and Perotti, E (1997), 'The Welfare State and Competitiveness', *American Economic Review*, 87.

Anderson, K M (1998), 'The Welfare State in the Global Economy: The Politics of Social Insurance Retrenchment in Sweden, 1990–1998', doctoral thesis, University of Washington.

Andrietti, V (2000), 'Occupational Pension Coverage in the European Union: An Empirical Analysis', Working Paper no. 2000–4, University of Essex (UK).

Ashenfelter, O, and Pencavel, J (1969), 'American Trade Union Growth: 1900–1969', *Quarterly Journal of Economics*, 83.

Askildsen, J E, and Ireland, N J (1997), 'Union–Firm Bargaining over Long Term Benefits', Working Paper no. 1297, Department of Economics, University of Bergen (Norway).

Baccaro, L (2000), 'Negotiating Pension Reform with the Unions: The Italian Experience in European Perspective', paper presented at the 12th International Conference of Europeanists, Chicago, 30 March–2 April.

Bertola, G, Boeri, T, and Nicoletti, G (2001), *Welfare and Employment in a United Europe*, Cambridge, Mass.: MIT Press.

Blanchard, O J, and Wolfers, J (2000), 'The Role of Shocks and Institutions in the Rise of European Unemployment: the Aggregate Evidence', mimeo, NBER.

Blöndal, S, and Scarpetta, S (1998), 'The Retirement Decision in OECD Countries', OECD Economics Department Working Paper no. 202/98.

Boeri, T, Börsch-Supan, A, and Tabellini, G (forthcoming), 'Would You Like to Shrink the Welfare State? The Opinions of European Citizens', *Economic Policy*.

Bonoli, G (1999), *The Politics of Pension Reform: Institutions and Policy Change in Western Europe*, Cambridge: Cambridge University Press.

Booth, A (1984), 'A Public Choice Model of Trade Union Behaviour and Membership', *Economic Journal*, 94.

——and Chatterji, M (1995), 'Union Membership and Wage Bargaining when Membership is not Compulsory', *Economic Journal*, 105.

Burdett, K, and Wright, R (1989), 'Optimal Firm Size, Taxes, and Unemployment', *Journal of Public Economics*, 39.

Calmfors, L, and Driffill, J (1988), 'Bargaining Structure, Corporatism and Macro economic Performance', *Economic Policy*, 6.

——and Horn, H (1986), 'Employment Policies and Centralized Wage Setting', *Economica*, 53.

Castellino, O (1995), 'Redistribution between and within Generations in the Italian Social Security System', *Ricerche Economiche*, 49.

Daveri, F, and Tabellini, G (2000), 'Unemployment, Growth and Taxation in Industrial Countries', *Economic Policy*, 30.

Davis, P E (1995), *Pension Funds: Retirement Income Security and Capital Markets, an International Perspective*, Oxford, Clarendon Press.

Di Tella, R, and MacCulloch, R (1995), 'The Determination of Unemployment Benefits', Applied Economics Discussion Paper no. 180, Institute of Economics and Statistics, University of Oxford.

Disney, R, and Cameron, L (1990), 'The Effect of Union Membership on Occupational Pension Coverage in Britain: A Disaggregated Analysis', mimeo, IFS, London.

Ebbinghaus, B (2000), 'When Labour and Capital Collude: The Varieties of Welfare Capitalism and Early Retirement in Europe, Japan and the USA', Working Paper PSGE no. 00.4, Center for European Studies, Harvard University, July.

—— and Hassel, A (2000), 'Striking Deals: Concertation in the Reform of Continental European Welfare States', *Journal of European Public Policy*, 7.

—— and Visser, J (1997), 'Der Wandel der Arbeitsbeziehungen im westeuropäischen Vergleich', in S Hradil and S Immerfall (eds.), *Die westeuropäischen Gesellschaften im Vergleich*, Opladen: Leske & Budrich.

—— and —— (2000), *Trade Unions in Western Europe since 1945*, London/New York: Macmillan/Grove.

EIRR (various issues), European Industrial Relations Review.

Esping-Andersen, G (1990), *Three Worlds of Welfare Capitalism*. Princeton: Princeton University Press.

—— (1996), 'Welfare States without Work: The Impasse of Labour Shedding and Familialism in Continental European Social Policy', in G Esping-Andersen (ed.), *Welfare States in Transition: National Adaptations in Global Economies*, London: Sage.

—— (1999), *Social Foundations of Post-industrial Economies*, Oxford: Oxford University Press.

European Federation for Retirement Provision (1996), *European Pension Funds: Their Impact on European Capital Markets and Competitiveness, Report*, London: EFRP.

Eurostat (1996), *European System of Integrated Social Protection Statistics ESSPROS Manual 1996*, Luxembourg: Office for Official Publication of the European Communities.

—— (1997), *Demographic Statistics 1996*, Luxembourg: Office for Official Publication of the European Communities.

—— (1998), *Social Protection Expenditure and Receipts 1980–1995*, Luxembourg: Office for Official Publication of the European Communities.

—— (1999), *Demographic Statistics: Data 1995–1998*, Luxembourg: Office for Official Publication of the European Communities.

—— (2000), *Yearbook*, Luxembourg: Office for Official Publication of the European Communities.

Feldstein, M (1976), 'Temporary Layoffs in the Theory of Unemployment', *Journal of Political Economy*, 84.

—— (1998), *Privatizing Social Security*, Chicago: NBER/University of Chicago Press.

Ferrera, M (1997), 'The Uncertain Future of the Italian Welfare State', *West European Politics*, 20.

Flora, P (ed.) (1986), *Growth to Limits: The Western European Welfare States since World War II*, iv, Berlin: W de Greuyter.

Freeman, R (1980), 'The Exit–Voice Tradeoff in the Labor Market: Unionism, Job Tenure, Quits and Separations', *Quarterly Journal of Economics*, 94.

Freeman, R (1981), 'The Effect of Unionism on Fringe Benefits', *Industrial and Labour Relations Review*, 34.

—— (1985), 'Unions, Pensions and Union Pension Funds', in D Wise, *Pensions, Labour and Individual Choice*, Chicago: NBER/University of Chicago Press.

—— and Medoff, J (1984), *What Do Unions Do?* New York: Basic Books.

Gillion, C, Turner, J, Bailey, C, and Latulippe, D (eds.) (2000), *Social Security Pensions: Development and Reform*, Geneva: International Labour Office.

Grossman, G, and Helpman, E (1994), 'Protection for Sale', *American Economic Review*, 84.

Gruber, J, and Wise, D (1999), *Social Security and Retirement around the World.* Chicago: NBER/University of Chicago Press.

Gustman, A L, and Steinmeier, T L (1986), 'A Structural Retirement Model', *Econometrica*, 54.

Hansen, H (1999). *Elements in Social Security*, Copenhagen: Danish National Institute of Social Research.

Hassel, A, and Ebbinghaus, B (2000), 'From Means to Ends: Linking Wage Moderation and Social Policy Reform', in G Fajertag and P Pochet (eds.), *Social Pacts in Europe*, Brussels: ETUI 2000, 61–84.

Hemerijck, A, Unger, B, and Visser, J (2000), 'How Small Countries Negotiate Change: Twenty-five Years of Policy Adjustment in Austria, the Netherlands, and Belgium', in F W Scharpf and V Schmidt (eds.), *Welfare and Work in the Open Economy*, ii, Oxford: Oxford University Press.

Holden, S, and Raaum, O (1991), 'Wage Moderation and Union Structure', *Oxford Economic Papers*, 43.

Holmlund, B, and Lundborg, P (1999), 'Wage Bargaining, Union Membership, and the Organization of Unemployment Insurance', *Labour Economics*, 6.

Huber, E, and Stephens, J D (1999), 'Welfare State and Production Regimes in the Era of Retrenchment'. Princeton: Institute for Advanced Studies, Occasional Papers.

Hutsebaut, M (1999), 'The Future of Social Protection in Europe: A European Trade Union Perspective', in V. Kari, *Financing Social Protection in Europe*, Helsinki: Finnish Ministry of Social Affairs and Health.

Johnson, P (1998), *Older Getting Wiser*, London: Institute for Fiscal Studies.

Kalisch, D, and Tetsuya, A (1998), *Retirement Income Systems: The Reform Process Across OECD Countries*, OECD: Paris.

Kersbergen, K v (1995), *Social Capitalism: A Study of Christian Democracy and the Welfare State*, London: Routledge.

Kjellberg, A (2000), 'Facklig organisering och arbetsmarknad: marginalisering av ungdomar och invandare?' (Unionization and the labour market: marginalization of youths and immigrants?) in S Tegle (ed.), *Har den svenska modellen överlevt krisen?* (Has the Swedish model survived the crisis?), Stockholm: Arbetslivsinstitutet.

Lazear, E P (1979), 'Why Is There Mandatory Retirement?', *Journal of Political Economy*, 87.

—— (1985), 'Incentive Effects of Pensions', in D Wise (ed.), *Pensions Labor and Individual Choice*, Chicago: University of Chicago Press/NBER.

Leonard, J S, and van Audenrode, M (1993), 'Corporatism Run Amok: Job Stability and Industrial Policy in Belgium and United States', *Economic Policy*, 17.

Levy, J D (2000), 'France: Directing Adjustment?' in F W Scharpf and V Schmidt (eds.), *Welfare and Work in the Open Economy*, ii, Oxford: Oxford University Press.

Lockwood, B, and Manning, A (1993), 'Wage Setting and the Tax System: Theory and Evidence for the United Kingdom', *Journal of Public Economics*, 52.

Manow, P, and Seils, E (2000), 'Adjusting Badly: The German Welfare State, Structural Change, and the Open Economy', in F W Scharpf and V Schmidt (eds.), *Welfare and Work in the Open Economy*, ii, Oxford: Oxford University Press.

Martin, J (1996), 'Measures of Replacement Rates for the Purpose of International Comparisons: A Note', *OECD Economic Studies*, no. 26.

Miles, D, and Iben, A (1998), 'The Reform of Pension Systems: Winners and Losers across Generations in the UK and Germany', mimeo, Imperial College, London.

Mortensen, D (1994), 'Reducing Supply-Side Disincentives to Job Creation', in *Reducing Unemployment: Current Issues and Policy Issues*, Proceedings from a symposium sponsored by the Federal Reserve Bank of Kansas City.

—— and Pissarides, C (1994), 'Job Creation and Job Destruction in the Theory of Unemployment', *Review of Economic Studies*, 61.

Mulligan, C, and Salai-i-Martin, X (1999), 'Gerontocracy, Retirement, and Social Security', NBER Working Paper no. W117.

Myles, J, and Pierson, P (forthcoming), 'The Comparative Political Economy of Pension Reform', in P Pierson (ed.), *The New Politics of the Welfare State*, Oxford: Oxford University Press.

Nickell, S (1997), 'Unemployment and Labour Market Rigidities: Europe versus North America', *Journal of Economic Perspective*, 11.

—— (1998), 'Unemployment: Questions and Some Answers', *Economic Journal*, 108.

Nilsson, M M (1998), 'Fördelarna med pensionsuppgörelsen Överväger', *LO-Tidningen* no. 1.

OECD (1991), *Employment Outlook*.

—— (1992), *Employment Outlook*.

—— (1994), *Employment Outlook*.

—— (1995), *Employment Outlook*.

—— (1998), 'Private Pensions Systems: Regulatory Policies', Working Paper no. AWP 2.2.

—— (2000), *Employment Outlook*.

Olson, M (1965), *The Logic of Collective Action*, Cambridge, Mass.: Harvard University Press.

Oswald, A J (1982), 'The Microeconomic Theory of the Trade Union', *Economic Journal*, 92.

Overbye, E (1998), 'The Politics of Voluntary and Mandatory Pensions in the Nordic Countries', *Labour*, 12.

Palier, B (1997), 'A Liberal Dynamic in the Transformation of the French Social Welfare System', in J Clasen (ed.), *Social Insurance in Europe*, Bristol: Policy Press.

Pedersen, P (1990), 'Arbejdsloshedsforsikring og faglig organisering, 1911–85' (Unemployment insurance and unionization), *Nationaløkonomisk Tidsskrift*, no. 128.

Pehkonen J, and Tanninen, H (1995), 'Institutions, Incentives and Trade Union Membership', Department of Economics Working Paper no. 156/1995, University of Jyväskylä School of Business and Economics.

Peracchi, F (1999), 'Patterns of Social Protection Expenditure in the European Union', mimeo, Tor Vergata, Rome.

Pierson, P (1994), *Dismantling the Welfare State? Reagan, Thatcher, and the Politics of Retrenchment*, New York: Cambridge University Press.

Regini, M, and Regalia, I (1997), 'Employers, Unions and the State: The Resurgence of Concertation in Italy?' *West European Politics*, 20.

Reynaud, E (1997), *Private Pensions in OECD Countries: France*, Paris: OECD Labour Market and Social Policy Occasional Papers, no. 30.

——(2000), 'Introduction and Summary', in E Reynaud (ed.), *Social Dialogue and Pension Reform*, Geneva: ILO.

Rothstein, B (1990), 'Labour Market Institutions and Working-Class Strength', in S Steinmo, K Thelen, and F Longstreth (eds.), *Structuring Politics: Historical Institutionalism in Comparative Analysis*, Oxford: Oxford University Press.

Saint-Paul, G (1995), 'Some Political Aspects of Unemployment', *European Economic Review*, 39.

——(1996), 'Exploring the Political Economy of Labour Market Institutions', *European Economic Review*, 39.

——(2000), *The Political Economy of Labour Market Institutions*, Oxford: Oxford University Press.

Scharpf, F W (1998), 'Employment and the Welfare State: A Continental Dilemma', MPIfG Working Paper 7, Cologne.

Schludi, M (1997), 'Kürzungspolitik im Wohlfahrtsstaat: Deutschland und Schweden im Vergleich', Diploma thesis, Konstanz University.

Stiglitz, J (2000), 'Democratic Development as the Fruits of Labor', Keynote Address, Industrial Relations Research Association, Boston.

Stokey, N L, and Rebelo, S (1995), 'Growth Effects of Flat-Tax Rates', *Journal of Political Economy*, 103.

Summers, L, Gruber, J, and Vergara, R (1993), 'Taxation and the Structure of Labor Markets: The Case of Corporatism', *Quarterly Journal of Economics*, 108.

Tabellini, G (1992), 'A Positive Theory of Social Security', NBER Working Paper no. 3272.

Topel, R (1983), 'On Layoffs and Unemployment Insurance', *American Economic Review*, 73.

Tyrvainen, T (1994), 'Real Wage Resistance and Unemployment: Multivariate Analysis of Cointegrating Relations in 10 OECD Countries', mimeo, OECD, Paris.

US Social Security Administration (1999), *Social Security Programs throughout the World*, Washington.

Verband Deutscher Renteversicherungsträger-VDR (1999), *Renteversicherung im internationalen Vergleich*, Frankfurt a.M.

Visser, J (1990), 'In Search of Inclusive Unionism', *Bulletin of Comparative Labour Relations*, 18, Deventer: Kluwer.

——and Hemerijck, A (1997), *A 'Dutch Miracle': Job Growth, Welfare Reform, and Corporatism in the Netherlands*, Amsterdam: Amsterdam University Press.

Wadensjö, E (2000), 'Sweden: Reform of the Public Pension System', in E Reynaud (ed.), *Social Dialogue and Pension Reform*, Geneva: ILO.

Walker, A (1999), 'Political Participation and Representation of Older People in Europe', in A Walker and G Naegele (eds.), *The Politics of Old Age in Europe*, Buckingham: Open University Press.

Western, B (1993), 'Postwar Unionization in Eighteen Advanced Capitalist Countries', *American Sociological Review*, 58.

—— (1994), 'Unionization and Labour Market Institutions in Advanced Capitalism, 1950–1985', *American Journal of Sociology*, 99.

—— (1997), *Between Class and Market: Postwar Unionization in the Capitalist Democracies*, Princeton: Princeton University Press.

Final Remarks

OLIVIER BLANCHARD

Some institutions die. Some keep being reborn. What will happen to unions?

The question is an important one. It is also a tough one. Economists (and others) have a hard time understanding why countries have different institutions, let alone predicting how these institutions are likely to change. We are well aware of how difficult the task is. Nevertheless, with the help of the two Reports in this volume, I believe we have made some progress.

A useful starting point is to think about what unions have done in the past. There are many ways of doing this. With an eye to what may happen in the future, let me organize my list around four functions:

1. first—and first historically—to provide insurance and help to their members, were the need to arise;
2. second, to protect workers against rent extraction by firms, in other words to fight exploitation;
3. third, to extract rents from firms and from the state. Clearly, the high unionization rates in sheltered sectors—including the public sector—stems not from an unusual risk of exploitation in those sectors, but rather from the presence of rents to be extracted;
4. fourth, to represent the interests of workers at the national level, either directly in consultation with business and government, or indirectly through political parties.

For each of these, it is useful to ask: which of these functions can/will/should unions continue to perform in the future? Let me take each one in turn. (Some of my arguments will have to do with 'can', some with 'should', some with 'will'.)

Insurance

It is fairly clear, both theoretically and empirically, that the state has a comparative advantage in providing unemployment insurance to workers. The state has the administration, the statistical records, and the economies of scale that unions just do not have. This was indeed the main motivation for the development of state-provided insurance, which is now the rule in most countries. It was a major accomplishment. But, in a way, it was a Pyrrhic victory for unions. The workers are better off, but the unions have lost one of their main functions.

The discussion of the so-called 'Ghent' system of unemployment insurance in Chapter 5 of Part II is interesting in this respect. In its pure form, the Ghent system is a system of co-provision of unemployment insurance by firms and workers. The unions like it, and the evidence is that it leads to higher membership rates. The authors of the paper contend that there might be good economic arguments in favour of such co-provision. But the argument they develop should actually make unions think twice: this is that, by forcing unions to internalize the cost of unemployment insurance, such co-provision will lead to more wage moderation. If this is the case, it may well be a poisoned gift. If the co-insurance system comes with large subsidies from the state, this is clearly more attractive to unions. But in this case the economic argument disappears. And, as we are currently seeing in France, the state may not then be eager to transfer the responsibility for running the system to unions and firms.

Rent Extraction by Firms

The opportunities for exploitation of workers by firms (or, to use more neutral semantics, the degree of monopsony power of firms in the labour market) have substantially decreased since the nineteenth century. But they have not disappeared. The issue here is how best to limit them. How much should be done by the state, how much should be left to the unions?

The answer is that it should mostly be done by the state. What is needed here are clear, across-the-board rules which limit abuse without interfering further with the decisions of most firms. This suggests the use of national laws and national minima, enforced by inspectors, rather than case-by-case bargaining.

And this is indeed what has happened over time. Working conditions are typically determined by national standards. In most countries, the minimum wage is determined by the state, rather than bargained sectorally.

Employment protection is a bit different. In many countries, the rules are complex, and the firms' decisions can be challenged by individual workers or by unions. But even there, there seems to be an increasing perception that the system is too complex, and that the costs are large, relative to the transfers to workers. The evolution—which, admittedly, is taking place only at glacial pace—seems to be towards simpler rules, more automatic payment of severance, and less room for recourse by either workers or unions.

All in all, the conclusion here seems to be the same as for insurance earlier. Limiting rent extraction by firms is probably better done through laws than by unions. And the role of unions in that dimension is indeed decreasing.

Rent Extraction from Firms
and from the State

We were warned in Part I that greater European integration does not necessarily imply a decrease in product market rents. The warning is important. But it is still the case that in many sectors increased competition, at either the national or the international level, is leading to a decrease in rents. Even the state sector is under increasing pressure to keep public-sector wages under tighter control.

What about the new economy? One might actually argue that in much of the new economy—think of the internet, or genetic engineering—marginal cost is close to zero, generating enormous rents. This is certainly the conclusion one must draw from the stock market's assessment of high-tech stocks. These rents may however be difficult for workers to appropriate. They come and go too quickly, both in time and in space, and most workers do not have much bargaining power anyway.

So the news on this third front is also bad for unions. The smaller the rents generated by firms, the smaller the rents the unions can appropriate, and so the smaller the appeal of unions.

National Representation

With the increasing focus on reform of labour market institutions, unions clearly have an important political role to play in the redefinition of these institutions. But one of the lessons I draw from the unemployment experience in Europe is that their role should go beyond that.

For an economy to grow at a steady pace, many conditions must be satisfied. One of these is that real wage growth must be consistent with the pace of total factor productivity (TPF). The lesson of the 1970s and early 1980s is that real wage growth in excess of TPF leads to lower employment, lower capital accumulation, and increasing unemployment. The lesson from the Netherlands or Ireland over the last fifteen years is that wage moderation—wage growth below TPF growth—leads to recovery and a decrease in unemployment.

Once upon a time, it was believed that active monetary policy could repair the damage created by inappropriate nominal wage growth. Whether or not this belief was right, it is no longer relevant. In the euro environment of a common currency and inflation targeting, appropriate real wage growth means appropriate nominal wage growth. And there are two ways to achieve this. One is to leave it to the markets: if nominal wage growth is too high, then unemployment will increase, and sooner or later pain will lead to wage moderation. The other is to try to avoid unemployment in the first place, and rely on coordination at the aggregate level to achieve the outcome—after all, the evolution of TPF, the appropriate nominal wage growth, are complex issues, and one may hope for a better outcome if these are discussed at the aggregate, coordinated level.

This takes us to social pacts and the role of unions in that context. It is fashionable these days to hail the Wassenaar agreements, which led to wage moderation in the Netherlands from the early 1980s, as an example of what should be done. And, in this case, I agree with fashion. Perhaps, given the state of the Dutch economy at that time, wage moderation would have come anyway. But the agreement almost surely helped show the way, and the results have been impressive.

Are social pacts the solution to all the problems of the labour market? Surely not. Wassenaar did not happen until unemployment was high in the Netherlands, and it may not have happened otherwise. And recent European history is full of failed social pacts, when circumstances were such that no trust existed, and no compromise could be achieved—such as in Spain in the early 1980s. But social pacts, or less formal coordination at the national level, can help. And, with the loss of national monetary policy, there are not many alternatives.

Conclusions

Suppose my conclusions are right. What is going to happen to unions?

On the one hand, they have less and less to offer to individual workers: Unemployment insurance and basic protection are increasingly provided by the state; and rents are getting smaller, leading to less room for rent extraction. As we have seen in the above reports, this decrease in attractiveness is reflected, in nearly all countries, by decreased membership and support.

On the other hand, unions have an increasingly important role to play at the national level. But they can do this only if they can claim to represent the workers. This question of legitimacy strikes me as the main challenge facing European unions today. Absent strong grass-roots support, there is clear danger of a 'squeeze play', in which either the government or the business organizations take note of the dwindling membership, and decide to ignore the unions.

The experience of France is interesting here. This is a country where membership numbers are between 5% and 10%, but where unions still play an important role at the national level. Will this remain the case? One of the exchanges in the discussion at the Naples conference suggests that the answer may be yes. When they are formally represented at the firm level (as in France), unions can help workers by ensuring that existing laws are enforced and that workers are aware of their rights, as well as by providing other services. Whether such a limited 'service' function at the firm level will be enough for them to retain their legitimacy at the national level remains to be seen.

STEPHEN NICKELL

It is evident from the above Reports that trade unions undertake an enormous range of activities. Here, I would like to summarize what unions do and to consider briefly the consequences. What unions do depends on what they *can* do, and this depends on the extent of product market competition.

Suppose we have reached the Nirvana of competitive product markets, which some believe we are approaching. Under these circumstances unions will find it hard to raise wages, but they can provide benefits. There are two kinds of benefits: those that do not impose costs on firms, such as the right to purchase cheap life insurance, and those that do, such as help with 'unfair' dismissal. These activities will have little effect on employment since, if they impose costs on the firm, wages will typically adjust to compensate.

Product market competition will not prevent unions from representing workers nationally, but what they then actually do depends on their place within the legal framework. Whatever they do, the macroeconomic effects will probably be minimal. Thus, while unions can benefit their members, they impose few if any costs on the rest of us if product markets are highly competitive. However, we are a long way from uniformly high levels of competition across all sectors. And if product markets are non-competitive, there are many more possibilities for trade unions. Some of these are as follows.

1. Unions can now raise wages significantly. If such activities are widespread, this will have macroeconomic effects, typically higher levels of unemployment.

2. Unions can capture product market rents in forms other than wages. For example, they can impose rigidities in the workplace to reduce the pace of work, or enforce discrimination against specific groups. Some of these activities may discourage innovation and result in lower productivity growth.

3. The above points bring unions into conflict with firms. But this is not always the case. Unions have a common interest with monopolistic firms to sustain and raise monopoly rents. Thus, unions and firms may join up to lobby for regulations that raise entry barriers and reduce foreign competition. In particular, they will push hard for laws that extend wage bargains to non-union firms in the same sector to prevent their monopoly power being undermined.

4. Because of the absence of competition, unions are often very active in the public sector, where they will attempt to exercise control over the rules governing their jobs as well as to press for monopoly public provision of whatever service they provide.

All these actions may benefit union members in the short run, but will often impose costs on the rest of us and even on the membership in the long run.

However, unions can also engage in more generally beneficial actions. The following are some examples.

- Unions and firms can set wages in a coordinated fashion, enabling the government to operate a more expansionary macroeconomic policy with lower average levels of unemployment.
- Unions can cooperate in the introduction of new technology, benefiting both outsiders and members in the long run.
- They can operate as a force against discrimination, again to the general social good.

Some of the activities in this list are mutually contradictory. Despite this, examples of all of them are readily available.

To summarize, there are two mutually opposing groups of activities open to unions in an environment where product market rents are widespread. Some unions in some countries operate in ways that favour their members in the short run but impose costs on the rest of us, and even on their own members, in the long run. Alternatively, other unions in other countries operate in ways that benefit both their own members and the rest of society.

Why do we see these contrasts? This is not a question I can even attempt to answer here. However, I would hazard a prediction. Unions that operate in the first way will come under pressure from the forces of competition and the activities of the rest of society on whom they impose costs. These unions are in danger of being eliminated in the long run. By contrast, the unions that generate benefits for the whole of society will probably survive and even thrive. We shall see if this prediction comes true.

Index

Names of countries are indexed only in cases of a substantial discussion of the country concerned.

acquis sociales 70
administration:
  social insurance 177–81
  unemployment insurance 241–2
age:
  ageing membership 29–30
  population trends 160
  problem of recruiting younger members 174
  public pensions, intergenerational effects
    202–4, 215
  seniority bias 187–210, 250–1, 265–7
Agell, J., with P. Lundborg 112
Akerlof, G. 17–18
Alesina, A., with R. Perotti 98–9
Allgemeinverbindlichkeitserklärung 79
allocative efficiency:
  impact of unions 49–50, 66
  see also efficiency
Alogoskoufis, G. C., with A. Manning 108
Amsterdam Treaty 125–6
Anderson, K. M. 220
Andreosso-O'Callaghan, B., with D. Jacobson
  48
Ashenfelter, O., with J. Pencavel 20, 236
Askildsen, J. E., with N. J. Ireland 190, 192,
  254, 267
Austria, austerity policies 232

Bain, G. S., with F. Elsheik 20
Ball, L. 106
  with D. Romer 107
bargaining 264–5
  bargaining power:
    factors determining 50–1
    foreign direct investment 58–9
    unemployment insurance 242–3
  bargaining structure:
    and macroeconomic performance 86–97
    tax and monetary policy 98–104
    and macroeconomic shocks 104–9
    European Monetary Union 109–12
    and economic outcomes 141
    and replacement rates 247
  centralization 34, 71–2, 238, 280
  collective bargaining:
    decentralization 118–21
    level of and centralization 34–6
    structure 70–5
  coordination 91–7, 125–9
  decentralization 8, 9–10, 50, 118–21
  density, impact 34–6, 51, 95–7
  foreign competition, impact 88, 89
  foreign direct investment 58–9
  forms of 52–3
  legislative environment 53–4

macroeconomic performance and 86–114
management attitudes 54–5
multi-level bargaining 89–91
transnational wage bargaining 9
wages 8, 108–11, 190–2
  and unemployment 104–5, 238–41
  see also wages
Barro, R., with D. B. Gordon 100
benefits, analytical framework 254–77
Bergström, Villy, comment 135–8
Bertola, G., with T. Boeri and G. Nicoletti
  56, 163
Blanchard, Olivier J.:
  comment 292–5
  with J. Wolfers 104–5, 239–40, 243
Blanchflower, D., with R. B. Freeman 34
Bleaney, M. 95
Boeri, T. *see* Bertola, G.
bonus wages 138
Booth, A. L. 17, 68
  with M. Chatterji 234
British Social Attitude Studies, motivations for
  joining unions 31
Brook, L. *see* Jowell, R.
Brown, W. 54
Bruno, M., with J. Sachs 69
Burdett, K., with R. Wright 246

Calmfors, L. 103
  with J. Driffill 280
Cameron, L., with R. Disney 198
capital:
  mobility of, and decentralization of bargaining 120
  organization 168, 169
  returns to human capital and work
    experience 65
  see also foreign direct investment;
    macroeconomics; multinational corporations
central bank, deterrent to wage increases 101–3
centralization:
  centralized bargaining 34, 71–2
  unemployment and wage bargaining 238, 280
  union density 34–6
  union policies 196–7
  wage flexibility 108
  see also conglomerate unions; coordination;
    decentralization
Chantiers de l'Atlantique, negotiated flexibility
  66
Chatterji, M., with A. Booth 234
Clegg, H. A. 55
closed shop, bargaining power 54
collective agreements 80
  see also contracts
collective bargaining *see* bargaining

comments:
 Bergström, Villy 135–8
 Blanchard, Olivier 292–5
 Flanagan, Robert J. 138–42
 Nickell, Stephen 296–7
 Saint-Paul, Gilles 278–81
 Salvati, Michele 281–5
Commons, John 19, 20
competition:
 foreign competition 49, 88, 89
 impact of unions 49–50
 labour markets and the unions 47–8, 50
 multinational corporations 140–1
 reciprocal dumping 56–7
 union's ability to appropriate surplus 47–9
concentration ratios, EU 48–9
conglomerate unions:
 decentralization 44–5
 see also centralization; decentralization
consumer price index, impact of wage rises 88–9
contracts 79–81
 wage contracts, length 105–6, 108
coordination:
 bargaining 91–7, 125–9
 European Monetary Union 9
 failure of and wage rigidity 106–7
 and monetary policy 100–4
 possible future developments 130–1
 social pacts 121–5
 transnational coordination 9, 127–31, 140–1
 unemployment and coordination of
  bargaining structures 98–104
 wage restraint 108–9
 see also centralization; decentralization
costs, union organizing 23
coverage (union) 83
 and bargaining coordination 95–7
 definition 206
 see also density; membership
cross-national diversity, membership density 32–4
Cukierman, A.
 with F. Lippi 100, 103
 with P. Rodriguez and S. Webb 102–3

Daveri, F., with G. Tabellini 99
decentralization:
 collective bargaining 118–21
 conglomerate unions 44–5
 multinational firms 129–30
 possible future developments 130–1
 wage bargaining 8, 9–10, 50
 see also centralization; coordination
decommodification 165–6
 and union density 171
Delsen, L. 27
density (union):
 and bargaining coordination 95–7
 changes in 139
 decline in 135
 decommodification 171
 definition 206
 deunionization 83
 economic cycle 19
 influence on bargaining power 51
 influence of changes in labour market 36–42, 43

multi-employer bargaining 34–6
non-active members 172–4
unemployment 239–41
unemployment insurance 22–3, 236–8
welfare state, scope of 168–71
 see also coverage; membership
deunionization 14, 83
Dickens, W., with J. Leonard 55
disability pensions, reform 213–14
Disney, R., with L. Cameron 198
Driffill, J., with L. Calmfors 280
dumping 56–7

early retirement 200–2, 212, 215
 and unemployment 220–3
 see also pensions; 'soft landing' schemes
Ebbinghaus, B. 200
 with J. Visser 33
economic cycle, and union density 19
efficiency:
 allocative efficiency 49–50, 66
 increasing 66–9
elasticity, of labour demand 71
Elmeskov, J., with J. Martin and S. Scarpetta 91, 93, 97, 99
Elsheik, F., with G. S. Bain 20
Employment Pact (1999) 126
Employment Relations Bill (1999) 53
erga omnes mechanisms 79, 84
Esping-Andersen, G. 165–6, 171, 282
EU:
 bargaining coordination:
  at European level 125–9
  and wage restraint 108–9
 bargaining power and foreign direct
  investment 58–9
 European Monetary Union (EMU) 137, 138
  bargaining structure 109–12
  incentives for national coordination 9
  Maastricht Treaty 75, 125–6
 European works councils (EWCs) 82
 Exchange Rate Mechanism (ERM),
  monetary policy 110
 future prospects for trade unions 115–34
 trade and competition 56–7
 unionization trends compared to USA 15
 wage shares compared to USA 17
European Central Bank 110
European Centre of Enterprises with Public
 Participation (CEEP) 127
European Commission, coordination 127
European Metalworkers' Federation 125
European Monetary Union (EMU) *see under* EU
European Trade Union Confederation (ETUC)
 127
Eurostat 164, 166
Exchange Rate Mechanism (ERM) 110
exit versus voice, and transactions costs 67–8
externalities, wage decisions 86–7

Feldstein, M. 245
Finland:
 buffer funds 123
 wage restraint 109
fiscal policy 138

Flanagan, Robert J., comment 138–42
flexibility 136
   allocative efficiency 66
   impact on membership 27
   wage flexibility 105–9, 108, 111–12
foreign competition:
   impact on wage bargaining 88, 89
   impact on wage negotiations 49
   see also competition
foreign direct investment (FDI), and bargaining
      power 58–9
France, fragmented social security system 223–4
Franzese, J., with P. A. Hall 103
free-rider, problem of 17–18
Freeman, R. B. 197
   pensions 188, 198
   with D. Blanchflower, level of bargaining 34
   with J. Medoff 67
      pensions 189–90
   with J. Pelletier
      legislative environment 54
      management attitudes to unions 55
full-time workers, membership 27, 30

Gallie, D. 32
game theory, membership rate and firm's options 11
gender:
   changing composition of labour market 24, 25
   and early retirement 221
   female unionization 45
   part-time jobs 27
   and union density 26–9
   wages, sex discrimination 64
general unions:
   decentralization 44–5
   see also conglomerate unions
Germany:
   erga omnes mechanisms 84–5
   as possible wage leader 128
   returns to human capital and work experience 65
   wage bargaining and monetary policy 110
gerontocracy 194
Ghent system 172, 241–2, 247, 251–2, 293
   and demand for union membership 234, 235–8
   reform of unemployment insurance 245
   and unemployment 238–41, 247
   and union density 22–3, 236
globalization, impact on bargaining power 51
Gordon, D. B., with R. Barro 100
governance 55–6
government activity:
   and union strength 139
   see also EU; macroeconomics; welfare state
Groth, C., with A. Johansson 108
Gruber, J.:
   with D. Wise 200
   see also Summers, L.
Gustman, A. L., with T. L. Steinmeier 198
Guzzo, V., with A. Velasco 100

Haffner, R. *see* Nicoletti, G.
Hall, P. A., with R. J. Franzese 103
Healy, J. *see* Slichter, S.
Hibbs, D. A., with H. Locking 90, 91

Hirschman, A. 67
history, membership trends 12–13
Holden, S. 103, 123
   with A. Rödseth 91
   with O. Raum 239
Holmlund, B., with P. Lundborg 234
Holzmann AG 67
Horn, H., with A. Wolinsky 52

IG Bau 67
IG Metall, as possible wage leader 128
income:
   income redistribution, intergenerational effects
      of public pensions 202–4, 215
   incomes policies, failure 16
   see also wages
industrial action, opposition to retrenchment 184–6
industrial relations 169
   decline in labour conflict 15–16
   prospects for a central unified system 127
inflation 68–9
   control of 137
   impact on union membership 19–20
   and wage rises 100–1
   see also macroeconomics
insiders 270
insurance 159, 160, 292–3
   administration of unemployment insurance 241–2
   reforms of unemployment insurance 244–6
   social insurance 167, 177–81
   'soft landing' schemes 199–202, 271–2
   unemployment insurance 172, 234–47
   unemployment insurance and union density
      22–3, 236–8
   wages and unemployment insurance 242–3
   see also Ghent system; 'soft landing' schemes
intergenerational effects *see* age
Ireland, N. J., with J. E. Askildsen 190, 192,
      254, 267
Italy, reform of social security system 232
Iversen, T. 72
   with D. Soskice 103

Jacobson, D., with B. Andreosso-O'Callaghan 48
Johansson, A., with C. Groth 108
Jowell, R., with S. Witherspoon, L. Brook and
      B. Taylor 31

Keynes, John Maynard, wage differentials 106
Klandermans, P. G. 18
Kleiner, M. M. 55
Kohaut, S., with C. Schnabel 83
Kok, Wim 76

labour conflict:
   decline in 15–16
   see also industrial action
labour markets:
   administration 178
   changing composition 24–6
   competition and unions 47–8, 50
   elasticity of demand 71
   structural and cyclical changes, influence on
      union density 36–42, 43
   see also unemployment

last-in-first-out rule (LIFO) 270–3
Layard, R., with S. J. Nickell 91, 93, 243
legal advice 69–70
Leonard, J. S.:
  with M. van Audenrode 200
  with W. Dickens 55
Lippi, F., with A. Cukierman 100, 103
Livernash, R. *see* Slichter, S.
Locking, H., with D. A. Hibbs 90, 91
Lundborg, P.:
  with B. Holmlund 234
  with J. Agell 112

Maastricht Treaty 75, 125–6, 252–3
Machin, S. 83
  with M. Stewart and J. van Reenan 52
macroeconomics:
  bargaining structures and macroeconomic
    shocks 104–9
  monetary policy:
    and bargaining coordination 100–4
    and wage bargaining in EU 110–11
  social pacts 75–9
management, attitudes to unions 54–5
Manning, A., with G. C. Alogoskoufis 108
manufacturing, decline 31
market power, effect of wage bargaining 87–9
Marshall–Hicks rule, elasticity of labour demand
  71
Martin, J. *see* Elmeskov, J.
Marwell, G., with P. Oliver 18
Medoff, J., with R. B. Freeman 67, 189–90
membership 11–45
  deunionization 83
  Ghent system and demand for union
    membership 234, 235–8
  history of membership trends 12–13
  inflation, impact 19–20
  levels of 8, 11–17
    cyclical explanations 19–23
    structural explanations 24–32
    institutional explanations 32–4
  private sector 24–6
  public sector 24, 26, 27
  reasons for joining and free-rider problem
    17–19
  welfare state and membership structure 172–5
  see also density
Metcalf, D., with M. Stewart 51, 54
Millward, N. 32
minimum wages 244
Moene, K.-O. 53
monetary policy:
  and bargaining coordination 100–4
  and tax 98–104
  and wage bargaining in EU 110–11
  see also macroeconomics
monopoly 159
  union's ability to negotiate wages 47–8
Mortensen, D. 246
Mulligan, C., with X. Sala-i-Martin 194
multi-employer bargaining:
  and centralization 34
  see also collective bargaining
multi-level bargaining 89–91

multi-unionism 52
multinational corporations (MNCs):
  and competition 140–1
  decentralization 129–30
  transnational bargaining 131
  see also foreign direct investment

national coordination, incentives for 9
Netherlands, Wassenaar Consensus 76
Nickell, Stephen J. 205, 208
  comment 296–7
  with R. Layard 91, 93, 243
  see also Nicoletti, G.
Nicoletti, G.:
  with R. Haffner, S. Nickell, S. Scarpetta and
    G. Zoega 47, 56, 105
  see also Bertola, G.
non-active members 172–4

occupational pensions 167, 180, 181–3, 197–9,
  225–30
  see also pensions
oligopoly, union's ability to negotiate wages
  48
Oliver, P., with G. Marwell 18
Olson, M. 17, 279
organizing:
  cost and membership level 23
  organizing agent, unions as 32

part-time workers, membership 27, 30
passive union membership, and pension spending
  209
payroll tax rate 191
Pedersen, P. 237–8
Pehkonen, J., with H. Tanninen 237–8
Pelletier, J., with R. B. Freeman 54, 55
Pencavel, J. H., with O. Ashenfelter 20, 236
pensions 165, 282
  bridging pensions 200, 201
  disability pensions 213–14
  early retirement 200–2, 212, 215
  governance, public and private pension
    schemes 180
  occupational pensions 167, 180, 181–3, 197–9,
    225–30
  pensioners as members of unions 172–4, 183–4
  privatization 216, 225–7
  public pensions:
    funding 217–20
    governance 180
    impact 190
    intergenerational effects of pay-as-you-go
      (PAYG) 202–4, 215
    reforms 211–33
  redundancies, early retirement and
    pre-retirement benefits 200–2
  spending on and youth unemployment 204–10
  union role 187–210
Peracchi, F. 206
Perotti, R., with A. Alesina 98–9
Phelps, E. 99, 105
Pochet, P. 128
political economy 265–73

political parties, unions' affiliation to 175–7
pre-retirement schemes 199–200
  see also 'soft landing' schemes
prices, consumer price index, impact of wage
    rises 88–9
private sector, membership 24–6
privatization, pensions 216, 225–7
productivity, and wages 67, 68
Produktivitätspeitsche 68
profit:
  profit sharing 108
  see also surplus
proportionality rules 53
public sector:
  union membership 24, 26
  women and membership 27
Putman, Robert D. 135

Raum, O., with S. Holden 239
reciprocal dumping, and competition 56–7
redundancies:
  early retirement and pre-retirement benefits
    200–2
  see also retrenchment
reforms:
  public pensions 211–33
  unemployment insurance 244–7
  welfare state 252–3, 283–4
regional bargaining 72
Rehn-Meidner 68
religion, religious union movements 175
rent-seeking 283, 293–4
  pension schemes 183
replacement rates, and bargaining structure
    244
restructuring:
  allocative efficiency 66–7
  mergers 10
retrenchment of the welfare state:
  and industrial action 184–6
  and shared policy-making 211–12
  see also redundancies
reward motive, union membership 20
Reynaud, E. 159
Rodriguez, P. *see* Cukierman, A.
Rödseth, A., with S. Holden 91
Romer, D., with L. Ball 107
Rothstein, B. 236

Sachs, J., with M. Bruno 69
Saint-Paul, Gilles, comment 278–81
Salai-i-Martin, X., with C. Mulligan 194
Salvati, Michele, comment 281–5
scale economies 42–5
Scandanavian countries, multi-level bargaining
    89–90
Scarpetta, S. *see* Elmeskov, J.; Nicoletti, G.
Schelling, T. C. 18
Schnabel, C., with S. Kohaut 83
sectoral bargaining 71
self-administration *see* administration
seniority bias 187–210, 250–1, 265–7
  see also age
services 69–70
  and union density 18–19

Shalev, M. 16
Sisson, K. 34
Skott, P. 100
Slichter, S., with J. Healy and R. Livernash 63
social custom:
  union membership 17–18
  and wage rigidity 107–8
social expenditure, and union density 170
social insurance 167
  administration 177–81
  see also insurance; pensions
social pacts 9
  and macroeconomic policy-making 75–9
  national coordination through 121–5
'soft landing' schemes 271–2
  pre-retirement and early retirement
    schemes 199–202
  see also Ghent system; insurance;
    unemployment; welfare state
Solow, Robert 136
Soskice, D., with T. Iversen 103
soziale Errungenschaften 70
Steinmeier, T. L., with A. L. Gustman 198
Stewart, M. B.:
  with D. Metcalf 51, 54
  see also Machin, S.
Streeck, W. 75
strikes *see* industrial action; labour conflict
structural explanations, membership levels 24–32
structure, non-active members 172–5
Summers, L., with J. Gruber and R. Vergara 99
surplus, union's ability to appropriate 47–9
Sweden:
  union density and unemployment 236–7
  wage bargaining and monetary policy 111
  wage drift 90

Tabellini, G. 204
  with F. Daveri 99
Tanninen, H., with J. Pehkonen 237–8
taxation:
  funding public pensions 217–20
  funding of welfare state 197
  tax policy and bargaining structure 98–100
Taylor, B. *see* Jowell, R.
Topel, R. 246
total factor productivity (TPF) 294
trade, competition, and reciprocal dumping 56–7
trade unions, future prospects 115–34
transactions costs, and exit versus voice 67–8
transnational coordination of bargaining 9, 127–31
  and competition 140–1
turnover 68

UK:
  occupational pensions 198–9
  welfare retrenchment 230–1
unemployment:
  and bargaining power 243
  coordination of bargaining structures 98–104
  and early retirement 220–3
  impact on membership 20–1
  and labour conflict 16
  unemployment insurance (UI) 172, 234–47
    administration 177–81

unemployment: (*cont.*):
   reforms 244–6
   and union density 22–3, 236–8
   and wages 242–3
   and wage bargaining 104–5, 238–41
   youth unemployment and pension spending
     204–10
   see also Ghent system; labour markets;
     redundancies; retrenchment; 'soft
     landing' schemes
Union of Industrial and Employers'
   Confederations of Europe (UNICE) 127
unionization *see* coverage; density; deunionization;
   trade unions
USA:
   unionization trends compared to Europe 15
   wage shares compared to EU 17

values, and membership 30–1
Van Audenrode, M., with J. S. Leonard 200
Van de Vall, M. 31
Van Reenan, J. *see* Machin, S.
Velasco, A., with V. Guzzo 100
Vergara, R. *see* Summers, L.
Visser, J. 72, 204
   with B. Ebbinghaus 33

wages:
   bargaining
     monetary policy in EU 110–11
     and pensions 190–2
     structure 8
     and unemployment 104–5, 238–41
   central bank as deterrent to increases 101–3
   determinants of union influence over 47–60
   differentials 106
   distribution 63–4
   fall in wage share 16
   and inflation 100–1
   minimum wages 244
   and productivity 67
   relationship with taxes 98–100
   returns to human capital and work
     experience in Germany 65
   sex discrimination 64
   and structural change 68

and unemployment insurance 242–3
wage drift 90–1
wage flexibility
   EMU 111–12
   response to demand shocks 105–9
wage restraint:
   bargaining coordination in EU 108–9
   EMU bargaining structure 109–11
   union's role 9, 16
   see also bargaining
Wallerstein, M. 23
Wassenaar Consensus 76, 295
Webb, S. *see* Cukierman, A.
Weber, Max 282
Weitzman, M. L. 108
welfare state 278
   membership structure of unions and non-active
     members 172–5
   reform 252–3, 283–4
   retrenchment and industrial action 183–6
   scope and industrial relations 164–71
   social insurance administration 177–81
   unions and affiliated political parties 175–7
   unions' interaction with 248–50, 283
   see also insurance; pensions; unemployment
Western, B. 236
Wise, D., with J. Gruber 200
Witherspoon, S. *see* Jowell, R.
Wolfers, J., with O. J. Blanchard 104–5, 239–40,
   243
Wolinsky, A., with H. Horn 52
workplace presence:
   membership level 21
   and union density 21
works councils 81–3
   European works councils (EWCs) 129
   relationship with unions 117
Wright, R., with K. Burdett 245

youth:
   youth unemployment, and pension
     spending 204–10
   see also age

Zetterberg, J. 95
Zoega, G. *see* Nicoletti, G.